THE LATIN AMERICAN VOTER

In this volume, experts on Latin American public opinion and political behavior employ region-wide public opinion studies, elite surveys, experiments, and advanced statistical methods to reach several key conclusions about voting behavior in the region's emerging democracies. In Latin America, to varying degrees the average voter grounds his or her decision in factors identified in classic models of voter choice. Individuals are motivated to go to the polls and elect public officials on the basis of demographic groups (class, religion, gender, and ethnicity), substantive political connections (partisanship, left-right stances, policy preferences), and politician performance (in areas like the economy, corruption, and crime). Yet evidence from Latin America shows that the determinants of voter choice cannot be properly understood without reference to context—the substance (specific cleavages, campaigns, performance) and the structure (fragmentation and polarization) that characterize the political environment. Voting behavior reflects the relative youth and fluidity of the region's party systems, as parties emerge and splinter to a far greater degree than in long-standing party systems. Consequently, explanations of voter choice centered on country differences stand on equal footing with explanations focused on individual-level factors.

Ryan E. Carlin is Associate Professor of Political Science at Georgia State University.

Matthew M. Singer is Associate Professor of Political Science at the University of Connecticut.

Elizabeth J. Zechmeister is Professor of Political Science and Director of the Latin American Public Opinion Project at Vanderbilt University.

NEW COMPARATIVE POLITICS

Series Editor
Michael Laver, New York University

Editorial Board
Ken Benoit, Trinity College, Dublin
Gary Cox, University of California, San Diego
Simon Hix, London School of Economics
John Huber, Columbia University
Herbert Kitschelt, Duke University
G. Bingham Powell, University of Rochester
Kaare Strøm, University of California, San Diego
George Tsebelis, University of Michigan
Leonard Wantchekon, Princeton University

The New Comparative Politics series brings together cutting-edge work on social conflict, political economy, and institutional development. Whatever its substantive focus, each book in the series builds on solid theoretical foundations; uses rigorous empirical analysis; and deals with timely, politically relevant questions.

The Latin American Voter

Pursuing Representation and Accountability in Challenging Contexts

Edited by
RYAN E. CARLIN
MATTHEW M. SINGER
ELIZABETH J. ZECHMEISTER

University of Michigan Press • *Ann Arbor*

Published in the United States of America by the
University of Michigan Press
Manufactured in the United States of America
⊗ Printed on acid-free paper

2018   2017   2016   2015   4   3   2   1

A CIP catalog record for this book is available from the British Library.

Library of Congress Cataloging-in-Publication Data

The Latin American voter : pursuing representation and accountability in challenging
contexts / edited by Ryan E. Carlin, Matthew M. Singer, and Elizabeth J. Zechmeister.
      pages   cm
   Includes bibliographical references and index.
   ISBN 978-0-472-07287-3 (hardcover : alk. paper) — ISBN 978-0-472-05287-5 (pbk. :
alk. paper) — ISBN 978-0-472-12143-4 (ebook)
   1. Voting—Latin America.   2. Representative government and representation—Latin
America.   3. Elections—Latin America.   4. Latin America—Politics and government.
I. Carlin, Ryan E.   II. Singer, Matthew M.   III. Zechmeister, Elizabeth J.

   JL968.L37   2015
   324.98—dc23

                                                                    2015017656

Contents

Preface and Acknowledgments

Just a decade and a half ago, when we editors first met, the proposition of rigorously studying voting behavior in Latin America in comparative perspective seemed remote. While some early pioneers in the field were producing innovative studies of voting behavior in single countries, there was no good way to talk about overall patterns within the region because survey data for the region were either incomplete or inaccessible. Voting behavior rarely figured into general discussions of Latin American politics, and colleagues who studied other topics or other regions often questioned us about whether traditional models of voting behavior were relevant in a region they perceived to be dominated by clientelism and populism. Today, by contrast, we have the good fortune of access to a goldmine of relevant resources and techniques: high-quality regional public opinion surveys are publicly available and advances in hierarchical modeling techniques allow us to assess theories about divergent cross-national patterns in voting behavior. In tandem with these developments, there has developed an ever-growing community of scholars producing innovative work on voter behavior in the region.

As we took stock of these developments, the three of us had at various points discussed the need for a project that would undertake a comprehensive assessment of Latin American voting behavior. Then Mike Lewis-Beck gave us a nudge. In a series of discussions at and following a meeting of the Midwest Political Science Association in 2010 and a workshop on elections and voter behavior sponsored by the Université Laval in 2011, he challenged us to write a broad book on "the basics" of voting behavior in Latin America. Throughout the project, we have benefited in many ways from our interaction with Mike, his critical insights, and his unwavering enthusiasm for our efforts.

As we took up the challenge to produce *The Latin American Voter*, the first systematic attempt to understand voting behavior across individuals and contexts in the region, we were united in our goal to create a book that made the most of the new developments with respect to the now-abundant cross-national comparative databases on public opinion in Latin America, new applications of statistical techniques, and the increasing number of experts on various facets of voter choice in Latin America. We decided early on that we would develop the project as an edited volume and over a series of meetings, so that we could benefit as much as possible from discussions among the contributors and by discussants at each stage in the process.

A project of this breadth and the activities that supported its development would not have been possible without a great deal of intellectual and financial support. We have the pleasure here of gratefully acknowledging the participation of many of the individuals and institutions who helped us bring this book to fruition. We thank them wholeheartedly and we are humbled by their generous efforts.

First of all, the editors would like to thank those organizations that made their data available to our contributors. Every chapter in the volume makes at least some use of AmericasBarometer surveys conducted under the auspices of the Latin American Public Opinion Project (LAPOP) at Vanderbilt University. The authors are grateful to LAPOP's founder and chief intellectual architect, Mitch Seligson, for the enormous amount of talent and energy that he has devoted to the AmericasBarometer, a hemisphere-wide regional survey project of the highest quality. LAPOP agreed to allow our contributors early access to some merged data files, which facilitated our work on this project. We thank all the supporters of LAPOP's AmericasBarometer, including USAID and Vanderbilt, for their roles in the development of the AmericasBarometer database and for making these data publically available. We also owe a debt of gratitude to the Democratic Accountability Linkages Project (DALP) at Duke University, under the direction of Herbert Kitschelt, and the Parliamentary Elites in Latin America (PELA) project at the University of Salamanca, under the leadership of Manuel Alcántara Sáez; we thank these two individuals for their expert leadership in these important survey projects and for sharing the data necessary to calculate the measures of programmatic effort and polarization that many chapters use. Our interpretations of the data and any and all mistakes in using these data are our responsibility, although we hope they are few.

We are grateful to the many people who participated in meetings where the content for this book was discussed. Our first attempt to organize the project was thwarted by Mother Nature, when a tropical storm led to the cancellation of the 2012 American Political Science Association meeting and a panel we had organized as an attempt to bring together early versions of manuscripts by the editors and several other contributors. We thank the students in Liz's political behavior graduate seminar at Vanderbilt, who read these papers and gave informative comments and feedback.

Our first large meeting on the project occurred at a one-day mini workshop at the January 2013 Southern Political Science Association Meeting in Orlando, Florida. Jana Morgan was instrumental in making that meeting happen. We thank Jana and the rest of the organizing committee for supporting the workshop. At that meeting we were fortunate to receive thoughtful feedback from those who generously agreed to serve as discussants for this event: Raymond Duch, Nathan Kelly, Michael Lewis-Beck, and James McCann. Their critiques, suggestions, and insights improved the quality of the individual papers and also helped improve the overall coherence of the volume.

In May 2013, we organized a meeting of all contributors and another set of discussants at Vanderbilt University. That conference was made possible by funding from a variety of sources, including the Tinker Foundation, LAPOP, the Department of Political Science at Vanderbilt University, and the Center for the Study of Democratic Institutions (CSDI) at Vanderbilt. The conference itself would have been impossible without tireless work behind the scenes by the administrative staff in the Department of Political Science, especially Darlene Davidson and Natasha Duncan. At the workshop we benefited from generous and very constructive criticism, feedback, and ideas offered by Larry Bartels, Damarys Canache, Scott Desposato, Cindy Kam, Jennifer Merolla, Vidal Romero, Mitch Seligson, and Carole Wilson, and the other conference attendees. Graduate students at Vanderbilt who helped with the conference and/or other aspects of the project include but are not limited to Fred Batista, Oscar Castorena, Margarita Corral, Brian Faughnan, Matt Layton, and Will Young. Vanderbilt continued to support us by hosting a meeting of the editors in Nashville two months after the conference for the purpose of in-depth editing of the chapters.

We had opportunities to present selections from the manuscript on several more occasions, which allowed us to receive feedback from a number of other individuals. In May 2013, Ryan taught the bulk of the chapters as a graduate seminar as a visiting professor at the Universidad Autónoma de Querétaro and received valuable insights into how the text might be used in the classroom from the students and his host, Rodolfo Sarsfield. Liz presented a portion of the project at Notre Dame and received trenchant feedback from Michael Coppedge and the participants in the workshop, which helped us fine-tune the introduction and conclusion, as well as her chapter. Some of the chapters were presented at the 2014 Midwest Political Science Association (MPSA) meetings, where Guillermo Trejo and Anibal Pérez-Liñán provided thoughtful comments. Matt presented an overview of the project at the 2014 Associação Brasileira de Ciência Política (ABCP) Meeting and is grateful to Luciana Veiga and the ABCP for arranging the presentation.

The three editors also benefited from support at their home institutions. At UConn, Molly Rockett researched the party positions that were used to generate the measure of left-right vote in parts II and III; Matt thanks Molly and the College of Liberal Arts and Sciences (CLAS) Alan R. Bennett Honors Professorship in Political Science for funding her research. At Vanderbilt, then-undergraduate student Christina Folds did amazing work in formatting and proofreading the entire manuscript. Ryan thanks Ilídio Nhantumbo, a graduate student at Georgia State University, for his work on preparing the manuscript for submission.

We are enormously grateful to Dr. Melody Herr at the University of Michigan Press for her support of the project. Her enthusiasm for the project motivated us and her input helped us to improve the manuscript in a number of ways. We thank Michael Laver for warmly welcoming the book into the New Comparative Politics series. We also thank the two anonymous reviewers for their extremely detailed reviews, which sharpened our argument and analyses and made the content of this volume more coherent. The feedback from these reviewers was astute, thought-provoking, and fair, and the project benefited tremendously from their input. We of course assume responsibility for any deficiencies that remain in the completed project.

Throughout this whole process, we have benefited from having an amazing group of contributors. The three of us have learned a great deal about voting behavior and the politics of the region through their analyses and in discussions with each individual contributor and in our group meetings, and we hope to have captured an imprint of this collective wisdom in the volume's introduction and conclusion, as well as within the book more generally. Each individual from this esteemed set of scholars responded generously, effectively, and quickly to feedback from the discussants and from us editors, which facilitated progress on the book and played a key role in making this a fun project for us to be engaged in over the past several years. We thank them for their collaboration on this project and we are delighted to have the opportunity to showcase the excellent results of their hard work and expertise in this volume.

Finally, as academic work often does, work on this project involved as many sacrifices by us as it did by our families. We want to thank our families for putting up with weekend and evening work to support our efforts and frequent email exchanges and Skype conversations over the project as well as for accommodating the travel time away from home that this project required. Deep thanks to our spouses, Molly, Cara, and Andy, and our children, Hugh, Mary, Andrew, Whitney, Annie, and Natalie, for being understanding during those times when we skipped away to develop the project, make revisions, and meet both internal and external deadlines, while giving us reasons to want to ignore it all and come back to you.

1 ✦ Introduction to the Latin American Voter

RYAN E. CARLIN, MATTHEW M. SINGER,
AND ELIZABETH J. ZECHMEISTER

Latin America's third wave of democracy has witnessed more than three hundred presidential and legislative elections.[1] Securing this fundamental political right is a monumental accomplishment because free and fair elections are the *sine qua non* of modern democracy (Dahl 1971). Elections alone are not sufficient for high-quality democracy; achieving political representation and accountability is more likely when there is also sustained citizen participation and monitoring between elections, as well as carefully designed institutions that create checks and balances (Smulovitz and Peruzzotti 2000; Mainwaring and Welna 2003). Yet elections provide a formal mechanism by which the "will of the people" determines who rules. The process may not always work as designed, and not all elections in the region have been flawless,[2] but elections have played the protagonists in the shift away from the unique politics of transitions and toward the normalization of democratic politics in Latin America.[3]

By casting votes, citizens connect to their broader community and, for a brief moment, join their voting compatriots in the spirit of political equality. Participating in elections can inculcate good habits of citizenship and, as exemplars of democratic politics, elections can help spread and reinforce democratic values (Blais and Gélineau 2007, 430; Brinks and Coppedge 2006; Lindberg 2006). The electoral process can allow the public to advance new issue agendas (Dalton 1996; Stoll 2013), especially to the extent that citizens use it to select representatives who reflect their interests and withdraw votes from those who do not. Moreover, elections can incentivize political actors to contest for power via routinized formal mechanisms rather than via rebellion and/or bullets. In this sense elections have the potential to legitimize democratic institutions and inoculate them against a range of maladies. Thus, where citizens use the popular vote to practice, defend, or improve democratic processes and to arbitrate between contending actors, elections can be agents of democracy from within and without.

In a region like Latin America, where modern democratic systems (re) emerged over the past fifty years,[4] it is all the more crucial for elections to fulfill these democratizing roles. In many places across the region, democracy persists in a fragile state and in others democracy has decayed in recent years (e.g., Diamond 2008; Puddington 2012). Democratic consolidation is secured when ordinary citizens and political elites accept and act according to the rules of the game (Linz and Stepan 1996; Przeworski 1991). To the degree that elections fail to achieve their potential in advancing democratic habits and processes, democracy is weakened and could be destabilized. Indeed, if elections repeatedly empower extremists or demagogues, fuel political brinkmanship and gridlock, and/or appear as little more than a baseless charade, then elections might unhinge already tenuous mass commitments to the rules of the democratic game in the region (Booth and Seligson 2009; Carlin and Singer 2011). Consequently, it is important to understand electoral processes, decision-making, and outcomes in Latin America.

Despite the importance of elections to politics and to democratic consolidation in the region, we know strikingly little about how Latin Americans decide their votes. That is not to say scholars of Latin American politics do not care about elections. In fact, scholarship on vote decisions in selected Latin American countries has increased steadily over the years, spurred on by the production of vote-oriented survey projects in particular in Brazil and Mexico (e.g., Ames, Baker, and Rennó 2008; Baker, Ames, and Rennó 2006; Domínguez and McCann 1996; Domínguez and Poiré 1999; Domínguez and Lawson 2003; Domínguez, Lawson, and Moreno 2009; Meixueiro and Moreno 2014; Moreno 2003, 2009b; see also Telles and Moreno 2013). Other studies take the vote tally as a point of departure to investigate how winners govern, how losers react, and how those in and out of government meld to craft policy. And others investigate the relationship between macro-economic and other system-level factors and electoral outcomes. But to truly understand elections in Latin America one must, figuratively speaking, crack open the ballot box and investigate what individual voters across the region are expressing by way of their votes. In our view, the study of voting behavior in Latin America and other new democracies provides a window into how elections function as tools of democracy.

Collectively the chapters in this volume answer three questions about national electoral behavior in Latin America: (1) Who votes? (2) What attributes and judgments influence voter choice? (3) What contextual factors distinguish voters across Latin American countries from each other and from voters in other contexts? In doing so this volume identifies group-based motivations for citizen involvement in elections, gauges how consistently voters link to politicians and parties based on the ideas and material goods they offer, and defines the role the public plays in holding politicians accountable for their actions. Throughout, we emphasize how political context influences citizens' decisions about whether to vote and for whom. By documenting what motivates citizens to take part in the democratic process and, subsequently, the judgments on which they draw when selecting their leaders and evaluating their performance, this volume helps determine the extent to which and when elections in Latin America provide voters meaningful control over the political agenda.

Generally speaking, we find that across the Latin American region the average individual is motivated to go to the polls and select officials on the basis of demographic group membership (class, religion, gender, and ethnicity); substantive political connections (partisanship, left-right stances, and policy preferences); and political outputs related to the economy, corruption, and crime. However, the extent to which these baseline propensities manifest in a given country at a given time depends critically on the nature of the substance (the specific cleavages, campaigns, and performance) and structure (e.g., party system fragmentation and polarization) that characterize the political environment.

With this conclusion we put a spotlight on the fact that democratic processes in most Latin American countries may be relatively normalized but, in many cases, they are not yet fully consolidated. Despite the vast democratic experience gained in the third wave, Latin American electoral politics remains unsteady and plagued by disruptions. Most transitions from authoritarianism to competitive party politics do not quickly result in a stable equilibrium. Political elites in comparatively new democracies face uncertainty about whether democracy will endure, the economic climate (especially if the economy is itself in transition due to market reforms and/ or globalization), and the stability of institutional rules (Lupu and Riedl 2013). Such dynamics encourage a great deal of policy experimentation, as entrepreneurial elites shift their positions to activate dormant and new cleavages, and even pursue radical policy switches (Stokes 2001). In this process, the birth and death of political parties (Lupu forthcoming; Morgan 2011) and the emergence of political outsiders (Carreras 2012; Seawright 2012) may disrupt the party system.

While not all countries have seen dramatic shifts in the nature of the party system, it is fair to say that on average today's Latin American political systems persist in flux. In most elections, the menu of political actors and parties ebbs and flows along with the content of the platforms they advocate and represent. To the extent Latin America is exemplary of post-transition politics in general, we can conclude that this political fluidity can last for decades. That enduring and coherent political options have not fully crystallized in most Latin American systems has implications for electoral behavior in the region. As a result of experimentations and disruptions, many citizens in the region face high uncertainty about what contending parties stand for and would do if elected. If becoming politically informed and casting a rational vote are challenging tasks for citizens in long-established systems with a small handful of comparatively coherent political options (Delli Carpini and Keeter 1996; Achen and Bartels n.d.), then the task facing the average Latin American voter is even more difficult.

In the face of weak party system institutionalization, we should expect to find entrepreneurial politicians seeking to activate new or dormant sociopolitical cleavages. When they succeed, voters should respond by connecting to politicians on the basis of group identities such as class, religion, gender, and ethnicity. Further, in such a climate partisan attachments and left-right identities should be less widespread, though voters may still take policy stances into consideration to some degree, especially when politicians emphasize substantively meaningful and distinct platforms. Finally, accountability voting—making electoral decisions based on retrospective assessments of the incumbent's performance, particularly with respect to the economy—should tend to be fairly commonplace as voters seize on this ubiquitous and comparatively less demanding electoral mechanism. Indeed, we find that the Latin American voter considers group identities to the extent they are activated, gives some consideration to political programs, and tends to punish poor policy outputs (in particular, those related to the economy).

Broad statements about common tendencies, however, skim over the significant intraregional political diversity that characterizes the Latin American region. Tremendous variation in electoral decision environments—the candidates stumping for office, the nature of the party system, and the outputs governments deliver—renders profoundly different answers to questions about voting behaviors across Latin American electorates. Voting scholars have long noted the importance of context (e.g., Campbell et al. 1960). Beginning from that foundation, we set out to explore how exactly context matters in a region such as Latin America. In fact, Latin American party systems differ on a number of dimensions that theoretically ought to produce differences in electoral decision-making: the number of parties among which voters choose, the stability of that menu of choices, and the content and distinctiveness of their appeals. This diversity allows us a singular lens through which to observe how voters' decision calculi change in response to the *substance* (e.g., the specific cleavages activated, the degree to which politicians campaign on issues, the salience of performance in various areas of governance) and the *structure* (e.g., fragmentation and polarization) of the political options elites present in a given election. And when we carefully assess this varied landscape we reach a core conclusion with great confidence: the extent to which and how the Latin American voter pursues representation and accountability at the polls hinges greatly on the substance and the structure that characterize his or her menu of electoral options.

Three Models of Voting Behavior

A primary objective of this volume is to consider how well, and under what conditions, extant models of voting behavior capture electoral dynamics in Latin America. We focus our attention on three fundamental schools of thought that undergird most theorizing about voter choice. In the first, individuals select candidates and parties whose socioeconomic or other personal characteristics mirror their own. A second holds that voters choose parties and candidates in line with their political ideas, packaged as partisanship, ideology, and issue stances. The third depicts citizens as monitoring the performance of elected officials and then voting to reward good output and to punish bad outcomes. Together, these models outline elections' essential democratic functions. When voters support parties that reflect their group's interests or champion policies they endorse, elections provide them *representation* in the political system. By judging parties and candidates on their performance, elections allow voters to hold officials *accountable* (Przeworski, Stokes, and Manin 1999; Powell 2000). Distinct as they may appear in their stylized versions, each of these models incorporates key elements of the others. And although they were largely substantiated in case studies of developed political systems in North America and Western Europe, early theorists recognized that these models' potency hinges on key aspects of the political context.

Two seminal books established the primacy of socioeconomic or demographic characteristics in voter choice, *The People's Choice* (Lazarsfeld, Berelson, and Gaudet 1944) and *Voting* (Berelson, Lazarsfeld, and McPhee 1954). According to these texts, many members of the public appear to hold pat vote decisions based on sociological groupings such as social class, religion, race, and urban/rural residency that stand impervious to political advertising tactics. Referred to by the name of the university where its founders were based, this "Columbia school" of voting behavior, and its core notion that group divisions (or "cleavages") anchor the vote, was accepted by many voting scholars of European democracies (e.g., Lipset and Rokkan 1967; Butler and Stokes 1969). Yet the political relevance of group identities across the continent is not considered to be entirely uniform. Rather, scholars of European politics have demonstrated that the extent to which ethnicity, class, or other social cleavages determine voter preferences varies as a function of how strongly political entrepreneurs appeal to groups, build group consciousness within them, and form ties to civil society organizations (see reviews in Knutsen 2004b; Thomassen 2005; Evans and de Graaf 2013).

Building on this foundation, an alternative theoretical framework argued that voting decisions ultimately reflect psychological and attitudinal motivations derived not only from individuals' social positions and upbringing but also from their issue concerns. Specifically, *The American Voter* (Campbell et al. 1960) linked voting decisions to long-term self-identification with political parties as well as assessments of specific candidates and opinions on issues of the day that, unlike sociological groupings, fluctuate in response to the environment. Known also by reference to its university home, this "Michigan school" of voting behavior became enormously influential in the United States and subsequently traveled to other continents (Thomassen 2005) and countries (Moreno 2003, 2009b; Lewis-Beck 2004), but had to be modified substantially to understand voting in multiparty elections (Thomassen 2005).[5] To their credit, Campbell et al. (1960) anticipated that the nature and leverage of attitudinal and psychological drivers of voter choice might vary with characteristics of the party system and other features of the "political atmosphere" (Campbell et al. 1960, 267).

A third perspective argues that individuals may initially focus judgment on the incumbent's policy performance and use their votes to punish or reward the incumbent accordingly. To be fair, the Michigan school (Campbell et al. 1960, ch. 13) did not overlook policy performance and the topic was also addressed in Downs's (1957) rational account of voter decisionmaking. Yet, it was Key's (1966) *The Responsible Electorate* and, later, Fiorina's (1981) *Retrospective Voting in American National Elections* that most clearly articulated how performance figured into the voting calculus. In short, this perspective holds that voters should be more inclined to retain the party in office if the country's overall situation has improved on its watch than if things have deteriorated. Performance judgments do not necessarily supersede partisan loyalty, as voters perceive the government's successes and failures through partisan-tinted glasses (Kayser and Wlezien 2011), but they represent distinct criteria on which voting decisions are made.

Though emphases differ across research domains, most voting scholars would likely agree that the menu of socio-demographics, identities and issues, and performance derived from these major approaches has relevance to democratic voters regardless of their geographic home. A focus on how group interests, issue concerns, and evaluations of government performance shape voter choices increases our understanding of the extent to which, and how, elections advance the democratic promise of representation and accountability. Thus, these models and their constituent parts are the primary emphases of this book.

We acknowledge, however, that they do not capture the universe of considerations that voters bring to the polls. Alternative models address voters' propensities to vote strategically, to incorporate heuristic aids and candidate traits, and to use candidate competency as a valence issue alongside candidates' policy positions, and further propose that the broader media and campaign environments shape these processes. Within Campbell et al.'s (1960) "funnel of causality" framework, many of these elements (strategic voting decisions, candidate traits, and campaigns) are quite proximate to the vote decision. But because they are often specific to a given campaign, they vary idiosyncratically from election to election in ways that are difficult to measure and analyze cross-nationally. While data limitations preclude us from fully addressing some of these considerations, the influence of candidates and campaigns, as well as the importance of party and candidate options and strategies for politicizing group divides, are common themes in part II of this volume.

We also recognize that voters, especially in less developed contexts, might vote on the basis of charismatic bonds (Madsen and Snow 1991; Merolla and Zechmeister 2011). As with candidate traits, studying how charisma affects electoral choice requires knowing how voters perceive candidates' qualities. Unfortunately, we lack cross-national survey data for the Latin American case on such questions. Yet to the extent that this volume shows Latin American voters systematically make considerations on the basis of factors that are related to party programs and output, we can— and do—conclude that their voting decisions are not entirely dominated by considerations of political elites' charismatic appeal.

Finally, extant models of democratic representation and accountability need to recognize that voters might care less about politicians' broad policy proposals or national-level policy outcomes but instead might focus on the tangible, material benefits that parties can provide to them and their family. Clientelism is pervasive in Latin America and we fold it into our study in a number of ways, including connecting it to turnout (Carlin and Love chapter); identifying it as a moderator of the connection between issues and left-right identifications, respectively, and the vote (Baker and Greene chapter; Zechmeister chapter); and presenting a rich portrait of its presence and effectiveness across the region (Kitschelt and Altamirano chapter). Moreover, just as with charisma, inasmuch as the contributions to this volume show that considerations related to policy and performance shape voter choice in the region, we can conclude that voters are not merely captured by political machines. In fact, Kitschelt and Altamirano's contribution suggests that clientelist mobilizing strategies in the region are fairly ineffective on average, which creates space for parties to win by emphasizing programmatic representation as they emphasize distinct policy positions to voters and work to activate latent social divisions.

The Electoral Context

The three classic models of voting behavior we identified in the previous section link voter choices to their demographic and personal characteristics, their issue positions and political identity, and their evaluations of government performance. Yet, consistent with insights offered by many scholars working in these traditions, we assert that the electoral relevance of these considerations for voting behavior varies greatly across contexts and countries (e.g., Lewis-Beck 1988; Powell and Whitten 1993; Evans 1999; Knutsen 2004b; Thomassen 2005; Singh 2010; Dalton and Anderson 2011; Dalton, Farrell, and McAllister 2011; Evans and de Graaf 2013; see also Anderson and Singer 2008). A key point that we take from this body of scholarship to inform our study of voter choice in Latin America is the following: elections provide voters differential access to representation and accountability depending on how they are structured and organized.

Though the list of all contextual factors that could theoretically condition voter behavior is extensive, they tend to fall into two dominant baskets, the first of which includes those that affect the *substance* of public demands—the specific issues that are salient and the groups that are mobilized—and the second of which relates to the *structure* of the choices provided by the party system. Obviously, these two dimensions are not independent; for example, a country's party system is connected to the social and economic divisions that generate and structure political conflict and demands (Kitschelt et al. 2010). Nevertheless, these dimensions help us distinguish contextual factors of *substance* that affect voter behavior, from the bottom up and in interaction with elite efforts, by shaping what voters ask for, from those of *structure* that shape voter behavior by limiting or clarifying the choices available to voters.

The substance of electoral competition often reflects specific cleavages that evolved as countries developed. Conflicts over the role of religion in society, over workers' rights and welfare provision, over the protection of ethnic groups, and between supporters and opponents of democracy all potentially can serve as axes of modern political competition if these fights are sufficiently strong and spawn organized interests within society to mobilize for their side (e.g., Lipset and Rokkan 1967; Collier and Collier 1991; Van Cott 2005; Moreno 1999; Kitschelt et al. 2010). Although history often creates the raw materials of political discourse, and patterns may get locked in as countries pass certain critical junctures in their development, these conflicts may also evolve as countries develop. New issues arise as societies change. In developed democracies, for example, increased wealth and the development of robust social safety nets have created space for politics to focus on post-material issues like social equality/tolerance and protecting the environment (Inglehart 1997; Knutsen 2004b) whereas these issues have not become as widely salient in much of Latin America (Rosas 2005). Other issues fade from the public agenda, such as has been the case of a democracy versus authoritarianism dimension in Latin America, which has become generally less relevant as democratic institutions became consolidated (Moreno 1999). Finally, the political agenda may shift episodically in response to new challenges. Economic crises and scandals, for example, focus media and public attention on government performance at the expense of other issues (Singer 2011, 2013a; Zechmeister and Zizumbo-Colunga 2013; Carlin et al. 2015). Thus, as we look across countries, we should expect the demands voters place on their representatives to vary systematically.

It would be a mistake, however, to assume that social processes deterministically define the electoral agenda and that politicians passively respond to issues that percolate from the bottom up. Issue concerns rarely surface and become important on their own. More often they emerge because an actor or an organization articulates a latent or emerging demand and mobilizes others around it. Politicians also have incentives to find issues that they can use either to build a coalition or to split an existing one (Schattschneider 1960; Riker 1988). Politicians can seldom create political conflict in the absence of social divisions to serve as fodder for political movements. They can, however, *activate* cleavages that would otherwise play a much smaller role.

While politicians may have incentives to make some issues or cleavages salient, they may also wish to deemphasize others. Indeed, they may face incentives to be vague about certain policy positions to avoid getting bogged down in minutiae that many voters will tune out or dislike and/or to give themselves flexibility to adapt and negotiate after elections (Shepsle 1972; Page 1976; Glazer 1990). Parties also may worry that focusing on specific issues and groups limits their ability to expand their coalition beyond their base. Parties may find it more effective to emphasize candidate personalities or to offer targeted material rewards to individuals across the electorate instead of talking about issues or targeting specific groups (Kitschelt 2000). In all of these circumstances, voters might have a hard time connecting issue priorities, ideology, or identities to the available electoral options because parties do not make them clear.

To understand voter behavior we need to consider the structure of the party system. Voters' choices are contingent on the options politicians present to them from the top down. For example, party systems differ in the degree to which parties take distinct policy positions. While extreme polarization can negatively affect democracy by hindering compromise and reducing political losers' perceived costs of advocating for their rivals to be deposed (Sartori 1976; Mainwaring and Perez-Liñán 2005),[6] it may be an asset to voters. By clarifying electoral options and potentially raising their stakes, a party system structured by polarized competition facilitates and even motivates voters to ground their electoral choices in identities, issues, and output (see Dalton 2008, 2011; Levendusky 2010; Evans and De Graf 2013; Singer forthcoming). In the absence of parties that present meaningful choices to voters, clientelism and candidate traits may be all that is left for voters to consider.

Party systems also differ in the degree of fragmentation (the number of parties). The theoretical effects of party system fragmentation on voter behavior, however, are not straightforward. On the one hand, fragmented party systems might increase the odds that voters find a party that represents them on ideological, issue, or group grounds (Klingemann and Wessels 2009). On the other hand, as the party system grows, so do the time and cognitive demands associated with learning and contrasting parties' various issue positions, especially if multipartism is associated with party system volatility (Kroh 2009; Singh 2010; Zechmeister and Corral 2013). Fragmented party systems that require negotiation to form legislative majorities should also frustrate voters' attempts to establish who is responsible for policy outcomes and, thus, hamper political accountability (Powell and Whitten 1993; Anderson 2000; Singer and Carlin 2013).

In sum, long-run social processes along with rapidly changing demands influence voting behavior and the nature of electoral competition from the ground up. Top-down decisions by political elites about which cleavages to activate, which issues to make salient (or ignore), and how to link to the voters largely determine the substance on which individuals can base electoral decisions. How elites structure electoral competition—by creating or dissolving parties and coalitions, by taking polarized rather than nebulous issue stances, by sending coherent instead of cacophonous policy messages—can shape voters' behaviors by determining how much information they can attain, how easily they can connect it to their personal preferences, and how simply they can find a party that reflects their interests. By emphasizing these particular factors, the chapters that follow offer a set of extensions to an impressive body of voting research that has developed principally (though far from entirely) with a focus on the United States, Canada, and Western Europe. Compared to Latin America, Western advanced industrialized countries have achieved higher levels of economic development and, thanks in part to unique historical circumstances, fairly stable electoral politics: the same parties compete in most elections, their ideological positions change slowly over time, and parties emphasize issue appeals in their campaigns. In short, by contrasting the Latin American electoral context with that of the more prosperous and consolidated systems, our study adds new perspectives on how the electoral context more generally influences voting behavior.

The Latin American Electoral Context

A guiding theoretical proposition of this volume is that important differences in electoral context condition how well classic models map onto the dynamics of voter choice in Latin America. While contributors to the canon of traditional voter choice studies recognized the importance of context, Latin America presents a singular landscape with respect to a number of indicators. Specifically, the confluence of two factors makes the Latin American region fecund terrain for comparative research on voter choice: its striking contrasts to countries and areas that have been the focus of classic scholarship on voting behavior and its significant intraregional variation. Taking as a given that the region's electoral democracies are comparatively young, we focus here on three key points of inter- and intraregional differentiation: levels of and fluctuation in development and societal organization, institutional arrangements, and party systems.

First, the economic and social context surrounding Latin America's elections differs significantly from that of Western democracies. The region experienced a series of deep economic crises in the 1980s and 1990s and economic volatility remains. Poverty is declining but still high[7] and, alongside pockets of incredible wealth, creates some of the highest levels of inequality in the world. In many countries of the region, poverty corresponds to racial and ethnic divisions, as indigenous and Afro-descendent communities struggle for economic and educational resources, and breaks down along gender lines as well (see Seligson, Smith, and Zechmeister 2012 for a review).

Civil society in Latin America also greatly diverges from that in the European context. Latin America's formal economies are strongly hierarchical, with large business conglomerates and multinational companies dominating production while labor unions are generally weak and labor market volatility is high (Schneider 2013). A massive informal sector further weakens labor unions. Thus, important exceptions notwithstanding (Collier and Collier 1991; Murillo 2001; Levitsky 2003), unions often lack strong ties to political parties and, more generally, civil society organizations tend to be weakly integrated into the political process (Oxhorn 2011). Social bonds are further frayed by unequal access to education and healthcare within comparatively weak welfare states (Haggard and Kaufman 2009) and endemic crime and corruption in most countries. As a result of these contextual differences, Latin American polities face a unique set of policy challenges in social contexts that are often diverse and weakly organized.

Another major distinction between Latin America and the regions that inspired the pioneering studies of voting behavior is the omnipresence of powerful, directly elected presidents in Latin America. Latin American presidents are generally perceived as the dominant political actor while other bodies are relegated to "reactive" status (Cox and Morgenstern 2001). Compared to parliamentary regimes, parties in presidential regimes organize and recruit candidates much differently, typically resulting in weaker party organizations and larger roles for political outsiders (Carreras 2012; Samuels and Shugart 2010). Presidential candidates can build an electoral base that diverges from their party's base by reaching out to different voters or emphasizing different policies, which can result in parties with flexible ideologies (Carreras 2012; Samuels and Shugart 2010). By placing the president at the center of political discourse, presidentialism may also tempt individuals to focus on leaders' personalities when voting (Tverdova 2011) and to discount other actors' influence on policy when holding presidents accountable (Samuels 2004).

Finally, Latin America's party systems are generally less institutionalized than in those countries where classic voting behavior models were crafted. All countries in the region experienced an authoritarian period at some point in the postwar period. Even after the "third wave" of democratization (Huntington 1991) installed formal democratic systems across nearly all the region, Latin America continues to confront episodic "interruptions" to basic political and electoral processes (Pérez-Liñán 2007; Valenzuela 2004). Additional pressure on party systems stems from the economic and societal shifts of the 1980s debt crisis and the economic restructuring in the decades that followed, weakening what were already (in many cases) tenuous party–civil society linkages (Roberts 2002).

The political change the region has witnessed since the third wave, particularly in some countries, includes the rise of new political movements, the fall of longstanding parties, and significant political learning by elites (Morgan 2011; Lupu forthcoming; Roberts 1998). Levels of new party emergence and electoral volatility in Latin America are roughly double those in Western Europe (Robbins and Hunter 2012, 921; see also Roberts and Wibbels 1999). Crises that shake the recently transitioned region from time to time only add to the state of flux, as parties and party systems may break down easily under exogenous shocks, such as economic decline, and recover only very slowly (Kitschelt et al. 2010; Lupu forthcoming; Morgan 2011). In fact, fragmentation has increased, not decreased, since the third wave began to wash over the region. Consequently, Latin American voters often face high-stakes decisions in which the electoral choices themselves are not always clear or stable.

Individuals embedded in such systems may not always or may not robustly conform to models of voting behavior that assume voters decide on the basis of group interests, party identification, ideology, policy appeals, and performance. Weak civil societies and high levels of labor volatility may reduce the linkage between group interests and political parties and work against the formation of a standing political identification. By weakening party organizations, presidentialism may have the same effect. Electoral volatility both reflects these weak party-voter ties and further exacerbates them, and can result in party system fragmentation and demise. These factors may shift voter behavior away from the models applied to voting patterns in other regions. These conditions have led some observers to characterize Latin American electoral politics as dominated by "floating politicians and floating voters" (Conaghan 1995, 540) and "catch-all [parties] . . . that are pragmatic or eclectic in ideology, multiclass in their support, and oriented to broad-based electoral appeals that go beyond the mobilization of a committed constituency" (Dix 1989, 27).

Alternatively, the contextual differences between Latin American democracies and those found in places such as Europe and the United States and/or their implications for voting behavior may be overblown. For example, Latin America's combination of high poverty, volatile economies, and weak governance could sharpen voter attention on performance while high levels of poverty and social exclusion may create latent cleavages that politicians in some contexts may be able to activate.

More likely, and at the core of the conclusion we reach in this volume, the key to understanding voting behavior in Latin America and the extent to which classic models fit electoral decision-making in this region is found in the substantial heterogeneity within the region. Levels of wealth vary significantly from country to country as does the political strength of organized labor, indigenous organizations, and other civil society groups. Even within countries, the relative salience of group-based identities varies across time as new issues and entrepreneurial politicians come and go. While Latin America's political parties are usually younger and less well defined than their European counterparts, some parties in the region have deep historical roots, campaign on the basis of issues, cultivate electoral connections with social groups, and show remarkable stability (Mainwaring and Scully 1995a).

Political (party system) fragmentation and polarization provide two windows into the political diversity of Latin America. With respect to the first, the most common way to gauge the number of parties seeking and winning seats is to calculate the effective number of parties by weighting them according to their size (Laakso and Taagepera 1979).[8] Due in part to proportional electoral rules for the legislature that allow multiple parties to win representation, the mean effective number of parties winning seats in Latin American legislatures in 2012 was 3.69.[9] This average, and the numbers for each country, are presented in the first column of table 1.1. The regional average for Latin America is only the slightest bit higher than the mean of level of legislative fragmentation (3.49) in West European parliamentary elections.[10] Yet the intraregional variation is great, with some countries approximating two-party competition in most elections (e.g., the Dominican Republic, Honduras, and Venezuela) while others have heavily divided legislatures (Brazil is the oft-cited example, but Colombia and Costa Rica have recently fragmented further). Most presidential contests

TABLE 1.1 Descriptive Statistics on Selected Party System Measures

	Effective Number of Parties	Left-Right Polarization (Singer)	Issue Polarization (DALP)	Programmatic Index (DALP)
Argentina	5.40	1.17[a]	0.20	0.09
Bolivia	2.29	1.98	0.41	0.22
Brazil	10.37	1.62[a]	0.43	0.14
Chile	2.02	1.75	0.60	0.25
Colombia	4.95	0.88	0.51	0.20
Costa Rica	4.13	0.71	0.46	0.22
Dominican Republic	2.01	0.21	0.15	0.06
Ecuador	3.80	1.66	0.51	0.23
El Salvador	3.04	3.28[a]	0.56	0.26
Guatemala	4.14	1.34	0.38	0.23
Honduras	2.30	0.26	0.10	0.04
Mexico	2.93	1.09	0.55	0.22
Nicaragua	3.16	2.47[a]	0.28	0.11
Panama	3.66	1.39	0.21	0.07
Paraguay	3.42	0.75	0.36	0.17
Peru	3.97	1.17	0.40	0.19
Uruguay	2.65	1.43	0.43	0.24
Venezuela	2.09	0.99[b]	0.17	0.10
Average	3.69	1.37	0.37	0.17

Sources: Authors, Singer (forthcoming), and Democratic Accountability and Linkage Project.
Note: See text for full descriptions.
[a] Data from 2010
[b] Data from 2005

also have several serious contenders (the effective number of presidential candidates is 3.07) although, again, important cross-country differences exist. There is a general correspondence between electoral fragmentation in the presidential and legislative electoral arenas, with the exception of Brazil and Chile, where parties routinely form two main coalitions in presidential elections. Fragmentation has increased in Latin America in past decades, though important cross-national and within-country variation remains in the number of candidates in contention.[11]

Additionally, the region's party systems also vary with respect to how clearly parties differentiate their programmatic profiles (Kitschelt et al. 2010). One measure of this variation comes from Singer (forthcoming), who looks at party distinctiveness on the left-right scale using data from the Parliamentary Elites in Latin America (PELA) surveys from the University of Salamanca (Alcántara 2012).[12] This measure starts by estimating each party's left-right position by looking at how members of the legislature described their own party. It then compares each party's ideological position to the legislature's average, weighting deviations from the mean by the size of the party. Table 1.1's second column presents the country estimate for the year closest to 2012 for which data are available (since most chapters in this volume focus on data from that year). Honduras and the Dominican Republic have the lowest levels of elite polarization while El Salvador, Nicaragua, and Bolivia have the largest differences in how the parties describe themselves in left-right terms. In addition to the significant variation across countries, the region has witnessed important cross-temporal change in levels of polarization (see Singer forthcoming). For example, in Argentina, Peru, Panama, and particularly Bolivia, ideological differences among the political elite have grown in recent elections. Honduras, in contrast, saw ideological distances shrink in the aftermath of the 2009 coup. Overall, elite polarization seems to have generally increased in most countries, particularly in those where left-populist leaders have been elected as part of Latin America's "left turn."

An alternative, issue-based measure of party system polarization comes from the Democratic Accountability and Linkage Project (DALP).[13] The DALP project surveyed academics, governance and election nongovernmental organization (NGO) employees, and political journalists in eighty-eight countries between 2007 and 2009 about party positions on five policy areas: support for redistribution, the state's role in managing the economy, spending on social programs (health, pensions, and education), support for minorities, and support for traditional values. The survey also asked about additional issues identified by country-experts as being particularly salient.[14] Based on responses to these questions, Kitschelt and Freeze (2010) coded party polarization on each issue first by comparing parties' positions (weighting parties according to their size) to the country average using a methodology similar to that used by Singer (see note 12). They then took the average polarization score of the most polarized economic issue, the ethnic rights question, and value question as well as the highest scoring question among the remaining questions (including the other economic and social policy questions) to generate an overall issue-polarization score. We list these polarization scores for each country in the third column of table 1.1. Levels of issue-based polarization are relatively low in Honduras, the Dominican Republic, Venezuela, Argentina, and Panama and comparatively high in Chile, El Salvador, Mexico, Ecuador, and Colombia.[15] The decision by authors in this volume to choose one of these two measures of party system polarization reflects, at least to some degree, whether they think differences on the left-right scale or on more specific issues are most relevant to their analysis, with results for the other measure usually presented in a note as a robustness test.

Although most of the comparative literature on voter behavior has focused on polarization, distinctiveness across political parties might not be sufficient for programmatic voting to occur (Kitschelt et al. 2010). Even if they stake out distinct positions, some parties may present a *cohesive* policy vision while for other parties infighting and internal disagreement introduce uncertainty about whether such policy positions will be enacted. We also must consider how well voters can even identify the party's position; if that position is not *salient* because parties are ambiguous about what they stand for or do not talk about issues, it is unlikely to have an effect.

Thus, Kitschelt and Freeze (2010) use DALP data to calculate additional measures of the party systems considered here: cohesiveness and salience. They gauge the cohesiveness of each party's stance by the disagreement (standard deviation) in how experts placed each party on the scale, and they capture the salience of those issues by counting the number of experts who failed to place the party on each issue.[16] Kitschelt and Freeze combine these cohesiveness and salience indicators with the polarization index discussed above to generate an overall *programmaticness* index for each issue area. Each component is normalized 0–1 and then the programmatic index score for each issue is calculated as the multiplicative interaction of those three components, treating them all as necessary components. They then take the average of each of the programmatic indexes for the economic issue with the highest programmatic score, the ethnic issue, the values issue, and the highest-scoring remaining issue to calculate summary estimates of programmatic efforts made by parties in each country. Table 1.1, fourth column, presents the DALP programmatic index (programmaticness) scores for each country and the regional mean. The DALP project also provides a measure of clientelist effort, as Kitschelt and Altamirano describe in their chapter.

The number of parties voters have to choose from and how programmatically distinct they appear are major workhorses in comparative voting behavior theory, and contributors to this volume assess their influence on voter choice in Latin America in a number of chapters. As outlined above, the theoretical expectation for polarization is very straightforward: as parties differentiate themselves, individuals should be better able to compare them and recognize which party is best positioned to represent them. It may also become easier for citizens to pick a side and form an identification with that party as parties grow more distinct. Several authors also consider whether an overall commitment to programmatic competition has a similar effect. The theoretical expectation for fragmentation is less clear-cut. In scholarship on stable democracies, a greater number of parties is thought to benefit voters by making it easier for citizens to find a party that represents their particular interests. Yet, especially where fragmentation is associated with party system flux, that complexity potentially makes it harder for voters to form ideological and partisan attachments or to identify who is responsible for policy outcomes (see Zechmeister and Corral 2013). At the same time, the substance and structure of party competition differs across Latin America in other ways, including the descriptive profiles of candidates running for office (see part II); the rise of leftist leaders (see parts II and III); and recent trends with respect to the economy, corruption, and crime (see part IV). Mindful of this, the authors in this volume incorporate points of contextual variation that are most theoretically relevant to the voting behaviors they are studying.

Given all this political diversity, to truly understand vote choice in Latin America we must analyze what Dalton and Anderson (2011) and Anderson and Singer (2008) call "nested" behavior by accounting for the ways in which regional heterogeneity in the electoral environment influences voters' decisions and behaviors. A guiding theme in this book is that understanding Latin American voters requires theorizing about voters *and* about context. The contributors are united in the pursuit of this objective, and therefore embed features of the electoral context into their expectations and empirical analyses of voter choice. Taking into account intraregional differences in political experiences and menus means that ultimately we observe that there is no single "Latin American voter." Rather, the modal form of electoral behavior differs substantially across countries. While this makes the theoretical and analytical tasks more demanding, we believe the payoffs are considerable. What results is a rich and textured portrait of voting behavior in Latin America, one that identifies conditions under which electoral decisions are more or less likely to be a function of group membership, issue stances, left-right identification, partisanship, and/or performance assessments.

Data and Methods

In stark contrast to the drought-like conditions that marked the field in decades past, today there is a bounty of survey data capturing citizens' attitudes, experiences, and behaviors across Latin America (Zechmeister and Seligson 2012). The availability of rich public opinion and political behavior datasets, combined with methodological advancements for analyzing them, make it an auspicious time for the study of voting behavior in the region. Due primarily to a lack of data, previous scholarship on voting behavior in

Latin America is of more limited quantity and scope. Some of the pioneering studies using survey data to study the vote include Dow's (1998) analysis of policy-relevant voting in Chile; Domínguez and McCann's (1996, 1998) "two-step" model of vote choice in Mexico, in which only those voters who rejected the dominant party considered factors relevant to a classic left-right orientation; and Mainwaring's (1999) study of weak party attachments in the case of Brazil. Over time, the number of single-case analyses of voter choice in Latin America has grown impressively, with key concentrations in Mexico and Brazil propelled in part by existing polling infrastructure and interest and in part by a steady production of election studies, including multi-wave panels (e.g., Ames, Baker, and Rennó 2008; Baker, Ames, and Rennó 2006; Domínguez and Lawson 2003; Domínguez, Lawson, and Moreno 2009; Meixueiro and Moreno 2014).

While single Latin American country election studies are prospering and are too extensive to comprehensively review, there have been fewer regional comparative studies. To gain leverage on voting behavior in Latin America, and to compare and contrast across the region, this volume draws on cross-sectional comparative survey data for eighteen Latin American countries[17] over multiple years, as well as multi-wave panel studies, survey experiments, and expert surveys. While most of these studies are not explicitly election studies, they provide information about electoral choices that allows insight into voting patterns in the region.

Because this volume's primary focus is individuals' political behavior, most chapters rely on data from public opinion surveys conducted using a common core of questions asked across the region. The primary source of these data is the AmericasBarometer survey conducted by the Latin American Public Opinion Project (LAPOP).[18] Though LAPOP's roots date to the 1970s, its regional AmericasBarometer survey project began in 2004 with eleven countries and, with a new wave every two years, expanded to include twenty-six countries in the Americas by 2010 and 2012. Most authors in the volume make use of data from the survey's 2006-12 waves.[19] The AmericasBarometer surveys are nationally representative studies based on complex (stratified and clustered) samples of a standard minimum of 1,500 voting-age individuals who are interviewed in their homes. Our analyses of these data take sample design features into account. The AmericasBarometer project employs an intensively pretested core of questions asked in the same way, according to the same protocol across countries, and the result is an extensive common core of questions. Because political scientists consider the country an appropriate unit of analysis, the authors in this volume weight each country in the pooled analyses equally.

This volume focuses on voter choice in national elections, in particular for the presidency. The AmericasBarometer is not designed as an election survey, yet it does contain the requisite vote-related questions to study choices related to national elections. AmericasBarometer surveys are implemented on a regular basis following a solar, as opposed to an electoral, calendar; in some cases, then, the surveys are conducted near election time while at other times the surveys are implemented several years out from an election. It is possible to cull out of the pooled AmericasBarometer dataset a subset of surveys that was conducted in relative proximity to national elections; we have assessed the robustness of a number of the analyses reported in this volume to that subset and the results lead us to similar conclusions (see, e.g., the introduction to part II). The particular studies the authors employ across the chapters in this volume vary, with some using multiple waves of the survey, between 2004 and 2012, and others using data from the year closest to the time of this book's production, 2012.

Two chapters employ data from annual surveys conducted by the Latinobarometer to illustrate changes in behavior patterns that date from the 1990s.[20] Eight countries have data available since 1995,[21] data from another nine countries are available since 1996, and then the Dominican Republic was added to the sample in 2004. Though we have every reason to expect it to increase in size, at the time of the writing of this volume only a subset of Latin American countries has been included in the Comparative Study of Electoral Systems surveys (the last module featured just five: Brazil, Chile, Mexico, Peru, and Uruguay); thus, we do not use it here.

While the primary focus of most chapters is on patterns within and across countries that emerge from cross-national survey data, several chapters use additional data to illustrate the specific mechanisms that underlie these patterns. Two chapters analyze panel studies from Brazil and Mexico, where respondents were interviewed multiple times in the months leading up to an election. By looking at the same individuals over time, these authors can examine whether changes in attitudes lead to changes in voting behavior. Additionally, one chapter reports on data from an original experiment designed to test whether individuals facing a hypothetical electoral choice change their voting behavior when provided with different information about the candidates. These studies are described in more detail in the chapters that utilize them.

Finally, one challenge in studying clientelism in Latin America is the lack of comparative survey data that asks about clientelist benefits in such a way that it can be included in models of voter choices. Yet our study of electoral behavior in Latin America would be incomplete without examining the extensiveness of this form of politics. Thus, Kitschelt and Altamirano take advantage of a DALP expert survey module that was designed to measure the extent to which parties offer clientelist goods, how those exchanges are organized, and their effectiveness.

An overarching theme in this volume is that voting patterns vary across countries. In short, context matters a great deal to Latin American voters. From the standpoint of analytical tools with which to assess this claim, we are also in an auspicious era with multiple available approaches. Most of our contributors conceptualize individuals as embedded within communities characterized by a set of political or economic conditions. To model this nested structure in analyses of survey data, authors in this volume frequently make use of hierarchical modeling techniques. They differ, however, in their specific approaches, with some estimating the relationship in each country/survey separately and then modeling the variance in those estimates (Jusko and Shively 2005) while others pool survey data and then interact individual-level variables with contextual variables with statistical techniques that generate appropriate standard errors given the limited number of countries (Steenbergen and Jones 2002). For the sake of space, we place some of the technical details related to analyses reported on in the manuscript in notes, chapter appendix material contained within this volume, and/or in an online appendix hosted by the University of Michigan Press. Appendix tables and figures that are found within this volume are denoted with an "A" (e.g., table A1.1), and those found within the online appendix are marked as "OA" (e.g., table OA1.1).

This volume's contributors all find the exploration of public opinion and political behavior to be an exciting enterprise. In the spirit of scholarly camaraderie and transparency, the authors have made code for their analyses available in the online appendix referenced above. Most of the survey data used in this book are also available online directly from the AmericasBarometer, the Latinobarometer, and other sources. We encourage students of public opinion and political behavior to use these code files to run analyses that replicate the results presented here and, even better, to draw out and test additional ideas to develop new insights.

Outline of the Book and Key Findings

This book is divided into four parts. Part I focuses on the choice Latin Americans make to vote or not. In their chapter, Carlin and Love show that demographic differences related to the life-cycle and religion most clearly distinguish the profile of the Latin American voter from that of the Latin American nonvoter, even after controlling for the main elements of the "civic voluntarism" model (Verba, Schlozman, and Brady 1995)—resources, mobilization, and psychological engagement. Compulsory voting laws and the degree of party system polarization, however, shape the impact of individual-level predictors of turnout, particularly those related to demographics and psychological engagement. In sum, descriptive characteristics appear to influence the decision to vote in Latin America more directly than the dominant model of participation suggests, but how pronounced these differences are depends on voting laws and how the party system is structured.

Part II shifts the analysis to the choices voters make among competing parties and models voting behavior within Latin America across social groupings. Many of the same sociological cleavages that influence the vote in other regions influence electoral behavior in Latin America. Class voting seems more prevalent in Latin America now than in the 1990s, a development Mainwaring, Torcal, and Somma link to the rise of leftist politicians who have put class back on the agenda. In their chapter, Boas and Smith show that religion affects voter choices in nuanced ways. Religiosity makes voters of *all* Christian denominations—Catholic or Protestant—more likely to support conservative candidates. Religious denomination shapes voter choices as well: Protestants are slightly more likely to support a non-Catholic (i.e., Protestant or explicitly secular) candidate over a Catholic one. Polarization in the party system, a structural feature of the electoral environment, magnifies religiosity's effects. Moreno's contribution suggests that ethnicity can also influence voter choice if activated by politicians. Though indigenous and mestizos are, on average, more supportive of left-leaning candidates than whites, Moreno shows that this result is driven by a handful of cases in which ethnicity is particularly salient; in most cases ethnicity is not a major voting divide after controlling for class. Moreover, while indigenous voters overwhelmingly supported an indigenous presidential candidate in Bolivia, there is less evidence that indigenous voters rallied behind an indigenous candidate in Guatemala. Thus, substantial ethnic voting only occurs where political entrepreneurs succeed in politicizing ethnicity in a given election. Finally, Morgan's study indicates that Latin American women voters exhibit a slight tendency to support conservative candidates, although this is less true among financially independent women. Women voters also tend to support female presidential candidates. Whether viable women candidates are on the ballot, however, depends on the nature of the electoral environment. Across part II, major social divisions are found generally to shape voting behavior in Latin America. We stress, however, that their impacts are contingent on parties nominating candidates who can activate a given social cleavage and strongly distinguish themselves from one another.

Part III examines voters' connections to the substantive offerings on which parties and candidates compete. As *The American Voter* (Campbell et al. 1960) and others have established, voting on the basis of policy stances is a cognitively demanding task for the average voter, who rationally pays little attention to politics (Downs 1957). Notwithstanding this difficulty and the added challenges posed by the frequently fluid and blurry policy divisions in much of the region, Baker and Greene provide evidence that economic issues influence the Latin American voter. Here the electoral context lends a hand; polarized party systems encourage such issue voting. Zechmeister, meanwhile, considers the extent to which policy-relevant voting is facilitated by the employment of left-right identifications in the voting calculus. She documents a tendency for many Latin Americans to eschew these terms and significant variation across countries in their substantive meanings. Again, the structure of party competition matters significantly. Polarization and programmaticness tighten the connection between left-right identifications and the vote, while fragmentation and clientelism undermine it. Lupu's chapter focuses on partisanship and finds tremendous variation in rates of partisan attachment across the region. At the same time, he shows that partisan identifications are predicted by and serve similar purposes in electoral politics in Latin America as in more established democracies. Particularly relevant to our theoretical framework, partisan attachments are higher where electoral completion is structured by a high degree of party system polarization and institutionalization and low levels of fragmentation. Finally, Kitschelt and Altamirano examine a factor of special significance to voting decisions in Latin America: clientelism. Their study paints a portrait of variation across the region and presents an intriguing empirical puzzle: Latin American parties concentrate great efforts on clientelism but it is not a very effective electoral tool. The authors attribute the ineffectiveness of clientelism to aspects of elections' substance—the recent and disruptive rise of left-populist leaders and parties in Latin America—and structure—overall levels of competitiveness as well as rising levels of development that make clientelism increasingly expensive.

In support of the performance model of voting, part IV shows that Latin America's voters do use the ballot to hold politicians accountable for outcomes on their watch. If voters perceive a weak economy (Gélineau and Singer), widespread corruption among political officials (Manzetti and Rosas), or high levels of insecurity (Pérez), they are likely to vote against the president's party while they generally reward politicians for improvements in these areas. However, and in line with the theoretical refrain of this volume, these effects hinge partially on the degree of control the president's party has over the policymaking process (fragmentation) and, in the case of the economy, party system polarization. The salience of these concerns also varies, with weak performance generally igniting voter ire while a strong economy might buy politicians space to survive corruption scandals. Thus, accountability in the region reflects voter priorities and takes into account structural features of the electoral choice environment.

Conclusion

Latin America provides us with a rich environment in which democracy is less deeply rooted and party politics is still quite fluid, where questions of democratic process take on greater significance, and where there are reasons to question how closely the elements of voters' decision calculi will mirror—in type and/or in degree—that which scholars have found in researching the advanced industrialized world. Despite all the environmental challenges Latin Americans face when it comes to deciding if and how to vote, the chapters in this volume collectively identify some common bases of voter behavior and decisions between advanced industrialized countries and Latin America. In particular, we find that entrepreneurial parties and candidates can activate selected socioeconomic and demographic cleavages in the region, such that voters then choose candidates in ways that align with their membership in socioeconomic, demographic, and related societal subgroupings. Further, we see that issue stances, left-right identifications, and party affiliations tend to play expected roles in electoral behavior, conditional on electoral politics being structured by programmatic competition. And we conclude that voters in Latin America do hold politicians accountable for output, though the weight of these factors depends on the political and economic environment.

Thus, one conclusion we reach in this volume is that the Latin American voter is not entirely unique when compared to others, such as the American voter or the European voter. In the foundational works on voters in established democracies, scholars have shown that group memberships, issue preferences, ideological orientations, party identifications, and performance assessments shape voter choice, but in ways that vary across electoral systems and contexts. We find the same to be true in the case of Latin America.

And yet this volume highlights important ways in which the Latin American voter does diverge. In some countries in the region, voters and nonvoters are virtually indistinguishable on most classic predictors of turn-out; in others they differ greatly, especially in their descriptive attributes. And for as many Latin American cases in which cleavages, ideational factors, or performance seem to matter for voter choice, we observe just as many in which they do not. To help us understand this intraregional heterogeneity, this volume places a spotlight on a set of core features of the electoral environment that correspond to its substance and its structure.

The evidence amassed here suggests that political elites and party systems play formative roles in shaping the nature of voting across the region: where politicians and parties activate group identities, insert issues into the repertoire of party competition, and present a clear menu of choices, Latin American voters are better equipped to pursue representation and accountability. Thus, we conclude that while electoral competition in Latin America is mostly regularized and voters in the region possess the necessary sophistication to behave in ways envisioned by classic models of voting behavior, the degree to which elections fulfill the roles envisioned by democratic theory varies according to the substance and the structure undergirding the choices offered to voters.

Chapter 1 Appendix

TABLE A1.1 Presidential and Legislative Elections in Latin America in the Current Wave of Democratization

	Period	Presidential	Legislative	Total
Argentina	1983–2013	7	13	20
Bolivia	1982–2013	7	7	14
Brazil	1985–2013	6	7	13
Chile	1989–2013	6	7	13
Colombia	1958–2013	14	18	32
Costa Rica	1948–2013	16	16	32
Dominican Republic	1978–2013	10	8	18
Ecuador	1979–2013	10	14	24
El Salvador	1984–2013	6	10	16
Guatemala	1985–2013	8	8	16
Honduras	1981–2013	9	9	18
Mexico	1994–2013	4	7	8
Nicaragua	1984–2013	6	6	12
Panama	1989–2013	5	4	9
Paraguay	1989–2013	5	6	11
Peru	1980–2013	8	8	16
Uruguay	1984–2013	6	6	12
Venezuela	1958–2013	12	12	24
Latin America	1978–2013	129	147	311

Source: International IDEA and International Foundation for Electoral Systems.

NOTES

1. See appendix table A1.1 for a list of elections by country.

2. On deficiencies in electoral processes in general, see O'Donnell (1994) and Achen and Bartels (2004). With respect to specifically flawed elections in Latin America, Hartlyn, McCoy, and Mustillo (2008) judge four presidential elections from 1980 to 2003 unacceptable (the Dominican Republic 1994, Panama 1989, Peru 2000, Venezuela 2000) and deem several others flawed (Bolivia 1985, 1989; Colombia 1990, 1994; the Dominican Republic 1986, 1990; Honduras 1981, 1985; Nicaragua 1996, 2001, 2011; Paraguay 1989; Peru 1995; Uruguay 1984; Venezuela 2000). Presumably, some legislative elections during the third wave and some presidential elections since 2003 could be qualified in similar terms.

3. On democratic transitions, see O'Donnell, Schmitter, and Whitehead (1986).

4. Most of the democratic movement associated with the third wave took place in Latin America beginning in the late 1970s and in the 1980s; we use "fifty" here to recognize the earlier emergence of electoral politics in a handful of countries (e.g., Costa Rica, Colombia).

5. To square the average voter's well-documented lack of knowledge about politics and low interest in campaigns with the demands of a model of choice that places policies and programs at the forefront of decision-making, many scholars turned to information short-cuts or, in the lexicon of this body of scholarship, "heuristic aids" (e.g., Fuchs and Klingeman 1990; Sniderman, Brody, and Tetlock 1991; Popkin 1994; see also Downs 1957).

6. Mainwaring and Pérez-Liñán (2013) see the danger not in ideological distinctiveness per se but in radicalism that makes parties unwilling to compromise.

7. See United Nations Economic Commission for Latin America and the Caribbean (ECLAC), Social Panorama of Latin America 2011, chapter 2.

8. If v_i is the percentage of legislative seats won by party i, then the effective number of parties is $1/\Sigma(v_i)^2$.

9. The authors compiled these data.

10. Authors' calculation based on Bormann and Golder (2013).

11. In some Latin American countries not only do the specific parties that compete often vary from election to election, but the sheer number of contenders may also differ as well. Several countries experienced spikes in the number of competitors (e.g., Argentina, Colombia's legislature, Ecuador, Venezuela) before returning to previous levels of fragmentation, albeit often with different parties after an economic crisis or corruption scandal reshaped the existing party system. Other countries have witnessed recent drops in the number of parties (e.g., Bolivia, Panama's presidential elections) while in Brazil the number of legislative parties has increased since the first third-wave elections. Party systems in Chile, the Dominican Republic, Honduras, and Uruguay, in contrast, have seen great stability in the number of parties, even if their specific identities have changed somewhat over time.

12. Singer follows Dalton's (2008) methodology whereby polarization for country-year j is defined as $\sqrt{\Sigma S_{ij}(LR_{ij} - LR_j)^2}$, where S_{ij} is the share of the legislature controlled by party i, LR_{ij} is the estimated left-right position of party i on the ideological scale, and LR_j is the average ideology for the entire legislature (weighted according to each party's size).

13. The Democratic Accountability and Linkages Project (DALP) was developed under the leadership of Herbert Kitschelt. See https://web.duke.edu/democracy/. Interestingly, polarization on the basis of issues does not always correspond with polarization along a general left-right dimension. Singer (forthcoming) shows, for example, that while the Dominican Republic and Honduras have low levels of polarization on both indices, Colombia and Mexico are less polarized on the Parliamentary Elites in Latin America (PELA) surveys' left-right dimension than on the DALP survey's issue-based measure. Bolivia and Nicaragua, in contrast, appear much more polarized according to legislators' left-right self-placements than experts' judgments of how parties differ across specific issues. It is important to keep in mind that left-right placements are not always indicative of ideological positioning, but may reflect symbolic (e.g., party) or even affective (e.g., antipathy for the opposition) positioning (see, e.g., Zechmeister's chapter on the left-right semantics among Latin American political elites in Kitschelt et al. 2010). Interestingly Singer's measure of left-right polarization correlates fairly strongly (r = 0.76) with polarization on the economic issue asked about by DALP (authors' analysis using data provided by Kent Freeze not reported here) and less well with the other issues.

14. These experts were asked about country-specific issues as well.

15. One potential issue with both the polarization measures we report here (DALP and Singer) is that they weight parties' ideologies by their legislative representation to create the overall country's score. The intuition behind this choice is that deviations from the average ideology by large parties are more important than deviations by smaller parties. Yet this means that if significant social movements boycott elections or fail to win significant representation due to institutional rules, these measures of political polarization may understate the degree of social polarization. One country where this may be in evidence is Venezuela, where the large numbers of strikes and protests surrounding elections diverge from the relatively low levels of polarization reflected in the data. Another factor that may explain the lower than expected polarization scores for Venezuela is that the DALP data was collected in 2007 while the PELA studies used by Singer are unavailable in Venezuela after 2005; thus, both measures predate the recent rounds of mobilization that appeared at the end of President Hugo Chávez's life and against the subsequent regime led by President Nicolás Maduro.

16. The specific measures for each of these countries are available in the online appendix or can be downloaded from the DALP project.

17. Argentina, Bolivia, Brazil, Chile, Colombia, Costa Rica, the Dominican Republic, Ecuador, El Salvador, Guatemala, Honduras, Mexico, Nicaragua, Panama, Paraguay, Peru, Venezuela, and Uruguay.

18. See http://www.vanderbilt.edu/lapop/ for more information about the survey, questionnaires, sample design, and data access.

19. In 2006 the survey included seventeen of the eighteen countries that are the focus of this book. Data from Argentina are available beginning in 2008.

20. See http://www.latinobarometro.org/latino/latinobarometro.jsp for information about these surveys and for data access.

21. Argentina, Brazil, Chile, Mexico, Paraguay, Peru, Uruguay, and Venezuela.

PART I

✦ VOTER TURNOUT ✦

2 ✦ Who Is the Latin American Voter?

RYAN E. CARLIN AND GREGORY J. LOVE

[T]he act of voting requires the citizen to make not a single choice but two. He must choose between rival parties or candidates. He must also decide whether to vote at all.

Campbell et al., *The American Voter*, 89

From 2000 to 2012, more than 71% of the voting-age population participated in the average first-round presidential election in Latin America (figure 2.1).[1] Our goal is to understand why some people participate while others stay home. Despite the staying power of elections since the third wave of democracy, most of what we know about turnout in the region relies on aggregate data and is related to the electoral and institutional context (Fornos, Power, and Garand 2004; Lavezzolo 2008; Ochoa 1987; Pérez-Liñán 2001; Kostadinova and Power 2007; Schraufnagel and Sgouraki 2005). But who are Latin America's voters? And how does context influence their decision to vote? Answering these questions is a necessary and analytically prior step to understanding voter choice in the region, the subject of the rest of this volume.

Our approach is two-pronged. First, we outline a causal sequence in which voting results from individuals' demographics, resources, mobilization, and psychological engagement with politics. Then we compare the explanatory value-added of each block of predictors to an overall accounting of individual-level turnout in Latin America. Our results indicate that voting is most heavily influenced by demographics, then psychological factors, with mobilization and resources mattering least. Second, and in line with the theoretical framework set forth in the introduction, we propose two contextual factors that condition the role individual factors play in Latin

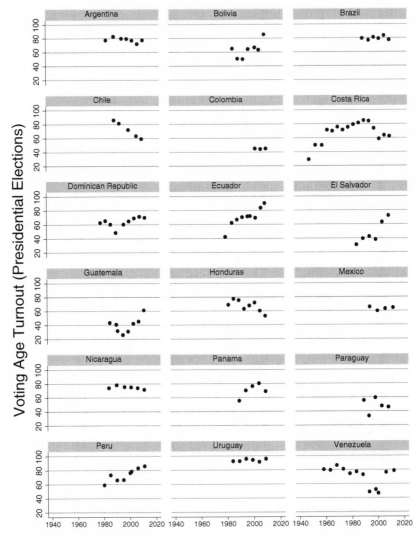

Figure 2.1   Presidential Voter Turnout in Presidential Elections by Country.
Source: International IDEA.

Americans' vote decisions. One is compulsory voting—laws are on the books of many countries in the region but unevenly enforced. The other is party system polarization, which varies mightily in Latin America. We then assess how compulsory voting and polarization condition the effects of each block of individual-level predictors in our causal sequence. Here we pay special attention to two of the most proximate drivers of voter turnout:

partisanship and political interest. We find that compulsory voting and party system polarization mainly moderate the roles of demographics and psychological engagement—especially partisanship—in the decision to vote. As such, our comparative analysis of Latin America helps identify the mechanisms by which electoral and institutional contexts condition voter turnout in the region and, perhaps, beyond.

Electoral Participation at the Individual Level: A Hybrid Framework

Why some citizens take part in elections and others do not is a fundamental political inquiry. To address this question we graft demographics onto the central tenet of the "civic voluntarism" model: that people do not participate in the political process "because they can't; because they don't want to; or because nobody asked" (Verba, Schlozman, and Brady 1995, 269). The civic voluntarism model assumes demographic links to participation via citizens' *resources*, networks of *recruitment and mobilization*, and *psychological involvement* with politics. Resources refer to the cognitive, monetary, and time-related facilitators of participation. Our theoretical framework supplements traditional networks of voter mobilization and recruitment found in Western democracies with the clientelistic networks widespread in Latin America. Finally, we expect psychological orientations and attachments to act as the most proximate motivators of electoral participation.

As depicted in the hybrid theoretical framework in figure 2.2, and in line with the Columbia (e.g., Lazarsfeld, Berelson, and Gaudet 1944; Berelson, Lazarsfeld, and McPhee 1954) and Michigan (e.g., Campbell et al. 1960; Lewis-Beck et al. 2008) schools, we assume that demographics shape individuals' initial priors for electoral participation. Whether demographics wield a direct influence or their effects are mediated by factors more proximate to the decision to vote, as the civic voluntarism model assumes, is an empirical question with real theoretical implications. Because these four blocks of predictors may be interrelated, gauging their total effects on the likelihood of voting requires consideration of their causal ordering.

Demographics

Demographics serve as the starting point for our causal story of voting in Latin America. By demographics, we mean largely descriptive characteristics that are either fixed or slow changing. Since voting is largely a habitual act, new entrants to the electorate may participate in elections at lower rates than long-enfranchised groups. At various points in time, suffrage

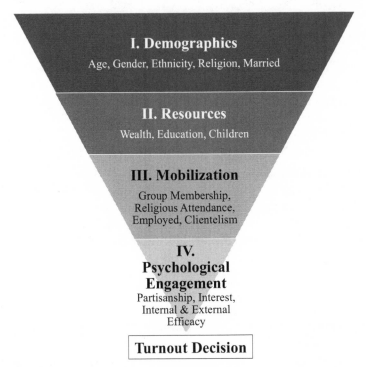

Figure 2.2   Causal Sequence of Individual-Level Determinants of Voter Turnout.

and other political rights in Latin America have been restricted, de jure or de facto, according to major demographic categories. Yet as new voters become more socialized into politics and organize, parties attempt to mobilize them and incorporate issues they care about. Eventually, these groups become habituated to electoral participation and shrink their turnout gaps, and in some cases, relatively rapidly. Movement between demographic categories—such as transitions into and out of marriage or religious faiths—may speed or slow political socialization and, potentially, create or break the habit of voting. Thus, demographics may be key inputs to the decision to turn out in contemporary Latin America.

Three theories compete to explain how electoral participation varies with age. According to the "life-cycle" theory, younger citizens vote less because they prioritize their budding careers and families over politics. Voting increases as they integrate into their communities and gain a stake in local affairs but decreases as they retire, withdraw socially, and become infirm (Milbrath 1965). In the "life-experience" model, familiarity with politics, political attachments, exposure to mobilizing agents, and the social-network rewards of voting increase with age (Rosenstone and Hansen 1993, 137). "Generational" theories connect diverging rates of voting across age cohorts to the lasting footprints of unique experiences of political socialization and highly competitive or salient elections (Miller and Shanks 1996; Franklin 2004). Comparative studies are inconclusive as to how age affects voting in Latin America. Seligson et al. (1995) observe life-cycle effects in Central America with the exception of Costa Rica, where the life-experience model is truer to data. Life-experience effects are also found in the 1979 Mexican and Venezuelan elections (Davis and Coleman 1983), seventeen Latin American countries in 2000 (Bratton, Chu, and Lagos 2010), and eighteen Latin American countries in 2010 (Carreras and Castañeda-Angarita 2014). To help resolve this tension, we explicitly probe life-cycle and life-experience effects for the region.

In Western democracies, women were excluded from elections for decades. In the United States, the gender gap following the Nineteenth Amendment (Merriam and Gosnell 1924) persisted among that cohort until the 1980s (Firebaugh and Chen 1995) but today is all but gone (Burns, Schlozman, and Verba 2001). The reversal of turnout gender gaps in established democracies owes to the greater party mobilization of women (Rosenstone and Hansen 1993) and new resources and cultural values that accompany economic modernization (Inglehart and Norris 2003). Analysts find that Latin American women are equally (Hinton, Moseley, and Smith 2012; Bratton, Chu, and Lagos 2010) or more likely (Carreras and Castañeda-Angarita 2014) to vote than men. We reexamine the relationship between gender and turnout here.

Ethnicity may also shape electoral participation. De jure and de facto disenfranchisement and political exclusion of ethnic and racial groups could, like gender, hinder participation. Early work in the United States supports this premise for southern blacks (Key 1949; Blalock 1967). Additionally, ethnicity may define important social cleavages around which parties form and mobilize voters (Lipset and Rokkan 1967; Birnir 2007). In line with this thesis is research emphasizing social connectedness, group identity, conflict, discrimination, and mobilization (Leighley 2001; Barreto and Pedraza 2009). Strong political and social hierarchies across ethnic lines have led some to dub Latin American society a "pigmentocracy" (Lipschutz 1944; Telles and Steele 2012). The rise of indigenous politics (Madrid 2012), the increasing importance of race (Wade 1997), and ethnicity's influence on voter choice in Latin America (Moreno, this volume) suggest these factors could increasingly matter for turnout. A case study in Guatemala finds lower turnout in more indigenous municipalities (Lehoucq and Wall 2004). Comparative studies of voter turnout in the region have virtually ignored ethnicity and race. A lone exception, Moreno's (2013) analysis of eighteen Latin American countries, finds higher voting propensities among indigenous self-identifiers compared to whites but lower propensities among black identifiers. Against this backdrop on diverging expectations, we further probe the link between race and electoral participation.

Religious beliefs may also shape voting turnout. Verba and Nie (1972) noted "a difference in political style between Protestants and Catholics, with the latter more likely to be involved in partisan activity" and to be classified as "voting specialists" (101). In Latin America, Boas and Smith (2013) find Catholics are indeed more likely to vote than other Christians, non-Christians, and the nonreligious. And as Boas and Smith (this volume) discuss, the spread of evangelicalism and increased public debate around moral issues has raised the salience of religion as a social cleavage in Latin America (see also Hagopian 2009 and Mainwaring and Scully 2003). Hence we test how religious affiliation influences the vote decision by looking at differences across denominations. Later, as part of the mobilization block, we examine turnout gaps between religious individuals and those who do not attend church at all.

A final demographic we consider is marital status. Conventional wisdom holds that "[m]arried people are more likely to vote than those who are single, separated, divorced, or widowed" (Wolfinger and Rosenstone 1980, 44). Theoretically, spouses influence electoral participation in three ways. First, marriage marks a significant step toward stabilizing one's personal life and establishing roots in the community. Second, marriages can serve as miniature social networks by which spouses mobilize each other: "The encouragement of a husband or wife might be the push necessary to get both partners to the polls" (Wolfinger and Rosenstone 1980, 45; see also Teixeira 1987; Strate et al. 1989). Third, any marital transition—from single to married, from married to widowed or divorced—may alter participation patterns (Stoker and Jennings 1995; Kinder 2006). Little is known about how marital status affects voting in Latin America. Our data allow a straightforward test of whether being married encourages Latin Americans to vote.

Resources

While voting is comparatively "cheaper" in terms of time and money than other forms of political participation, it is clearly not "free" and, thus, is more widespread among citizens of higher socioeconomic status (Verba and Nie 1972). Verba, Schlozman, and Brady's (1995) civic voluntarism model reframes the mechanism in terms of resources—time, money, and civic skills. Those authors find resources mightily shape other forms of political participation, though their effects on voting are more idiosyncratic. The logic is that these classes of assets facilitate participation; without them taking part in politics is more daunting. Free time heavily depends on employment and family circumstances, especially children in the home. Money may matter marginally for turnout but is considered more crucial to non-electoral participation. Civic skills flow from education and are honed by exercising them in the workplace, nonpolitical organizations, and churches. In our analysis, we use education as a proxy for civic skills along with proxies for time (children) and money (wealth).

Recruitment and Mobilization

While resources and psychological engagement constitute individual-level traits that facilitate political activity or compel involvement, it is naïve to think that people will universally participate without an invitation. While nonpolitical "secondary institutions" (the workplace, voluntary associations, churches, etc.) are arenas for forging civic skills, they also serve as recruitment networks into which parties, candidates, activists, and peers can tap to mobilize voters. Rosenstone and Hansen (1993) describe two forms of mobilization. Direct mobilization is when leaders or activists personally encourage would-be voters and, in effect, "subsidize" the information needed to vote (e.g., pamphlets about issues, Election Day reminders, discussing key issues, etc.) and the costs of voting (e.g., distributing voter registration cards, offering rides to the polls, etc.). Indirect mobilization consists of encouraging people to vote via social networks: "Leaders need not communicate with every person directly. Instead, leaders contact their associates, associates contact their colleagues, and colleagues contact their friends, families, and co-workers. Through social networks, leaders get the word out, and citizens get the word" (Rosenstone and Hansen 1993, 27). Indirect mobilization effectively multiplies the impact of direct mobilization because it creates "social expectations about the desirable course of action" (Rosenstone and Hansen 1993, 29). To enforce compliance, network members reward voters and sanction nonvoters. Scholars have proffered alternative logics by which social networks boost participation (e.g., Edlin, Gelman, and Kaplan 2007; Franklin 2004) that lead to the same prediction.

Indirect mobilization seems to function similarly in Latin America. Voting rates are higher among Latin Americans who are employed, are active in civic groups and in churches, and live in tight-knit rural communities (Boas and Smith 2013; Bratton, Chu, and Lagos 2010; Carreras and Castañeda-Angarita 2014). Direct mobilization should also work as theorized. While our data preclude a test of direct mobilization through canvassing, we can test whether clientelistic offers—which are fairly common in Latin American party systems (Kitschelt et al. 2010)—directly mobilize Latin Americans to vote (Carreras and Castañeda-Angarita 2014; Nichter 2008). This proposition is less obvious than it seems given the slippage between clientelistic effort and effectiveness pointed out by Kitschelt and Altamirano (this volume).

Psychological Engagement with Politics

Lastly, the civic voluntarism model assumes resources and social networks enhance the sorts of civic attitudes and engagement that foster participation in political life. Thus, it subsumes a key insight of the Michigan model, namely, that voting is a behavioral manifestation of one's psychological engagement with politics and buttressed by attitudes and affective orientations to politics, elections, and political actors. As a recent work in this tradition concludes, "[t]urnout behavior is guided by the following rule: The stronger a person's psychological involvement in politics, the higher the propensity to participate in politics by way of voting" (Lewis-Beck et al. 2008, 92). Below we review the basic arguments and decidedly mixed evidence regarding the major political-psychological predictors of turnout in Latin America: party identification, political efficacy (internal and external), and political interest.

Party identification was originally conceived as "an affective attachment to an important group object in the environment" (Campbell et al. 1960, 143). As such, it is a "psychological identification with a party" (Lewis-Beck et al. 2008, 112) that contains an element of social identification (Greene 1999, 2004). Social identity is "that part of an individual's self-concept which derives from his knowledge of his membership in a group (or groups) together with the value and emotional significance attached to the membership" (Tajfel 1978, 63). Thus, identifying with a political party can make one more likely to vote by raising the expressive benefits of voting. It also shapes people's preferences among competing candidates and gives them "a dog in the fight" (Lewis-Beck et al. 2008, 90). Many studies in American and comparative politics (e.g., Kittilson and Anderson 2011; Verba, Nie, and Kim 1978) concur: citizens with stronger party attachments vote at higher rates.

Given its prominence in a range of political systems and the variance in levels of partisanship in Latin America, the uneven attention to partisanship in voter turnout models in the region is striking. However, all studies in the region that analyze partisanship conclude that it dramatically raises the likelihood of voting. In eighteen Latin American democracies, partisanship emerges as the most robust psychological correlate of voting (Carreras and Castañeda-Angarita 2014). Moreno (2003) found that identifying with and, in most cases, leaning toward a party heightened voting intentions in the 2000 Mexican election. This suggests that Mexicans, like their counterparts elsewhere (Hinich and Munger 1997; Aarts and Wessels 2005), are driven to vote by both the directional and intensity dimensions of partisan identification. Moreover, Lupu (this volume) demonstrates that party identification in Latin America has similar correlates and predicts vote choice in line with classic theories derived from the United States and Western Europe. We have every reason to expect partisanship to bolster turnout in Latin America.

Campbell, Gurin, and Miller's (1954) foundational conception of political efficacy refers to "the feeling that individual political action does have, or can have, an impact upon the political process . . . the feeling that political and social change is possible, and that the individual citizen can play a part in bringing about this change" (187). Scholars have since unpacked these motivations into *external* and *internal* political efficacy. Internal efficacy refers to the belief that one can personally influence the political process, whereas external efficacy refers to the belief that the political system is responsive to one's views (Balch 1974; Niemi, Craig, and Mattei 1991). Though both forms of efficacy are expected to boost turnout, the literature in American politics swirls with debates about their measurement. Most research in broad comparative perspective has prioritized external over internal efficacy (e.g., Kittilson and Anderson 2011; Norris 2004).

Comparative turnout studies in Latin America have employed both concepts, though rarely together and always with varied results. Starting with Davis and Coleman (1983), Mexican and Venezuelan voters were found to be more internally efficacious than nonvoters but only the Mexican voters were more externally efficacious. Seligson et al. (1995) observed a positive but nonlinear relationship between external efficacy and turnout in El Salvador, a negative relationship in Honduras, and null effects elsewhere in Central America. McCann and Domínguez's (1998) inspection of turnout in the 1988 and 1991 Mexican elections revealed a positive influence of external efficacy. Carreras and Castañeda-Angarita

(2014) showed external efficacy *lowered* voting in the region, though the effects were miniscule and reproduced in just two country analyses. Thus, political efficacy appears only weakly related to voter turnout in Latin America and possibly in unexpected ways, reflecting the conflicts seen in the U.S. literature.

Expressing an interest in politics indicates a psychological involvement that, presumably, motivates individuals to further their understanding of politics via the press, social networks, and direct participation in political processes. This logic implies that "[c]itizens who are interested in politics—who follow politics, who care about what happens, who are concerned with who wins and loses—are more politically active" (Verba, Schlozman, and Brady 1995, 345). Although research in the Michigan tradition is equally focused on voters' interest in the campaign and concern over its outcome (cf. Lewis-Beck et al. 2008), other landmark works in American politics (Rosenstone and Hansen 1993; Verba, Schlozman, and Brady 1995) and most comparative studies (e.g., Aarts and Wessels 2005; Almond and Verba 1963; Powell 1986; Verba, Nie, and Kim 1978) incorporate *general* interest in politics into models of electoral participation along with stalwarts, partisanship, and efficacy.

Political interest has figured in Latin American turnout models in various forms and with differing degrees of success. Merging political interest and political knowledge into an "involvement in politics" index, Davis and Coleman (1983) found that it boosted turnout in Venezuela but depressed it in Mexico. Case studies of Mexico (McCann and Domínguez 1998; Lawson and Klesner 2004; Moreno 2003, 2009b) and Chile (Carlin 2006, 2011) link political interest to voting. Bivariate analyses reveal positive associations between vote intention and political interest throughout Latin America (Payne 2007). Together the evidence implies that political interest should be associated with turning out to vote in the region.

By way of summary, the first part of this chapter seeks to identify Latin American voters' demographic profiles, resource levels, degree of insertion into mobilization networks, and psychological engagement with politics. Our expectations differ little from the conventional wisdom on voter turnout in established democracies. Nevertheless, the empirical record in Latin America is quite thin and, thus, some anomalous or null results should not be surprising. Our first set of analyses seeks to build up this empirical record and provide more conclusive answers as to who votes in Latin America. With this in mind, and modest about what any model of voter turnout can hope to explain, we now describe our data, research design, and methods.

Individual-Level Research Design and Analysis

Our dependent variable is self-reported turnout in the previous presidential election. The data we use are responses to the biennial AmericasBarometer surveys of the eighteen Latin American countries that are the subject of this volume (see chapter 1, note 18). We code as having voted respondents who say they went to the polling booth in the past election,[2] regardless of whether they claim to have voted for a specific candidate or cast a blank ballot. Because voting self-reports suffer from social desirability bias and inaccurate recollection, individually validated survey data of turnout are the gold standard. No such data exist for the region. Thus, to test our expectations we rely on survey data, and make the choice to pool all AmericasBarometer surveys 2008–12[3] for all eighteen Latin American countries into one model.[4] Not surprisingly, there is over-reporting of turnout in the data (8 percentage points on average). Yet a strong correlation ($r = 0.8$) between turnout as reported by national election institutes and aggregate levels of self-reported turnout across these surveys provides some validity to our claim that the survey question is related to actual turnout.

Block I: Demographics

The first block of explanatory factors includes basic demographics and social identities. *Age* is measured in years and we include *Age* and *Age²* to gain leverage over life-cycle versus life-experience debate.[5] Because in some countries (e.g., Chile) common-law type marriage is widespread because of recent restrictions on divorce and other social factors, we include a dichotomous variable coded for respondents who are *Married* or living in marriage-like relationship (*unión libre*). Gender gaps in voting will be assessed with a dichotomous variable coded 1 for respondents who are *Male* and zero for *Female*. Dummies for self-identified ethnicity and religion are also included. Specifically, for ethnicity we have *Mestizo, Indigenous, Black,* and *Other* as compared to *White*, the reference category. For religion mainline *Protestant, Evangelical, Mormon/Jehovah's Witness, No Religion,* and *Other* are judged against the reference category *Catholic*.

Block II: Resources

We analyze three forms of theoretically relevant resources. A respondent's level of *Wealth* is measured in national quintiles and constructed from a principal component analysis of ownership of a series of household material goods (Córdova 2009). Since many Latin Americans make their livelihoods from subsistence agriculture or in the informal sector, wealth better captures material resources than income. We gauge time resources with the respondent's *Number of Children*. According to the civic voluntarism model, having children reduces the time and money available for civic and political participation. However, children may also motivate parents to model good citizenship by voting. Finally, we proxy civic skills with *Education*: a 19-point scale running from no formal education to more than 18 years of schooling.

Block III: Mobilization and Recruitment

To test if social connectivity and civic involvement expose Latin Americans to mobilizing agents we model five potential mobilizing factors. Most are chiefly arenas of *indirect* mobilization. *Membership*, for instance, is the average level of participation in five types of social groups (religious, parent-teacher, community improvement, professional, and political). The scale ranges from zero (no participation) to 4 (weekly participation in *all* group types); the sample mean of this scale sample is 0.60, and country means vary from a high of 0.79 in Guatemala to a low of 0.32 in Uruguay.

Separate from the membership scale we include a 5-point scale measuring frequency of attendance at religious services. It ranges from never or nearly never to more than once a week. Houses of worship and the pulpit are often key loci of electoral mobilization. They also widen one's social network and provide links to the community that can increase the odds of voting. We include this *Religious Attendance* measure in addition to the *Membership* scale that counts religious groups to capture the more casual or passive effects church attendance may have on turnout. Essentially, it can test whether voters can be mobilized just by being in the pews. While frequency of religious service attendance and attending religious groups are related, they are not perfect substitutes ($r = 0.58$).

Rural indicates that the respondent resides in a rural rather than an urban setting. Rural areas may feature dense social networks and extensive associational life, which could spur electoral participation. Of course, this effect may be attenuated by the socially disruptive processes of urbanization as people leave their historic communities for cities. Moreover, urban areas are easier for parties to canvass. To see what effect, if any, geographic location has we include a dichotomous variable for rural residents. We also use a dichotomous variable for individuals who are *Employed* to gauge the mobilizing impact of the workplace on turnout.

The final factor in our mobilization block is a measure of clientelistic targeting. In many developing democracies direct quid pro quo mobilization via a patron-client relationship is pervasive. Our *Clientelism* measure taps whether the respondent has received "gifts" from candidates or parties in exchange for his or her vote or support in recent elections on a 3-point scale from never (0) to frequently (2). Since this question was only asked broadly in the 2010 AmericasBarometer (and even then not in Honduras) we restrict our analysis of mobilization to 2010.

Block IV: Psychological Engagement

First among the psychological motivators of turnout is *Partisanship*: a dichotomous variable coded 1 if respondents identify with a party and zero if not. Ideally we could tap strength of partisanship; yet the comparative literature on partisanship strongly argues that concepts of party attachment vary extensively with the nature of party systems. In addition, survey questions about strength of partisanship may lack cross-context reliability if parties play differing social roles across polities. Thus, we employ a dichotomous measure of identification to help ensure a more reliable and valid measure of partisanship in Latin America.

Internal Efficacy is measured on a 7-point scale (linearly recoded to run 0–1) gauging respondents' subjective assessment of their understanding the most important political issues. *External Efficacy* is a 7-point scale (recoded 0–1) gauging how much respondents think national leaders are interested in people like themselves. *Political Interest* is a 4-point measure of how much interest the respondent has in politics, recoded from zero, none, to 1, a lot.

In keeping with the causal sequencing of our hybrid theoretical framework, we empirically model the influence of individual characteristics in the step-wise block approach illustrated in figure 2.2. It shows how the blocks build on each other and which variables are tested in each. Namely, we estimate the substantive effect of each block of variables (demographics, resources, mobilization, psychological) with *only those controls that theoretically precede it*. For example, the effect of gender on voting turnout is only estimated including the other demographic variables (age, married, ethnicity, and religion) that in theory should not be affected by gender itself. By the same token, the influence of resources on voting is estimated with demographics variables in the model but not the variables from the mobilization or psychological engagement blocks. Mobilization variables, for their part, are estimated along with the demographics and resources variables that causally precede them but without the variables in the psychological engagement block. Finally, the effects of the variables in the psychological engagement block—partisanship, political interest, and external and internal political efficacy—on the decision to turn out are gauged while controlling for all the variables in the preceding three blocks. Our motivation for using this step-wise block approach is to gauge predictors' effects before they are diluted by intervening variables farther down the causal chain.

Since our dependent variable is binary, we use logistic regression along with country and year fixed effects. To ease interpretation we report logistic regression coefficients in appendix table A2.1 and in figures 2.3 and 2.4 show the change in probability of voting (and its standard error) when a particular variable's value is changed from its observed minimum value to maximum values while holding all other causally prior variables at either their mean or mode (for binary variables). We also calculate adjusted count R^2, a measure of model fit that represents the percentage of observations correctly predicted adjusted by the mean value of y. In the simple intercept model adjusted count R^2 is zero. Essentially, then, adjusted count R^2 indicates how much the model improves on the average reported turnout rate in the sample. We use this approach over competing pseudo-R^2 measures because our models' improvement over a naïve model is the characteristic of central interest to our research question. Moreover, with survey-adjusted weighting, the model does not produce a log-likelihood, which is required for all non-count-based pseudo-R^2s.

Individual-Level Results

First among the variables in the demographics block is *Age*. Breaking with previous work on Latin America (Bratton, Chu, and Lagos 2010; Carreras and Castañeda-Angarita 2014; Seligson et al. 1995), we find convincing evidence in favor of the life-cycle, as opposed to the life-experience, thesis—a finding echoed in well-established democracies (Smets and van Ham 2013). Because the curvilinear effects of *Age* can only be appreciated graphically, we analyze them separately in figure 2.3. It demonstrates that both the young and very old are much less likely to vote than individuals toward the middle of the age distribution. The propensity to vote rises until around the age of 56 and then starts declining. The substantive impact of these combined effects makes *Age* the most potent determinant of

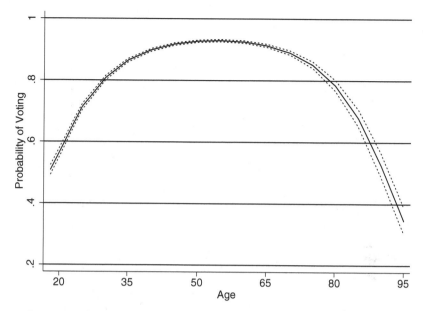

Figure 2.3   Life-Cycle Effect on Voter Turnout. *Source:* Americas-
Barometer 2008–2012. *Note:* Predicted probability of voting across the
life cycle with 95% confidence-intervals (dotted lines). Based on estimates
from a pooled model that are adjusted for complex survey design.

voter turnout under study. In a country-by-country analysis not reported
here the same pattern emerges in every case.

Discrete change values in predicted probabilities for all demographic
factors besides *Age* are displayed in figure 2.4. We observe a small gender
gap, with *Males* slightly more likely to vote. While this finding goes against
the grain of trends in established democracies (Smets and van Ham 2013),
it presages the traditional gender gap in vote choice that predominates in
Latin America (Morgan this volume).[6] *Marriage*, an understudied correlate
of voting in Latin America, raises the likelihood of voting by roughly 4.4
percentage points. Considering the historical discrimination and political
exclusion of Latin America's indigenous groups it is somewhat noteworthy
that, when compared to self-identified *Whites*, only self-identified *Blacks*
vote at lower rates. When it comes to religion, *Evangelical* and mainline
Protestants along with the *Nonreligious* are less likely to turn out than *Catholics*, adherents of the region's dominant faith.[7]

Figure 2.4 also displays the substantive effects of the variables in the
resources block. *Wealth* has a minor but positive relationship to voting.

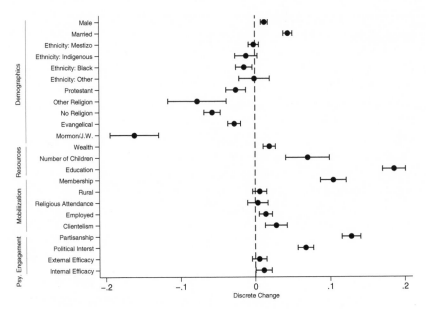

Figure 2.4   Predicted Substantive Effects of Individual-Level Factors on
Voter Turnout. *Source:* Data come from waves 2008, 2010, and 2012 of
the AmericasBarometer for all blocks *except* Mobilization. Because of data
availability only the 2010 wave (excluding Honduras) was used to estimate
the Mobilization block. *Note:* Point estimates were adjusted for complex
survey design. Change in probability of voting going from a variable's
min to max value holding all variables from the same or preceding blocks
(demographics, resources, and mobilization) constant at their means or
modes.

In long-standing democracies, Smets and van Ham (2013) also uncover
inconsistent if moderately positive effects of wealth on turnout. Perhaps
surprisingly, *Number of Children* is positively associated with voter turnout.
Its effects are on par with *Wealth*, and analyses not reported here suggest
that they do not vary across men, women, or housewives. So unlike wealthy
democracies, where the number of children and turnout are inversely related (Smets and van Ham 2013) because it drains free time (Verba, Schlozman, and Brady 1995), the opposite holds true in Latin America. *Education*,
for its part, has one of the largest overall effects on turnout. We observe
an 18.6 percentage point difference in the probability of voting between
those with 18 years of education and those with none. As such, the effect of
education on turnout in Latin America is more in line with that of Western democracies (Smets and van Ham 2013) than democracies in Africa or

East Asia, where education and turnout do not appear to be linearly related (Bratton, Chu, and Lagos 2010).

The third block, mobilization, incorporates five measures, three of which significantly predict turnout. Being *Employed* is related to voting but its substantive effect is quite small. But group *Membership* matters a great deal. The most active group members are 10 percentage points more likely to vote than people who are not involved in any group. Although *Religious Attendance* is insignificant in this model, other analysis indicates that its effects flow entirely though religious group membership. Regarding *Clientelism*, those who were frequently targeted for vote-buying were just 2.8 percentage points more apt to turn out than those not targeted. These modest effects speak to the gulf between how much effort Latin American parties put into clientelism and its electoral yield (Kitschelt and Altamirano this volume). *Rural* residents and *Urban* dwellers appear equally likely to vote.[8] While in line with Smets and van Ham's (2013) meta-analysis of established democracies, this result contradicts previous work in Latin America (Carreras and Castañeda-Angarita 2014; Bratton, Chu, and Lagos 2010) and the pessimistic participatory portraits of "agrarian apathy" (Campbell et al. 1960), "farmers" (Milbrath and Goel 1977), and "farm workers" (Wolfinger and Rosenstone 1980) in the American politics literature.

In the final block, two indicators of psychological engagement are significantly and positively related to going to the polls. Identifying with a party increases the probability of voting by 12 to 13 percentage points. Thus, as observed in developed (Smets and van Ham 2013) and developing (Carreras and Castañeda-Angarita 2014; Bratton, Chu, and Lagos 2010) democracies alike, partisanship motivates turnout. Political interest has an effect roughly as large. Compared to the uninterested, respondents very interested in politics are around 6.7 percentage points more likely to vote. Neither internal nor external efficacy is consistently related to turning out.[9]

In sum, consistent with life-cycle theories the likelihood of Latin Americans voting varies with age and marital status. We also observe turnout gaps—with Catholics voting at higher rates than non-Catholics and some evidence suggesting men vote more consistently than women. Ethnicity has two noteworthy effects: black Latin Americans have a participation gap compared to that of whites but the indigenous—another historically excluded group—do not. Latin American voters are mobilized on the job, in civic associations, and via clientelistic parties; mobilization is not systematic vis-à-vis religious attendance or residential setting (i.e., rural or urban).

While Latin American voters indeed have more resources in the forms of wealth (financial), education (civic skills), and time (children) than their nonvoting counterparts, incorporating such factors improves very little on a basic sociological model of turnout. Those individuals who identify with a political party are much more likely to go to the polls. Similarly, those who are most interested in politics are the most likely to vote; however, in contrast to what is often observed in developed democracies, efficacy, internal or external, appears to play little if any role in turnout in Latin America.

Finally, figure 2.5 reports how well each block predicts an individual's decision to vote on models restricted to 2010 in order to include *Clientelism*.[10] Demographics play a central role.[11] The adjusted count R^2 for a demographics-only model is 0.20, meaning the demographics block improves model fit by 20% over a model with just country dummies. The addition of the resources block—wealth, education, and children—increases the model's performance to an adjusted count R^2 of 0.22 (a 10% increase). But adding the mobilization block has no effect (0.22) and neither does addition of the psychological block (0.22).

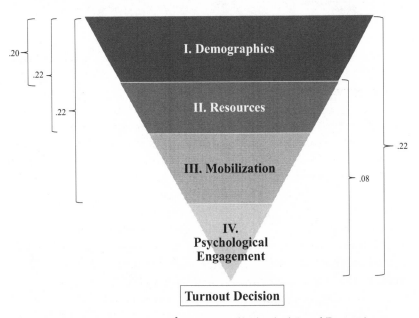

Figure 2.5 Adjusted-Count R^2 by Blocks of Individual-Level Determinants of Voter Turnout. *Note:* Because of data availability, all blocks are estimated using the 2010 wave excluding Honduras, which is missing data for the *Clientelism* variable.

Intriguingly, the civic voluntarism model only marginally improves our understanding of why Latin Americans vote over demographics. Indeed, the adjusted count R^2 of a model that includes all blocks *except* demographics is a paltry 0.08. This suggests that demographic factors like age, gender, religion, ethnicity, and marriage have effects on the vote decision that do not run through resources, mobilization, or psychological factors. This conclusion goes against the conventional wisdom in the United States (Verba, Schlozman, and Brady 1995) and recent comparative research in Latin America (Carreras and Castañeda-Angarita 2014) that emphasize the roles of psychological engagement and resources, respectively. Overall, though in line with previous models of turnout in the region (Carreras and Castañeda-Angarita 2014), our model has limited ability to explain turnout. To explore why, the following section examines how variation in the political contexts of Latin American elections shapes the models' explanatory power.

Context and the Decision to Vote: Compulsory Voting and Party System Polarization

Does the explanatory power of each block of individual-level factors—demographics, resources, mobilization, and psychological—vary with institutional and political contexts? First-cut analysis by country suggests so.

Since these contexts are unlikely to change between elections (or at all with institutions) we address this question by estimating the same model specifications (with the exception of *Clientelism*) as above using the AmericasBarometer survey that occurred within twenty-four months of each country's most recent presidential election. By using the surveys most closely following an election we expect the estimates to be more valid than using a survey distant from the election. Mirroring the pooled analysis, the country-by-country analysis shows that baseline demographics and the psychological factors most proximate to the vote decision wield the most explanatory power. More important, the country-by-country models highlight vast variance in the blocks' predictive abilities. Specifically, large standard deviations in the mean adjusted-count R^2's by country and block[12] indicate that context likely plays a role in shaping how well individual factors can explain the turnout decision.

If the effects of individual-level factors on voter turnout indeed vary across Latin America, a crucial theoretical question is why. Answering this question, we argue, requires an appreciation for the political milieus in which citizens vote. But which aspects should theoretically condition the link between the blocks of individual traits and turnout?

Powell's (1986) pioneering article serves as a useful starting point. It was motivated by a paradox: compared to their counterparts in other advanced industrial democracies, Americans were more psychologically inclined toward voting but voted far less. Powell concluded that voluntary voter registration was partially to blame but cautioned, "there is little doubt that adopting automatic registration or other measures to encourage turnout of the less well-off would bring to the polls a total electorate somewhat less interested, efficacious, and informed than the present voters" (37). One common "other measure" used to "encourage turnout" in Latin America is compulsory voting, and it tends to boost voter turnout substantially (Ochoa 1987; Pérez-Liñán 2001; Fornos, Power, and Garand 2004; Schraufnagel and Sgouraki 2005; Lavezzolo 2008; Carreras and Castañeda-Angarita 2014).

A second culprit Powell identified were weak linkages between parties and differentiated social groups. Where such linkages are strong, "[p]arty choice should seem simpler to the less involved; cues from the personal environment of the individual (friends, family, and co-workers) should be more consistent; party organizers can more easily identify their potential supporters in making appeals and in helping voters to the polls on election day" (22). In Latin America, Pérez-Liñán (2001) argued that party competition incentivizes mobilization agents to turn out the vote via networks much as observed in the American case. And evidence suggests turnout is higher where ethnic parties mobilize voters around ethnic cleavages (Schraufnagel and Sgouraki 2005).

Together these findings imply that voting is less informationally and psychologically demanding where voting laws and party linkages facilitate electoral participation. Based on this premise, we deduce a set of theoretical expectations regarding how compulsory voting and party linkages should condition the relationship between individual characteristics and voter turnout.

Compulsory Voting

Perhaps the most ironclad conclusion in the comparative turnout literature is that enforced compulsory voting laws boost turnout (cf. Blais 2006; Franklin 2004; Gallego 2014). While compulsory voting regimes are the norm in Latin America they vary in degrees of enforcement. Powell's (1986) intuitions notwithstanding, the implications of compulsory voting laws for the individual basis of voting in the region are rarely explored (but see Maldonaldo 2011).

We advance a simple hypothesis: where voting is voluntary, citizens must rely more heavily on demographics, resources, mobilization, and psychological orientations to propel them to participate in elections, which are low-cost, low-benefit activities (Aldrich 1993). But compulsory voting laws backed by enforced sanctions relieve the need for such high levels of political-psychological involvement. If voting is easy, common, and legally coerced, then voters should be less dependent on the informational heuristics gained by group identity, material resources, mobilization, or psychological engagement. In short, compulsory voting regimes should weaken the civic voluntarism model's explanatory leverage vis-à-vis turnout.

Party System Polarization

Political parties can link with the electorate in several ways (Kitschelt 2000). When engaged in programmatic competition, parties craft unambiguous, consistent, and interrelated sets of policy stances on the basis of social or political cleavages, ideology, or appeals to particular issue publics (Kitschelt and Freeze 2010). To the extent parties reach polarized positions, the electorate benefits in the form of easily differentiable electoral options. A positive externality of such party polarization may be heightened voter turnout. Indeed, evidence that turnout is higher when parties are more polarized (Dalton 2008; Brockington 2009) and when lines of responsibility in the policymaking process are clear (Carlin and Love 2013) suggests that citizens are more apt to vote when their electoral options are discrete and obvious.

We expect party system polarization to weaken the influence of individual characteristics on turnout based on the following logic. Polarized party systems make voting less demanding in terms of resources and psychological involvement. Individuals with resources and motivation have comparatively smaller advantage over non-identifiers if the latter can rely on parties to highlight the unmistakable differences between themselves. Moreover, if parties are nearly indistinguishable, the cost-benefit analysis of voting (Downs 1957)[13] loses traction and affective motivations, such as psychological attachments, and informational resources, such as education or group identities, gain traction on the decision to vote. In sum, if party system polarization bolsters turnout, then it also decreases the differences between voters and nonvoters.

The alternative hypothesis, that polarization increases the influence of individual factors, is worth considering. Elections that present voters with very distinct choices are more meaningful since the policy goals and priorities of the competing parties permit substantial change via the ballot box (Kittilson and Anderson 2011, 38). In polarized systems the resource-rich and mobilized electorate may perceive elections as high-stakes games and, thus, turn out more systematically than their nonpartisan and disinterested counterparts. Nonpolarized systems, on the other hand, could reduce elections' stakes and, thus, weaken the influence of individual factors on voting. We will test our proposed hypothesis against this alternative.

Cross-Level Empirical Approach and Analysis

To test the conditional expectations laid out above, we run a country-level analysis in which the dependent variable is adjusted count R^2 from the country-by-country analyses discussed above. Because the dependent variable is itself an estimate, we follow Lewis and Linzer's (2005) advice and estimate Efron robust standard errors to correct the sampling variance of the estimated dependent variable and the small sample size. Since using measures of model fit as dependent variables is relatively rare, we performed a validity check based on the following logic: as turnout rates increase, the purchase individual attributes grant us on the question of who votes should decrease. To test this notion, we predicted country-specific adjusted count R^2s from our models with the official turnout rates for each election under study. As expected, the coefficient on official turnout levels is negative. In other words, our individual-level model performs worse, in terms of adjusted count R^2, in high-turnout countries. So in high-turnout countries, such as Uruguay, Nicaragua, and Argentina, few if any characteristics systematically distinguish voters from nonvoters. This result helps validate our empirical approach.

To test our hypotheses concerning how context influences individual traits predictive power vis-à-vis turnout, we measure *Compulsory Voting* with a dichotomous variable scored zero where voting is not compulsory and enforced and 1 for where it is (International IDEA). Since 2000, countries in Latin America with strongly enforced compulsory voting laws have, on average, turnout rates more than 15 percentage points higher than countries that do not; we find a similar pattern in the AmericasBarometer data. Our *Party System Polarization* measure is generated by Singer (forthcoming) from the Universidad of Salamanca's Parliamentary Elites in Latin America (PELA) survey described in the introductory chapter of this volume. Its scores represent the mean ideological placements of a country's parties by parliamentary elites. Polarization ranges from a low of 0.14 (Dominican Republic) to a high of 3.3 (El Salvador). Voting-age turnout in the most polarized party systems of the region since 2000 is, on average, 8 points higher than in the least polarized systems.

The level-2 results reported in table 2.1 show strong support for our contention that electoral and institutional contexts condition the importance of individual traits on the decision to vote. *Compulsory Voting* has its largest effect by far on the links between demographics and voting. Where enforced compulsory voting laws do not exist, such as in Colombia, Nicaragua, or Mexico, demographic characteristics are much stronger predictors of who votes than in places with enforced compulsory voting laws, like Bolivia and Uruguay. And as each additional block of individual characteristics enters the model, the difference in predictive power of the model between compulsory and noncompulsory systems tends to increase. After demographics, *Compulsory Voting* most significantly conditions the power of the psychological engagement block. In sum, enforcing compulsory voting laws dramatically reduces the ability of individual-level factors to distinguish voters from nonvoters.

Party System Polarization has similar if slightly more nuanced effects. Like compulsory voting, the explanatory purchase of individual-level predictors diverge between polarized and nonpolarized party systems. A unit increase in the polarization scale (range 0.14 to 3.3) cuts in half the adjusted count R^2 (0.05) for the demographics block alone. However, *Party System*

TABLE 2.1

Blocks	I	I+II	I+II+III	I+II+III+IV
Compulsory Voting	−0.082**	−0.107**	−0.106**	−0.115**
	(0.026)	(0.028)	(0.025)	(0.031)
Party System Polarization	−0.053*	−0.055*	−0.057**	−0.052*
	(0.022)	(0.023)	(0.017)	(0.023)
Constant	0.175**	0.196**	0.198**	0.205**
	(0.044)	(0.047)	(0.035)	(0.043)
Observations	18	18	18	18
R-squared	0.404	0.43	0.511	0.425

Source: Because of data availability all blocks are estimated using the 2010 AmericasBarometer excluding Honduras.

Note: Dependent variable is adjusted count R^2 after each block is added to logistic regression analysis. Blocks: I, Demographics; II, Resources; III, Mobilization; IV, Psychological Orientations. Efron robust standard errors in parentheses. ** $p < 0.01$, * $p < 0.05$, two-tailed.

Polarization seems to have much smaller, if any, effects on the other blocks of the model. To delve more deeply into this result, we consider whether compulsory voting and polarization have differential effects across the four measures of psychological engagement, the most proximate predictors of voting choice affected by context.

We begin by visually inspecting the effect sizes—measured as the change in predicted probabilities of voting for a discrete change (minimum to maximum)—of the four psychological variables across the eighteen countries. The results, reported in figure 2.6, indicate heterogeneity in

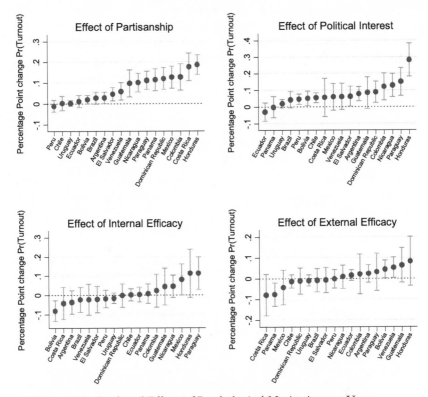

Figure 2.6   Predicted Effects of Psychological Motivations on Voter Turnout: Discrete Change Probabilities and Standard Errors from Country-by-Country Logit Models. *Source:* Only the AmericasBarometer surveys that most closely followed the most recent presidential elections were used. The 2008 wave is used for: Mexico, Guatemala, Colombia, Venezuela; 2010 wave for: El Salvador, Honduras, Panama, Ecuador, Bolivia, Paraguay, Chile, Uruguay, Dominican Republic; 2012 wave for: Nicaragua, Costa Rica, Peru, Brazil, Argentina.

the depth of the psychological roots of turnout across Latin America. Yet only *Partisanship* and *Political Interest* vary significantly across the region. While *Partisanship* has significant positive effects in a majority of cases, they are much greater in some cases than others. A similar pattern is observed for *Political Interest*. However, *External Efficacy* and *Internal Efficacy* appear completely unrelated to turnout in nearly all country-level models (and the pooled ones above).

Following on the theory and method outlined above, we test whether *Compulsory Voting* and *Party System Polarization* moderate, that is, reduce, the degree to which *Partisanship* and *Political Interest* predict the decision to vote. As table 2.2 shows, our expectations are generally upheld. In countries without well-enforced compulsory voting laws, having a partisan attachment makes citizens much more likely to vote. On average, *Partisanship* boosts the probability of turning out by 9% in such contexts. Furthermore, the more polarized a party system becomes, the less determinant of voting partisanship becomes, even controlling for differences in compulsory voting regimes. Across the roughly 3-point range of *Party System Polarization* in our sample, then, its reductive effects on the influence of *Partisanship* on voting are on par with, if not slightly larger than, that of *Compulsory Voting*. When it comes to *Political Interest* the results are more mixed. Whereas enforced compulsory voting laws systematically diminish its influence on voter turnout, the degree of polarization in the party system has no effect. The coefficient is, however, signed in the expected, negative, direction,

TABLE 2.2   Conditional Effects of Context on Psychological Foundation of Voter Turnout

	DV. Effect of Partisanship	DV. Effect of Political Interest
Compulsory Voting	−0.09**	−0.06*
	(0.017)	(0.029)
Party System Polarization	−0.035*	−0.031
	(0.013)	(0.026)
Intercept	0.15**	0.13*
	(0.023)	(0.052)
R^2	0.62	0.30
N	18	18

Source: Only the AmericasBarometer surveys that most closely followed the most recent presidential elections were used. The 2008 wave is used for: Mexico, Guatemala, Colombia, Venezuela; 2010 wave for: El Salvador, Honduras, Panama, Ecuador, Bolivia, Paraguay, Chile, Uruguay, Dominican Republic; 2012 wave for: Nicaragua, Costa Rica, Peru, Brazil, Argentina.

Note: Dependent variables are the effects of partisanship and political interest, respectively, on voting measured as the change in predicted probabilities for a discrete change (minimum to maximum) of these variables. Efron robust standard errors are in parentheses. $^{**}p < .01$, $^{*}p < .05$, two-tailed.

which is suggestive given the fact that these effects are estimated from a relatively small national-level sample ($n = 18$).

Overall, compulsory voting regimes and party system polarization combine for a parsimonious yet relatively powerful explanation of the power of our demographics cum civic voluntarism model and its most proximate (psychological) factors on voter turnout in Latin America. Working through distinct mechanisms, these features of the electoral and institutional context reduce the demographic bias within and the psychological demands on the electorate.

Conclusion

From this attempt to paint a portrait of the Latin American voter, we offer several preliminary conclusions. According to our individual-level analysis, Latin American voters and nonvoters are chiefly distinguished by their demographic characteristics and psychological orientations and, to a lesser extent, by their resources and exposure to mobilizing agents. The average Latin American voter is, in order of substantive significance, in the middle of his or her life-cycle, educated, civically active, married, wealthy, employed, partisan, and interested in politics. Painted in those terms, Latin American voters bear a striking resemblance to their cousins in Western democracies. At the same time, our analysis suggests that Latin American voters are more likely to be, again in order of effect size, a parent with multiple children, Catholic, mobilized by selective clientelistic benefits, and male. Considered this way, the Latin American voter takes on a more unique profile.

Theoretically, the individual-level analysis shows the potential limits or scope conditions of the civic voluntarism model. In contrast to the United States, in Latin America the influence of the fundamental demographics of age, gender, religion, and race are not realized solely, or even mostly, through factors farther down the causal sequence. Rather, they have strong independent effects on turnout that are not mediated by factors associated with resources, mobilization, and psychological engagement. Together these micro-level findings foreshadow a motif of this volume: there is no single Latin American voter.

At the contextual level we encounter another incarnation of this motif: the profile of the Latin American voter changes from context to context. Distinctive, yet decontextualized, profiles of voters and nonvoters based on demographic attributes and psychological engagement fade away under certain electoral and institutional conditions. Specifically, well-enforced sanctions for not voting and high degrees of polarization in the party system iron out voting differentials across demographic and social groups. Such findings resonate with Powell's (1986) theorizing about the centrality of electoral laws and partisan linkages for fostering electoral participation. Our results also provide evidence to support Lijphart's (1997) normative argument that compulsory voting should be used as a tool for raising electoral and, in turn, political equality.

Yet a critical reflection on the findings reported in this chapter also reveals some tensions among basic democratic ideals. If we take seriously Lijphart's insistence that a broad and active electorate is a public good, then how we reach such an equilibrium has normative implications. The easiest and swiftest approach to increase turnout in Latin America is almost certainly to introduce compulsory voting laws with strict sanctions and to enforce more effectively such laws already on the books.[14] Yet this solution carries a potentially high price tag. Responsive and accountable government requires voters who are engaged enough in politics to articulate their demands to parties, to monitor party performance with respect to those demands, and to vote on that basis. If compulsory voting can bring this about, as Lijphart claims, then such laws would potentially advance the democratic ideal. However, experimental evidence casts doubt on this supposition (Loewen, Milner, and Hicks 2008), and, indeed, we find no significant differences between the system types with regards to political interest or internal efficacy levels. So if compulsory voting means the politically involved and those weakly invested in politics vote at roughly the same rates, it introduces a greater potential for moral hazard among elites and, thus, slippage on these democratic ideals. Even though strong and clear party competition also diminishes the weight of partisanship in the voting calculus, it encourages turnout by making it easier to distinguish which parties to reward and which to punish. So, like compulsory voting, polarized party systems may facilitate higher electoral participation—along with greater accountability—without the coercion. Perhaps this is why Powell (1986) rejected tinkering with registration and voting laws and, instead, prescribed tighter party-group linkages.

Chapter 2 Appendix

TABLE A2.1   Pooled Block Model of Voter Turnout in Latin America

		Logit Coefficient (std. err.)
Demographics	Male	0.096***
		(0.018)
	Age	0.210***
		(0.004)
	Age-squared	−0.002***
		(0.000)
	Married	0.296***
		(0.020)
	Ethnicity: Mestizo	−0.012
		(0.026)
	Ethnicity: Indigenous	−0.085
		(0.054)
	Ethnicity: Black	−0.105***
		(0.040)
	Ethnicity: Other	−0.006
		(0.077)
	Protestant	−0.179***
		(0.045)
	Other Religion	−0.491***
		(0.110)
	No Religion	−0.377***
		(0.033)
	Evangelical	−0.193***
		(0.029)
	Mormon/Jehovah's Witness	−0.909***
		(0.076)
Resources	Wealth	0.037***
		(0.008)
	Number of Children	0.026***
		(0.007)
	Education	0.077***
		(0.003)
Mobilization	Membership	0.455***
		(0.047)
	Rural	0.060
		(0.049)
	Religious Attendance	0.008
		(0.017)
	Employed	0.131***
		(0.042)
	Clientelism	0.144***
		(0.042)
Psychological Engagement	Partisanship	0.720***
		(0.028)
	Political Interest	0.504***
		(0.041)
	External Efficacy	0.039
		(0.036)
	Internal Efficacy	0.081**
		(0.040)

Source: AmericasBarometer surveys 2008–2012.

NOTES

1. Only presidential elections held during democratic periods (Polity score > 5) are displayed.

2. With the exception of Peru in 2010, in countries with a two-round presidential election system, the question asked about turnout for the first round of the election.

3. We use all countries and surveys during the five-year period to estimate an average effect of individual traits across the region and for the time period. Including multiple surveys for each country also helps estimate tighter confidence intervals. In a sample that includes only one survey per country (the one most closely following a presidential election), results are largely similar, with the main difference being church attendance has significant positive relationship with voting.

4. For the mobilization set we are restricted to the 2010 wave because it is the only one that systematically includes a question on vote-buying, Honduras being the lone exception.

5. Our models cannot properly address generational theories because we lack longitudinal data.

6. If we restrict the data to 2012 AmericasBarometer surveys, there is no gender gap, which may indicate that the gender gap is closing.

7. *Mormons* and *Jehovah's Witnesses* as a combined group are significantly less likely to vote than any other group, but the number of identifiers for these two religions is much smaller.

8. This finding holds even if we remove from the equation the wealth variable, whose aggregation method incorporates the urban/rural distinction.

9. In a sample with those surveys conducted within twenty-four months of an election, *External Efficacy* shows a significant yet small correlation with turnout.

10. As noted above, the sample includes all countries except for Honduras.

11. The adjusted count R^2s for each block are estimated on the same sample. Non-survey weighted models produce McFadden pseudo-R^2s that follow a similar pattern (see replication code).

12. After each model we calculate adjusted count R^2 after each block is added for each country and analyze its distribution. For the demographics block the mean adjusted count R^2 is 0.077 with a large standard deviation (0.087). After adding the resources block, the mean adjusted count R^2 rises to 0.089 (s.d. = 0.097); the addition of the mobilization block (without clientelism) adds no explanatory value on average (mean = 0.088; s.d. = 0.09). A final block of psychological variables brings the country-by-country average adjusted count R^2 to 0.1 (s.d. = 0.1). See online appendix figure OA2.1 for a graphical distribution by country and block.

13. Downs argued that when parties have identical platforms, one receives the same utility regardless of who is elected; thus, it is rational to abstain to avoid wasting resources on voting.

14. While some may suspect increasing baseline levels of democracy would be helpful, the level of democracy as measured by Freedom House (average of *Political Rights* and *Civil Liberties* scores) is not significantly correlated with turnout in our sample or as measured at the aggregate level by International IDEA, nor does it condition the effects of our individual predictors of turnout.

+ DEMOGRAPHICS AND THE VOTE +

Introduction to Part II:
Demographics and the Vote

RYAN E. CARLIN, MATTHEW M. SINGER,
AND ELIZABETH J. ZECHMEISTER

Electoral coalitions often reflect social divisions. Socioeconomic and demographic divides can come to undergird political competition through three general processes. First, in some cases groups from one or more of these social subdivisions participate in the founding of a political party and there may be formal ties between civil society organizations that advocate for specific groups (e.g., labor unions, indigenous rights organizations, churches) and political parties that guarantee these groups a role in selecting candidates and determining the party's platform. Second, voters may support candidates with similar backgrounds and demographic characteristics to attain descriptive representation. Third, group interests may shape voters' policy preferences on issues such as the welfare state and income distribution, education and cultural policy, and moral values; with the goal of advancing those policy preferences, voters might select parties that share those values.

While other parts of the world have seen party systems develop and endure around deep societal cleavages (Lipset and Rokkan 1967; Deegan-Krause 2007), many scholars of Latin America have argued that parties there have aimed at mass inclusion so that they "catch all sides" of extant or potential divisions (Dix 1989). Yet societal divisions are likely to matter in the Latin American context in those particular cases in which they are activated. In fact, scholars point to several Latin American cases in which civil society groups like unions (Collier and Collier 1991; Levitsky 2003), churches (Mainwaring and Scully 2003), and indigenous rights organizations (Yashar 2005; Van Cott 2005; Madrid 2012) helped establish political parties or purposefully forged formal linkages with existing parties. In turn, parties in many countries have structured political competition along religious, class, and identity lines via church-state conflicts; debates over moral issues like divorce, gay rights, and abortion; battles against income inequality and poverty; and the political inclusion and social rights of indigenous movements (Kitschelt et al. 2010). By revisiting old social cleavages and activating latent ones, parties have the potential to make societal divides relevant to Latin American voters.

We focus in this part of the book on four social divides that are particularly relevant to Latin America: class, religion, ethnicity, and gender. Historic and current wealth disparities make class an important social divide in Latin America, and one that has been activated from time to time by parties and political entrepreneurs. Political conflict over the question of state-church relations marked the early period of Latin American politics, and issues related to religion have found new life in debates over moral issues and in the rise in evangelical denominations, on the one hand, and the drop in church attendance in a once-predominantly Catholic region, on the other hand. Ethnicity is a salient social divide in those countries across the region in which large portions of the population identify with indigenous groups and customs and where these groups have often been marginalized both economically and politically. And cultural norms and divergent outcomes contribute to gender gaps in the Latin American region as they do in most other parts of the globe, though little has previously been said about the extent to which Latin American political gender gaps mirror those found in other democracies.

The principal dependent variable in this part and in part III is respondents' reported vote choice, with the options arrayed on a left-right dimension according to expert ratings of the parties' ideological positions. Several chapters also look at whether groups vote for candidates who have the same demographic traits that they have (e.g., whether Protestant voters support Protestant candidates, women vote for women, and indigenous voters vote for indigenous candidates). However, group-based interests can manifest themselves even when there is not a candidate who shares the same social or economic markers of the group whose support is being courted. Group-based theories of voting thus generally focus on explaining voters' propensity to support parties or candidates with distinct political leanings and the chapters in this part follow suit.

Generally speaking, one can expect traditionally economically marginalized groups, such as lower classes, to be more supportive of left-leaning parties that emphasize welfare programs and endorse social equality as a goal. Religious identities and practices are expected to lead voters to support right-leaning candidates who endorse traditional social values. On average, we might expect voters oriented toward an indigenous identification to find left-leaning candidates in Latin America attractive, given the tendency for left ideological platforms to emphasize natural resource protection, indigenous rights, and state-sponsored services to marginalized groups; however, we recognize that there is considerable diversity across countries, and across time, in the ways in which indigenous issues have been politicized. And scholarship focused on advanced industrialized countries has identified an ideological gender gap, with women leaning toward the left. As Morgan explains in her chapter in this part, Latin American women have customarily espoused conservative social values and supported right-leaning parties and candidates, but life circumstances, choices, and changes in women's social and economic roles may leave them increasingly more likely to vote for left-leaning candidates.

To assess the extent to which individuals sort into electoral options according to their group memberships and/or identities, we need a measure of voter choice that captures the political options represented on the ballot. Consequently, the core dependent variable in this part and the following is based on a question from the Latin American Public Opinion Project's (LAPOP) AmericasBarometer surveys that asks respondents for whom they voted in the first round of the previous presidential election.[1] To construct a "left-right vote choice" variable, we follow an approach offered by Baker and Greene (2011). Namely, we recode answers to this question according to Wiesehomeier and Benoit's (2009) expert scorings of the ideology of the presidential candidates' political parties on a scale from left (1) to right (20).[2] If a voter supported a party that was not included in the expert survey, we exclude him or her from the analysis.[3] If a candidate was nominated by a coalition of parties, we use the average of the nominating parties weighted according to the size of their electoral representation after the election.

To provide a sense of these data, figure II.1 presents the mean values on the voter choice variable for each of the eighteen Latin American countries, based on the 2012 AmericasBarometer data. The figure shows significant

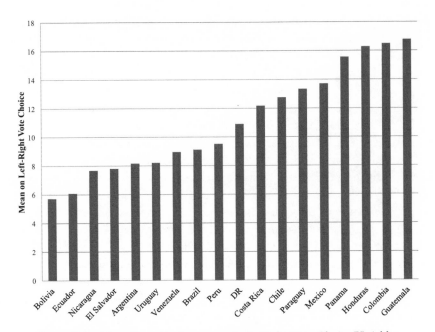

Figure II.1   Mean Voter Preference on Left-Right Vote Choice Variable.
Source: AmericasBarometer 2012. *Note:* Data adjusted for complex survey
design. Chart shows mean responses to the vote choice question, which
has been coded to correspond to the parties' placements on an array
from 1 (far left) to 20 (far right), as determined by the Wiesehomeier and
Benoit (2009) expert survey.

variation across the region. The voting public in some countries (e.g., Bolivia, Ecuador, and Nicaragua) strongly favors candidates who stand clearly
on the left of the political spectrum, while in other countries the vote leans
decisively toward candidates on the right end of the scale (e.g., Honduras,
Colombia, and Guatemala).

One potential concern with this approach to developing a vote choice
dependent variable is that the results are conditional on a coding that has
been generated on the basis of a single elite survey. To address this concern, we ran a series of robustness checks that pitted a model in which our
left-right voter choice variable is a function of social divides and identities
against the same model but with alternative left-right voter choice measures.
Specifically, in these alternate models we coded respondents' votes using (1)
legislators' placements of parties in their own countries based on the Parliamentary Elites of Latin America (PELA) survey data from the University

of Salamanca (Alcántara 2012) and (2) the average self-placement on the left-right scale of individuals who reported voting for any given party in the AmericasBarometer survey. Models based on these different coding schemes yield very similar estimates of left-right vote choice[4] and, thus, suggest that our substantive conclusions about the predictors of voter choices in Latin America do not depend on the particular indicator used.

Another potential concern with the dependent variable is that it is based on a survey question that asks about behavior in an election that may have occurred, in some countries, up to six years prior to the survey. Although this could be viewed as predicting past electoral behavior with respondents' current characteristics, certain key independent variables (e.g., gender, race) do not change over time while others (e.g., wealth and religiosity) tend to change slowly. Still, gaps in time may aggravate faulty recall or willful misstatement of the vote. While the vote recall question does overstate the vote for the incumbent president,[5] we observe a very strong correlation ($r = 0.94$) between the percentage of respondents who reported voting for a candidate in 2012 and the percentage of the vote that candidate actually received in the previous election. As a second set of robustness checks, we pooled data from various AmericasBarometer surveys and created a second dataset that included only the survey that most closely followed the last national election. Using the same general model referenced above, we find that the correlates of vote choice in 2012 are roughly equivalent to those found in analyses based on this alternative dataset of surveys most proximate to the last election. Convergence with respect to the results from these two different datasets gives us reason to believe that basing our dependent variable on a question that asks respondents for whom they voted in the first round of the previous presidential election is a sound approach.[6]

A final way to assess the validity of our vote choice measure is to observe the extent to which it confirms the predictions of relatively well-established hypotheses (see Adcock and Collier 2001, 542–43). If our measure lacks validity and/or introduces a great deal of "noise" into the analyses, observing hypothesized differences in vote choice across subgroups becomes more difficult. Throughout parts II and III, and in the conclusion to this book, we present evidence that the factors that, in theory, ought to predict the vote, in practice, do. Thus, while we are cognizant that our left-right vote choice measure and models are not perfect representations, we are confident that the dependent variable is a reasonable proxy for left-right voter choice in Latin America and that our models allow us to trace core patterns in voters' decision-making calculi.

The chapters in this part collectively demonstrate that the vote in Latin America often divides along societal subgroup lines. And yet this tendency varies across elections and countries. Certain socioeconomic and demographic divisions are more heavily politicized in some countries than in others, and, moreover, certain candidates and parties are better poised to prime this dynamic by incorporating ethnic and class appeals, religion, or gender policies into their campaigns. In short, whether individuals connect to political options on the basis of characteristics that stem from social divides such as those marked by class, religion, ethnicity, and gender depends on whether parties and candidates can activate those distinctions in the electorate and attract voters who might not otherwise be predisposed to them. While there is variation across the studies of societal divides presented in this part, the reader will note three core take-away messages: first, the nature and electoral relevance of particular social divides changes significantly from country to country; second, a societal divide in and of itself is only a necessary but not a sufficient condition to generate group-based voting patterns; and, third, in a number of cases, contexts in which political options take clearly distinct (i.e., polarized) positions are ones in which group-based voter choice is more likely to emerge.

More specifically, Mainwaring, Torcal, and Somma show that class voting, while highly variable across time and space in Latin America, appears more prominently in the contemporary period than in the 1990s. Further, they find that the presence of a left-of-center candidate is a successful recipe for engendering class-based voting, while polarization itself does not. Boas and Smith identify distinct voting patterns across Christian denominations (Catholics versus Protestants) and between believers and secular individuals in the Latin American region. They pay particular attention to the potential for religious clergy and politicians to activate the religious cleavage, and find that polarization is positively associated with a tendency for the nonreligious and religious churchgoers to split into left and right voting camps. Moreno finds that the ethnic vote in Latin America is difficult to pin down, as exemplified by crosscutting results for indigenous self-identity and language across the region. Of all the countries Moreno examines, ethnicity is most consistently and highly politicized in Bolivia, where Evo Morales has found success in cultivating a strong base of indigenous support. The lack of consistency in patterns of ethnic voting in the region tells us that the presence of a large indigenous population may be a necessary condition for ethnic-based voting, but not sufficient. Finally, Morgan demonstrates that traditional gender gaps (with women preferring political options to the right of men) are found on average across the Latin American region, though there is some evidence that this gap is dissipating as a new modern gap (with women to the left) shows signs of diffusing across the region. Once again, the structure of the party system is shown to matter: the more polarized the party system, the greater the tendency for women and men to sort into vote groups that create a traditional gender gap.

In summary, the chapters in this part document how, and the conditions under which, parties and candidates who politicize class, religion, ethnicity, and gender are likely to activate identity voting in Latin America. Across the region candidates from traditionally marginalized groups— lower classes, women, ethnic minorities, and non-Catholics—are increasingly viable and often successful presidential candidates. Candidate supply is typically met by voter demand, but the supply of candidates willing and able to engage in identity politics is inconsistent across time and space. In addition, ideological differences in voting patterns across social groups depend, at least to some extent, on the structure of the party system. In particular, the more polarized the political options, the more religion and gender appear to influence the vote; and polarizing left populist presidential candidates have the potential to—but may not always—activate class voting and ethnic voting.

NOTES

1. Respondents were provided a list of the candidates who ran for president along with their party affiliations (or the coalitions of parties that supported them) to make it easier to remember which party they supported.

2. In the cases of Argentina and Ecuador, the incumbent party was not listed in the expert survey but the experts scored the incumbent president (Ecuador) or her husband (Argentina) and so we use those measures as a proxy for the more general party position.

3. One downside to our approach is that some party systems have experienced major shifts in the time since the expert survey was conducted in the mid-2000s. We have adopted case-specific solutions as follows. We code a vote for Reyes Villa and the right-wing opposition in Bolivia in 2010 as being an ideological continuation of the right-wing coalition that coalesced around Quiroga in the 2005 election. But there is no analogous solution to some of the new parties that emerged in recent elections in several other countries. As a result 40% of voters who report casting a valid vote in Guatemala cannot be coded, nor can 19% in Nicaragua, nor 10% in Colombia. All other cases have fewer than 2% of the vote that cannot be coded ideologically. We have carried out several robustness checks to ensure that these cases with missing data are not unduly affecting the results. First, we have run analyses reported in this introductory essay and in the conclusion of this volume using the other measures of party position described in the text and the

results are generally comparable. Second, we have run the models without Bolivia, Colombia, Guatemala, and Nicaragua. The substantive results do not change if these four countries are excluded. Third, we have pooled these data with previous rounds of the AmericasBarometer survey and modeled voter choice in the 2005 Bolivian elections, 2006 Colombian elections, 2007 Guatemalan elections, and 2006 Nicaraguan elections. Doing so reduces the independent variables available to us due to changes in the survey content over time, but the main substantive conclusions about the role of wealth, gender, ethnicity, religion, and policy and left-right stances on average across the hemisphere are not affected by this change. Nonetheless, specific results for these countries in the chapters that follow should be interpreted with an appropriate degree of caution given the comparatively larger amount of missing data.

4. The estimates of party positions based on the left-right position of their voters are correlated with the measures generated using academic experts or parliamentary elites at $r = 0.69$ or higher. The expert surveys and parliamentary elite estimates are correlated at $r = 0.89$.

5. The percentage of people who said they voted for the eventual winner is about 15.5 percentage points higher on average than the percentage of the vote that he or she got in the first round of the election. The average runner-up candidate loses about 8 percentage points of his or her vote in the survey compared to the actual vote share while the third-place candidate loses 5 percentage points.

6. As an additional robustness check, Singer and Tafoya (2014) replicated the pooled analyses we report in the conclusion using a 2010 Latinobarometer survey that asked respondents whom they would vote for if the election were held today. They coded responses using the Wiesehomeier and Benoit (2009) data with updates from Baker and Greene (2011) to generate a measure of left-right vote that is not retrospective but instead reflects the voters' current attitudes. The correlations they report between that measure and respondents' demographics and issue positions are consistent with those reported in this volume with the exception of gender—Singer and Tafoya find no gender gap with regards to left-right voting while Morgan (this volume) finds women to be somewhat more supportive of conservative candidates. Otherwise, the overall similarity in the two sets of findings suggests that these patterns are robust to measurement concerns.

3 ✦ The Left and the Mobilization of Class Voting in Latin America

SCOTT MAINWARING, MARIANO TORCAL,
AND NICOLÁS M. SOMMA

Dating as far back as late nineteenth-century debates about whether workers would be able to achieve socialism through elections, class voting has been an issue of long-standing interest. In the second half of the twentieth century, class voting became a key scholarly issue as sociologists and political scientists analyzed the degree to which different cleavages structured party systems. Over decades, an abundant literature emerged on class voting in Western Europe and the United States. In contrast, until recently there were few empirically solid cross-national studies of class voting in Latin America. With the resurgence of the Latin American left since the election of Hugo Chávez in 1998, interest in this subject has rekindled.

In light of the massive changes in class structures, the great socioeconomic inequalities, increased electoral competition, and electoral instability in Latin America in recent decades, it is timely to examine class voting. Class voting reveals insights into how different classes perceive their interests and hence cast their ballots. Variance across countries and over time provides insights into the political construction of class voting. Because of the fairly recent advent of cross-national surveys that cover much of the region, for the first time it is possible to compare class voting across most of Latin America.

Class voting also has consequences for the institutionalization of party systems. Stable and enduring social links between political parties and citizens' preferences are one of the four dimensions that characterize institutionalized party systems (Mainwaring and Scully 1995a; Mainwaring and Torcal 2006). Understanding cross-national differences and the evolution of class voting could help explain how these social links develop, and by extension, the potential mechanisms to increase the level of the institution-alization of party systems.

This chapter has three objectives. First, we present the most compre-hensive-to-date description of class voting in Latin America. It covers eighteen countries, far more than any previous scholarship on class voting in Latin America. We use two different dependent variables (presidential and legislative voting), two different measures of class, and three cross-sectional surveys (AmericasBarometer 2006, 2008, and 2010). Contrary to what Torcal and Mainwaring (2003a) found for seven Latin American countries in 1995, today there is huge variance in class voting across the eighteen countries. In contrast to earlier analyses that reported weak class voting in almost all countries of the region (Dix 1989; Roberts 2002; Tor-cal and Mainwaring 2003a), in recent years it has been strong in Argen-tina, Bolivia, Brazil, Guatemala, Peru, and Venezuela—though still weak in many countries.

Second, we analyze the degree to which results are consistent with Lip-set's classic hypothesis that the poor vote for the left and the better off for the right (we call this "conventional class voting").[1] In contemporary Latin America, where there is class voting, it overwhelmingly supports this well-known hypothesis. However, whereas previous analyses argued or assumed that the primary agent of class voting, consciousness, and mobilization would be the organized working class (Bartolini 2000, 240–63; Clark, Lip-set, and Rempel 2001, 84; Roberts 2002), in contemporary Latin America, class voting is strongest among highly disadvantaged sectors—the poor self-employed and unskilled workers—and weak among skilled workers.

Third, we argue that class voting must be mobilized by viable left-of-center presidential candidates and parties and by policies implemented by left-of-center governments. Class is an objective condition, but class vot-ing depends on the political activation of class issues. This activation of class issues does not occur automatically. In Latin American party systems without viable left-of-center presidential candidates, class voting has con-sistently been feeble. In the absence of a viable left-of-center presidential alternative, parties have not mobilized voters along the issues that foster class voting: income redistribution, empowering the poor, social programs for the poor, creating popular organizations, and so on. Most leftist gov-ernments and presidential candidates have politicized class issues and in-duced class voting. In contemporary Latin America, having a competitive left-of-center presidential contender seems to be a necessary though not sufficient condition to produce class voting.

Class voting has increased sharply in several Latin American countries relative to the mid-1990s. Because the structural and cultural variables that are used to explain class voting change only slowly, they cannot explain the rapid changes that have occurred. Instead, we argue that leftist governments and presidential candidates have emphasized class issues and induced class voting by proposing and promoting specific social policies (Handlin 2013a). The fact that class voting sometimes surges suddenly from one election to the next with the rise of strong leftist presidential contenders means that the dominant perspectives, which have emphasized long-term conditions favorable to class voting, do not explain recent changes in Latin America or variance among countries.

The Theoretical Framework: Political Agency and Class Voting

The comparative literature beyond Latin America has been divided between authors who emphasize the political construction of class voting from top to bottom (Chhibber and Torcal 1997; Esping-Andersen 1985; Heath 2009a, 2009b; Hout, Brooks, and Manza 2001; Przeworski and Sprague 1986; Sartori 1969; Torcal and Mainwaring 2003b) and explanations based on structural and cultural variables (Clark and Lipset 1991; Franklin 1992; Inglehart 1984, 1990; Lipset 1960, 1964, 2001; Nieuwbeerta and Ultee 1999). Both, however, share the idea that class voting emerges as a consequence of long historical processes. We share the top-down approach that class voting is politically activated and needs to be mobilized by social or political actors, but we show that it does not always require favorable long-term social and economic conditions such as historically strong leftist parties or a well-organized welfare state.

Even in contexts of high inequality and considerable poverty, individuals do not necessarily vote on the basis of redistributive claims. In agreement with the chapters in this volume on ethnicity, religion, and gender, class can become a politically activated identity but does not in and of itself dictate vote choice. Political parties, labor unions, social movements, and, in Latin America above all, governments and competitive presidential candidates activate class voting by politicizing class issues. Unless some political actors emphasize class issues, there is no reason to assume that class voting will occur. Indeed, the evidence presented in this essay indicates that it will *not* occur. Historically, leftist and populist parties and governments were the main agents that created a class vote by politicizing class issues.

The argument about the formation of class voting in the region has two alternative versions. The first emphasizes the political and structural aspects of class voting to explain cross-national differences (Dix 1989; Roberts 2002). In this approach, class voting is the product of a long historical process that went hand in hand with the institutionalization of party systems with strong social democratic or socialist parties and the development of the welfare state (Esping-Andersen 1985, 1999). According to this line of analysis, class voting is stronger in countries with a larger blue-collar workforce and a solid welfare state, and indirectly in countries with a longer democratic history. However, with the possible exception of two countries with early and long democratic histories and a tradition of competitive leftist parties (Chile and Uruguay), this long-term path to class voting did not exist or has been historically dismantled in Latin America.

In several Latin American countries, a different path has boosted class voting since the late 1990s: the emergence of leftist governments and viable leftist presidential contenders who propose and implement new social policies (Handlin 2013a). Our perspective emphasizes the role of political agency and electoral supply as a more active and recent promoter of class voting. It is consistent with studies that have shown sharp increases in class voting in Venezuela under Hugo Chávez (Handlin 2013b; Heath 2009a).

Class Voting in Latin America

Latin America has the starkest income inequalities in the world. In 2008, Latin American and Caribbean countries, considered as a whole, had a Gini index of 48.3, far above the high-income countries (with a Gini of 30.9) and also Middle East and North Africa (39.2) and Asia (40.4) (Ortiz and Cummins 2011, 26). Today, the region hosts a plethora of billionaires, but also has urban slums and vast rural areas of terrible destitution. Class issues such as poverty, income distribution, land reform, social policy, repression of poor groups, discrimination against poor ethnic groups, and the cultural and legal empowerment of poor citizens have often been at the core of democratic politics. Yet class voting has historically been weak according to most previous studies (Dix 1989; Domínguez and McCann 1995; Singer 2009, 85; Torcal and Mainwaring 2003a).

While acknowledging the weakness of Latin American class voting compared to that of Western Europe, some scholars argued that some countries (especially Chile) developed stronger class cleavages than the rest (Dix 1989). Other studies have demonstrated strong associations between class and vote in Venezuela in recent years (Handlin 2013a, 2013b; Heath 2009a, 2009b, 189), in Argentina in some periods (Cataife 2011; Lupu and Stokes 2009), and in Brazil (Hunter and Power 2007; Singer 2009; Zucco 2008).

The reemergence since 1998 of viable leftist presidential candidates and leftist governments made class issues the center of the political agenda and political debate in many Latin American countries. It has produced a rapid appearance of class voting in some party systems. Defying conventional wisdom, class voting has been strongest among the poor self-employed and unskilled workers.

Dependent and Independent Variables

Presidential voting is our primary dependent variable because of how important the presidency is, and also because the data are available for most countries in all AmericasBarometer surveys, which is not the case with the legislative vote. In the multinomial models presented below, the reference category is the candidate (for presidential voting) located most to the right among those who obtained at least 10% of the valid preferences among survey respondents. We determined the most conservative option by the mean ideological self-placement of voters who supported that candidate.

Our primary independent variable is the class of the respondent. We constructed this variable in two different ways, each of which has some advantages over the other. In the United States, "class" often refers to income or household wealth. Accordingly, our first measure is based on household wealth, which is commonly used as an indicator of class (Handlin 2013b). The construction of this measure is more straightforward, and it is available for almost all individuals in the surveys.

Most Western European analyses of class voting have focused on a structural understanding of class rather than on income or household wealth. The most prominent is the Erikson-Goldthorpe (1992) class schema, which is based on individuals' employment status and their position in production processes. Our second measure roughly approximates this class schema, which is more aligned with the way most sociologists and political scientists conceptualize class.

Measuring Household Wealth

We estimated household wealth using a principal component analysis of ten household assets listed in the AmericasBarometer surveys. The principal component analysis used dichotomous variables to indicate whether or not a household has a television, a refrigerator, a landline telephone, a cellular phone, one vehicle, two vehicles, three vehicles, a washing machine, a microwave oven, indoor plumbing, an indoor bathroom, or a computer.[2]

The wealth index assigns a larger weight to assets that vary the most across households; an asset found in all households is given a weight of zero. Our wealth index is based on the entire region rather than individual countries, and it does not differentiate between urban and rural areas.

We use household wealth rather than income for several reasons.[3] First, the coding for income is not commensurable across all countries. Second, a measure of wealth based on household goods is more stable than one based on income. A middle-class person could leave the labor market for a short time without experiencing a pronounced decline in household wealth (Booth and Seligson 2009, 115–16). Third, wealth based on household goods correctly codes relatively well-off retired individuals, whereas these individuals might have little or no income. Fourth, misreporting and underreporting are higher on income than on household wealth (Handlin 2013b, 150–51). Fifth, if we used income, we would need to adjust for size of household. A certain household income could be more than adequate for one person but put a household of seven below the poverty line. A measure based on household wealth is much less vulnerable to this problem. Finally, there are far fewer missing cases for household wealth (in 2006, only 5 out of 28,216 respondents compared to 3,613 missing observations for the family income question).

Online appendix table OA3.1 shows the distribution of the mean household wealth variable by country. The data array in an intuitively sensible way; average household wealth ranges from 1.6 standard deviations above the regional mean in Costa Rica in 2006 to 1.7 standard deviations below it in Nicaragua in 2010. Table A3.1 also shows the per capita GDP (in 2010) and the number of respondents in each country. Mean country household wealth correlates very strongly with per capita GDP: 0.90 for 2006, 0.91 for 2008, and 0.87 for 2010.

Predicting Presidential Vote with Household Wealth

We carried out a multinomial logistic model with robust standard errors in each country using the AmericasBarometer surveys of 2006, 2008, and 2010. If more than one survey referred back to a given presidential or legislative election, we used only the survey that immediately followed that election. The dependent variable is categorical, and indicates the candidate for whom respondents voted in the last presidential election.

For both measures of class, we employ simple models with three demographic variables as controls in addition to our primary variable of interest (household wealth or class): population size where the respondent lives (metropolitan area and large cities = 1; medium cities, small cities, and rural = 0),[4] sex (male = 1, female = 2), and age.[5]

Because of the strong overlay between class and race in the Latin American countries with large indigenous or Afro-Latin American populations (Cannon 2008), we did not control for ethnicity. Doing so would probably reduce the coefficients for class in a misleading way.

Most parties and presidential candidates in Latin America do not choose between mobilizing people by appealing to class issues (redistribution, social policies targeted at the poor, rhetorical denunciations of the wealthy, etc.) as opposed to ethnic or racial issues, but rather present messages that could appeal to voters because they are poor *and* indigenous (or Afro-descendents). We excluded respondents who did not answer the question, did not know for whom they voted, or stated that they did not vote at all or did not vote for any candidate. Full results from these analyses are available in online appendix table OA3.2.

Table 3.1 summarizes the results of regressions using household wealth as the main independent variable for all thirty-one elections for which data are available. The penultimate column provides a summary of class voting based on household wealth. It is the average of the statistically significant change in probabilities (the difference between how the wealthiest and the poorest voted), weighted by the vote share of candidates (other than the reference category) who won at least 10% of the valid vote according to the survey. Non-significant coefficients (at $p < 0.10$) count as zero change in voting probabilities.

Table 3.1 is ordered from strongest to weakest class voting, using the means of absolute values to array the countries. The variance across countries is huge; Chile, the Dominican Republic, Ecuador, Honduras, and Uruguay have a score of zero, meaning that household wealth consistently had no statistically significant impact on any pair of candidates. Conversely, seven countries—Brazil, Bolivia, Venezuela, Argentina, Peru, Guatemala (2007), and Paraguay (2008)—exhibited strong conventional class voting (the rich vote for the right and the poor for the left) in at least one election. Strikingly, four of the countries with strong conventional class voting—Bolivia, Peru, Guatemala, and Paraguay—have large indigenous populations.

Conventional class voting occurs if the regression results (available online in appendix table OA3.2) obtain negative and significant associations between household wealth and the dependent variable. Seven leftist and center-left candidates won great support from poor voters. Simulations based on the regression results indicate that according to the 2008

TABLE 3.1 Summary of Statistical Associations between Household Wealth and First Round Presidential Vote by Country

Country	Year of Survey	Year of Presidential Election	Left-of-Center Candidate with > 10% of Valid Survey Preferences	Number of Paired Comparisons in which Higher Household Wealth is Associated with More Conservative Presidential Vote	Number of Paired Comparisons in which Higher Household Wealth is Associated with More Leftist Presidential Vote	Number of Paired Comparisons with No Significant Associations	Election Weighted Change in Voting Probabilities from Poorest to Wealthiest Voters	Country Mean Weighted Change in Voting Probabilities from Poorest to Wealthiest Voters
Brazil	2006	2006	won	1	0	0	-0.51	-0.51
Bolivia	2008	2005	won	1	0	0	-0.48	-0.42
	2010	2009	won	1	0	0	-0.36	
Venezuela	2008	2006	won	1	0	0	-0.42	-0.42
Costa Rica	2006	2006	2nd	0	1	0	0.37	0.37
Argentina	2008	2007	won	1	0	1	-0.34	-0.34
Peru	2006	2006	lost runoff	2	0	0	-0.25	-0.25
Guatemala	2006	2003	lost runoff	1	0	1	-0.04	-0.17
	2008	2007	won	1	0	0	-0.29	
Colombia	2006	2006	not competitive	0	1	0	0.14	0.14
Paraguay	2006	2003	none	0	0	1	0.00	-0.12
	2010	2008	won	1	0	0	-0.24	
El Salvador	2006	2004	2nd	0	1	0	0.24	0.12
	2010	2009	won	0	0	1	0.00	
Mexico	2006	2000	3rd	2	0	1	-0.14	-0.10
	2008	2006	2nd	1	0	1	-0.05	
Nicaragua	2006	2001	2nd	0	0	1	0.00	0.05
	2008	2006	won	0	1	1	0.10	

Panama	2008	2004	none	0	1	1	0.06	0.03
	2010	2009	none	0	0	1	0.00	
Chile	2006	2005	won	0	0	2	0.00	0.00
	2010	2009	3rd	0	0	2	0.00	
Dominican Republic	2006	2004	none	0	0	1	0.00	0.00
	2010	2008	none	0	0	1	0.00	
Ecuador	2006	2002	won	0	0	1	0.00	0.00
	2008	2006	won	0	0	1	0.00	
	2010	2009		0	0	1	0.00	
Honduras	2006	2005	none	0	0	1	0.00	0.00
	2010	2009	none	0	0	1	0.00	
Uruguay	2006	2004	won	0	0	1	0.00	0.00
	2010	2009	won	0	0	1	0.00	
Total	—			13	5	22		

Source: Based on regression results using AmericasBarometer surveys 2006–2010.

survey respondents, in 2007 the wealthiest Argentine voters were a whopping 57 percentage points less likely than the poorest to vote for Cristina Fernández de Kirchner rather than Roberto Lavagna.[6] For example, among Fernández de Kirchner and Lavagna voters, if 80% of the poorest voters chose Fernández de Kirchner, only 23% of the wealthiest did. In Bolivia, poor voters were far more likely than wealthy voters to choose Evo Morales over Jorge Quiroga in 2005 (–48%) and over Manfred Reyes in 2009 (–36%). In Brazil, the poorest voted 51 percentage points more than the wealthy for President Lula da Silva in 2006. In Venezuela, the poor flocked to Hugo Chávez in 2006 (–42%), Ollanta Humala in Peru in 2006 (–38%), and Fernando Lugo in Paraguay in 2008 (–24%); and Alvaro Colom in Guatemala in 2007 (–29%) also fared much better among the poorest voters. Alvaro Colom in 2003 (–7%), Cuauhtémoc Cárdenas in Mexico in 2000 (–5%), and Andrés Manuel López Obrador in Mexico in 2006 (–11%) also fared somewhat better among the poorest voters in the competition with the most conservative candidates.

But this result was far from consistent across all countries. In El Salvador, in the competition with the conservative candidate, Alianza Republicana Nacionalista's (ARENA) Antonio Saca, the old Communist Party leader and Farabundo Martí National Liberation Front (FMLN) candidate Schafik Hándal won 24 percentage points more among the wealthiest voters than he did among the poorest. Given the strong connections between business groups and ARENA, and given the revolutionary and largely rural genesis of the FMLN, this result is surprising. In the competition with the most conservative candidate, Daniel Ortega in Nicaragua (2001), Michelle Bachelet in Chile (2005), and Tabaré Vázquez in Uruguay (2004) did no better among the poorest voters than among the wealthiest.

Table 3.1 also shows how often "conventional" and "reverse" class voting occurred (by "reverse" class voting, we mean that wealthy voters were more likely than poor voters to choose the more progressive candidate). In thirteen of the forty paired comparisons of presidential candidates in online appendix table OA3.2, poor voters were more likely than the wealthy to prefer the more progressive of two candidates. In twenty-two of the forty paired comparisons of candidates, household wealth had no statistically significant influence on the vote.

Conversely, in five paired comparisons, wealthy voters preferred candidates to the left of the most conservative candidate (reverse class voting). Two involved center-left candidates whose primary base of support was the urban middle class: Ottón Solis of the Citizens' Action Party in Costa Rica in 2006 and Carlos Gaviria, who finished a distant second to Alvaro Uribe in Colombia's 2006 presidential election. Both campaigned more on civic than class issues. Urban educated middle classes sometimes prefer progressive candidates, while some conservative candidates and parties have made significant inroads in the lower classes (e.g., the Partido Revolucionario Institucional, or PRI, in Mexico and Fernando Collor de Mello, the winning presidential candidate in Brazil in 1989).

Results are fairly stable from one election to the next. For the thirteen countries in table 3.1 for which surveys covered at least two presidential elections, the correlation between the summary score in the first election and the score in the second is 0.65. This overall consistency conceals some important changes between the first and second elections. In El Salvador and Panama, in the first election registered in table 3.1, reverse class voting occurred; wealthy individuals were more likely than poor voters to support the more progressive of two candidates. They are the only countries with reverse class voting in table 3.1 for which results for a subsequent election are available. In the subsequent election, in both countries, household wealth had no effect on presidential vote. Based on these two cases, it appears that reverse class voting might be ephemeral in Latin America. When it occurs, it does not endure. In contrast, all three cases with two elections in table 3.1 that featured conventional class voting in the first election (Bolivia, Guatemala, and Mexico) reproduced it in the second. Thus, when leftist candidates and governments mobilize poor voters, the effects seem to stick more from one election to the next.

In two countries, voting based on household wealth increased sharply from the first election to the second: Guatemala (from –0.04 to –0.29) and Paraguay (from 0 to –0.24). Both involved successful runs by left-of-center presidential candidates who emphasized tackling poverty: Alvaro Colom (2008–12) in Guatemala, who became his country's first left-of-center president since 1954; and Fernando Lugo (2008–12) in Paraguay, a former Catholic priest and bishop known for his commitment to the poor, who became the first non-Colorado president since 1947. In Paraguay, the left-of-center had hitherto not been a powerful electoral contender, and in Guatemala, it had not had a credible presidential contender from 1954 until 2003. The increase in class voting in Paraguay and Guatemala supports our argument that class voting is the product of the political mobilization of class issues. In Latin America, this occurs primarily through left-of-center governments and powerful presidential contenders.

Among the candidates running in elections covered in table 3.1, two or three had profiles as radical leftists: Evo Morales, who won the Bolivian elections of 2005 and 2009; Hugo Chávez in Venezuela; and perhaps

Ollanta Humala in Peru.[7] If class voting gets activated by clear class signals and conflicts created by campaigns, political styles, and government policies, it should be strong in these cases. The data strongly confirm this hypothesis for all three candidates; they fared vastly better among the poorest voters.

Results for legislative voting using household wealth as the primary independent variable of interest were extremely highly correlated ($r = 0.97$) with results for presidential voting. These results, however, are limited to nine countries in the 2006 survey; the 2008 and 2010 surveys did not include this question. See online appendix table OA3.3 for a summary of legislative results.

Class: Erikson and Goldthorpe's Schema

The Erikson-Goldthorpe (1992) schema is based first on whether an individual is self-employed, an employer, or an employee, and second, on the individual's occupation.[8] No major Latin American survey has used the detailed occupational coding that is needed to fully reproduce Erikson and Goldthorpe's class schema. Because the AmericasBarometer's occupation categories are not detailed enough to accurately code all respondents based just on employment status and occupation, we used questions on education and household wealth to help build some class categories. However, the beginning point of our coding was always employment status and occupation.

The most commonly used organization of the Erikson-Goldthorpe schema has five class categories. The service class (large owners, professionals, administrators, managers, and high-level supervisors) holds the most privileged economic position. The petty bourgeoisie includes small owners, farmers, and self-employed workers in primary production. The routine non-manual class includes workers in administration and commerce and sales personnel. The final two classes are skilled and unskilled workers.

The Erikson-Goldthorpe schema was developed with advanced industrial democracies in mind. Using this schema for coding class in Latin American countries requires some adjustments because of deep cross-regional differences in class structure. We added a sixth category, the poor self-employed, which is essential for understanding class in Latin America. With the explosive growth of the informal sector in most countries in recent decades, the poor self-employed constitute a sizable share of the labor force in most Latin American countries—much larger in most countries than skilled workers. These six categories, which are based on objective positions in the productive structure, differ from categories based on subjective (self-reported) class, income, or household wealth.

Following Erikson and Goldthorpe, we first divided respondents by employment status into four groups: (1) employees, (2) employers, (3) self-employed, and (4) unpaid workers.[9] We then classified them according to each AmericasBarometer occupational category. Where employment status and occupation did not suffice to code class, we also used education and/or household wealth. Table 3.2 provides coding details.

Figure 3.1 shows the breakdown into six classes in the eighteen Latin American countries included in our analysis. There are stark cross-national differences in class composition that conform closely to differences in level of development. The service class is much larger in the more developed countries (Chile 13.8%, Costa Rica 12.8%) than in the poor countries (Guatemala 3.2%, Nicaragua 3.0%, Honduras 2.6%, and Paraguay 2.2%). The bivariate correlation between the size of the service class and per capita GDP is very high at 0.75.

Conversely, the poor self-employed class is much larger in the poor countries. They range from 3.1% of the samples in Argentina and Costa Rica to 46.9% in Nicaragua. The bivariate correlation between the size of the poor self-employed class and per capita GDP is –0.86. The skilled working class is larger in the more developed countries (18.1% of the sample in Uruguay compared to only 3.6% in Nicaragua). The bivariate correlation between its size and per capita GDP is 0.73.

Predicting Class Voting with the Erikson-Goldthorpe Schema

The full set of presidential results of multinomial logistic regressions predicting vote choice with the Erikson-Goldthorpe class measure (and control variables) is available in online appendix table OA3.4. Figure 3.2 summarizes the results for the twenty-four presidential elections and eight legislative elections for which data are available. The summary score for each election weights the statistically significant change in voting probabilities by party size and class size (exclusive of the reference class, the petty bourgeoisie). A country score of 9% means that on average, being in a class other than the petty bourgeoisie changes the likelihood of voting for a candidate other than the reference candidate by 9 percentage points.

Figure 3.2 again registers great cross-country variance and some variance over time. Class voting in presidential elections was strongest in Guatemala (8% in 2003 and 18% in 2007), Brazil (12% in 2006), Venezuela (10% in 2006), Bolivia (9% in 2005 and 11% in 2009), Peru (9% in 2006), Nicaragua (8% in 2001), and Argentina (7% in 2007). All nine elections featured a left-of-center presidential candidate who won (Guatemala 2007,

TABLE 3.2 Using AmericasBarometer Surveys to Code the Erikson-Goldthorpe Class Variables

Occupation[c]	Private Employers (OCUP1A)		Employees[a] (government or private)		Self-Employed[b]		Unpaid Worker
	Subdivided by education (ED) and wealth	Our class coding	Subdivided by education (ED) and wealth	Our class coding	Subdivided by education (ED) and wealth	Our class coding	Our class coding
Professional, manager	15+ years education and wealth top 20%*	Service class	15+ years education and wealth top 20%*	Service class	15+ years education and wealth top 20%*	Service class	Routine non-manual
	less than 15 years education OR wealth bottom 80%**	Petty bourgeoisie	less than 15 years of education OR wealth bottom 80%**	Routine non-manual	< 15 years of education OR wealth bottom 80%**	Petty bourgeoisie	
Technician	15+ years education and wealth top 20%*	Service class	15 years + education and wealth top 20%*	Service class	15+ years education and wealth top 20%*	Service class	Skilled worker
	less than 15 years education OR wealth bottom 80%**	Petty bourgeoisie	less than 15 years of education OR wealth bottom 80%**	Routine non-manual	If not service class and wealth top 50%**	Petty bourgeoisie	
					Wealth bottom 50%	Poor self-employed	
Office worker	15+ years education and wealth top 20%*	Service class	15 years + education and wealth top 20%*	Service class	If 15+ years education and wealth top 20%*	Service class	Routine non-manual
	less than 15 years education OR wealth bottom 80%**	Petty bourgeoisie	Less than 15 years of education OR wealth bottom 80%**	Routine non-manual	If education < 15 years or wealth bottom 80%**	Petty bourgeoisie	

	15+ years education and wealth top 20%*	Service class	15+ years education and wealth top 20%*	Service class	If 15+ years education AND wealth top 20%*	Service class	Routine non-manual
Merchant	15+ years education and wealth top 20%* less than 15 years education OR wealth bottom 80%**	Service class Petty bourgeoisie	15+ years education and wealth top 20%* Less than 15 years of education OR wealth bottom 80%**	Service class Routine non-manual	If not service class and wealth top 50% wealth bottom 50%	Petty bourgeoisie Poor self-employed	Unskilled worker
Peasant or farmer	15+ years education and wealth top 20%* less than 15 years education OR wealth bottom 80%**	Service class Petty bourgeoisie	9+ years education AND wealth top 50% < 9 years education OR wealth bottom 50%	Skilled worker Unskilled worker	wealth top 50% wealth bottom 50%	Petty bourgeoisie Poor self-employed	Unskilled worker
Farmhand	NA	NA		Unskilled worker	NA	NA	Unskilled worker
Artisan		Petty bourgeoisie	9+ years education and wealth top 50% < 9 years education OR wealth bottom 50%	Skilled worker Unskilled workers	wealth top 50% wealth bottom 50%	Petty bourgeoisie Poor self-employed	Unskilled worker
Domestic service	NA	NA		Unskilled worker	NA	NA	Unskilled worker

(continued)

TABLE 3.2 (Continued)

	Private Employers (OCUP1A)	Employees[a] (government or private)	Self-Employed[b]	Unpaid Worker			
Other services	15+ years education and wealth top 20%*	Service class	15+ years education AND wealth top 20%*	Service class	If 15+ years education AND wealth top 20%*	Service class	Unskilled worker
	less than 15 years education OR wealth bottom 80%**	Petty bourgeoisie	9+ years education and wealth top 50%	Routine non-manual if not in service class	If not service class and wealth top 50%	Petty bourgeoisie	
			< 9 years education OR wealth bottom 50%	Unskilled worker	wealth bottom 50%	Poor self-employed	
Skilled worker		Petty bourgeoisie		Skilled worker	wealth top 50%	Petty bourgeoisie	Skilled worker
					wealth bottom 50%	Poor self-employed	
Unskilled worker		Petty bourgeoisie		Unskilled worker	wealth top 50%	Petty bourgeoisie	Unskilled worker
					wealth bottom 50%	Poor self-employed	

Notes:
* Top 20% of household wealth within the individual's country *and* for the region as a whole.
** Bottom 80% of household wealth within the individual's country OR for the region as a whole
[a] In the AmericasBarometer 2006 mother questionnaire (Spanish version) the variable with this information is OCUP1A. In the 2006 pooled dataset the variable is ocup1a.
[b] *Trabajador por cuenta propia* in the mother questionnaire.
[c] In the LAPOP 2006 mother questionnaire (Spanish version) the variable with this information is OCUP1. In the AmericasBarometer 2006 pooled dataset the variable is ocup1_06.

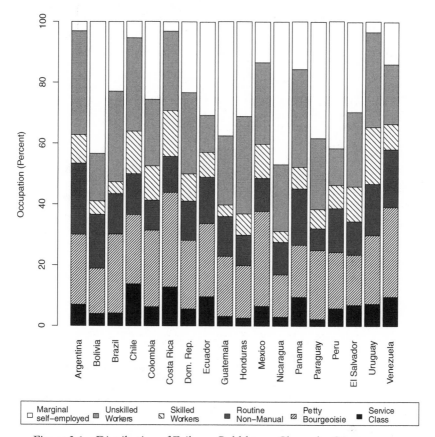

Figure 3.1   Distribution of Erikson-Goldthorpe Classes by Country.
Source: Based on 2006 AmericasBarometer for all countries except Argentina, Bolivia, Brazil, Ecuador, Panama, and Venezuela, for which we used 2008.

Brazil 2006, Venezuela 2006, Bolivia 2005 and 2009, and Argentina 2007) or came in a close second (Guatemala 2003, Peru 2006, and Nicaragua 2001). Between these seven countries with strong class voting and the rest, there was a yawning gap. Class voting in presidential elections was weak (1% or less) in Costa Rica in 2006, the Dominican Republic in 2004, Ecuador in 2006 and 2009, El Salvador in 2004, Honduras in 2005, Mexico in 2000, Chile in 2005, Panama in 2004, Paraguay in 2003, Uruguay in 2004, and Colombia in 2006.

Both countries with winning radical leftist candidates, Bolivia (with Evo Morales) and Venezuela (Hugo Chávez), had strong class voting, consistent

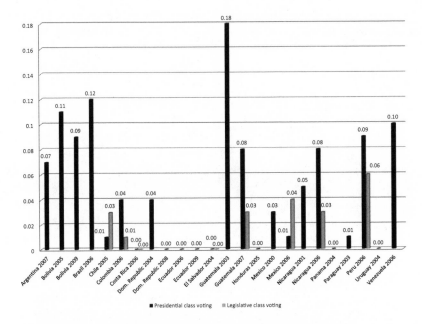

Figure 3.2   Summary of Erikson-Goldthorpe Class Voting Scores.
Source: AmericasBarometer 2006–2010. *Note:* Scores are the absolute values of the changes in probabilities, weighted by party sizes and class size. The figure provides the election years. Corresponding years of surveys are provided in table 3.1. Based on online Appendix table A3.5 and similar results for legislative voting.

with results based on household wealth. Peru, with Ollanta Humala as a candidate with some radical leftist characteristics in 2006, also had strong class voting that year. This is not by chance. In their discourse and policies, radical leftist presidents and candidates emphasize solidarity with the poor and economic redistribution, and they criticize the wealthy as enemies of the nation (Hawkins 2010). Class issues have been front stage on the national political scene in these countries. Class polarization provoked by leftist governments and highly competitive presidential candidates is favorable to strong class voting.

Class voting is not necessarily ideological or programmatic. Perhaps surprisingly, Latin American countries with strong class voting are not generally countries with strong associations between left-right identification and voting. Zechmeister (this volume) identifies Mexico, Chile, El Salvador, Venezuela, and Uruguay as the countries with the strongest association between left-right identification and voting. Among them, only Venezuela is a case of strong class voting. Moreover, although class voting has increased greatly in several countries because of the growth of the left, Zechmeister reports that this growth has not significantly affected ideological leanings and structuration in the Latin American region.

As was the case for results based on household wealth, results for the Erikson-Goldthorpe schema are fairly consistent across presidential and legislative voting for the eight countries for which we have this information. The correlation between countries' scores for presidential voting and their scores for legislative voting is 0.63. On average, class voting was stronger in presidential elections (mean = 0.044) than in legislative elections (mean = 0.025), probably because many left-of-center presidents and presidential candidates, especially radical leftists, are polarizing.

Assessing Conventional Class Voting with the Erikson-Goldthorpe Schema

To what degree do the Latin American cases circa 2006 demonstrate conventional class voting? Table 3.3 synthetically summarizes the results by each of the five classes other than the petty bourgeoisie. The data cover the twenty-four presidential elections and eight legislative elections for which Erikson-Goldthorpe scores are available. Each comparison of paired presidential candidates for each class counts as one case.

Four findings stand out. First, the statistically significant results overwhelmingly support the hypothesis that the poor vote for more progressive candidates. Thirty-three of the thirty-eight statistically significant results for presidential voting and all sixteen statistically significant results for legislative voting are consistent with this expectation. Overall, forty-nine of fifty-four statistically significant results support the traditional hypothesis. Only one case of reverse class voting out of 250 comparisons of candidates and parties in table 3.3 involved a segment of the working class (skilled workers, unskilled workers, or the poor self-employed) supporting a conservative candidate over a left-of-center candidate: unskilled workers were more likely than the petty bourgeoisie to support the incumbent president, center-right populist Alvaro Uribe, rather than the center-left candidate, Carlos Gaviria, in Colombia in 2006.

Second, most cells (78% for presidential voting and 80% for legislative voting) are not significant. Class voting is not ubiquitous.

Third, the magnitude of class voting varies greatly by class (because the class variables are entered individually as independent variables in

TABLE 3.3   Assessing Conventional and Reverse Class Voting: Erikson-Goldthorpe

Class	Presidential Vote			Legislative Vote		
	# cases where poorer class voted for more progressive candidate	# cases where poorer class voted for conservative candidates	# cases with no class voting	# cases where poorer class voted for more progressive candidate	# cases where poorer class voted for conservative candidates	# cases with no class voting
Service class	4	3	27	1	0	15
Routine non-manual	7	0	27	1	0	15
Skilled workers	1	1	32	1	0	15
Unskilled workers	12	1	21	6	0	10
Marginal self-employed	9	0	25	7	0	9
Total	33	5	132	16	0	64

Note: Results are for the twenty-four presidential elections and eight legislative elections shown in figure 3.2.

the model, we can determine which of the class categories significantly predict the vote and how often this is the case). Relative to the petty bourgeoisie, unskilled workers and the poor self-employed engaged in far more class voting than other classes. These two categories occupy the bottom of the wealth hierarchy in Latin America. The poor self-employed have historically been known to have difficulties with collective action and political mobilization.[10] In contemporary Latin America, however, several leftist and center-left presidential candidates have successfully appealed to this sector. Evo Morales in Bolivia (+14% in 2005 and +16% in 2009), President Lula da Silva in Brazil (+17%), center-left candidate Alvaro Colom in Guatemala (+16% in 2003, +21% in 2007), center-left candidate Cuauhtémoc Cárdenas in Mexico (+4%), and leftist candidate Ollanta Humala in Peru in 2006 (+16%) did well among the poor self-employed. In light of some literature about their low levels of politicization and their difficulties in engaging in collective action, it is striking that the poor self-employed, along with unskilled workers, are at the core of pro-left voting. Most of the literature posited that the unionized working class would be the primary agent of class voting (Bartolini 2000, 240–63; Clark, Lipset, and Rempel 2001, 84; Roberts 2002). Because the poor self-employed outnumber skilled workers in all Latin American countries but Argentina, Chile, Costa Rica, and Uruguay,[11] left-of-center governments and presidential candidates have electoral incentives to appeal to the unorganized poor. With the decline of the political importance of organized labor in many countries and the explosive growth of the informal sector, the potential political gain from appealing to the latter has grown.

Likewise, seven leftist and center-left candidates successfully mobilized the vote of unskilled workers: Cristina Fernández de Kirchner in Argentina (+27%), President Lula in Brazil (+12%), Daniel Ortega in Nicaragua (+17% in 2001 and +15% in 2006), Hugo Chávez in 2006 (+14%), Cuauhtémoc Cárdenas in Mexico (+3%), Ollanta Humala in Peru (+3%), and Alvaro Colom in Guatemala (+14% in 2003 and +21% in 2007). The discourse, mobilizational efforts, and social policies of the radical left are aimed at the marginalized populations, so the strong support of poor people for radical left presidents and presidential candidates is not surprising.

This pattern of leftist and center-left electoral success among unskilled workers and the poor self-employed was not uniform. Michelle Bachelet in Chile, Schafik Hándal in El Salvador, and Tabaré Vázquez in Uruguay did not fare better among unskilled workers or the poor self-employed than among the petty bourgeoisie.

Table 3.3 shows very limited class voting by skilled workers, who according to some analyses were expected to be the politically most progressive sector of the working class. The voting patterns of skilled workers were similar to those of the petty bourgeoisie, diverging in only three of the fifty cases (combining the presidential and legislative vote). In some accounts, the decline of the organized working class in recent decades supposedly contributed to the decrease in class voting. Recent experience in Latin America, however, shows that the organized working class need not be the primary generator of class voting. The Venezuelan experience, in which Chávez mobilized poor sectors primarily through neighborhood organizations and dismantled opposition unions, is revealing of the potential for a different organizational path for mobilizing class voting. The results hint at a broader political change in many Latin American countries: growing political mobilization of the formerly unorganized popular sectors coupled with the decrease of the size of the unionized blue-collar working class.

Fourth, in the four years covered by the three surveys we analyzed, there was considerable stability from one election to the next in the Erikson-Goldthorpe summary scores. Based on the limited sample of seven countries for which data are available for two presidential elections, the correlation between their scores in the first and second elections is 0.70.

Consistency between Household Wealth and the Erikson-Goldthorpe Class Schema

How consistent are the results between the two different measures of class? For the twenty-four presidential elections shown in table 3.2, the results are correlated at 0.61. This shows good, though far from perfect, consistency between the two measures.

Differences between the two measures arise for several reasons. The number of individuals coded by household wealth was much higher than those coded by Erikson-Goldthorpe, mainly because the Erikson-Goldthorpe variable includes only individuals who are in the labor force. For this reason and because the Erikson-Goldthorpe measure divides respondents into six different classes, the number of individuals in each comparison in the regressions is on average about ten times higher with the household wealth measure. Additionally, the household wealth variable is continuous, while the Erikson-Goldthorpe variable contains six dichotomous variables. Parameters with the Erikson-Goldthorpe model are based on the comparison of five classes with the petty bourgeoisie in predicting individual voting preferences, whereas parameters with the household wealth variable include all individuals together. The Erikson-Goldthorpe schema can produce statistically significant results for different classes that are offsetting according to household wealth. For example, in Nicaragua in 2001 some poor classes (unskilled workers and routine non-manual) and the service class voted disproportionately for Daniel Ortega, resulting in a high score for Erikson-Goldthorpe but producing no effect according to household wealth.

Change over Time

The ability to track change over time is crucial for understanding how class voting is constructed and why it varies over time and space. The best way to track change over time, through many repeated surveys using the same questions over decades, is not available. However, three kinds of evidence provide a reasonable amount of information about change over time in a fair number of countries.

First, for seven Latin American countries (and seven Western European countries), we have an earlier measure of class voting that is very similar to the Erikson-Goldthorpe measure presented here (Torcal and Mainwaring 2003a). Like the measure employed here, it was based on changes in voting probabilities, weighted by class size and party size. Among the seven

Latin American countries included in the analysis of 1995, class voting was weak or modest everywhere, and differences across countries were small compared to a decade later. The Erikson-Goldthorpe scores for 1995 were far below the highest scores for presidential class voting in the 2000s: Brazil (0.04), Uruguay (0.03), Argentina (0.03), Peru (0.03), Mexico (0.03), Chile (0.02), and Venezuela (0.02). Scores for the seven Western European countries ranged from 0.12 for Spain to 0.04 for Switzerland. Two Latin American presidential elections (Brazil in 2006 and Guatemala in 2007) had higher scores than *any* Western European country in 1995.

In the mid-1990s, class voting was much stronger in Western Europe than in Latin America. The finding of weak class voting in the mid-1990s is consistent with Roberts's (2002) argument that during the neoliberal era in Latin America, social inequalities widened while class cleavages in party systems were muted. Roberts attributed the weakness of class cleavages in Latin America in the 1990s primarily to structural changes wrought by neoliberalism.

In contrast, our primary explanation for weak class voting in the 1990s in most Latin American countries is political. Few major parties and governments politicized class, as many important formerly left-of-center parties engaged in radical policy shifts toward market-oriented policies (Lupu forthcoming; Stokes 2001; Weyland 2002). Programmatic and ideological differences among major parties eroded in Argentina, Bolivia, Peru, and Venezuela, among other countries (Lupu forthcoming; Morgan 2011; Seawright 2012) during a short-lived era of neoliberal dominance. Major parties that had once waved the banners that attracted multitudes of poor voters while repelling some wealthier voters—income redistribution, land reform, social justice, empowerment of the poor—did an about face. Few major presidential candidates positioned themselves on the left.

The heightened class voting in many Latin American countries in recent years shows that market-oriented reforms and the structural changes they brought about did not in and of themselves dampen class voting. With the ascendance of Hugo Chávez in Venezuela in 1999 and other leftist leaders elsewhere a few years later, a new group of presidents and close contenders assumed a discourse and implemented policies that politicized class and mobilized class voting—both for and against them. Class voting became stronger in most countries that had leftist presidents or competitive leftist presidential candidates.

The results for 2006–10 are very different from those for 1995. Among the seven countries in the 1995 analysis, in 2006 class voting was strongest in Argentina, Brazil, Venezuela, and Peru. After 1995, class voting declined in Chile (Bargsted and Somma forthcoming) and Uruguay. Conversely, in Argentina, Brazil, Peru, and Venezuela, it increased greatly. The Argentine and Venezuelan cases are especially striking. Under President Carlos Menem's (1989–99) market-oriented economic policies, class voting was very limited; under President Fernández de Kirchner (2007–present), who has implemented left-of-center economic policies, it is very strong. Likewise, class voting was weak in Venezuela in the 1990s, and it became strong under the polarizing influence of Hugo Chávez.

The dilution of class voting in Uruguay and Chile and its growth in Argentina, Brazil, Peru, and Venezuela cannot be explained on the basis of structural variables such as income inequalities or level of development. These variables did not change much between 1995 and 2006. What did change because of the electoral growth of the left in most of Latin America was the nature of electoral competition. In Chile and Uruguay, middle-class voters flocked to support the moderate left, diluting the modest class vote that had existed earlier. Conversely, in the 1980s and until the late 1990s, the two main parties in Venezuela of the 1973–88 period converged ideologically and programmatically around the center-right (Coppedge 1994; Morgan 2011; Seawright 2012), and the same was true in Peru in the 1990s (Seawright 2012). Without a left-of-center party that could realistically compete for the presidency, class voting withered. In countries where class voting was weak in the 1990s, if the radical left came to power (Venezuela and Bolivia) or nearly did so (Peru 2006), class voting expanded dramatically (Handlin 2013b; Heath 2009a, 2009b). Radical leftist presidents and presidential contenders mobilized class voting.

A second form of evidence about change over time comes from a few papers that give longitudinal data about specific countries. Handlin (2013a) and Heath (2009a, 2009b) show that class voting in Venezuela intensified greatly after Hugo Chávez's rise to power and implementation of "mobilizational" policies. Chávez's discourse, actions, and policies won the support of a decisive majority of poor Venezuelans and alienated the better off. Torcal and Mainwaring (2003b) show that class voting in Santiago, Chile, was much stronger during the highly polarized years of Salvador Allende's presidency (1970–73) than in the mid-1990s, when the new democratic governments pursued conciliatory and moderate policies and eschewed class mobilization. These changes over time support our theoretical argument, and it is difficult to explain them through alternative theoretical approaches.

Third, although the data presented in this essay cover a short time span (2006–10), two countries present ideal opportunities to examine the impact on class voting of the emergence of strong left-of-center contenders where previously none had existed: Ecuador, where Rafael Correa won the 2006 election, and Paraguay, where Fernando Lugo won the 2008 contest. For both countries, we have data points before and after the emergence of a winning left-of-center candidate. The left had been electorally weak throughout the history of both countries before then. The Paraguayan results fully substantiate the argument that the emergence of the partisan left can spark class voting; the country shifted from a score of zero in the 2003 election to strong class voting (–0.24) in 2008. In contrast, Correa did not boost class voting in 2006 or in his 2009 reelection. But the Ecuadoran experience is an outlier: there is no other case in table 3.1 (household wealth) or figure 3.2 (Erikson-Goldthorpe) of a somewhat radical left with a summary score of zero for class voting.

The Left and the Activation of Class Voting

In contemporary Latin America, viable left-of-center presidential candidates are not a sufficient condition to induce class voting, but they seem be a necessary condition. Where there was no viable left-of-center presidential candidate, conventional class voting was consistently feeble: Ecuador and Peru before 2006, Guatemala before 2003, Paraguay before 2008, Colombia, Panama, the Dominican Republic, and Honduras. Class voting does not emerge spontaneously as a result of individuals' objective positions in the material hierarchy or the productive structure. If it did, class voting would be ubiquitous throughout Latin America. Rather, it has reemerged recently as the result of the politicization of class issues by leftist presidents and strong presidential contenders, appealing in several cases to the most disadvantaged sectors (unskilled and marginal self-employed sectors).

We used the expert survey of political parties by Wiesehomeier and Benoit (2006–7) to assess the relationship between the presence of a major left-of-center candidate and class voting. Experts located the major Latin American parties on a scale from 1 (farthest left) to 20 (farthest right). Of the 31 presidential elections in table 3.1, in 8 no candidate with at least 10% of the survey preferences had a score below 9 on the Wiesehomeier-Benoit left-right scale from 0 to 20. If we operationally define a competitive candidate as one who comes within 20 percentage points of the first-round winner or 10 percentage points of the first-round runner-up, in 3 other elections, Colombia in 2006, Mexico in 2000, and Chile in 2009, the left-of-center was not competitive. In 10 of these 11 elections without a competitive left-of-center candidate, there was either no class voting (8 cases) or moderate *reverse* class voting (2 cases). Among these 11 elections, there is only one case, Mexico in 2000, of (modest) conventional class voting. The average country score for conventional class voting based on household wealth in 20 elections with a competitive left-of-center candidate was 0.17 compared to 0.01 for 11 elections without one.[12] In the absence of a viable left-of-center presidential candidate, parties do not mobilize voters along class lines.

The data largely support a secondary hypothesis. We expected, following Handlin (2013a), that the radical left, with its concerted efforts to implement and emphasize mobilizational class issues, would politicize class and induce class voting more than the moderate left such as the Frente Amplio in Uruguay, the Chilean left, and the Partido dos Trabalhadores (PT) in Brazil, which tends to promote more technocratic social policies. Radical left candidates and presidents constantly emphasize class issues, making them the center of the political and electoral agenda. The radical left (Hugo Chávez in Venezuela, Evo Morales in Bolivia) has mobilized the popular sectors around class issues, often through neighborhood groups (Handlin 2013a; Hawkins 2010).[13] The moderate left has been more successful at reducing poverty than the radical left, but it has not mobilized the popular sectors to the same degree, nor has it been nearly as polarizing. As a result, we expected sharper class divisions in elections with the radical left.

Bolivia under Evo Morales, Venezuela under Hugo Chávez, and Ollanta Humala in Peru in 2006 (strong class voting) and Chile and Uruguay (weak class voting) fully conform to this expectation. However, Brazil was a case of strong class voting in 2006 even though President Lula and the PT are widely seen as part of the moderate left. Class voting increased significantly due to a combination of social policies that greatly benefited the poor, corruption scandals that drove away many middle-class voters in 2006, and Lula's ability to win support from the poor based on his own humble background and modest self-presentation. Moreover, despite President Rafael Correa's (2007–present) confrontational style and somewhat radical policies, Ecuador experienced weak class voting in his first two elections (2006, 2009). Because of Correa's technocratic decision-making style and failure to mobilize civil society, this result is only partly at odds with our theoretical expectations.

The critical difference in terms of class voting was between countries that had a competitive left-of-center and those that did not; empirically it did not matter how far left the left candidate was, as long as she or he was left-of-center. The correlation between the left-right position of the farthest left party according to the expert survey and conventional class voting based on household wealth and using presidential choice in the first election for each country shown in table 3.1 as the dependent variable ($n = 18$) was 0.31 (stronger conventional class voting was associated with a more left-wing candidate). However, this correlation stemmed wholly from the six elections without a viable left-of-center candidate. Without these six elections, conventional class voting had no correlation with candidates situated farther on the left (-0.09, $n = 12$). Likewise, against our expectations, higher party system polarization (Singer forthcoming) using data of the Parliamentary Elites in Latin America (PELA) database from the University of Salamanca was not correlated with stronger class voting.

Party agency is a necessary but probably not sufficient condition for the consolidation of class voting. Leftist governments might be a key ingredient for consolidating class voting, not only because of the visibility of leftist presidents and the central role of class issues on their political agendas, but also because they implement policies that might solidify subsequent party preferences (Chhibber and Torcal 1997). The consolidation of class voting might depend on social and economic policies that build lasting partisan loyalties and antipathies. The priming effect of class issues has been reinforced and highlighted by the policies implemented by some left-of-center governments in power—for example, Chávez in Venezuela and Lula in Brazil. However, on this point, too, the evidence from Latin America is mixed. Leftist governments in Chile, Ecuador, and Uruguay did not boost class voting, and, in Chile and Uruguay, they presided over *decreasing* class voting.

This argument about the effects of left-of-center candidates on class voting does not mean that any such candidate can spark class voting at any moment in history. The deep economic turmoil and transformations most Latin American countries underwent in the 1980s (extending into the 1990s in many) forged a temporary elite consensus around the need for economic stabilization and market-oriented policies. During those years of triple- and quadruple-digit inflation rates in many countries, the abject failure of heterodox policies discredited left-of-center economic policies. Leftist candidates who attempted to navigate against the tide were not successful in those circumstances. Poor voters (like others) prioritized economic stability. By the late 1990s, the discrediting of market-oriented policies in many countries created space for leftist candidates. The revitalization of class voting required leftist presidents or presidential candidates, and it also required popular disenchantment with neoliberal economic policies, such that poor citizens were again receptive to voting for candidates who emphasized class issues.

Several authors have argued that class voting diminished in Western Europe as social inequalities diminished (Clark and Lipset 1991; Clark, Lipset, and Rempel 2001) or as the working class became wealthier (Clark and Lipset 1991; Clark, Lipset, and Rempel 2001; Dalton 1996, 174; Lipset 1960, 1964, 2001). These arguments might be correct for Western Europe, but the level of inequality and the level of development do not explain differences in class voting among Latin American cases. Circa 2006, the correlation between countries' income inequality and class voting approximated zero (–0.02 for household wealth and 0.04 for the Erikson-Goldthorpe measure). Likewise, the correlation between per capita GDP in 2006 and class voting was feeble and not statistically significant (–0.07 for household wealth and –0.16 for Erikson-Goldthorpe).[14] Moreover, class voting increased sharply in many Latin American countries in the 2000s even as poverty declined steeply in much of the region.

Although strong class voting could forge durable ties between voters and parties and hence foster party system institutionalization, for the short time span covered in this chapter, this effect has not appeared. In the 1990s and 2000s, Guatemala had one of the most weakly institutionalized party systems in Latin America, and Bolivia, Venezuela, and Peru experienced party system collapses. These countries ranked first, third, fourth, and fifth, respectively, in class voting in figure 3.2. There is a good chance that the strong class voting that has emerged in Bolivia and Venezuela is leading to the institutionalization of a new, post-collapse party system—but the Guatemalan party system remains very weakly institutionalized despite strong class voting in 2007. Some of the region's most institutionalized party systems, including the Chilean, the Uruguayan, the Mexican, the Salvadoran, and the Honduran, are cases of weak class voting.

Conclusion

We have made three main arguments. First, class voting in Latin America varies greatly across space and time. The conventional wisdom was that class voting in Latin America was historically weak in most countries (Dix 1989; Torcal and Mainwaring 2003a). We cannot fully judge whether that wisdom was true before the 1990s (Argentina, Chile, Peru, and possibly Uruguay in some historical periods were exceptions). It was largely correct in the 1990s but is no longer the case as a generalization. Since the 2000s, the intensity of class voting has varied greatly by country. In the 2000s, it was very strong in Argentina, Bolivia, Brazil, Guatemala, Peru, and Venezuela, and weak in Chile, the Dominican Republic, Ecuador, Honduras, Panama, and Uruguay.

The differences from the highest scores to the lowest are huge—which was not the case circa 1995 (Torcal and Mainwaring 2003a).

Second, to the degree that there is class voting in Latin America, it is almost always conventional class voting. But contrary to this classic hypothesis, strong class voting is not ubiquitous. Surprisingly, in light of earlier arguments, class voting is far more intense among the poor self-employed than among skilled workers.

Finally, class voting must be politically activated. Even in countries with huge social gaps, voters do not necessarily cast their ballot based on class issues. In the absence of parties, governments, and presidential candidates who emphasize class issues, citizens are unlikely to vote based on those issues. In Latin America, presidents and presidential candidates to the left-of-center have been the main actors who have raised the banners of social justice, income redistribution, social programs for the poor, and empowering the poor. In their absence, class voting is feeble. Left-of-center parties do not ensure vigorous class voting, but they are a necessary condition for it.

NOTES

María Victoria De Negri and Krystin Krause provided helpful research assistance. Ryan Carlin, María Victoria De Negri, Jean Paul Faguet, Tasha Fairfield, Sam Handlin, Peter Kingstone, Andrés Mejía, Ken Shadlen, Mitchell Seligson, Matthew Singer, Elizabeth Zechmeister, and participants of the Latin American Voter conference at Vanderbilt University, May 16–18, 2013, gave us excellent comments. Nicolás Somma acknowledges the support of the Center for Social Conflict and Cohesion Studies (CONICYT/FONDAP/15130009 grant, Ministry of Education of Chile).

1. Lipset (1960, 234) wrote that "[m]ore than anything else, the party struggle is a conflict among classes, and the most impressive single fact about political party support is that in virtually every economically developed country the lower-income groups vote mainly for parties of the left, while the higher income groups vote mainly for parties of the right."

2. Following Córdova (2009), the wealth index for household i is the linear combination,

$$y_i = \alpha_1\left(\frac{x_1 - \bar{x}_1}{s_1}\right) + \alpha_2\left(\frac{x_2 - \bar{x}_2}{s_2}\right) + \dots + \alpha_k\left(\frac{x_k - \bar{x}_k}{s_k}\right)$$

where $\bar{x}k$ and s_k are the mean and standard deviation of the asset x_k and α is the weight for each variable x_k for the first principal component.

3. We draw on Handlin's (2013b) excellent discussion of the advantages and disadvantages of different conceptualizations and operationalizations of "class."

4. This dichotomous variable parsimoniously captures the relationship between population size and the ideology of the presidential candidate for whom respondents voted. The differences between respondents of medium cities and those of smaller locales were not statistically significant.

5. The model to be estimated is: $P_i (P_n/P_o) = \alpha_i + \beta_1 \text{ class}_i + \beta_2 \text{ age}_i + \beta_3 \text{ residence size}_i + \beta_4 \text{ gender}_i + \mu_i$, where $P_i (P_n/P_o)$ is the respondent's probability of voting for party P_n rather than the most conservative party P_o.

6. In the simulations, the control variable for age is held constant at the mean value. The simulations are based on male residents of large cities.

7. On the radical left and its differences in relation to the moderate left, see Levitsky and Roberts (2011a); Weyland, Madrid, and Hunter (2010).

8. The occupation and employment status variables were not asked in the 2006 surveys in Brazil, Bolivia, and Ecuador. We did not include these countries in the 2006 analysis because it was impossible to approximate the Erikson-Goldthorpe schema.

9. The category of unpaid workers does not exist as a separate category in Erikson and Goldthorpe's schema. In 2006, there were only eighty individuals in this category (less than 1% of the sample).

10. Expressive of this view, Roberts (2002, 22) wrote that "many informal workers occupy an ambiguous class position. Labor fragmentation has made it increasingly difficult for workers to engage in collective action in either the workplace or the partisan sphere, severely eroding the organizational dimension of class cleavages." He attributed declining class voting in part to the growth of the informal sector, and he argued that structural changes and the weakening of unions would lead to a continuation of weak class voting (26). However, the poor self-employed have engaged in far more class voting than skilled workers.

11. In the rest of the countries combined, the ratio of poor self-employed to skilled workers is four to one.

12. We counted elections with reverse class voting as having a score of zero for conventional class voting.

13. Levitsky and Roberts (2011b) and Weyland, Madrid, and Hunter (2010) viewed Morales, Chávez, and Correa as the leading expressions of the radical left. In Peru, Ollanta Humala situated himself in this camp in his second-place 2006 presidential campaign before switching to a much more moderate platform in his victorious 2011 election.

14. The source for data on the Gini index and per capita GDP is the World Bank's *World Development Indicators*. Per capita GDP is based on purchasing parity power, in constant 2005 international dollars.

4 ✦ Religion and the Latin American Voter

TAYLOR BOAS AND AMY ERICA SMITH

Religion—at least organized religion in the monotheistic, Judeo-Christian tradition—is deeply, inherently political. In prescribing moral tenets, precepts not only for individuals' relationship to the divine, but also for their relationships to each other and to society at large, religious traditions provide one basis for ethical discourse, ideology, and the legitimation of political organization. But religion's impact on politics is due not only to its moral precepts, as important as such teachings are. In providing a regular, organized setting for communities to gather, religious groups help to generate the social capital necessary for political action and constitute a platform for political persuasion and activism. Finally, religion can serve as an important social identity for many people, facilitating the development of political in-groups and out-groups. Religion is profoundly political despite most contemporary states' adoption of some form of secularism; in fact, secularism is a response to religion's almost inevitable encroachment on the public sphere.

Latin America's political and social development has been heavily influenced by religion, from the first days of colonialism through the development of contemporary, third wave democracies. At the same time, the relationship between religion and politics in the region has changed dramatically in the past three decades. Until recently, the Catholic Church—the region's religious monopolist—faced little competition from other religious groups. The Church was far from monolithic or homogeneous; both its ideology and level of involvement in politics varied across time and space. States also varied in the strength of their support for or opposition to the Church. Still, the Catholic Church's constant presence in Latin American social life throughout much of history—and the consequent lack of variation in citizens' nominal religion—would have frustrated attempts at quantitative analysis even if appropriate survey data had been available.

Much has changed in the past few decades. No longer do Latin Americans identify as Catholic "by default." On the one hand, citizens who once might have considered themselves Catholics, albeit non-practicing, now increasingly identify as having no religious affiliation at all. On the other hand, Protestant churches—especially those of the evangelical and Pentecostal variety—have made increasing inroads into the territory of the faithful (for reviews of these trends, see Chesnut 2003, 2009; Garrard-Burnett 2009). The 2012 AmericasBarometer survey indicates that while 70% of Latin Americans still consider themselves Catholic, 19% now identify with non-Catholic Christian denominations and 9% claim no religious affiliation at all.[1]

What are the political implications of the increasing diversity and competitiveness of Latin America's religious marketplace? As religious affiliations and practices become more varied, do the political preferences and behaviors of the religious and nonreligious, or Catholics and Protestants, diverge? In this chapter, we seek to understand how Latin Americans' voting decisions are shaped by religion. In answering these questions, we provide what we believe to be the first systematic, survey-based examination of the role of religion across the entire region.

Our analysis pays particular attention to two increasingly salient religious cleavages in Latin America: between believers and nonbelievers, and between Catholics and Protestants. These cleavages often manifest themselves in voting behavior in the region, though in different ways and only under certain conditions. First, we find that the religious-secular cleavage has a clear effect on ideological voting, with nonbelievers supporting more left-wing candidates and more frequent churchgoers voting to the right. However, the magnitude of effects depends on the degree to which parties span the ideological spectrum and appeal to voters in programmatic terms. Second, while Catholics and Protestants do not consistently differ ideologically, this cleavage leads to identity voting when a non-Catholic candidate is among the options. That is, mainline and evangelical Protestants are more likely than Catholics to favor a Protestant for president; evangelicals even incline toward secular politicians when given the chance to vote against their religious rivals.

Like the other chapters in this part of the volume, we emphasize the conditions under which identities are activated and become salient for voting. One clear conclusion is that identity matters in part because voters seek candidates sharing those identities. Just as Latin American indigenous voters and women respond to the ethnicity and gender of candidates in their choice set (see chapters in this volume by Moreno and by Morgan), religious minorities seek politicians sharing their background. Thus, identity should matter more in political systems offering greater candidate diversity. Like Moreno, we conclude that identity matters when politicized by candidates or other opinion leaders. At the same time, as with class (Mainwaring, Torcal, and Somma this volume) and gender, religious identity only sometimes shapes the ideological direction of the vote. Like Morgan, we find that identity translates more readily into ideological voting in party systems that offer clearer differences between parties. In highlighting one input for ideological identification and voting, we also speak to topics addressed in the second part of this volume.

The Religious Marketplace in Latin America

Data from the 2004–12 AmericasBarometer surveys underscore the changing nature of religion in Latin America.[2] As figure 4.1 indicates, the strength of Catholicism varies substantially across our eighteen countries, with 80% or more identifying as Catholic in Ecuador, Mexico, Paraguay, and Venezuela, and as few as 36% of Uruguayans describing themselves as Catholic in 2012. Examining the AmericasBarometer since 2004 (prior years' data not shown in the figure), however, we find a clear trend: in most countries Catholicism is losing ground to secularism or to other Christian denominations. Other Christian groups have gained significant ground in every country in the region but Chile. Likewise, those claiming no religious identification have significantly encroached on Catholic territory in Bolivia, Brazil, Colombia, the Dominican Republic, Mexico, and Uruguay.[3] At the extreme, in Uruguay, secularism has overtaken Catholicism in recent years, with nearly half of all respondents claiming no religion in 2010 and 2012. Conversely, the Catholic Church has lost a significant share of identifiers in every country but Argentina, El Salvador, and Venezuela.

Across Latin America, 8% of citizens are classified as mainline or historical Protestants and 10% as evangelical or Pentecostal.[4] The latter traditions place an emphasis on conversion, missionary work, the authority of scripture, and, in the case of Pentecostalism, speaking in tongues and faith healing (Freston 2008; Pew Research Center 2006). While evangelicals in many countries were initially reluctant to engage in worldly pursuits such as politics, they have largely overcome this reluctance, and evangelicalism's proselytizing bent often makes its adherents particularly influential in electoral politics. As figure 4.1 indicates, evangelicals and Pentecostals

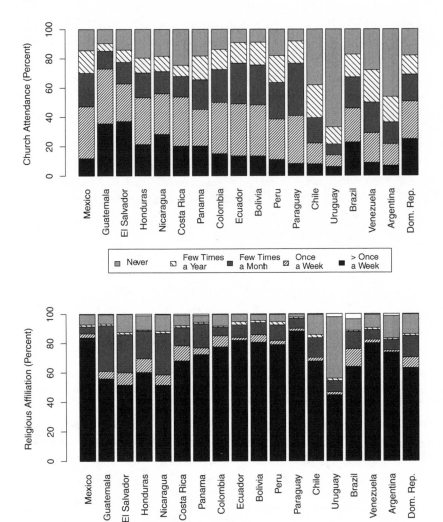

Figure 4.1 Religious Affiliation and Church Attendance. *Source:* Americas-Barometer 2012.

outnumber traditional Protestants in most countries, especially in Central America. In a few countries—Bolivia, Brazil, Colombia, and Mexico—mainline Protestants are predominant.[5] Even so, the intensity with which evangelicals participate in politics often gives them outsized political influence, especially in Brazil.

Just as important as religious identification is religious practice. Figure 4.1 also underscores that some countries that are nominally quite Catholic, such as Chile and Argentina, have few regular churchgoers; in 2012, only 18 to 20% in those countries attended one or more times per week.[6] Uruguay again stands out as particularly secular, with 81% rarely or never attending church. At the other end of the spectrum, countries with high rates of evangelicalism, especially those in Central America, tend to have large numbers who attend religious services at least weekly (75% in Guatemala). As this discussion suggests, the intensity of religious practice varies across religious groups: while just 42% of Catholics say they attend church at least weekly, 75% of evangelicals and 69% of historical Protestants do so.

Religion and the Vote in Latin America: Who, Where, How

Do religious differences across Latin America translate into differences in voting behavior? As Latin America's third wave democracies matured, scholars of religion and politics turned from investigating religion's role in authoritarianism and democracy (e.g., Fleet and Smith 1997; Gill 1994; Klaiber 1998; Johnston and Figa 1988) to address religion's impact on electoral and party politics. As an institution, the Catholic Church has become more politically neutral, moving away from both liberation theology and religious parties. Hagopian (2008, 2009) argues that the Church has nonetheless sought to retain the faithful by promoting either progressive economic policies (e.g., in Brazil) or conservative stances on issues such as women's reproductive rights (particularly in Argentina, Chile, and Mexico). Protestant churches' political agendas have coincided with the Catholic Church's positions on poverty and sexuality, while contesting the Church's historical privileges (Smith 1998). On the other side of the political spectrum, leaders of many Marxist-inspired, left-wing political movements have historically been atheist, agnostic, or, at the very least, non-practicing Catholics. The growing salience of issues such as abortion and same-sex marriage—absent from the political agenda even a decade ago, but now major topics of debate—reinforces these divides.

Scholars have indeed found a strong religious-secular cleavage among Latin American voters. For instance, Catholics and, especially, non-Catholic Christians are substantially less tolerant than the nonreligious and non-Christians toward gays seeking office (Seligson and Moreno 2010). In Costa Rica, Chile, Argentina, and Mexico, research shows that religiosity is associated with conservatism and secularism with leftist voting

(Camp 2008; Patterson 2004a, 2004b; Steigenga 2003; Valenzuela, Scully, and Somma 2007).

A second potential cleavage relates to differences among the religious. While Catholics and Protestants often vote differently from one another, differences vary greatly across countries and over time. Many scholars emphasize that Latin American evangelicals and Pentecostals exhibit considerable ideological variety (Fonseca 2008; Ireland 1991, 1997). Sometimes evangelicals vote on the right, such as for Mexico's Calderón in 2006 (Camp 2008), or they mobilize against leftist candidates, including Lula in Brazil's 1989 election and Dilma Rousseff in 2010 (Freston 1993, 2004; Smith 2013). But Brazil's evangelicals have also voted for left-of-center politicians: Garotinho in 2002 and Marina Silva in 2010, both evangelicals themselves (Bohn 2004, 2007; Smith 2013). In El Salvador, Chile, and Venezuela, there is also evidence of evangelicals voting to the left of Catholics (Aguilar et al. 1993; Smilde 2004; Valenzuela, Scully, and Somma 2007).[7] For their part, Mexico's evangelicals have historically aligned with the centrist Partido Revolucionario Institucional, or PRI (Barraca 2008). Finally, evangelicals sometimes vote no differently from citizens of other religions. This was the case in Brazil's 2006 election (Bohn 2007), when no evangelical candidates were running, and in Nicaragua's 1990 and 2006 elections, when evangelicals and Catholics similarly supported Daniel Ortega (Dodson 1997; Gooren 2010; Smith and Haas 1997; Zub 1992).[8]

Even if Latin American Protestants do not vote in a consistent ideological direction, religious minorities—especially evangelicals—often favor fellow believers (Bastian 1999). Despite few ideological differences with Catholics, Guatemalan Protestants generally rated coreligionist politicians more favorably (Steigenga 2003). In Brazil, where many evangelical churches have adopted a "Brother votes for Brother" stance, there have been dramatic increases in the number of evangelicals (including clergy) elected to office in the past two decades (e.g., Boas 2014; Fonseca 2008; Freston 2004).[9] Bohn (2007) argues that evangelicals had no common ideology in Brazil's 2002 and 2006 presidential elections, but were mobilized only as an "identity group" responding to coreligionists in the candidate choice set.

Existing studies of religion and voting behavior in Latin America address important questions, but they do so in a somewhat piecemeal fashion. While some authors array the religious vote on the left-right spectrum, others focus on candidates' religious identities. Few consider both candidates' ideology and religion (for an exception, see Bohn 2007). Further, we lack systematic, region-wide evidence enabling broad generalization. Most work consists of single-country case studies, with cross-national comparisons usually limited to two or three countries. Though several important studies address religion and politics region-wide, these studies have not focused on voting behavior (Freston 2008; Garrard-Burnett 2009; Gill 2002; Hagopian 2009; Mainwaring and Scully 2003).

Another important question is *how* religion shapes vote choice. Studies of the Catholic-Protestant voting cleavage suggest that evangelicals favor fellow believers because of identity-based heuristics (or information short-cuts), while Catholics might vote against these same candidates because of out-group cues. Even nonbelief might come to serve as a group identity, with those who reject religion seeking secular candidates and avoiding the religious. Yet religion might also affect voting behavior through social mechanisms. Those who attend church more regularly are exposed to political information and opinions from clergy and other parishioners. While lay Catholics are often skeptical of the Church's political leadership (Amuchastegui et al. 2010; Blancarte 2009), Catholic clergy may nonetheless exercise indirect influence, in part through pastoral letters (Camp 2008; Oro 2006). And evangelical and neo-Pentecostal clergy campaign more overtly, mobilizing followers as a voting block (Campos 2005; Oro 2003; Smith 2010, 2013). Bohn (2004) found that Brazilian evangelicals were likely to mention church as the most important source of electoral information and religion as a key criterion in choosing a political party.

Religion and the Ideology of Vote Choice

Do religious voters seek presidential candidates who are ideologically compatible, or simply ones who share their religious identities? We begin by assessing the extent to which religion shapes ideological voting, using AmericasBarometer data from 2008 to 2012. We estimated a series of OLS regression models in which the dependent variable was the ideological position of the respondent's vote in the last presidential election, as described in this volume's introduction. Our key independent variables included frequency of attending religious services and indicator variables for mainline Protestants, evangelicals, and those claiming no religion (with Catholic as the reference category).[10] As is standard throughout the volume, the model included controls for household wealth, education, size of place of residence, age, and gender and indicator variables for black and indigenous. For this chapter we also included indicators for Mormons/Jehovah's Witnesses and non-Christians. For a region-wide model, we pooled all countries, using fixed effects for country and for survey waves. We also estimated separate models for each country, replacing country fixed effects with those for subnational regions. Where multiple waves of the survey covered a single election, we used all observations but applied weights so that each election counted equally.

The results are summarized in figure 4.2. We find that across all eighteen Latin American countries church attendance is associated with a more right-wing vote, while those with no religion are significantly to the left. Mainline and evangelical Protestants do not differ from Catholics. Hence, the religious-secular cleavage in Latin America is expressed in ideological voting, but interreligious differences are not. Nonetheless, recall that Protestants attend church much more frequently than Catholics; while 47% of evangelicals and 40% of historical Protestants attend more than once a week, only 12% of Catholics do. Thus, the groups differ slightly (but not significantly) in actual ideological voting due to varying religiosity.[11]

Looking at individual countries, we find further support for these conclusions. Evangelicals or mainline Protestants vote significantly to the left of Catholics in Nicaragua, Panama, Ecuador, Bolivia, and Uruguay; evangelicals vote significantly to the right of Catholics in El Salvador and Paraguay. We can think of no obvious contextual features, such as the nature of the party system, to explain these varied effects. The effects of religiosity and secularism, however, are more consistent: the nonreligious vote significantly to the left in Mexico, Chile, Uruguay, and Venezuela, while church attendance pushes voters significantly to the right in Mexico, Nicaragua, Uruguay, and Argentina.

Party system features such as polarization and programmaticness might help explain cross-national variation in religion's effects. Religious views may influence voters' personal ideology, but whether these attitudes are expressed at the polls should depend on the options presented to voters. In polarized party systems, where candidates tend to differ clearly from one another on the left-right spectrum, religious conservatism and secular leftism should be more likely to translate into voting behavior. Indeed, in those countries in figure 4.2 where church attendance or secularism has a significant effect, recent presidential elections have tended to feature clear left- and/or right-wing options. Similarly, whether voters' issue stances matter for voting behavior should depend on programmaticness—the degree to which parties appeal to voters on the basis of issue positions rather than clientelism or charisma.

To examine whether religion's effect on ideological voting varies systematically with features of a country's party system, we estimated two hierarchical linear models. At the individual level, we used the same

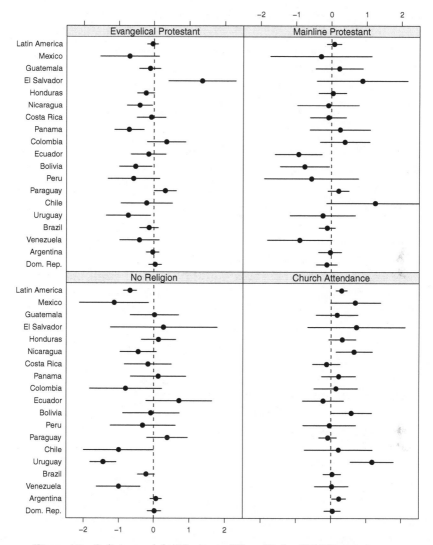

Figure 4.2   Religion and the Ideology of Vote Choice (OLS Regression Coefficients). *Source:* AmericasBarometer 2008–2012. *Note:* Dots represent OLS multiple regression coefficients; dependent variable is ideology of vote choice (0–20 scale, higher numbers indicate the ideological right). Catholic is the references category for the religion dummy variables. Lines give 95% confidence intervals (design-effect based). Church attendance runs from 0 (never) to 1 (more than weekly). Models include controls for non-Christians, Mormons/Jehovah's Witnesses, household wealth, education, town size, age, gender, race, and country/region/year fixed effects.

specification as in the pooled model described above, along with fixed effects for each survey wave. As before, when multiple survey waves cover an election, we applied weights to count each election equally. For the first model, we included an additional country-level variable: an index of parties' programmaticness derived from the expert surveys of the Democratic Accountability and Linkages Project, or DALP (Kitschelt and Freeze 2010). For the second model, we included an election-level variable: party system polarization, constructed using data from the Parliamentary Elites in Latin America (PELA) study on how elected legislators locate their own parties on the left-right spectrum.[12] We measured the polarization of the legislature in session at the time of each presidential election. In each case, we interacted the higher-level index with the key religious variables (mainline Protestant, evangelical Protestant, no religion, and church attendance, with Catholic again serving as the baseline).

The results of these hierarchical linear models underscore that secularism and church attendance matter for ideological voting in Latin America only where parties span the ideological spectrum or present clear programmatic options to voters. Consistent with the argument that interreligious cleavages are expressed in terms of identity rather than ideological voting, we obtain null results for the evangelical and mainline Protestant dummy variables (i.e., dichotomous measures that are coded as 1 if they have the characteristic and zero otherwise), as well as the interactions between these variables and the country-level measures. However, for church attendance and the no religion dummy variable, we find several interactions that are significant in the expected direction.

In figures 4.3 and 4.4 we present the statistically significant interactions. In the first figure we plot the interaction between no religion and DALP's programmaticness index—that is, the marginal effect of not having a religion across countries with different levels of programmaticness.[13] The top horizontal axis presents the actual value of each country on the programmaticness index. In the second figure, likewise, we plot the effects of the interaction between church attendance and polarization, or the marginal effect of church attendance in elections with higher or lower levels of polarization. Since the polarization measure varies by election, the top horizontal axis in this latter figure presents the coding of different country-election years.

At the lowest levels of the programmaticness index, secularism has no significant effect on ideological voting, but at moderate and high levels—where most countries are located—it pushes voters significantly to the left. Likewise, church attendance makes no difference for ideological voting at

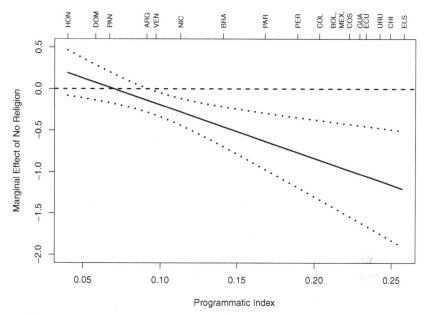

Figure 4.3   Marginal Effect of Having No Religion on Ideology of Vote Choice. *Sources:* AmericasBarometer 2004–2012 and DALP. *Note:* Dotted lines give 95% confidence intervals (design-effect based). See text for details of model specification.

lower levels of legislative polarization. However, in presidential elections held when legislative polarization is moderate or high, it is associated with right-wing voting.[14] The more relevant ideology and issues are for elite politics, the more the secular-religious cleavage matters in Latin American electorates.

Religion and Identity Voting

Religion might also affect vote choice in ways not captured on the left-right spectrum. Religious minorities, such as non-Catholic Christians or the nonreligious, might vote disproportionately for a group member when one is on the ballot, even if religious minority candidates occupy ideological positions similar to those of others in the race. Especially for Protestants and evangelicals, identity might trump ideology, pulling voters to the left in some elections and to the right in others. Out-group effects may also be present; Catholics might be reluctant to vote for evangelicals or mainline Protestants, and vice versa, while the religious may shy away from

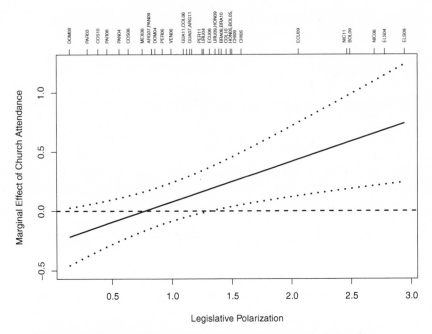

Figure 4.4   Marginal Effect of Church Attendance on Ideology of Vote
Choice. *Sources:* AmericasBarometer 2004–2012 and PELA. *Note:* Dotted
lines give 95% confidence intervals (design-effect based). See text for
details of model specification.

avowed atheists or agnostics. Effects of this sort are particularly likely in
countries where competition for believers has spilled over into competition at the ballot box (Boas 2014).

To examine identity voting, we used publicly available news sources to
score the professed religious beliefs of all major presidential candidates
covered in the 2008–12 AmericasBarometer.[15] We identified six Protestant
candidates: Roberto Madrazo (Mexico 2006), Manuel Baldizón and Harold Caballeros (Guatemala 2011), Humberto Lay (Peru 2006), Nicanor
Duarte (Paraguay 2003), and Marina Silva (Brazil 2010). Seven candidates
were classified as secular: Carlos Gaviria Díaz (Colombia 2006), Jorge Arrate and Marco Enríquez-Ominami (Chile 2009), Michelle Bachelet (Chile
2005), José Mujica (Uruguay 2009), Tabaré Vázquez (Uruguay 2005), and
Hermes Binner (Argentina 2011).[16] We also found a handful of candidates
who were Jewish or practiced traditional religions, but not enough to warrant separate analysis. The vast majority of candidates were identified as
Catholic. On the 0–19 scale for candidate ideology (rightists receive higher

values), secular candidates average 4.6, adherents of traditional religions 8.4, Jews 9.7, Protestants 12.0, and Catholics 12.2.

Religion and the presence of a non-Catholic candidate were salient during at least some of these campaigns. Baldizón finished second in Guatemala's 2011 election, campaigning with phrases like "I will govern with the Bible in one hand and the Constitution in the other" (Palomares 2011). In Brazil's 2010 election, controversy surrounding Dilma Rousseff's shifting position on abortion helped draw attention to Marina Silva's status as an evangelical candidate opposing it (Smith 2013). In Chile in 2005, right-wing candidate Sebastián Piñera made a play for centrist Christian Democratic votes by criticizing the agnosticism of front-runner Michelle Bachelet (Campusano 2005).

We proceeded to estimate two logistic regressions in which the dependent variable was, alternatively, "vote for a Protestant" and "vote for a secular candidate." In each case, the baseline category was voting for any other candidate; in nearly every instance this meant voting for a Catholic.[17] We pooled all countries and survey years in which each choice was relevant, weighting the data so that elections counted equally. We used the same individual right-hand-side variables as in the models described above, along with country and year fixed effects. We then generated predicted voting probabilities, varying church attendance and religion for all observations while holding other variables at their observed values.

The results (figure 4.5) underscore that Latin America's Catholic-Protestant cleavage, though not expressed consistently in ideological voting, shapes religious identity voting. When given the option, mainline and evangelical Protestants are substantially more likely than Catholics to support a Protestant candidate (32% versus 25%).[18] Nonreligious demographics are poor predictors, and only education is significant; having higher education as opposed to no education is associated with a 9% drop in the probability of voting for Protestants.

For evangelicals we also see evidence of out-group identity voting. When choosing between secular and Catholic candidates, evangelicals are significantly more likely than Catholics to vote for the secular competitor (43% versus 39%)—presumably not because they favor a godless president, but because they fear that a Catholic one might endorse state prerogatives for Catholicism.[19]

Finally, we see evidence that the religious-secular cleavage, which matters for ideological voting, also shows up in terms of identity voting. Voters with no religion are significantly more likely than Catholics or evangelicals to vote for a secular candidate (51% probability); this effect holds up even

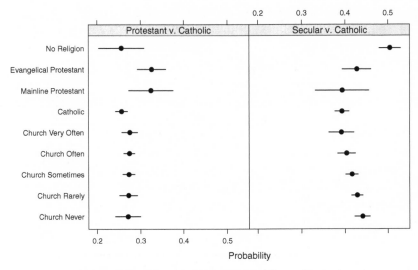

Figure 4.5   Voting for Religious Minority Candidates. *Source:* Americas-Barometer 2004–2012. *Note:* Lines give 95% confidence intervals (design-effect based). Models include controls for household wealth, education, town size, age, gender, race, non-Christians, Mormons/Jehovah's Witnesses, and country-year fixed effects. Probabilities are estimated setting all observations to the value of interest, and leaving all other variables at the observed values.

when controlling for individual left-right identification. Secular candidate support is also significantly higher for the well-educated, for younger voters, and for those in larger urban areas.[20]

Thus, there is clear evidence of both religious-secular and Catholic-Protestant voting cleavages in Latin America, but these cleavages manifest themselves differently. The religious-secular cleavage shows up in ideological voting, with religiosity leading to support for candidates on the right. Yet church attendance and secularism have larger effects on ideological voting when party systems are more polarized and programmatic, and a null effect where they are least so. Finally, while interdenominational cleavages do not consistently push voters to the left or right, they do influence identity voting in elections featuring non-Catholic candidates.

Case Study: Clergy Influence in Brazil

Our analysis of the AmericasBarometer suggests that, under some conditions, religion affects voting in Latin America. Yet causality and causal mechanisms are difficult to explore using these data. Voters might prefer a candidate of their own faith because of in-group identity, but ideology might also drive the relationship, particularly for the religious-secular cleavage. Church attendance may be associated with right-wing voting, but it remains unclear whether sitting in the pews each Sunday has a causal effect on vote choice—for example, because of politically tinged sermons—or whether these variables are merely correlated.

In this section, we delve deeper into religion's effect on voting in Brazil, drawing on two survey experiments. We argue that religion matters for vote choice directly, through identity voting, and indirectly, via clergy endorsement of candidates and voters' positions on issues such as gay rights.

Brazilian legislative elections present a context in which we would expect religion to shape voting behavior. The combination of open-list proportional representation, high district magnitude, and a highly fragmented party system means that there are hundreds of candidates for most legislative offices. This system gives citizens the freedom to vote their preferences, rather than encouraging them to vote strategically. The difficulty of gathering information about so many contenders also boosts the influence of shortcuts like clergy voting recommendations or a candidate's religion. Furthermore, low levels of mass partisanship (Samuels 2006) and frequent party switching among legislators (Desposato 2006) mean that a candidate's party affiliation is less useful for reaching a decision, leaving room for religion to matter more.

Brazilian politicians also span a wide range of religious affiliations and ideological positions, giving voters who are motivated by faith or ideology the chance to choose candidates with similar characteristics. Brazil ranks sixth out of eighteen countries in the ideological distance between its leftmost and rightmost political parties, ahead of Bolivia and Venezuela. Moreover, open list proportional representation gives party leaders strong incentives to diversify candidate lists by including representatives of particular identity groups, like evangelical Christians.

Finally, both religious-secular and Catholic-Protestant cleavages have been salient during recent Brazilian campaigns. Controversy surrounding abortion saw many Catholics and evangelicals campaigning side by side against Dilma Rousseff in the 2010 presidential election, while secular activists rushed to her defense. Yet evangelicals' political ambitions have also led to conflict with Catholics. In São Paulo's 2012 mayoral election, the Catholic hierarchy mobilized against front-runner Celso Russomanno, who, though not evangelical himself, had strong ties to the Universal Church of the Kingdom of God. The archbishop of São Paulo released a letter calling Russomanno a "threat to democracy" and instructed priests to read it during Mass, arguably helping to derail Russomanno's candidacy (Lima 2012; Gama and Roncaglia 2012).

To test the effect of religious cues on voting in low-information elections, we conducted a survey experiment during the two and a half weeks before Brazil's October 7, 2012, municipal election.[21] Advertising on Facebook, we recruited 1,820 registered voters age 18 or older for an online survey. Though selection was nonrandom, we ended up with a strikingly representative sample on variables such as region, race, party identification, and 2010 presidential vote. The sample over-represents the young, wealthy, males, and residents of larger cities, though we still have decent variation here. We also obtained disproportionately large subsamples of Protestants/evangelicals (30%), atheists/agnostics (4%), and those who believe in God but subscribe to no organized religion (14%), allowing us to examine the effect of religious cues among these minority groups.

Our first experiment examined the effect of clergy candidates using their official electoral names to signal religious leadership (Boas 2014). Brazilian electoral law gives candidates broad leeway to use nicknames or professional titles, and many take advantage of this opportunity; an evangelical minister named Paulo Rodrigues de Souza might present himself as "Pastor Paulo."[22] To test this cue's effect, we provided a brief description of a city council candidate, including party, age, marital status, and education. Respondents in the treatment condition were given the candidate's electoral name with a religious title; those in the control condition received the candidate's full legal name.[23] We then asked respondents how likely they would be to vote "for a person like this," on a scale of 1 to 7.[24]

The top half of figure 4.6 summarizes the "pastor" treatment effect on vote intention. On average, receiving a candidate's religious title has a significant *negative* effect on vote intention. However, the effect is positive among evangelicals, and even larger (and significant) among the subset who identify with Pentecostalism. This positive effect is offset by a negative one among every other religious category, reaching statistical significance for atheists/agnostics, all Catholics, and Charismatic Catholics. The findings for the latter group are particularly striking. The Charismatic movement, Catholicism's answer to Pentecostalism, involves a similar worship style and draws from a similar social base. However, our survey provides clear evidence of divergent identity voting for these two groups. Charismatic Catholics are turned off from voting for an evangelical pastor, despite seemingly aligned stances on important issues—just as evangelicals across numerous Latin American countries favor secular candidates over Catholic opponents.

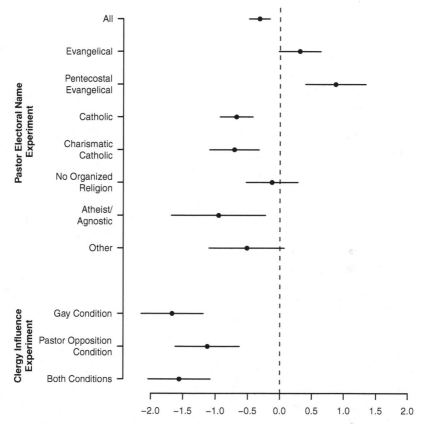

Figure 4.6 Treatment Effects on Vote Intention, Brazil 2012. *Source:* Authors' original data collection. *Note:* Dots give point estimates; lines represent 95% confidence intervals. Results of the clergy influence experiment are for the evangelical subsample.

Our second survey experiment sought to test the effect of clergy voting recommendations as a mechanism by which church attendance might affect voting (Smith 2013). In the real world, it is difficult to disentangle the impact of clergy recommendations from that of other political information, as well as the weight of the issues clergy and the media address. We sought to separate these potential influences experimentally. All respondents read the following message: "Suppose that José Vargas dos Santos is a candidate for city council from [PARTY]. He has been working in the community for more than 20 years."[25] The control condition received just this message, but three treatment conditions received the following additional information:

Treatment 1: "He participates actively in the gay movement."

Treatment 2: "Various evangelical pastors have spoken out against his political positions."

Treatment 3: "He participates actively in the gay movement. Various evangelical pastors have spoken out against his political positions."

Once again, respondents reported their likelihood of supporting "a person like this."

The bottom half of figure 4.6 summarizes each treatment's effect among evangelicals, vis-à-vis the control condition.[26] Voters are clearly swayed by both issues and clergy endorsements. While simple clergy opposition lowers responses by 1.1 points on the 7-point scale, information about the candidate's activism for gay rights pushes down responses by 1.7 points. When both messages combine, the effect is 1.6 points. Thus, religious Protestants take into account *both* issues and clergy preferences, though clergy endorsements matter less than issues.

Though both scenarios were described as fictitious, they approximate conditions under which religion matters for voting in the real world: the presence of religious minority candidates and the politicization of religion during the campaign. Religion's effect is enhanced by the broader electoral context—Brazil's fragmented party system, low party identification, and an electoral system with numerous candidates for legislative office. These results underscore that religion exerts both direct and indirect effects on voting. Consistent with our region-wide analysis, we find in-group and out-group identity heuristics matter when an evangelical pastor runs for office. In such cases, identity may trump issue voting; charismatic Catholics were turned off by "Pastor Paulo" even though he would probably agree with their stance on abortion or same-sex marriage. Yet in other contexts, religion influences voting behavior indirectly, via issue positions and clergy endorsements. We find evidence of both in the decision to vote against the gay rights activist.

Conclusion

Across eighteen countries and a decade's worth of presidential elections, two religious cleavages have mattered for the Latin American voter: between the religious and nonreligious, and between Catholics and Protestants. The religious-secular cleavage manifests itself in ideological voting, with the nonreligious voting to the left and more frequent churchgoers to the right. Protestants and Catholics tend to vote similarly in ideological terms, but this interreligious cleavage shows up in identity voting; each group prefers candidates of the same faith. Our first survey experiment confirms the importance of both in-group and out-group identities: evangelical clergy candidates appeal to evangelical voters, though they also generate rejection from both Catholic and secular voters. Yet the second survey experiment suggests that religion also shapes the vote through mechanisms other than identity. Religious congregations and clergy channel key information to the faithful on issues such as sexual politics, and they also shape voting by directly endorsing or explicitly rejecting candidates, regardless of religious affiliations. These social and informational mechanisms may contribute to interreligious differences in the ideology of vote choice.

Yet both identity-based and ideological effects depend on the characteristics of elections or of countries' political systems. Religiously motivated ideological voting requires that party systems be at least somewhat polarized and that parties appeal to voters on at least moderately programmatic terms. When parties fail to differentiate themselves on the policy issues that most distinguish religious voters from the nonreligious—in particular, issues of sexual politics and the family—there is little room for religion to affect the ideological direction of the vote. By contrast, as party polarization grows and left and right increasingly take distinct positions on issues such as abortion and homosexuality, religion exerts greater effects.

For its part, identity-driven voting for religious minorities (either Protestant or secular) requires that one be included among the ranks of candidates—something that still happens only infrequently in presidential elections across Latin America.[27] Non-Catholics are more likely to run at lower levels of office, particularly in legislative elections with a large number of candidates. In such cases, religious heuristics and socially supplied cues may have particularly strong effects on vote choice, as we find in Brazil.

Our findings provide interesting parallels and contrasts with gender and ethnicity, the other two identity group categories examined in this volume. All three chapters uncover important identity voting effects. Just as religious minorities seek coreligionist candidates, Morgan shows that women voters are more likely to vote for women candidates, and Moreno finds strong links between indigenous voters and candidates. Moreover, just as Morgan finds that Latin American women often vote to the right of men, and that the strength of the gender-ideology association is stronger in countries with more polarized party systems, we find that religion and religiosity push voters to the right, but only in more polarized and programmatic party systems.

Nonetheless, we suspect that in other ways the electoral impact of religion is different from that of gender or ethnicity. Though Morgan does not find evidence of countries with significant modern gender gaps (women to the left of men) in present-day Latin America, scholars argue that socioeconomic development causes gender gaps to close and then to reverse. By contrast, it is hard to imagine a long-term social process that would cause Latin America's "religion gap"—the ideological divide between the religious and nonreligious—to reverse in direction. While the political meaning of any group identity is socially constructed by its members, the political implications of religion are constrained to a much greater degree by authoritative texts and traditions, as well as by the overlapping and mutually reinforcing influences of local, national, and transnational religious institutions.

Proponents of an assertive vision of state secularism are often uncomfortable with the normative ramifications of religious voting since religious beliefs can be contentious and can make it difficult to negotiate a consensus regarding the common good. Regardless of any normative qualms one might hold, our analysis suggests that religious voting is likely to be a continuing feature of the Latin American political landscape. Religion's impact on electoral outcomes might actually increase over time as greater percentages of citizens identify as nonreligious, on the one hand, and evangelical, on the other. If the maturation of party systems leads to greater polarization and programmaticness, religion's influence on ideological voting should grow even further.

From a normative standpoint, we suggest that the growing role of religion in Latin American elections is actually a positive development. Historically, having viable and competitive parties that give both leftists and rightists a stake in the system has strengthened the prospects of Latin American democracy by reducing the likelihood of either insurgencies or coups. Though the threat of an armed secular or evangelical movement sounds remote, incorporating a diverse set of interests and identities into the electoral process is no less important to regime legitimacy and to citizens' satisfaction with democracy. As secular and Protestant Latin Americans grow in numbers, their presence at the ballot box contributes to a more diverse and vital democracy.

NOTES

Thanks to Scott Desposato, Kirk Hawkins, Michael Lewis-Beck, the editors of this volume, and participants in Vanderbilt University's Latin American Voter

Conference for comments on previous drafts of this chapter; to Joe Gettemy, Ryan Washburn, and Marisa Wilson for excellent research assistance; and to the Latin American Public Opinion Project (LAPOP) for survey data.

1. These percentages weight each country's sample by its population. Using unweighted percentages (i.e., treating each country in Latin America as having the same population), we find that 66% identify as Catholic, 22% as other Christian, and 10% as religiously unaffiliated.

2. In the 2008 AmericasBarometer, question **Q3** asked: "What is your religion?" [Do not read options] (1) Catholic, (2) Mainline Protestant or Protestant non-Evangelical (Adventist, Baptist, Calvinist, The Salvation Army, Lutheran, Methodist, Nazarene, Presbyterian), (3) Non-Christian Religions (Jewish, Muslims, Buddhists, Hinduisms, Taoists), (5) Evangelical and Pentecostal (Pentecostals, Charismatic non-Catholics, Light of World), (6) Mormons, Jehovah's Witness, Spiritualists and Seventh-Day Adventists, (7) Traditional Religions or Native Religions (Candomble, Vodoo, Rastafarian, Mayan Traditional Religion), (4) None, secularist or atheist (Do not believe in God). In the 2010–12 AmericasBarometer question **Q3C** asked: "What is your religion, if any?" [Do not read options. If the respondent says that he/she has no religion, probe to see if he/she should be located in option 4 or 11] (1) Catholic, (2) Protestant, Mainline Protestant or Protestant non-Evangelical (Christian; Calvinist; Lutheran; Methodist; Presbyterian; Disciple of Christ; Anglican; Episcopalian; Moravian), (3) Non-Christian Eastern Religions (Islam; Buddhist; Hinduism; Taoist; Confucianism; Baha'i), (4) None (Believes in a Supreme Entity but does not belong to any religion), (5) Evangelical and Pentecostal (Evangelical; Pentecostals; Church of God; Assemblies of God; Universal Church of the Kingdom of God; International Church of the Foursquare Gospel; Christ Pentecostal Church; Christian Congregation; Mennonite; Brethren; Christian Reformed Church; Charismatic non-Catholic; Light of World; Baptist; Nazarene; Salvation Army; Adventist; Seventh-Day Adventist; Sara Nossa Terra), (6) LDS (Mormon), (7) Traditional Religions or Native Religions (Candomblé, Voodoo, Rastafarian, Mayan Traditional Religion; Umbanda; Maria Lonza; Inti; Kardecista, Santo Daime, Esoterica), (10) Jewish (Orthodox; Conservative; Reform), (11) Agnostic, atheist (Does not believe in God), (12) Jehovah's Witness. For all three survey waves, separate variables are coded 1 for respondents of each of the following religious affiliations, zero for respondents who listed other religious affiliations, and missing for those who did not respond: Catholic (Q3C and Q3 option 1), Historical/Mainline Protestant (Q3C and Q3 option 2), Evangelical Protestant (Q3C and Q3 option 5), Mormon (LDS)/Jehovah's Witness (Q3C options 6 and 12; Q3 option 6), No religion (Q3C options 4 and 11; Q3 option 4), Non-Christian (Q3C options 3, 7, and 10; Q3 options 3 and 7).

3. In each of these countries, the slope coefficient for a logistic regression of the respective religious identification on year is statistically significant in the direction mentioned.

4. Throughout most of Latin America, the Spanish and Portuguese term *evangélico* is applied to both mainline/historical and evangelical Protestants. Moreover, national censuses and surveys often do not distinguish between the two variants of

Protestantism, and historical Protestant denominations may adopt practices typical of evangelicals.

5. In Brazil, however, those classified as Pentecostals outnumber mainline Protestants in other recent LAPOP waves, including 2008, 2010, and 2014, as well as in the 2010 census.

6. Based on AmericasBarometer question **Q5A**. "How often do you attend religious services?" [Read options] (1) More than once per week; (2) Once per week; (3) Once a month; (4) Once or twice a year; (5) Never or almost never. Recoded on a scale from zero to 1, with higher values representing more frequent church attendance: 1 = attends church more than once a week, 0 = never or almost never attends church.

7. In Chile, however, other studies suggest little ideological difference between Catholics and Protestants (Patterson 2004b) or claim that evangelicals are disconnected from politics (Fontaine Talavera and Beyer 1998).

8. Zub (1992), however, does find that evangelicals were slightly less likely to vote for the Frente Sandinista de Liberación Nacional (FSLN) in 1990.

9. In contrast, relatively few Catholic clergy have run for office in Brazil, with limited success (Oro 2006).

10. Frequency of religious services was recoded to run from zero to 1, with higher numbers indicating more frequent attendance.

11. In addition, church attendance matters somewhat more for ideological voting among Catholics and evangelicals than among historical Protestants.

12. We develop a three-level hierarchical model, with survey waves nested within countries. Weights adjust for both the survey's complex design and the use of multiple waves for some election years. The interactive effects are robust to various alternative specifications, including ones using cross-classified random effects (but without weights).

13. Complete results can be found in the online replication files.

14. For the programmaticness model, the marginal effect of church attendance was insignificant across nearly the entire range of values. Likewise, in the polarization model, the marginal effect of no religion was insignificant across nearly the entire range. However, estimated marginal effects were always of the expected sign.

15. In two-round voting systems, variable VB3 asks about the first-round election.

16. Candidate secularism comprises atheism, agnosticism, and public disavowal of religion.

17. There were no cases including both secular and Protestant candidates. Tomás Hirsch, a minor candidate in Chile's 2005 election, is Jewish and is included in the baseline along with votes for Piñera and Lavín. Three percent of the 2008 sample supported Hirsch.

18. The logistic regression coefficients are significant at $p = 0.015$ (mainline Protestants) and $p = 0.0011$ (evangelicals). However, these effects are only statistically significant among mainline and evangelical Protestants attending church at least weekly.

19. The logistic regression coefficient for evangelicals is significant at $p = 0.039$.

20. There is little evidence that the effect of church attendance on secular voting varies across denominations.

21. The survey was conducted jointly with F. Daniel Hidalgo; approval was obtained from the institutional review boards of each of our institutions.

22. About three-quarters of clergy city council candidates use a religious title. "Pastor," denoting a Protestant minister, is the most common. Catholic priests, who rarely run for office, would use the title "Padre" (Father).

23. This treatment is stronger than simply mentioning a candidate's religion, but is externally valid in a way that religion is not; candidate names routinely include professional titles, but rarely other religious cues. To further enhance external validity, respondents from a municipality with real "pastor" ballot name candidates were randomly given either one of these candidates (37%) or the fictional candidate Paulo Rodrigues de Souza/Pastor Paulo (37%). We pool these groups since effects were statistically indistinguishable.

24. Respondents were asked to evaluate a single candidate rather than choose among several. This question format has several methodological advantages, such as allowing for more reliable 7-point scales. It deviates from actual voting practice (entering the chosen candidate's number into the electronic voting machine), but prompting voters to choose among named alternatives would do so as well. Moreover, voters arguably do evaluate candidates in isolation during the campaign, as they are presented with numerous individual self-promotion efforts.

25. Party was randomly assigned from among the Partido dos Trabalhadores (PT), the Partido da Social Democracia Brasileira (PSDB), and the Partido do Movimento Democrático Brasileiro (PMDB).

26. Elsewhere (Smith 2013) we present the coefficients for evangelicals, Catholics, and the nonreligious. Here we present coefficients only for evangelicals since cues from evangelical pastors should have the greatest impact precisely among evangelicals.

27. Though in the more secular countries of the Southern Cone, the presence of secular candidates appears to have become something of a new norm.

5 ✦ Ethnicity and Electoral Preferences in Latin America

DANIEL E. MORENO MORALES

Latin America is a region with great ethnic diversity. Descendents of the original indigenous inhabitants coexist with people of European descent whose ancestors migrated in several waves during the past five centuries. Large black and mulatto populations descending from Africans make up sizable minorities in many countries across the region, and in some countries Asians form relevant minority groups. The largest group across the region, and the majority group in most countries, is the mestizo population, consisting of individuals of mixed descent (indigenous and European).

In this chapter I aim to contribute to the understanding of the relationship between ethnic and racial factors and electoral choice in Latin America by discussing findings related to two different but complementary empirical questions. First, are electoral preferences determined by ethnicity? More specifically, are indigenous individuals and members of other minorities more likely to vote for candidates who embrace a particular ideological orientation? And second, can we find evidence of ethnic identity voting in the region? That is, are members of minority groups likely to vote for candidates of their same ethnicity? Results indicate that ethnicity is a relevant predictor of voting preferences only in a few cases in the region, and that ethnic voting is prevalent only in those few cases in which ethnicity has become important for politics.

There are three relevant features of ethnicity in Latin America that are worth keeping in mind for understanding its effects on politics across the region. The first is that social stratification is usually consistent with ethnic divides. Black and indigenous individuals tend to be poorer and less educated than mestizos and whites, and even controlling for those factors discrimination affects indigenous and blacks more frequently than other citizens, resulting in lower wages and fewer opportunities for upward social mobility (Hall and Patrinos 2006; Pascharopoulos and Patrinos 1994).

A second important feature of ethnicity in the region is that its measurement is problematic because of the use of ambiguous measures and lack of state efforts to define it. Despite the importance of ethnic diversity in the region, official figures that account for the size of each ethnic group are unreliable and problematic; national census offices have until very recently ignored ethnic self-identification, and the items they have included are often incomplete and problematic (Del Popolo 2008; Nobles 2000). Most available estimates suggest that around 10% of the population in the region is indigenous, while another 10 to 15% are blacks or mulattos of African descent, but these figures vary substantially from source to source. The data used for this chapter overcome some measurement limitations by relying on self-identification in relation to different ethnic/racial categories and, as well, examining the independent effects of linguistic background.

The third and final feature of ethnicity that needs to be considered is its "fluid" character, the fact that the resulting groups vary from one measure to another and across time. Despite a strong correlation between skin color and self-identification (see below), identification with a particular ethnic category depends very much on two different factors: the question employed to record self-identification; and the social and political context.[1] Slight changes in the way the self-identification question is asked can result in huge differences in the results. And identification can also change across time, depending on the social and political context, which gives meaning to the ethnicity categories used in the self-identification question.[2] The fluidity of ethnic identifications and categories should be considered when projecting across time and contexts from the findings presented in this chapter; as well, they suggest the fact that ethnicity can be activated, or made to be more salient, by different political contexts and actors. This latter point will be noted later in this chapter.

A Portrait of Ethnicity in the Region

The AmericasBarometer dataset contains valuable information about the self-identification of individuals with the main ethnic categories in each country. Individuals identify with a particular ethnic group as a result of complex identity construction processes, in which political factors play relevant roles and in which the naming of the categories is crucial (Chandra

and Laitin 2002; Hoddie 2006; Moreno Morales 2008). The question employed in the AmericasBarometer asks the respondent to identify herself
or himself as part of any of the following categories: white, mestizo, indigenous, black, or other.[3] Figure 5.1 shows the response distribution for each
category by country.[4] The self-identification categories were recoded into
dummy variables (meaning they are given the value of 1 if the respondent
has that trait and zero otherwise) for the analyses, leaving the larger "mestizo" category as the reference group.

While the AmericasBarometer question provides insight into ethnic
self-identification across the region, ethnicity is fundamentally a complex
concept, consisting of different dimensions often measured in different

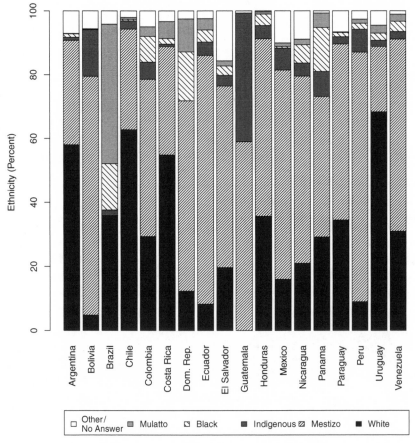

Figure 5.1   Identification with ethnic categories by country.
Source: AmericasBarometer 2012.

manners (Abdelal et al. 2006; Brubaker 2004; Chandra 2006). Ultimately, ethnicity (just like the relevant identities that it creates) is a socially constructed phenomenon (Chandra 2001), and the specific process of constructing ethnic identities, including how ethnic identities change across time for a single individual and what particular markers become more relevant, is driven by historical context (Chandra and Laitin 2002; Laitin 1998).

Besides self-identification there are other relevant social markers that define ethnic belonging; the most relevant in Latin America are language and race.[5] So, how well does self-identification match these other theoretically relevant dimensions of ethnicity? While some variation exists, subjective identification with these categories is consistent with other objective traits, such as skin color, which is the main feature of race.[6] The relationship between self-identification and skin color seems to follow a predictable pattern. Individuals who identify as whites tend to have lighter skin tones than members of other groups, while those who define themselves as blacks are significantly darker. However, self-identification does not seem to match well with language, which is another often used approach to defining ethnic groups (Alesina et al. 2003; Fearon 2003) and in Latin America is particularly relevant for indigenous groups. Only 31% of all individuals in the pooled AmericasBarometer dataset who report an indigenous language as their first language identify themselves as "indigenous," while 50% of them identify as "mestizo" and 15% as "white."

Ethnic Politics in the Region

During the past couple of decades, ethnicity has gained increasing importance in Latin American politics, modifying the political map of the region and receiving attention from scholars from different disciplines. The emergence of indigenous politics has been recognized as the most visible manifestation of the increasing salience of ethnicity in the region (see, e.g., Sieder 2002); the evidence of other ethnic minority groups, such as blacks, emerging as relevant political actors is weaker.

Some authors claim that this emergence has been a tense process that has challenged traditional political institutions and even compromised the existence of the national state itself (Yashar 2005). Others have seen this process as more moderate, gradually channeling itself into the system via new institutional forms (Degregori 1998; Van Cott 2000a, 2002, 2005). It is likely that the process has had both tense and gradual elements at different moments and under different contexts, as some observers have argued (Aguilar 2011). What is certain is that the number of political actors who campaign on ethnic grounds has become conspicuous throughout the region, both at the national level and in subnational politics (Madrid 2005; Rice and Van Cott 2006; Van Cott 2005).

Without doubt, at the start of the twenty-first century, the most relevant news in ethnic politics in Latin America was the electoral success of Evo Morales and the Movimiento al Socialismo (MAS) in Bolivia. Morales, an Aymara indigenous from the highlands, won the 2006 and 2009 elections with wide margins, campaigning on ethnic and populist platforms; since being elected, he and his administration have enjoyed support from an ample majority of the population.[7]

But Morales is not the only politician to campaign recently on an ethnic discourse, nor the only member of an ethnic minority competing for power in the region. A plethora of indigenous candidates have taken on electoral races in different countries, campaigning on demands of recognition and inclusion of their ethnic groups. A small number of ethnic parties have been formed and they have competed in elections in different countries in the region (Madrid 2005; Van Cott 2005). While success varies substantially, given that ethnic minority groups are usually concentrated in some geographical areas, they have proven to be more successful in subnational-level politics than at the national level.

But why should ethnicity ever be relevant for politics? That is, what are the theoretical bases that could account for ethnic voting patterns? Existent research on ethnic voting discusses a number of different reasons that individuals might be more likely to vote for a member of their own ethnic group; however, very few studies on these issues have been conducted in Latin America,[8] and even fewer in a cross-national setting.

One explanation holds that the appeal of ethnic politics is based on the idea that ethnicity creates a sense of belonging to broader categories, to communities that are "imagined" (Anderson 1983). Under the assumption of common ancestry, represented by either cultural or phenotypic characteristics, ethnicity generates horizontal "communities," groups of individuals who feel that they share something. Ethnic politics is then based on that sense of mutual belonging, of intragroup solidarity (whether imagined or real), that defines ethnic groups (Chandra 2004).

However, there is more to ethnicity than just "imagined" communities. Members of ethnic minorities are usually exposed to similar socio-economic conditions, which can include discrimination, social exclusion, or simply poverty and unequal access to resources. In Latin America, both indigenous and Afro individuals are usually poorer, less educated, and less represented than members of the majority white and mestizo groups (Hall and Patrinos 2006; Pascharopoulos and Patrinos 1994; Telles 2004; Wade 1994), and exclusion seems to be even worse for those of African descent than for indigenous individuals (Hooker 2005). This average lower socioeconomic level suggests that indigenous and blacks could express particular political preferences based on their disadvantaged conditions. One example is a tendency for disadvantaged ethnic minorities to band behind populist leaders, an orientation that has been dubbed "ethno-populism" (Madrid 2008).

And there are other reasons that ethnicity should matter for politics. Individuals might be driven to vote for candidates of their own ethnic group for the satisfaction of having someone similar to them in office and as a form of reaffirming their own identity (Birnir 2007; Horowitz 1985). In either way, voting for a member of an individual's own ethnic group might be seen as an expression of allegiance to the individual's identity group.

Voters could also choose to vote for a candidate of their own ethnic group because of instrumental reasons. Depending on the information given by the candidate, voters could expect that a particular candidate might be more willing to allocate state goods, or even gifts and other forms of patronage, to their group or community (Chandra 2004; Ichino and Nathan 2013; Posner 2005). This "instrumental" explanation is based on the combination of interests and beliefs about the candidates as the basis for electoral choice.

Despite its potential appeal to voters, ethnic politics is not an automatic key to success for politicians. It is well known that, depending on the specific context, other cleavages usually aggregate social interests more efficiently, and that ethnic categories cannot be automatically translated into actual "groups" with common interests (Brubaker 2004). And even if they did, ethnic minorities in Latin America have historically had less participation and influence than the ruling white and mestizo majority in national politics, and thus, it could be inefficient for politicians competing for national office to concentrate appeals on a group with historically inferior levels of political participation.

Hypotheses and Data

Two main hypotheses are put to test in this chapter. The first relates to the question of whether racial and ethnic groups differ in their preferences for particular candidates along a general ideological dimension. One potential expectation (H1) is related to the fact that members of the indigenous and black communities in Latin America are more likely to be poor and socially excluded than whites and mestizos. For this, or potentially for other reasons (such as candidate supply, which would be relevant if indigenous or Afro candidates are more likely to run on the left), we might expect indigenous and Afro-descendents to be more likely to vote for candidates embracing pro-poor discourse, championing minority rights, and/or offering more general leftist ideology. The second hypothesis (H2) addresses the main idea behind ethnic identity voting, and suggests that voters will be more likely to vote for members of their own ethnic group, or for parties that clearly represent their ethnic group.

The main data source for this project is the 2012 round of the AmericasBarometer, a comparable survey conducted on twenty-six countries in the Americas by the Latin American Public Opinion Project (LAPOP) consortium.[9] Data are analyzed at the individual level both within the region and in each country treated individually. The analytic approach I employed for testing these hypotheses includes a pooled region-wide analysis and a series of case studies that featured major ethnic candidates, which is presented in the following section. All models presented below take into account the complex sample design, and robust standard errors clustered on country are estimated for the pooled models. The analyses do not include cross-level interactions, as other chapters in this book do, because of the low number of national cases with candidates from ethnic minority groups, which would make the interpretation of on-average results problematic.

Operationalization

Dependent Variables

Two dependent variables are considered in the analyses. The first is the ideological orientation of the candidate for which the person voted in the last national election; this variable is also analyzed in other chapters of this volume.[10] Second, I analyze the probability that individuals vote for members of their own ethnic group; I specifically analyze the vote for indigenous candidates in key recent national elections across the region.

Independent Variables

The main independent variable used in this chapter is individuals' self-identification with one of the categories employed within LAPOP's ethnic identification variable. As described above, the original question was recoded into dummy variables for "white," "indigenous," "black," and "mulatto," leaving the larger "mestizo" category as the reference group.

And as mentioned before, the self-identification variable seems to be a valid measure for the racial dimension of ethnicity, but not of the ethnolinguistic one. That is why the analyses also consider information about the first language the person spoke during childhood;[11] in the data analyses this variable was coded with a zero in case the person spoke Spanish (or Portuguese in Brazil) or a foreign language and 1 if the person spoke an indigenous language, but it is used only in the analyses for countries with a sizable proportion of native speakers of an indigenous language.[12]

A series of other controls measured at both the national and individual levels are included in the statistical models of this essay. At the country level, the following variables were included to control for as many potentially relevant system-level measures as possible: the effective number of parties; programmaticness (measured by the Democratic Accountability and Programmatic and Linkages Project's, or DALP's, programmatic index); level of clientelist effort (also from DALP); and the level of polarization, calculated using data collected by the Parliamentary Elites in Latin America (PELA) project. At the individual level, I include a set of controls found throughout this volume: church attendance, household wealth, education level, age, gender, and size of place of residence.

Analyses

The first question that needs to be answered is whether there is a relationship between ethnicity and ideological preferences. I first check whether such a relationship holds at the regional level; to do that, an OLS regression model for the left-to-right ideological position of presidential candidates variable was fitted on the eighteen-country pooled database of the 2012 AmericasBarometer. The model was fitted over an effective N of 15,034 individuals in 18 countries. The results for the key variables are summarized in the first row of table 5.1.

Focusing on Latin America as a region, and controlling for individual- and national-level factors, table 5.1 shows that self-identification with a particular ethnic category seems to have little effect on ideological voting preferences. Individuals who identify as "whites" and "indigenous" tend to vote more to the right than "mestizos," but differences are small and only marginally significant in the case of "indigenous." "Mulattos," on the other hand, tend to vote to the left of the mean mestizo individual when the pooled data are considered.

TABLE 5.1   Summary of Regression Results of Ethnicity Variables on Left-Right Vote Choice

	White Self-ID	Indigenous Self-ID	Black Self-ID	Mulatto Self-ID	Other/no Self-ID	Indigenous Language
Pooled	0.003** (0.001)	0.009** (0.003)	0.001 (0.002)	−0.010*** (0.002)	−0.001 (0.003)	NA
Argentina	−0.0018*** (0.0004)	NA	NA	NA	−0.003** (0.001)	NA
Bolivia	0.030*** (0.009)	−0.008** (0.003)	NA	NA	0.018* (0.009)	−0.013*** (0.003)
Brazil	0.001 (0.001)	NA	0.0003 (0.001)	RG	0.0017 (0.0015)	NA
Chile	0.003 (0.006)	0.024* (0.010)	NA	NA	NA	NA
Colombia	0.002 (0.003)	0.002 (0.003)	−0.0002 (0.005)	−0.019 (0.014)	−0.001 (0.008)	NA
Costa Rica	0.001 (0.001)	NA	NA	−0.001 (0.003)	0.001 (0.007)	NA
Dominican Republic	0.003 (0.002)	NA	−0.003 (0.002)	−0.002 (0.002)	−0.004 (0.003)	NA
Ecuador	0.005 (0.006)	0.011 (0.013)	0.012 (0.010)	0.010 (0.010)	−0.001 (0.008)	−0.017 (0.013)
El Salvador	0.006 (0.008)	−0.006 (0.013)	NA	NA	0.013 (0.012)	NA
Guatemala	NA	−0.0001 (0.0004)	NA	NA	NA	−0.0001 (0.0004)
Honduras	−0.003* (0.001)	−0.001 (0.003)	−0.002 (0.004)	NA	NA	NA
Mexico	0.002 (0.007)	−0.003 (0.005)	NA	NA	0.006 (0.006)	0.001 (0.009)
Nicaragua	−0.001 (0.001)	−0.0005 (0.003)	0.005 (0.004)	NA	0.001 (0.002)	NA
Panama	−0.002 (0.003)	−0.002 (0.005)	−0.007 (0.004)	−0.009 (0.005)	NA	−0.021** (0.007)
Paraguay	0.001 (0.001)	−0.004 (0.004)	NA	NA	0.0001 (0.003)	0.001 (0.002)
Peru	0.001 (0.006)	−0.002 (0.006)	−0.023 (0.013)	NA	−0.010 (0.009)	−0.023*** (0.005)
Uruguay	0.007* (0.003)	NA	0.0005 (0.007)	−0.0008 (0.007)	0.003 (0.006)	NA
Venezuela	0.009*** (0.002)	−0.006* (0.003)	−0.004 (0.004)	0.006 (0.007)	NA	NA

Source: AmericasBarometer 2012.

Note: Reference group is Mestizo, with the exception of Brazil (mulatto). Ethnic identification categories with a share of less than 2% were combined with the reference group. Other controls in the model: Wealth, education, gender, age, church attendance, size of place of residence.

*** $p \leq 0.001$; ** $p \leq 0.01$; * $p \leq 0.05$; NA: Not available.

When the level of comparison is shifted to countries, there is a different and richer panorama of the relationship between ethnicity and electoral preferences. Table 5.1 summarizes the results of similarly specified regression models fitted on each single Latin American country dataset from the AmericasBarometer round of 2012; the full results of each model are included in the online appendix. The dependent variable is still the left-to-right ideological position of candidates (a positive effect means "right"), and the same individual-level controls are included as noted above. Only results that are statistically significant at least at the 0.05 level are reported.

Table 5.1 shows, in the first place, that the relationship between ethnicity and electoral preferences is not constant across countries in the region; more often than not, the effect of ethnicity on ideological preferences is nonexistent or very limited. In the handful of cases where it does matter, its effects vary substantially.

All other factors controlled for, self-identification as white has a positive effect on the choice of a right-wing candidate in Bolivia, Uruguay, and Venezuela, but has the opposite effect in Honduras and Argentina (where whites are the majority group). Similarly, Bolivian and Venezuelan indigenous voters prefer a candidate on the left, while indigenous voters in Chile tend to prefer a candidate on the right of the scale. And individuals who identify with other ethnic categories are more likely to vote for the left in Argentina but tend to vote for the right in Bolivia.

The other three variables included in the analyses show more stable patterns. Self-identification as black and mulatto consistently fails to have any significant effect on ideological voting preferences across the region; once all other factors are controlled for, self-identification as Afro-descendent does not seem to be related to particular voting preferences in any country in Latin America.

On the other hand, being a native speaker of an indigenous language has a negative (left-inclining) effect on the left-to-right scale in all three countries in which the variable has a significant effect. It is worth noting that the variable was employed only in the analyses of six countries. In these cases, when it matters, this cultural dimension of indigenous identity seems to be related to a preference for candidates on the left of the scale.

Finally, it is also relevant that there is only one country in the region where all the ethnicity measures considered in the analysis produced statistically significant independent effects: Bolivia. In this Andean nation "whites" and individuals who identify with other ethnic categories (or with none of the available options) tend to vote for candidates to the right of those chosen by the average "mestizo voter," while the indigenous tend to prefer candidates on the left. Independent of self-identification, native speakers of an indigenous language also tend to vote for candidates to the left of those chosen by native speakers of Spanish. These are signs that suggest the high salience of politicized ethnic cleavages in the case of Bolivia, something that is discussed more in depth during the specific case study below.

Evidence of Ethnic Voting in the Region

The previous section presented evidence that suggests that the importance of ethnicity as a predictor of electoral preferences varies substantially across the region. This section tests for the existence of ethnic voting patterns in the region by analyzing voting patterns in countries where at least one candidate from an ethnic minority group participated in the last national election. If the hypothesis that suggests that individuals are more likely to vote for members of their own ethnic group holds, candidates with an ethnic origin different from that of the majority group should be favored by the vote of their co-ethnics.

But finding ethnic variation among presidential candidates in recent Latin American elections is not an easy task. While there has been a clear opening in gender relations allowing for the inclusion and successful electoral competition of women in many countries (as the successful stories of Michelle Bachelet, Dilma Rouseff, Laura Chinchilla, and Cristina Fernandez illustrate), most candidates in the region still come from the same white or mestizo ethnic background. The participation of black and indigenous candidates running for top office in national-level elections is still very limited, and suggests a pervasive exclusion of these groups from mainstream politics in the region.

The only countries with ethnic variation among candidates in the latest presidential elections are Guatemala and Peru in 2011 and Bolivia in 2009.[13] Because the cases of Guatemala and Bolivia illustrate two divergent patterns for ethnicity and voting, I focus here on these two elections.[14] The dependent variable in the analysis is vote choice.[15]

Guatemala 2011

Despite the large size of its indigenous population, Guatemala is a country where ethnic variables do not seem to have any effect on electoral preferences (or at least not in the 2011 national election), as the results presented in table 5.1 illustrate. Indigenous individuals do not seem inclined to vote for candidates with any particular ideological orientation. But would indigenous voters prefer an indigenous candidate over other candidates? If they do, this would support the hypothesis of ethnic voting in this particular country in the region.

The first round of the 2011 presidential election in Guatemala was held on September 11 of that year. The winning candidate was Otto Pérez Molina, who would later also win the second round of the election, receiving 1.6 million votes, around 36% of the total. The only indigenous candidate in the race was Rigoberta Menchú, who had previously and unsuccessfully run as presidential candidate;[16] in 2011, Menchú received a mere 146,353 votes, around 3.3% of the national vote. As we are interested in the relationship between ethnicity and electoral behavior, we want to know whether indigenous voters were more likely to vote for the only indigenous candidate, Rigoberta Menchú.

It is worth recalling that Guatemala is a country where the indigenous population has been particularly deprived, enduring poverty conditions at much higher rates than the "Ladino" white-mestizo population. Also, indigenous groups in the country were particularly targeted by state-sponsored violence during the war years in the 1980s, and their social capital and political organizations were heavily affected and decimated of leaders (Moreno Morales 2008).

Figure 5.2 illustrates the standardized coefficients of a logistic regression modeling the probability that a person voted for Menchú. As in previous analyses, data come from the 2012 round of LAPOP's AmericasBarometer.

Self-identification as indigenous fails to have an effect on the probability of voting for Menchú once language, skin color, wealth, education, gender, age, church attendance, ideology, and size of place of residence are taken into account. The odds of voting for Menchú are not statistically different for indigenous individuals when compared to "Ladinos."

However, the linguistic variable employed as an alternative measure of belonging to an indigenous group has a very large positive effect on the probability of having voted for Menchú. The odds that a person who had an indigenous language at home as first language voted for this candidate are approximately seventeen times higher than the odds that a Spanish speaker did so.

The only two variables included as statistical controls that have a significant effect on the probability of voting for the only indigenous candidate in the Guatemalan elections are gender and ideology. In accord with findings highlighted by Morgan (this volume), women were more likely to vote for the female Nobel Prize winner indigenous leader. Further, individuals

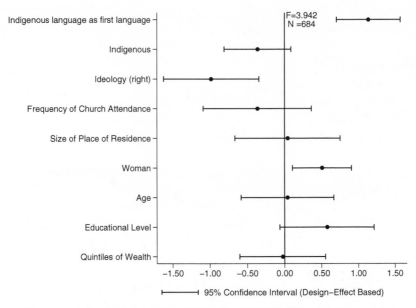

Figure 5.2   Logistic regression results for voting for Menchú, Guatemala 2011. *Source:* AmericasBarometer 2012.

who place themselves to the right in the ideology scale were less likely to vote for her.

It is important to consider here that among the 837 respondents who gave a valid answer when asked about whom they voted for, only 24 (almost 3%) claim to have voted for Rigoberta Menchú. This results in an extremely low N with a positive outcome for the dependent variable; this low N might explain the absence of a statistically significant effect of indigenous identification on the preference for the only indigenous candidate on the list.

Bolivia 2009

Bolivia is the only country in the region currently ruled by an indigenous leader; it is also the only country in which variables for all ethnic categories have an effect on the analysis of ideological electoral preferences, as table 5.1 has shown. But the Bolivian is a particular case, as the successful candidate, Evo Morales, is both an indigenous and a leftist leader. Any potential pattern of ethnic voting seems to be confounded with ideological preferences and economic voting.

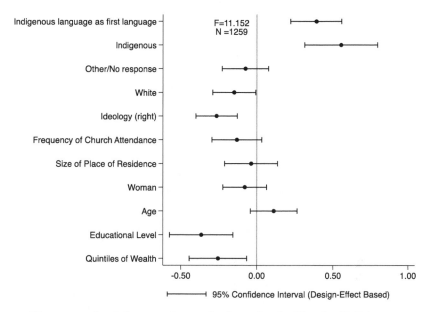

Figure 5.3   Logistic regression results for voting for Morales, Bolivia 2011. *Source:* AmericasBarometer 2012.

Evo Morales won a second term in an election held on December 9, 2009. Morales was running for reelection and all pre-electoral polls suggested an easy victory for the incumbent and his party, the Movimiento al Socialismo, or MAS. Morales was one of four candidates running for president in that election who publicly identified themselves as indigenous, the others being Román Loayza, Alejo Véliz, and Rime Choquehuanca. Morales received more than 64% of the national vote, while the other indigenous candidates obtained only between 0.38 and 0.22%.[17]

Were indigenous voters more likely to vote for Evo Morales and the other indigenous candidates during the 2009 national election? Figure 5.3 shows the logistic regression standardized coefficients for the probability of voting for Morales or any of the other indigenous candidates, versus another choice.

The results are strikingly clear and show the relevance of ethnicity in contemporary Bolivian politics. First of all, self-identification as indigenous has a huge positive effect on the probability of voting for Morales; once all other factors are controlled for, the odds of voting for an indigenous candidate are 380% higher for indigenous individuals compared to those who identify as "mestizo." And the odds that a person who identifies as "white" voted for Morales or any of the other indigenous candidates are only half of the odds for a member of the majority "mestizo" group. In fact, the relationship between ethnic identity and voting preference is so strong that among indigenous voters who declared their vote, 91% voted for an indigenous candidate (in the vast majority of cases the vote was for Evo Morales). The same proportion among non-indigenous voters is only 56%.

The alternative measure of indigenous belonging, being a native speaker of an indigenous language, also fares well in predicting the vote for an indigenous candidate. Independent of all other factors in the model, the odds of having voted for an indigenous candidate are 150% higher for speakers of an indigenous language when compared to those individuals who spoke Spanish as their first language during childhood.

Left-right self-identification is also a strong predictor of the preference for an indigenous candidate; people on the left are more likely to vote for Morales than people on the right. And the inclusion of this variable in the models does not affect the predicting power of ethnic and racial variables. In other words, independent of their own ideological position, indigenous voters tend to prefer indigenous candidates; and consistently, white voters are less likely to vote for an indigenous candidate even after their own ideological position is taken into account.

But the effects of education and wealth are also independent of ideological identification: less educated and poorer individuals are more likely to vote for Morales and the other indigenous candidates no matter what their own ideological position might be. This confirms that Morales's support comes from both indigenous and poorer individuals, combining ethnic with socioeconomic voting patterns.

The variable that does not show an independent effect on the likelihood that a person voted for an indigenous candidate is size of place of residence. Some researchers have placed the emergence of the MAS and its political success on rural areas (Zuazo 2008); however, results show that once other factors are controlled for, living in a rural area does not increase the odds that a person votes for Morales or another indigenous candidate.

Discussion

The findings presented in this chapter suggest that the capacity of ethnicity to predict electoral preferences varies substantially across countries in the region, and depends highly on the level of politicization of ethnic cleavages. By "politicization of ethnic cleavages" it is understood that ethnicity has become important for a political system at a particular moment. In other words, the relevance of ethnicity as a stable political referent is a manifestation of the politicization of ethnic cleavages.

In general, ethnic identities are not strong predictors of voting along a left-to-right ideological candidate scale and the national cases in which they matter are limited. Indigenous identity seems to be more relevant than black and mulatto self-identification, and the ethnolinguistic dimension of belonging to an indigenous group seems to be a more powerful predictor than self-identification as indigenous itself.

When voting for candidates with a particular ethnic origin is considered, self-identification with one of the identity categories offered to respondents in the AmericasBarometer questionnaire matters only in one of the two countries considered in the analyses. Indigenous voters are not more likely to vote for an indigenous candidate in Guatemala, but they prefer a member of their own identity group in Bolivia. In fact, voting patterns in Bolivia seem to align clearly with ethnic divides, with whites being least likely to vote for Morales and indigenous being the most likely group to do so.

But the conditions in which ethnic politics has thrived in Bolivia are very specific and hard to find in other Latin American countries. During the past two decades, Bolivia has seen a process of organization and political mobilization of its large indigenous population that has resulted in the organization, consolidation, and electoral success of the Movimiento al Socialismo, Evo Morales's party. This process can be traced back to multicultural reforms and recognition of diversity in Bolivia's Constitution during the decade of the 1990s; likewise, the Law of Popular Participation of 1994 opened the possibility to organize and compete for local (municipal) office, inaugurating a process of political organization that would result in the formation and strengthening of national-level organizations. And Evo Morales's *caudillo* type of leadership also plays a relevant role in the political mobilization of indigenous and poor voters by practicing a personalized form of politics.

In Guatemala, the emergence and consolidation of an indigenous movement has been nonexistent, despite the relevant share of indigenous population. In the case of Guatemala, the systematic violence suffered by indigenous communities during the internal war in the early 1980s has resulted in a demobilization of civil society and a significant loss of social capital.

Besides leadership and the process of organization and mobilization of the indigenous movement, other factors that could have relevant roles in the politicization of ethnic cleavages in Latin America are the size of the minority population (Posner 2004) and the representation system (Huber 2012; Lijphart 1977). In countries where the minority population is relatively large, it is likely that competition is guided along ethnic lines. And proportional representation should also result in better alignment of parties with ethnic identities.

However, the number of elections at the national level in which indigenous or other ethnic minority candidates have participated is very limited. This makes it impossible to produce a research design that could reasonably test competing explanations using voting behavior at the national level as the unit of analysis. A different research strategy has to be designed to explore the causes of politicization of ethnic cleavages in Latin America.

While ethnicity seems to be a poor predictor of ideological voting preferences in the region, it plays a more relevant role in determining the vote for particular candidates. This conclusion, though, depends on the measure of ethnicity. Where there is diversity among presidential candidates, individuals are more likely to vote for members of their own linguistic group than members of other groups. In the two country cases analyzed in this chapter, Bolivia and Guatemala, indigenous presidential candidates performed much better among individuals who are native speakers of an indigenous language.

The main measure of identity considered here, self-identification as indigenous, has contrasting results between Bolivia and Guatemala. While in Bolivia indigenous self-identification follows a predictable pattern (indigenous individuals are more likely to vote for indigenous candidates), in the case of Guatemala this relationship is not statistically significant. One of the main problems in trying to solve this apparent contradiction is the small number of votes for Menchú in Guatemala, which does not permit further analyses that could shed light on this issue.

In a third case not reported on in detail here, Peru, I examined the preference for Ollanta Humala in the latest national election. Peru is a country where, despite the relatively large indigenous population, the ethnic cleavage has not become politically salient (Yashar 2007). While Humala does not identify as part of an indigenous group, his lower-class mestizo background and populist discourse make him closer to indigenous individuals than to the white and mestizo elites who have traditionally ruled the country (Madrid 2011b). The evidence presented in my analyses (again, not shown here for sake of space) seems to support this claim: individuals who had an indigenous language as their first language were more likely to vote for this candidate in the latest national elections than native Spanish speakers; however, self-identification as indigenous is not statistically related with a preference for Humala.

Being a native speaker of an indigenous language is the only variable with a positive and significant effect in all three cases. Native speakers of a particular language share many of the cultural traits and values that are associated with that particular language and with the way of naming and understanding the world linked to it; and if they come from a marginal and historically excluded community, the opportunity for the politicization of ethnic identity seems greater.

Conclusion

The effect of ethnicity on voting preferences varies substantially across Latin America as a region. Ethnic identification variables affect electoral preferences only in a few countries in which ethnicity seems to be politicized along polarized political systems and it often does so in different and contradicting ways.

Despite the variability in the relationship between ethnicity and voting preferences in the region, a few constants can be observed. First, there is no consistent significant effect of identification as black or mulatto on electoral preferences defined by the ideological position of the elites; despite the fact that the effect of being mulatto on voting is significant in the pooled sample, this does not happen in any of the countries observed here. Second, in all the countries where the language variable was employed and was found to be statistically significant, it is linked with a preference for candidates on the left. Related, the language variable also proved to be a good predictor of voting for an indigenous candidate in all three countries for which the data allow an analysis of vote for an indigenous candidate (Bolivia, Guatemala, and Peru). Sharing a specific language since childhood seems to be a distinctive element of ethnicity that can be translated into aggregated political interest better than other features such as subjective self-identification.

This research found evidence of highly politicized ethnic identities in one of the countries considered in the analyses, Bolivia. But in this particular case it seems that ethnicity is part of a more complex and wider process of political polarization including other socioeconomic factors, such as education and wealth. And it is also very likely that this polarization revolves around the leadership of Evo Morales and that it is not entirely based on ethnic identities.

The success of ethnic politics in the region, and more generally, the possibility of politicizing identities seem to rely on a series of conditions, including individual leadership. Perhaps this is not surprising given the fluidity of ethnic and racial categories and identifications noted at the beginning of this chapter and it is also perhaps not surprising given the broader societal divisions (along socioeconomic lines that overlap with ethnicity, and thus provide fodder for political campaigns). Consistent with other chapters in this part of the volume, it appears that political entrepreneurs who emerge in opportune contexts can have transformative effects on the political preferences expressed by subgroups in the country at the polls.

NOTES

This chapter benefited from valuable comments made by Cindy Kam, the editors of this volume, and participants of the Latin American Voter conference held in Nashville, Tennessee, in May 2013. All errors and omissions are the author's only.

1. For a recent discussion of the "fixed" or "fluid" nature of ethnic identity in the region, see Telles and Paschel (2012).

2. Identification as "indigenous" in Bolivia is a good example of how sensitive ethnicity is to both context and the question employed to record it. Previous research has shown that context is responsible for the doubling of the proportion of the population who identifies as indigenous during the period of time in which the indigenous movement gained political salience and Evo Morales won office (Moreno Morales 2008; Seligson et al. 2006). And the LAPOP questionnaire includes two different questions for self-identification, which produce strikingly different results (Moreno Morales 2012).

3. The question (**ETID**) presents slight differences across countries. In Guatemala, the only available options are "Ladino" (which represents the white and mestizo majority) and "indígena"; in Brazil the options are "branca," "preta," "parda," "amarela" ("parda" was coded as mulatto and "amarela" as "other"); in the Dominican Republic the "mestizo" and "indigenous" categories were merged; and in Venezuela a "morena" option was added to the list and was subsequently coded as "mestizo." No responses and other answers were grouped together as valid answers under "Other/No response." Ethnic identification categories with a share of less than 2% were combined with the reference group.

4. All analyses are adjusted for complex sample design and pooled analyses weight each country equally.

5. Race, understood as a visible characteristic of individuals, can be viewed as one dimension of ethnicity, one socially relevant marker that can define boundaries and establish categories that individuals recognize as ethnic groups (Gabbert 2006).

6. Skin color is registered in the AmericasBarometer with the use of a color palette developed by the Project on Ethnicity and Race in Latin America (PERLA) at Princeton. The values on the palette run from 1 to 11, representing a range from the lightest to the darkest skin tones. The palette is used discretely by the

interviewer when the interview has concluded. A complete explanation and discussion of the color palette can be found at the PERLA website (www.perla.princeton. edu). See also Telles and PERLA (2014); Telles and Steele (2012).

7. Over the past couple of years, however, the Morales administration has lost support among indigenous organizations and individuals (Moreno Morales 2011); to some observers this suggests a shift from an indigenist model of government toward a more development-oriented one.

8. Some notable exceptions are the works of Madrid (2012) and Van Cott (2000b), for example.

9. For more information on LAPOP, its surveys, and its databank, see the introduction to this volume and LAPOP's website (www.lapopsurveys.org).

10. This variable creates a tough test of the hypothesis that ethnicity matters because changes in the party systems in several countries with large indigenous populations resulted in the exclusion of candidates who entered only a single electoral contest and were not still viable or had not yet been formed at the time of the expert survey on which the measure is based; in these countries, these candidates might have captured some of the indigenous vote.

11. The question in the AmericasBarometer is **LENG1**. "What is your mother tongue, that is, the language you spoke first at home when you were a child? [Mark only one answer] [Do not read the options] [Coding: the 'X' is replaced by the country code as found in variable "PAIS"] (X01) Spanish, (X02) Indigenous language [NB; list the name of the most common indigenous languages], (X04) Other (indigenous), (X05) Other foreign.

12. The countries where at least 2% of the population declared having an indigenous language as native language in the 2012 LAPOP survey are Paraguay, Bolivia, Guatemala, Peru, Mexico, Panama, Honduras, and Uruguay.

13. The criterion used here to identify what candidates are members of an ethnic minority is whether the candidate publicly and noticeably declared to be part of these minorities.

14. While Ecuador has had indigenous candidates in previously held presidential elections, in the 2009 elections no candidate publicly identified himself or herself as indigenous. The Brazilian 2010 presidential election had one mulatto ("pardo") candidate in the race, Marina Silva. Despite her self-identification, ethnicity was not an important issue in her electoral platform, and it would be incorrect to try to find patterns of ethnic voting in this specific case.

15. The corresponding AmericasBarometer question is **VB3**. "Who did you vote for in the last presidential elections of 2008?" [DON'T READ THE LIST] [IN COUNTRIES WITH TWO ROUNDS, ASK ABOUT THE FIRST.] (00) none (Blank ballot or spoiled or null ballot), (X01) NAMES AND PARTIES . . ., (77) Other, (88) DK, (98) DA, (99) N/A (Did not vote). In Bolivia, voting for an indigenous candidate was coded 1 when the respondent said that he or she voted for candidates: Morales, Loayza, Véliz, and Choquehuanca. In Guatemala the variable was coded 1 when the person voted for Rigoberta Menchú. In Peru it was coded 1 when respondent voted for Ollanta Humala. In the three cases, nonvoters were treated as missing data, which also include DK and DA responses.

16. Rigoberta Menchú is a visible public figure in Guatemala; as an indigenous leader she has campaigned nationally and internationally defending indigenous people's rights, which led to her being awarded the Nobel Peace Prize in 1992.

On the previous candidacy of Menchú and the political participation of indigenous people in Guatemala, see Moreno Morales (2008).

17. The dependent variable used in the analyses is a dichotomous measure combining the vote of all three indigenous candidates, though obviously the Morales vote represents the vast majority of the indigenous vote.

6 ✦ Gender and the Latin American Voter

JANA MORGAN

Historically, Latin American women have faced economic inequalities, social injustices, and political exclusion, and despite some advances these patterns persist. Do broad societal divisions between the sexes translate into different preferences at the voting booth? Interestingly, authors of the seminal and eponymous book about the American voter and some of their successors largely relegated discussion of gender differences to brief asides (Campbell et al. 1960; Miller and Shanks 1996). But recently scholars of advanced democracies have brought attention to political gender gaps (Box-Steffensmeier, De Boef, and Lin 2004; Inglehart and Norris 2003; Kaufmann and Petrocik 1999; Manza and Brooks 1998). Women in these countries typically embraced conservative attitudes and behaviors with greater frequency than men, resulting in so-called traditional gender gaps. But over the past thirty years, patterns have shifted. In some countries women today are more supportive of left-leaning candidates, parties, and ideological positions than men, outcomes we can call "modern gender gaps."

Gender differences in voting behavior and ideology have received considerably less attention outside advanced (post)industrial societies.[1] A handful of studies that include cases from the developing world suggest traditional gender gaps have largely persisted in these countries as women have remained more conservative in their attitudes and less engaged in politics than men (Arana and Santacruz Giralt 2005; Desposato and Norrander 2009; Inglehart and Norris 2003; Montero 1975). However, theories explaining the evolution of gender gaps as well as findings from the United States and Europe hint that this pattern might be in transition. Existing studies of the developed world have argued that processes such as the declining influence of religion (Boas and Smith this volume; DeVaus and McAllister 1989), women's increasing independence (Box-Steffensmeier,

De Boef, and Lin 2004; Carroll 1988; Giger 2009), and the advancement of post-material values (Inglehart and Norris 2003) contribute to shifts from traditional to modern gender gaps. If these processes are also relevant for understanding gender differences in the developing world, then movement from traditional toward modern gender gaps may well be occurring across Latin America. Moreover, regional variation in processes like secularization, values transformation, and women's economic and personal empowerment has the potential to yield interesting cross-national differences in the direction and significance of gender gaps.

This chapter describes and analyzes gender differences in vote choice across the region and explores the factors that influence voting for Latin America's recent wave of female presidential candidates. After outlining the contours of gender gaps in the region, I build a theoretical model of gender gaps in vote choice. I assess how the voting decisions of women and men are shaped by individual-level factors, including childhood socialization, adult socialization, female autonomy, and issue attitudes as well as contextual variables such as development, female advancement, and party system features. The findings indicate that limits on female autonomy, particularly female employment which produces both individual- and contextual-level effects, and the conservatizing influence of motherhood (but not fatherhood) have contributed to the persistence of traditional gender gaps in the region. Thus, expanding women's independence has the potential to promote movement toward more modern gender gaps. Additionally, analyzing voting for female candidates demonstrates that women vote for women. In so doing, they opt for descriptive representation, in part calculating that female leaders are more likely attuned to their concerns than the male-dominated political establishment. This finding, paired with evidence that party system polarization does not prompt more ideologically motivated voting among women, suggests that Latin American party systems may not effectively incorporate women's interests into their programmatic appeals.

Gender Divides in Latin America

While inequities remain, notable progress has been made in reducing gender-based marginalization in the region. Women are much more likely to engage in paid work than they were twenty years ago.[2] Average female labor force participation in the region now surpasses 55%, ranging from highs in Peru and Uruguay of 71% and 67%, respectively, to a low in Honduras of 44%. Latin American women have entered professional occupations at significant rates as well, surpassing half the workforce in this sector in several countries including Uruguay, Argentina, and Venezuela (Hausman, Tyson, and Zahidi 2011). Women have also made gains in the social realm. While Latin America's Catholic Church hierarchy still opposes abortion and contraception, average fertility rates have fallen from 3.7 in 1990 to 2.5 in 2011. Brazil, Chile, and Costa Rica have fertility rates slightly below the United States' rate of 1.9. However, abortion remains illegal throughout most of the region despite moves in places like Mexico City and Uruguay to allow at least some access during the first trimester.

Female presence in politics has also grown (Buvnic and Roza 2004). Due at least in part to many Latin American countries enacting gender quota laws requiring parties to nominate women for elected office, women held 22.1% of seats in the region's legislatures in 2012. This marks a significant increase over the 7.8% occupied by women in 1990. Female representation in executive cabinets has also expanded from 7% of ministerial posts in 1990 to 18% in the mid-2000s (Escobar-Lemmon and Taylor-Robinson 2005).

Previous research on the developed world suggests that this sort of progress toward greater equality for women has the potential to promote political engagement and progressive attitudes among women, thereby reshaping gendered dimensions of political behavior. But despite these changes, traditional gender gaps in voting behavior persist in the region. While early research on the gendered dimensions of Latin American voting behavior was limited, evidence from 1960s Chile and Argentina suggests that women typically voted for conservative and confessional parties at higher rates than men (Gil and Parrish 1965; Lewis 1971). Survey data from the first decade of the twenty-first century indicate that Latin American women remain more conservative than men, but only slightly so.

Throughout the chapter, I calculate gender gaps so that positive scores signify modern gender gaps in which women are to the left of men, while negative scores denote traditional gaps in which women are to the right of men. Figure 6.1 displays region-wide gender gaps in voting (dashed line) and ideology (solid line) over time.[3] The negative values that we observe demonstrate that gender gaps in voting and ideology across the region are traditional, with women slightly but consistently more right-leaning than men.[4] Given that the standardized ideology and vote choice scales used in these figures surpass 300 points, the depicted gender gaps are quite small. These slight gender differences in ideology are statistically significant in all years, but the gaps in voting are only statistically distinguishable from zero in 2006 and 2012.[5]

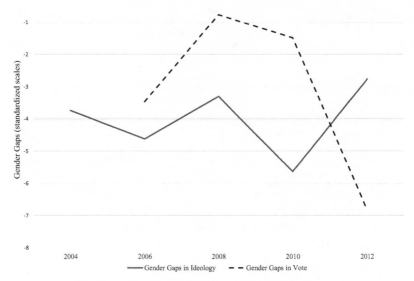

Figure 6.1   Gender Gaps in Ideology and Voting over Time.
Source: AmericasBarometer 2004–2012. *Note:* Positive values indicate modern gender gaps in which women are to the left of men; negative values indicate traditional gaps in which women are right of men. To make voting and ideology more comparable for presentation in a single figure, each scale is divided by its standard deviation before calculating the gender gap shown. The over-time pattern looks exactly the same as unstandardized versions of the scales. The rest of the analysis uses unstandardized scales.

Figure 6.2 breaks down gender gaps by country, depicting gaps in voting (light gray) and ideology (dark gray) as reported in the 2012 AmericasBarometer survey. Six countries have statistically significant traditional gender gaps in voting: the Dominican Republic, Chile, Peru, Bolivia, Colombia, and El Salvador. Traditional gaps in ideology are found in Argentina, Uruguay, Bolivia, and El Salvador. The only significant modern gender gaps are for voting in Panama and ideology in Costa Rica. Interestingly, the data demonstrate very little in-country congruence in the observed gender gaps for both ideology and vote choice. El Salvador is the only country that manifests significant gaps in the same direction for both measures, while eight countries have a negative sign on one scale and a positive sign on the other. The lack of congruence in the patterns for ideology and voting indicates that ideological divides are not translated directly into differences in voting preferences, suggesting that the gaps in voting

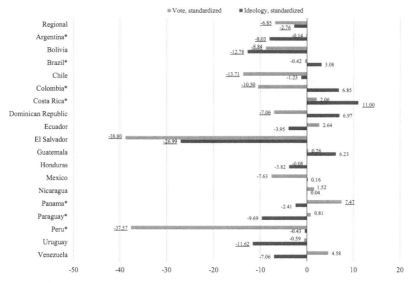

Figure 6.2   Gender Gaps in Ideology and Voting by Country.
Source: AmericasBarometer 2012. *Note:* Positive values indicate modern gender gaps in which women are to the left of men; negative values indicate traditional gaps in which women are right of men. Underlined numbers indicate a significant gender gap. To make voting and ideology more comparable for presentation in a single figure, each scale is divided by its standard deviation before calculating the gender gap shown. The pattern looks exactly the same as unstandardized versions of the scales. The rest of the analysis uses unstandardized scales. *Female candidate in the last presidential election.

are likely moderated by factors such as electoral context, party system, and candidate characteristics. I explore these possibilities below.

Overall, these data on Latin American gender gaps indicate that where they exist, gaps are frequently traditional, with women being more ideologically conservative and voting for more right-leaning candidates. However, most countries exhibit small or nonexistent gender gaps. It is possible that gender simply does not shape political behavior in the region. On the other hand, Latin America is in transition toward more gender equality in the home and the workplace, and these economic and cultural changes may be reshaping political attitudes and behavior, creating the illusion of insignificant gender effects as gaps shift from traditional toward modern. I explore this possibility by examining how gender differences in Latin

American voting behavior are shaped by a range of factors with the potential for promoting convergence or divergence among women and men.

Individual-Level Explanations of Gender Gaps

Previous research on gender gaps in political attitudes and behavior suggests several theories concerning the existence and evolution of voting differences between women and men in Latin America. Here I focus on four individual-level accounts of gender gaps: childhood socialization, adult socialization, female autonomy, and attitudinal.[6] Through the discussion that follows, I adapt existing research findings to the Latin American context because despite a few notable exceptions (e.g., Desposato and Norrander 2009; Inglehart and Norris 2003; Morgan and Buice 2013), most scholarship in this vein focuses on the United States and Western Europe.

The childhood socialization argument is rooted in the idea that boys and girls are treated differently as they grow up, and these divergent socialization experiences produce different political attitudes and behavior (Manza and Brooks 1998). Under this view, parents play a vital role in the attitude formation of children. If parents inculcate boys and girls with distinct views of their appropriate roles, with girls being encouraged toward nurturing and boys taught to be more concerned about strength, they are also likely to promote traditionally gendered stances toward politics (Gilligan 1982). Given mothers' centrality to childrearing, their experiences and orientations are of particular importance. A mother's education may be especially influential, as educated women are more likely to experience the feminist consciousness-raising that frequently accompanies more schooling. As a result, children raised by educated mothers have greater opportunities to develop modern gender norms, while those with less educated mothers may be inclined toward traditional gender roles (Bolzendahl and Myers 2004; Ciabattari 2001). Although Latin American women now approach or even surpass educational parity with men, previous generations of women did not have such opportunities (Duryea et al. 2007). Their limited education and resulting missed opportunities for feminist consciousness-raising may contribute to the perpetuation of traditional gender gaps among their children, who are today's adults.

The adult socialization argument moves beyond early upbringing and emphasizes gendered experiences more temporally proximate to present voting behavior. This approach argues that adult family dynamics are central in shaping gender differences (Sapiro 1983). One view of adult socialization suggests that women in nontraditional family arrangements, such as not having children or being divorced, are likely to take more progressive stances toward politics because such experiences transform their attitudes and interests in liberalizing ways (Klein 1984). Thus, women who are not mothers are likely to hold less conservative political attitudes than women who follow a more traditional path (Campbell et al. 1960; Plutzer 1988). If this perspective is correct, motherhood will contribute to traditional gender gaps.[7]

Arguments that emphasize female autonomy, or lack thereof, in shaping political attitudes and behavior suggest that more independent women who are able to form preferences outside the context of the traditional family will be more politically progressive. More autonomous women are likely to prioritize their individual self-interest rather than primarily considering the interests of their partners or households (Box-Steffensmeier, De Boef, and Lin 2004; Buvnic and Roza 2004; Carroll 1988; Desposato and Norrander 2009; Giger 2009; Morgan and Buice 2013). Factors that promote female autonomy include participating in paid work, greater economic power within the household, and being unmarried. Because the Latin American left has typically promoted more pro-female policies (Sacchet 2009), I expect women with greater autonomy to vote for more left-leaning candidates. Given gender inequalities in labor force participation and wages (Ñopo 2012), lower levels of autonomy among women as compared to men may contribute to traditional gender gaps in voting preferences.

Attitudinal accounts of the gender gap argue that men and women have different positions on gender and political issues, which translate into more general divides in political orientations and behavior (Kaufman and Petrocik 1999; Studlar, McAllister, and Hayes 1998). This line of thinking suggests that the advancement of feminist ideals among women and women's disproportionate support for government provision of social welfare push women toward supporting left candidates who align with these positions, fostering modern gender gaps (Conover 1988; Kaufman and Petrocik 1999; Manza and Brooks 1998; Plutzer and Zipp 1996).

Analysis of Individual-Level Explanations for the Gender Gap

To assess the extent to which these various accounts help us understand gender gaps in Latin American voting, I conduct region-wide analysis of vote choice, assessing how the gender gap varies after taking account of each of these potential explanations in turn.[8] Based on this analysis, figure 6.3 presents the regression coefficient for female—that is, the effect of being female on vote choice—after separately introducing four sets of

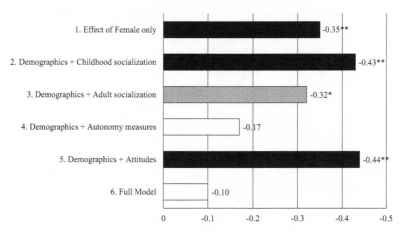

Figure 6.3   Traditional Gender Gaps in Left-Right Vote Choice.
Source: AmericasBarometer 2012. *Note:* Figure displays coefficient for female from hierarchical linear analysis of vote choice in 18 Latin American
countries. Negative values indicate that women vote for more right-leaning candidates than men – traditional gender gaps. White bars indicate
insignificant effect for female. *Light gray bars indicate effect with p-value
<0.10. **Dark bars indicate effect with p-value <0.05. All models include
random coefficients for respondent sex as well as contextual-level controls
for the Gender Inequality Index and lack of religiosity. Models 2–6 include
demographic controls for age, church attendance, education, household
wealth, and skin color. Model 1 includes sex plus contextual measures of
gender inequality and lack of religiosity. Model 2 adds mother's education plus individual demographics. Model 3 drops mother's education and
includes parenthood. Model 4 drops parenthood and adds measures of
autonomy – employment, marriage and gender inequality in household
incomes. Model 5 drops the autonomy measures and adds measures of
attitudes about social policy, women's political leadership, abortion attitudes and views of female employment. Model 6 includes all variables in
previous models.

variables designed to assess each theoretical explanation. Specifically, the
figure depicts how variation in female and male childhood socialization
(row 2), adult socialization (row 3), levels of autonomy (row 4), and issue
attitudes (row 5) contribute to gender gaps in voting. In essence, this analysis allows us to evaluate how the gender gap changes after controlling
for each of these potential sources of voting differences between women
and men. Recall that in this chapter the vote choice measure is coded
so that higher values indicate support for more left-leaning presidential

candidates. As a result, negative and significant coefficients in the figure denote traditional gender gaps, while positive and significant coefficients would point to modern gaps. Insignificant coefficients, indicated by white bars, reflect the elimination of a measureable gender gap in voting after including a particular set of explanations in the analysis. The disappearance of the gender gap suggests that differences between women and men on a given factor (or factors) play an important role in explaining gender gaps in vote choice.

The first model, represented by the dark bar at the top of the figure, depicts the effect of being female only controlling for contextual effects. The traditional gender gap observed in this base model reiterates the evidence in figure 6.1—women reported voting for right-leaning presidential candidates more than men (model 1), even in the presence of demographic controls for respondent's age, church attendance,[9] household wellbeing,[10] education,[11] and skin color[12] (model 2). The next four rows separately add variables assessing each theoretical explanation in succession: childhood socialization (model 3), adult socialization (model 4), autonomy (model 5), and feminist as well as policy attitudes (model 6).

The black bar associated with model 3 indicates that childhood socialization, measured using the education of the respondent's mother,[13] does not reduce the size or statistical significance of the traditional gender gap. While mother's education has a significant effect on vote choice, with children of less educated mothers more likely to vote for left candidates, the effect of female is unchanged compared to model 1. Based on this evidence, mother's education does not explain the gender gap in voting. Moreover, in additional analysis not shown here I considered whether the same childhood socialization experiences influence women and men differently, with less educated mothers potentially having a greater conservatizing influence on daughters than sons. However, this analysis revealed no gender difference in the way mother's education shapes voting preferences.[14]

Including parenthood as a measure of adult socialization[15] in model 4 appears to have a similarly unremarkable effect on the gender gap. Being a parent does not alter the magnitude of the coefficient for female and only slightly reduces its statistical significance. But here analyzing women and men separately is important. Considering how a respondent's sex interacts with being a parent reveals significant differences in the ways that mothering and fathering influence vote choices. Being a mother is linked to more electoral conservatism for women, while fatherhood has the opposite relationship and is associated with more left voting. The conditional effect of parenting among men = 0.42, $p < 0.01$, while the conditional effect among women = −0.37, p < 0.10 (see online appendix table OA6.1, column 2). Thus, women who engage in the traditional female role of motherhood are also more likely to take traditional stances toward politics and vote for right-leaning candidates. The divergent effects of parenting on vote choices of women and men play an important role in perpetuating traditional gender gaps in the region. After accounting for this interaction between parenthood and respondent sex, being female has no significant relationship with vote choice, and among non-parents the gender gap actually becomes positive (but still insignificant).

Returning to figure 6.3, incorporating measures of autonomy (marital status,[16] employment,[17] and relative financial power within the household[18]) also significantly reduces the magnitude of the gender gap and, in fact, eliminates its statistical significance. Among the three autonomy measures, only employment has a statistically significant effect on vote choice, with those in the workforce more likely to vote for the left than those not currently working. Women are much less autonomous than men in this regard, with female respondents' workforce participation half that of males. Thus, many women are not experiencing the liberalizing effect of working outside the home. As a result, non-working women maintain traditional political stances, while their husbands, brothers, fathers, and sons enter the workforce and develop more left-leaning orientations. Differences in levels of workforce participation between women and men help explain the existence of a traditional gender gap in Latin American voting.[19]

The last set of individual factors considered in figure 6.3 includes attitudes toward social policy and feminist issues. I measure support for social policy using a scale built from four survey items about the role of the state in promoting social welfare by guaranteeing wellbeing, creating jobs, reducing inequality, and providing healthcare.[20] Feminist attitudes include three separate items: support for female political leadership,[21] support for abortion access if the mother's health is at risk,[22] and opposition to prioritizing male over female employment.[23] The effect of being female after controlling for these factors demonstrates that they do very little to alter the size or significance of the gender gap. Attitudinal differences between women and men are not drivers of the traditional gender gap. In fact, while female voters hold more feminist attitudes than men concerning employment and descriptive representation, there are no differences in women's and men's attitudes about abortion or social policy. In additional analysis, I explored whether these issue attitudes might differentially shape the vote choices of men and women. The only issue with a significantly different effect among females and males is abortion attitudes, with support for abortion rights associated more strongly with left voting among men than women.[24] This finding suggests that men link their abortion preferences to the general ideological positioning of presidential candidates, while women do not necessarily see candidates' positions on abortion as aligning with candidates' ideologies.

The final model in figure 6.3 incorporates all the independent variables discussed above. The unshaded bar indicates that there is no significant gender gap in voting after controlling for differences in socialization, autonomy, and issue attitudes among men and women. As the above discussion indicates, limited female autonomy due to lack of employment perpetuates conservative political behavior among women. Higher male workforce participation means that as more men than women enjoy the autonomy of paid work, they are more likely to experience consciousness-raising in the workplace, which tends to promote more left-leaning orientations. The divergent influence of parenthood among women and men, with mothers being significantly more conservative than fathers, also contributes to the traditional gender gap in voting. Additional analysis of ideology as the dependent variable, which is not shown here, offers further support for this conclusion. Motherhood has a significant negative relationship with left ideology, and taking account of this effect shifts the ideology gender gap in the more modern direction, just as we observed for vote choice.

Context and the Gender Gap

Thus far, the discussion has focused on individual-level explanations of the gender gap suggested in previous research. However, country context might also shape observed gender differences in the electoral arena. While little attention has been paid to the way context shapes gender gaps in Latin American voting, a growing literature points to the significance of context for explaining gender differences in political engagement, efficacy, and attitudes (Atkeson 2003; Desposato and Norrander 2009; Hansen 1997; Morgan and Buice 2013).

Existing scholarship concerning gender gaps suggests that socio-structural factors related to modernization, such as economic development and secularism, create a socialization context that might promote modern gender gaps. These indicators of modernization are largely viewed as operating mechanistically in ways that contribute to over-time change in the gender gap. Religiosity, for example, is a conservatizing factor, the decline of which might push women in particular (who tend to be more religious) toward the left (DeVaus and McAllister 1989; Moore and Vanneman 2003). Similarly, economic development might encourage post-material and feminist values, which are associated with modern gender gaps (Buvnic and Roza 2004; Inglehart and Norris 2003; Iversen and Rosenbluth 2006). However, the models presented in figure 6.3, which included an aggregate measure of secularism, found no effect for country-level religiosity on the gender gap. In an additional analysis detailed below in table 6.1 (column 3), I consider the potential influence of economic development,[25] but find no evidence that economic modernization affects gender gaps in Latin American voting.[26] These results run contrary to developmental theories but align with previous cross-national research on gender gaps in Latin America (Desposato and Norrander 2009).

The individual-level analysis above and previous research together point toward other contextual effects. The finding that female autonomy plays an important role in promoting left voting among women in the workforce suggests that women's economic independence may produce society-wide effects as well. Moreover, previous research has found that women and men respond differently to female advancement in terms of their political behaviors and attitudes, indicating that societal-level measures of women's progress may offer analytical leverage in our understanding of gender differences in voting behavior (Beaman et al. 2009; Desposato and Norrander 2009; Morgan and Buice 2013; Morgan, Espinal, and Hartlyn 2008). The analysis here considers two indicators of female advancement: the Gender Inequality Index (GII) and the share of professional jobs filled by women.[27] GII is a composite index of women's equality developed by the United Nations Development Programme (UNDP). The share of female professionals, which is not part of the composite index, provides a specific indicator of women's economic opportunities (Hausman, Tyson, and Zahidi 2011).[28]

As the results of the hierarchical linear model in column 1 of table 6.1 show, GII has no significant direct or interactive effects on vote choice or the gender gap. However, the share of female professionals has a significant effect in interaction with respondent sex such that the share of professional women shapes how women vote. The top panel of Figure 6.4 plots this interactive effect. In countries where the share of female professionals is low, women are significantly more conservative in their political orientation than men, voting for more right-leaning presidential candidates. However, once women constitute at least 48% of the professional sector, female respondents, regardless of their own employment status, are no more likely to vote for candidates on the right than men are. In other words, the presence of a critical mass of women in professional jobs

TABLE 6.1   Contextual Predictors of Vote Choice: Female Autonomy, Party System Polarization, and Economic Development

	(1)	(2)	(3)
Individual-Level Variables			
Female	−2.77*	0.32	−0.23
	(1.53)	(0.28)	(0.20)
Age	−0.10	−0.10	−0.10
	(0.19)	(0.19)	(0.19)
Church attendance	−0.36***	−0.36***	−0.36***
	(0.10)	(0.10)	(0.10)
Well-being	−0.43***	−0.43***	−0.43***
	(0.10)	(0.10)	(0.10)
Less education	−0.03	−0.04	−0.04
	(0.15)	(0.15)	(0.15)
Darker skin color	0.75***	0.75***	0.75***
	(0.20)	(0.20)	(0.20)
Parent	0.14	0.14	0.14
	(0.09)	(0.09)	(0.09)
Married	0.03	0.03	0.03
	(0.08)	(0.08)	(0.08)
Not working	−0.13*	−0.13*	−0.13*
	(0.07)	(0.07)	(0.07)
Household inequality	0.12	0.12	0.13
	(0.19)	(0.19)	(0.19)
Pro-social policy	0.43***	0.43***	0.43***
	(0.16)	(0.16)	(0.16)
Pro-female politicians	0.14*	0.14*	0.14*
	(0.08)	(0.08)	(0.08)
Country-Level Variables			
Gender Inequality Index	−18.66		
	(14.53)		
Female professionals	1.89		
	(14.94)		
Female Professionals*Sex	5.15*		
	(3.07)		
Party system polarization		7.43**	
		(2.92)	
Polarization*Sex		−1.63***	
		(0.62)	
Gross national income, per capita (PPP)			0.00
			(0.00)
Constant	−3.90	−13.94***	−11.54***
	(10.35)	(1.27)	(2.10)
Variance Components			
Sex, random effect	0.43	0.35	0.51
	(0.17)	(0.14)	(0.20)
Country-level	11.76	9.56	13.03
	(3.94)	(3.20)	(4.36)
Individual-level	13.50	13.50	13.50
	(0.16)	(0.16)	(0.16)
Individual-N	14,045	14,045	14,045
Country-N	18	18	18

Source: AmericasBarometer 2012.

Note: Standard errors in parentheses. * $p < 0.10$, ** $p < 0.05$, ***, $p < 0.01$. Significance levels of variance components not shown. Model calculated in Stata 11.0 using xtmixed, MLE option, and unstructured covariance matrix.

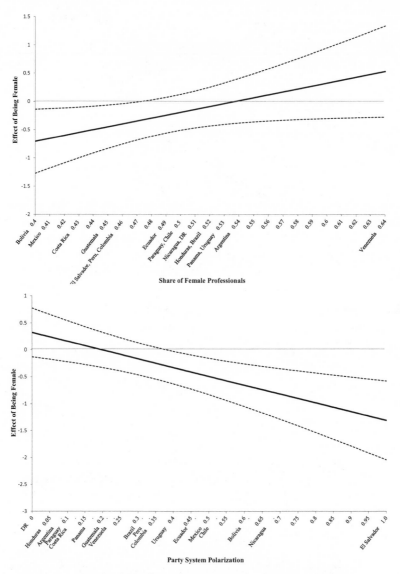

Figure 6.4 Conditional Effects of Being Female on the Gender Gap in Left-Right Vote Choice. *Sources:* AmericasBarometer 2012; polarization from Singer (forthcoming). Female professionals data from Hausman, Tyson, and Zahidi (2011). *Note:* Solid lines indicate estimated effects; dotted lines indicate 90% confidence interval. Effects calculated using multilevel analysis of vote choice with xtmixed command in Stata 11.0. Both models include random coefficients for sex as well as measures of demographics, adult socialization, respondent autonomy, social policy attitudes, and support for female political leadership. Mother's education, abortion attitudes, and views of female employment are not included because they were only asked in half of the sample.

fosters more progressive attitudes among women across society, eliminating the gender gap in contexts like Venezuela, Argentina, and Uruguay, where women have attained significant economic empowerment through professional employment. This suggests that while economic development itself has no effect on the gender gap, economic opportunities for women can play an important role in reducing and even eliminating traditional gender divides, encouraging women to vote more progressively. Moreover, this finding reinforces the results of the analysis above, which pointed to the importance of female workforce participation in promoting more left-leaning attitudes among individual women and thereby closing traditional gender gaps.[29]

I also explore if party system dynamics shape gender gaps. The structure of the party system and the nature of the appeals made at election time are likely to shape voters' electoral calculus. For instance, voters presented with distinct ideological options at the polls might be more inclined to vote based on policy appeals rather than clientelist ones. Alternatively, in less programmatic systems voters may opt for descriptive representation, hoping for some responsiveness from elected officials who share similar backgrounds, rather than prioritizing substantive policy congruence with candidates. Moreover, these party system features may have different effects among women and men, influencing gender gap patterns in the region. If party programs are primarily targeted to appeal to male voters, then (lack of) ideological structure in the party system might influence men more than women.

To explore these effects, I consider how party system polarization interacts with respondent sex to shape gender gaps in voting. Polarization is estimated using data from the Parliamentary Elites in Latin America (PELA) study.[30] Higher scores on the polarization measure signify a more defined programmatic space while lower scores denote greater overlap across parties. Analysis in table 6.1 (column 2) incorporating this measure indicates that the traditional gender gap widens as polarization in a country's party system increases; this pattern is depicted in the bottom panel of Figure 6.4. Where polarization is low, women and men make similar voting decisions. But as polarization increases (largely because there are parties on the ideological left instead of just the center and right), men become more supportive of left-leaning presidential candidates, while women's behavior does not change. Therefore, the effect of being a woman is increasingly negative at higher polarization levels, and as a result, greater party system polarization is associated with a widening in the *traditional* gender gap. This evidence indicates that the ideological signals transmitted in more polarized party systems shape the behavior of male but not female voters.

This finding suggests the possibility that Latin American party systems do not effectively incorporate women's interests into their programmatic appeals.

Gender Gaps in Voting for Female Candidates

In the final portion of this chapter, I move beyond analysis of vote choice generally and explore voters' decisions to cast their ballot for *female* presidential candidates. In recent years, a growing number of Latin American women have contested and even won elections for their country's highest political office. At the time of this writing, there are three female chief executives in the region—Argentina's Cristina Fernández, Chile's Michelle Bachelet, and Brazil's Dilma Rousseff; several other countries in the region have former female presidents. Moreover, women have contested the presidency under major party banners in the most recent elections held in Colombia, Mexico, Peru, Panama, and Paraguay.

Here I consider the factors that shape voters' decisions to cast their ballot for these female candidates.[31] Again, the main variable of interest is respondent's sex. In addition to sex, all versions of the analysis incorporate a series of individual-level measures: age, church attendance, household wellbeing, education, and skin color. The results show that younger people as well those from poorer households with less education and with darker skin are more likely to have voted for a female presidential candidate. At the contextual level, the models consider the effects of GII and female professionals, with less gender inequality and more professional women associated with greater support for female candidates. Most important for our focus here, the analyses presented in columns 1 and 2 of table 6.2 demonstrate that women are significantly more likely than men to support female presidential candidates, even controlling for these socio-demographic and contextual factors. This finding aligns with evidence from existing single-country studies analyzing voting for female candidates (Yanez 2001).

To explore if this effect for respondent sex is more than simply an artifact of parties that typically appeal to women choosing to nominate a female candidate, I compared the gender gap in voting for the woman candidate to the gender gap in voting for the male candidate from the same party in the most recent all-male presidential contest using data from the AmericasBarometer survey conducted closest to that election.[32] In Costa Rica, Panama, and to a lesser extent Colombia, female voters did not disproportionately support the male candidate backed by the same party that later nominated a female candidate. In Brazil, there is no significant

TABLE 6.2   Multilevel Logit Analysis of Voting for Female Presidential Candidates

	(1)	(2)	(3)	(4)	(5)	(6)
Individual-Level Variables						
Female	0.27***	0.27***	0.26***	0.20**	0.25***	0.10
	(0.06)	(0.06)	(0.07)	(0.10)	(0.06)	(0.13)
Age		−0.33**	−0.32*	−0.34**	−0.32*	−0.40*
		(0.16)	(0.18)	(0.16)	(0.16)	(0.23)
Church attendance		0.14	0.19**	0.13	0.14	0.12
		(0.09)	(0.10)	(0.09)	(0.09)	(0.12)
Well-being		−0.22**	−0.24**	−0.22**	−0.25***	−0.21*
		(0.09)	(0.10)	(0.09)	(0.09)	(0.12)
Less education		0.69***	0.65***	0.66***	0.70***	0.56***
		(0.15)	(0.16)	(0.15)	(0.15)	(0.20)
Darker skin color		0.46***	0.54***	0.50***	0.53***	0.64***
		(0.17)	(0.19)	(0.17)	(0.17)	(0.21)
Ideological distance			−0.14			
			(0.14)			
Pro-social policy				0.09		
				(0.15)		
Perceived insecurity				−0.29**		
				(0.14)		
Insecurity*Sex				0.20		
				(0.20)		
Pro-female leadership					0.16**	
					(0.07)	
Abortion is justified						−0.04
						(0.11)
Abortion justified*Sex						0.28*
						(0.16)
Country-Level Variables						
Gender inequality index	−24.46***	−25.41***	−24.65***	−25.43***	−25.45***	−26.76***
	(7.87)	(7.73)	(7.53)	(7.71)	(7.70)	(7.53)
Female professionals	20.87**	21.10**	20.53**	20.89**	20.78**	19.48**
	(10.07)	(9.87)	(9.63)	(9.85)	(9.83)	(9.60)
Constant	−0.49	−0.51	−0.49	−0.36	−0.48	0.98
	(5.19)	(5.09)	(4.97)	(5.08)	(5.07)	(4.93)
Country variance component	0.96	0.93	0.88	0.93	0.92	0.86
	(0.53)	(0.51)	(0.49)	(0.51)	(0.51)	(0.49)
Individual-N	6,868	6,708	5,455	6,598	6,480	3,655
Country-N	7	7	7	7	7	7

Source: AmericasBarometer 2012.
Note: Standard errors in parentheses. * $p < 0.10$, ** $p < 0.05$, ***, $p < 0.01$. Significance levels of variance components not shown. Model calculated in Stata 11.0 using xtmixed, MLE option, and unstructured covariance matrix. Analysis only includes the 7 countries where female candidates received at least 5 percent of the vote in the most recent presidential election: Costa Rica, Panama, Colombia, Peru, Paraguay, Brazil, and Argentina.

bivariate gender gap in voting for Dilma Rousseff nor for her co-partisan and predecessor President Lula da Silva. Unexpectedly, in Paraguay there was significantly less female support for Colorado party nominee Blanca Ovelar than for the male candidate in the previous election. Despite this anomaly, the pattern suggests that parties generally attract more female voters when they have women heading their presidential tickets than when a man is the nominee, reinforcing the consistent finding in table 6.2 that women disproportionately vote for women if the option is available.

At first blush then, women appear to be opting for descriptive representation in voting for other women, perhaps hoping that female presidents might prioritize women's policy concerns, thus converting descriptive representation into substantive representation. But this pattern of descriptive representation might belie other forms of substantive congruence in ideology or issue positions between female voters and candidates. Models 3 through 6 in table 6.2 explore this possibility. In model 3, I assess whether ideological congruence with female candidates encourages voters to support women at the polls. To measure congruence, I take the absolute value of the distance between respondents' ideological self-placement and the expert-scored ideological position of the female candidate's party from Wiesehomeier and Benoit (2009). Higher values indicate greater ideological distance between voter and candidate, and we would expect a significant negative coefficient for this variable if people vote for female candidates based on ideological affinity. However, we observe no such effect, and this insignificant relationship is uniform across female and male respondents.[33] In additional analysis not shown, I explored whether women's support for female candidates was more pronounced in voting for women on the left like Dilma Rousseff (Brazil) or for women on the right like Keiko Fujimori (Peru). However, the effect of respondent's sex remained constant regardless of the candidate's ideology. These findings indicate that women across Latin America are choosing descriptive representation and voting for female candidates at disproportionately high rates regardless of the candidate's ideological position.

Model 4 explores whether gender stereotypes about the issue positions of female politicians shape voting for women presidential candidates. The common perception is that women in public office will emphasize compassion issues, like healthcare, education, and other social policies. Moreover, if female leaders and female voters both agree that compassion issues are important, social policy attitudes might be particularly influential in encouraging women to support female candidates. Conversely, female leaders are frequently perceived as being weak on crime. Thus, those who view their community as especially unsafe may be less likely to vote for women, favoring male candidates who stereotypically have a heavier hand in fighting crime. The results in model 4 indicate that support for social policy has no effect on female or male decisions to vote for women contesting the presidency. Perceived congruence on social issues is not a source of women voting for female candidates. Perceived insecurity[34] does have the expected negative relationship with the pro-female vote, but after accounting for the interaction with respondent sex, perceived insecurity only undermines support for female candidates among Latin American *men*. Women do not succumb to the negative stereotype that female leaders are not capable of dealing effectively with insecurity and are therefore not less likely to vote for a female candidate if they feel unsafe in their community.

Finally, models 5 and 6 examine the effects of attitudes toward female political leadership and abortion rights. As we would expect, support for female leadership in the abstract is positively associated with voting for real-world female candidates, but this effect is uniform for both sexes and does not account for the gender gap we observe. Attitudes about abortion rights, on the other hand, have differential effects among men and women. Specifically, support for access to abortion increases the likelihood that a woman will vote for a female candidate while abortion attitudes play no role in shaping male support for female candidates.[35] Moreover, among abortion opponents there is no significant gender gap in voting for female presidential candidates, whereas women who support abortion access are much more likely than male supporters to vote for women.[36]

Thus, while gender stereotypes influence male voting decisions regarding female candidates, women who vote for women seem to be doing so in pursuit of substantive as well as descriptive representation. Male voters accept gender stereotypes and reduce their support for female candidates if they feel insecure, but female voters do not allow crime perceptions to color their judgments of women running for president. What's more, women who support some access to abortion embrace female candidates, perhaps in the hope that women, regardless of their ideological orientation, will hold more feminist views on this as well as other issues important to women. The fact that women vote for women, no matter what the candidate's party label or ideological leaning, suggests that Latin American political systems offer more meaningful policy outcomes for women's concerns through descriptive representation than through traditional left-right conceptions of substantive representation. Combined with the evidence above that polarization influences the voting behavior of men but not women, the significance of descriptive representation in the calculus of female voters implies that the programmatic offers extended by Latin American parties do not successfully appeal to women and instead seem to neglect their concerns. Therefore, rather than being influenced by the ideological orientations of parties, women opt to vote for other women, hoping that their shared identity will result in political and policy decisions that address their most pressing concerns. Given previous research suggesting that female politicians in Latin America prioritize women's issues (e.g., Jones 1997; Schwindt-Bayer 2006), these perceptions may be well founded.

Discussion and Conclusion

This chapter indicates that small but significant traditional gender gaps dominate the Latin American electoral landscape. The analysis of voting preferences provides some indication of the factors most important in shaping gender differences. In particular, motherhood is associated with more conservative choices among women, while women without children behave more like their male counterparts. This evidence lends support to theories of the gender gap that emphasize adult socialization as pivotal in explaining gender differences. Moreover, the evidence supports the idea that women's employment at the individual level and professional advancement at the societal level close the traditional gender gap. These findings suggest that if women enter the workforce at rates similar to that of men or constitute a large share of professional workers, traditional gender differences in voting may disappear. Thus, the process of empowering women economically promotes progress toward modern gender gaps.

The significance of factors pertaining to women's ability to assert independence from home and family and to attain professional status offers some insight into how gender gaps may be in transition across the region. As women throughout Latin America obtain greater autonomy by delaying or avoiding traditional gender roles in the family and by achieving economic independence, a transition from traditional toward modern gender differences is more likely. The absence of significant gender gaps in many individual countries across the region suggests that this process may well be under way, and as women are more frequently in the workplace, especially in professional positions, movement toward modern gender gaps is a likely outcome.

Another important finding indicates that Latin American women are motivated by the opportunity for descriptive representation when women are on the ballot. Throughout the region, female presidential candidates attracted significantly higher levels of support from women than from men. This finding was consistent across the ideological spectrum, with female candidates on both the left and the right drawing support from female voters. The importance of female political leadership in shaping Latin American gender attitudes has been emphasized in previous research (Morgan and Buice 2013), but these findings go further to indicate that the presence of female candidates may alter voting behavior in ways that promote descriptive representation for women as they pursue substantive influence. This result aligns with other studies, primarily in the developed world, which find gender cues transmitted by highly visible female candidates or politicians to be important in fostering political engagement and pro-female voting among women (Atkeson 2003; Desposato and Norrander 2009; Hansen 1997).

Finally, the analysis suggests that Latin American parties and party systems are not connecting effectively with women through typical policy appeals and ideological position-taking. Where party systems present distinct ideological options to voters, these programmatic positions primarily influence men. Women's votes are not influenced by party system polarization. As a result, the traditional gender gap is wider in countries where distinct ideological choices are available. Moreover, on an issue of particular salience among women—abortion rights—female voters do not view traditional left-right ideological orientations as meaningfully connected to positions on abortion. While men's abortion attitudes are linked to voting through the general ideological orientations of presidential candidates, women do not see the abortion issue reflected in the left-right divide. Instead, women who favor abortion rights vote for female candidates in pursuit of representation. While abortion is the only women's issue for which we have data, it is possible, even likely, that other gendered concerns such as protection from domestic violence and equality in education and employment follow a similar pattern, with women failing to see the male establishment as responsive to their concerns and thus turning to female leaders, irrespective of ideology. These findings point to a shortcoming in party systems' capacity to reach female voters through programmatic appeals. Instead, descriptive representation is a strong motivation for female voters, who are seeking to be heard and who may not find meaningful substantive representation in the conventional, male-dominated political process.

NOTES

I am grateful to Damarys Canache, Scott Desposato, Cindy Kam, Nate Kelly, Michael Lewis-Beck, Aníbal Pérez-Liñán, Noam Lupu, Jim McCann, Jenn Merolla, Tracy Osborn, Leslie Schwindt-Bayer, Adrienne Smith, Amy Erica Smith, and the volume's editors as well as participants in conferences held at Vanderbilt University and the University of Tennessee for their helpful comments and suggestions on earlier drafts of this chapter. Any remaining errors or oversights are my own.

1. A rich body of scholarship explores other topics pertaining to women in Latin American politics such as analyses of women's movements (Baldez 2002), descriptive and substantive representation (Schwindt-Bayer 2010), and gendered facets of social policy (Blofield 2012; Ewig 2010; Htun 2003).

2. Unless otherwise noted, all statistics in this paragraph are averages of the eighteen Latin American countries included in this volume and were calculated using data from the World Bank's GenderStats database (World Bank 2013).

3. Data are from the 2004–12 Americas Barometer surveys in eighteen Latin American countries described in the introduction to this volume.

4. The vote choice measure employed here is essentially the same as that utilized throughout this part of the book, with respondents' ideology identified according to the candidate for whom they cast their vote in the most recent presidential election. Ideology is measured using a survey question in which respondents are asked to place themselves on a 10-point left-right scale. To facilitate identification of traditional versus modern gender gaps, both variables are coded here so that higher scores indicate more left-leaning positions.

5. The standardized scale for ideology has a 360-point range, and the range on the standardized vote scale is 308. To make the gaps in voting and ideology more comparable in figures 6.1 and 6.2, the scales were divided by their standard deviation before calculating gender gaps. Given that the original scales are not inherently meaningful and that the figures are intended to identify and compare the *direction* of gender gaps over time and across countries, the raw numbers are not of much relevance and standardizing the scales merely facilitates presentation. The rest of the analysis uses unstandardized versions of the scales.

6. These categories build on Manza and Brooks (1998).

7. An alternative view of adult socialization suggests that motherhood primes women to seek left-oriented policies that support their role as caregivers, such as public investment in education and healthcare (Manza and Brooks 1998). This view is not supported in the analysis below.

8. The analysis employs hierarchical linear models because the intra-class correlation coefficient indicates that 48.5% of the variance in vote choice is cross-national. The analysis includes random slope coefficients for sex, which demonstrate there are statistically significant differences in the relationship between sex and vote across countries. All models in figure 6.3 include two country-level controls: lack of religiosity, measured using the share of AmericasBarometer respondents who do not affiliate with any religion, and the Gender Inequality Index, which captures gender differences in health, education, political representation, and unemployment (United Nations Development Programme 2011b). While in theory

these variables could matter, neither has a significant effect on vote choice nor does their inclusion alter the size or significance of the gender gap.

9. **Q5A**, "How frequently do you attend religious services? More than once per week, once per week, once per month, one or two times a year, and never or practically never?" Higher values are coded to indicate greater religiosity.

10. An index of wellbeing based on ownership of a series of twelve household items (Córdova 2009) equivalent to the measure of individual wealth used in other chapters in this volume. Scores account for cross-national and urban-rural differences in access. Higher scores indicate greater wellbeing.

11. **ED**, "What was the last year of school that you completed?" Response options range from none to completed university and are coded so that higher scores indicate *lower* levels of education.

12. **COLORR**, Based on interviewer-identified skin color using a provided color pallet. Higher scores indicated darker skin color.

13. Question **ED2** asked, "Up to what level of education did your mother complete?" Response options range from: (0) None, (1) Primary incomplete, (2) Primary complete, (3) Secondary incomplete, (4) Secondary complete, (5) Technical school/Associate degree incomplete, (6) Technical school/Associate degree complete, (7) University (bachelor's degree or higher) incomplete, (8) University (bachelor's degree or higher). Thus, higher scores indicate higher levels of education. This question was only asked of half the sample in most countries.

14. Online appendix table OA6.1 (column 1) contains details of this interaction effect between respondent's sex and mother's education.

15. Based on a question (**Q12**) asking whether or not the respondent has children. Those with children receive a score of 1 on this variable; those without children score zero.

16. **Q11** "What is your marital status?" Those who indicated that they were married or part of a common-law marriage (*union libre*) receive a score of 1 on this variable; all others score zero.

17. **OCUP4A.** How do you mainly spend your time? Are you currently working, not working at this moment but are employed, actively looking for work, being a student, taking care of household duties, or retired/disabled?" Those who indicated that they were working or currently employed score a zero on this item; all others score a 1.

18. To measure relative financial power in the household, I employ an item asking: "Thinking only about you and your partner and the salaries that you earn, which of the following phrases best describe your salaries: you earn nothing and your partner earns everything, you earn less than your partner, you and your partner earn more or less the same, you earn more than your partner, you earn all the income and your partner earns nothing?" Using this item, I create an ordinal scale with four categories coded to assess the extent to which women have economic power in their household, with higher values indicating less economic power. Men score zero, women who do not have partners or who earn more than their partner score 0.33, women who earn something but less than their partner score 0.67, and women without any income score 1.0.

19. None of the autonomy measures have significant interactions with respondent sex, indicating that while gender differences in *levels* of autonomy contribute

to more conservative female voting, there are no differences in the *way* autonomy influences women and men.

20. These questions follow the same prompt: "Now I am going to read some items about the role of the national government. Please tell me to what extent you agree or disagree with the following statements. We will continue using the same ladder from 1 to 7." **ROS2.** "The (Country) government, more than individuals, should be primarily responsible for ensuring the well-being of the people. To what extent do you agree or disagree with this statement?" **ROS3.** "The (Country) government, more than the private sector, should be primarily responsible for creating jobs. To what extent to do you agree or disagree with this statement?" **ROS4.** "The (Country) government should implement strong policies to reduce income inequality between the rich and the poor. To what extent do you agree or disagree with this statement?" **ROS6.** "The (Country) government, more than the private sector, should be primarily responsible for providing health care services. How much do you agree or disagree with this statement?" The scale is created by averaging responses across the four items; respondents who answered at least two of the questions receive a score based on the non-missing data. Factor analysis of these four questions reveals one factor with an eigenvalue of 2.29. The Cronbach's alpha score is 0.83. Additional analysis using each individual component separately produces the same substantive effects as those reported for the scale.

21. **VB50.** "Some say that in general, men are better political leaders than women. Do you strongly agree, agree, disagree or strongly disagree?" Responses are thus coded so that higher scores indicate more egalitarian answers.

22. **W14A.** "And now, thinking about other topics. Do you think it's justified to interrupt a pregnancy, that is, to have an abortion, when the mother's health is in danger?" Those who indicate that abortion is justified score a 1; those who do not see abortion as justified score zero.

23. **GEN1.** "Changing the subject again, some say that when there is not enough work, men should have a greater right to jobs than women. To what extent do you agree or disagree?" Responses are coded 1–7 so that higher scores indicate more egalitarian answers. The final two items were only asked of half the respondents; results on the other variables remain the same if these items are excluded and the full sample remains intact.

24. The conditional effect of abortion support among men = 0.21, $p < 0.10$; among women the effect = −0.27, $p < 0.10$.

25. Development is measured using gross national income (GNI) per capita in constant 2005 U.S. dollars, adjusted for purchasing power parity (United Nations Development Programme 2011a). Additional analysis also found no significant interaction between GNI and respondent sex.

26. The individual-level variables included in the models assessing contextual effects parallel those analyzed in figure 6.3. Only mother's education, attitudes regarding abortion, and female employment are excluded because they were asked of only half of the respondents.

27. I also considered potential effects for women in the legislature, female labor force participation, women in managerial positions, and the presence of a female presidential candidate in the election, but none altered the gender gap or influenced voting behavior.

28. This sector includes occupations such as architects, engineers, scientists, doctors, nurses, teachers, clergy, lawyers, and artists.

29. Also see Morgan and Buice (2013) for a discussion of the importance of female economic empowerment in promoting gender egalitarian attitudes among women.

30. This particular measure of polarization is based on legislators' self-placement on an ideological scale. From this information, each party received an average ideology score. Using these party scores, polarization was calculated following Dalton (2008). Other measures of polarization based on the PELA data and the Democratic Accountability and Linkages Project (DALP) (Kitschelt and Freeze 2010) revealed results similar to those presented here. I also considered potential effects for measures of clientelism, party system cohesion, and effective number of parties but found no significant effects.

31. The analysis includes Chinchilla, Fernández, and Rousseff as well as Balbina Herrera in Panama, Noemí Sanín in Colombia, Keiko Fujimori in Peru, Blanca Ovelar in Paraguay, and Marina Silva in Brazil. The Mexican elections that included Josefina Vázquez were held after the 2012 AmericasBarometer surveys were conducted.

32. The comparison in Colombia is between the Conservative candidate Sanín in the 2012 data and the independent Uribe who was backed by the Conservative Party in the 2006 elections (data from 2008). Suitable comparisons are not possible in Argentina, where Fernández was the candidate in both elections for which AmericasBarometer data are available, or in Peru, where the previous election was not an all-male contest.

33. One explanation for this null finding might lie in the general paucity of ideological content to left-right identifications in the Latin American region (see Zechmeister this volume).

34. **AOJ11**. "Speaking of the place or neighborhood where you live and about the possibility of being a victim of an assault or robbery, do you feel very safe, somewhat safe, somewhat unsafe, or very unsafe?" Scores are coded so that higher values indicate greater perceived insecurity.

35. The conditional effect of abortion attitudes among women is 0.23, $p < 0.01$; among men the conditional coefficient is -0.04, $p > 0.50$.

36. I also considered the possibility that female candidates mobilize or demobilize female voters depending on their degree of ideological affinity with the candidate. If like-minded women are more likely to turn out and vote while ideologically distant women stay home, the significant pro-female vote from women may reflect ideological and policy considerations beyond those offered as a result of descriptive representation. However, a comparison of the average ideology of women who voted in races with female presidential nominees versus the ideology of women who turned out in previous presidential contests reveals no such pattern. It does not seem that women who share the ideology of the female candidate are especially mobilized to vote.

✦ SUBSTANTIVE OFFERINGS
AND THE VOTE ✦

Introduction to Part III:
Substantive Offerings and the Vote

RYAN E. CARLIN, MATTHEW M. SINGER,
AND ELIZABETH J. ZECHMEISTER

At its core politics is about distribution (Lasswell 1936) and, quite often, political choices reflect different preferences over a menu of distributive stances and styles. One way voters can select among choices at the ballot box is by taking into consideration the substantive propositions explicitly or implicitly expressed by political parties and candidates. These might be ideational (an issue-defined policy platform), material (clientelistic offerings), and/or broader packages consisting of these or other offerings tagged with a partisan label or a specific location in ideological space. To signal their preferences over how goods are distributed, voters can ground their electoral decisions in policy stances, left-right ideological orientations, partisanship, and/or the private material goods that political parties may offer as selective inducements in exchange for a vote.

When citizens connect to parties and candidates who compete on the basis of policy stances bundled into coherent and distinguishable platforms, we consider this evidence of programmatic party structuration (Kitschelt et al. 2010). Such linkages are a core component of the mandate representation model, which presumes that political competition takes place mainly over bundles of issues (programs) (see Powell 2000; Przeworski, Stokes, and Manin 1999; Luna and Zechmeister 2005). In some ways, voting based on policy stances is considered a gold standard for citizens in the electoral arena, as classic conceptions of representative democracy conceive of elected officials as agents who represent the viewpoints of their constituents (Powell 2004). Yet even where parties offer relatively clear and stable programs, policy voting is cognitively demanding: individuals must recognize their own stances on the issues and perceive the parties or candidates as taking distinct stances on those issues (Campbell et al. 1960). In Latin America, where electoral and political fluidity frequently obscures meaningful differences in the policy platforms of those competing for office (e.g., Stokes 2001), voting based on policy stances can be particularly challenging. Perhaps this is why one gloomy account of Latin American voters views them as beholden to non-programmatic appeals (see discussion in Baker and Greene this volume). And yet politicians and parties throughout the region often do compete for election on the basis of issue stances. Thus, we should not be surprised to find *some* connections between individuals' policy stances and their vote choice.

Compared to policy stances, left-right markers theoretically offer voters a simpler way to navigate the marketplace of political ideas at election time. It is not uncommon for analysts of voter choice to present left-right identifications as indications of a citizen's "ideology" and to link them to specific policy concerns we often associate with the ideological scale. Yet, as Zechmeister notes in her chapter in this volume, empirical research provides extensive evidence that left-right identifications often better reflect group membership (e.g., partisan preferences and identities) than policy stances, at least at the mass level. So while left-right orientations are tools citizens can use to locate themselves in the political arena and to facilitate choices, this convenience comes at the cost of abstraction away from a specific menu of policy options. Given a dearth of rich, shared content to the left-right semantics, perhaps it is not surprising that, as Zechmeister shows, many Latin Americans do not (or are unable to) make effective political use of left-right labels, either by refusing to place themselves on the left-right spectrum or by failing to connect left-right identifications to their vote choice in a systematic way.

Another fundamental way individuals can and do connect to parties and candidates is via party identification. As Lupu (this volume) relates, partisanship is a much-discussed concept in the field of comparative political behavior. And while variations on its conceptualization abound, most would agree that partisanship reflects some balance of deep-rooted affective ties to political parties and cognitive evaluations that form a "running tally" of assessments of parties' platforms and performances in office. Yet questions linger with respect to whether the nature of partisanship in a comparatively less consolidated region is unique and, as well, whether partisan identities translate into vote choices in Latin America with the same reliability as in long-standing democracies. These questions are valid, as Lupu's chapter argues, because of the fluid nature of political competition, the lack of party system institutionalization, and the prevalence of clientelism in the region.

Finally, as alluded to above, Latin America is not immune to clientelistic party-voter linkages. Like voters in other developing contexts around the globe, Latin American voters may select candidates based on the promise or actual exchange of private material goods for votes. Conceptions of clientelism are even more varied than partisanship, arguably, but Kitschelt and Altamirano (this volume) offer this definition: "a targeted, contingent exchange of votes for benefits." Whereas policy stances, left-right identifications, and partisanship are typically considered inputs into a voter's selection among candidates located in a given ideational space, clientelism can run orthogonal to that political space. Thus, rather than examine the relationship between vote-buying and voter choice per se, Kitschelt and Altamirano examine the gap between the effort parties spend on clientelism and the effectiveness of this effort in attracting voters. While this chapter differs from the others in this volume in that it does not rely on public opinion data, its key finding that clientelist parties often struggle to effectively convert those efforts into electoral support provides further evidence that there is electoral space for programmatic electoral competition in Latin America.

The dependent variable used in three of the four chapters in part III is the same left-right vote choice variable presented in the introduction to part II and featured across the chapters in that part. We refer the reader to the introduction of part II for a description of this variable and discussion of its limitations as well as checks on its general validity as a measure of vote-relevant political preference.

Within this part, the chapters by Baker and Greene and by Zechmeister illustrate that issue appeals and left-right labels constitute tools that Latin America's parties can use to earn votes, and they explore some of the mechanisms underlying these relationships. Importantly, they show that the strength of the associations between issues or left-right identification and voter choices varies across countries. Lupu's chapter investigates the individual-level and country-level characteristics that foster partisan identification in Latin America. Kitschelt and Altamirano first analyze the scope of clientelist organizing in Latin America and then attempt to explain relatively high degrees of inefficiency in clientelistic efforts that plague much of the region. Taken as a whole, the chapters suggest that electoral contests in Latin America offer voters a highly diversified set of the substantive and material packages, and the extent to which they inform voter choice varies across the region.

How, specifically, does context matter for the nature of the relationship between voters and political elites? Both directly and indirectly the discussion and evidence in this part's chapters point us toward the two sets of contextual factors we identified in the introduction: the substantive content and the structure of party competition. With respect to the former, the extent to which elites campaign on the basis of issues, make relevant left-right semantics and partisanship, and pursue votes by offering material incentives has obvious implications for the nature of party competition as well as the ways that voters connect to elites within it. With respect to structural features, we see that the presence of high levels of clientelism is negatively associated with voting on the basis of both issues and left-right identifications. Further, party system fragmentation undermines partisanship and the association between left-right placements and the vote in Latin America. At the same time, polarization appears as a consistent, positive influence on the political and vote relevance of issues, left-right identifications, and partisanship. Where the political choices presented to voters are clearly distinct and fairly distant from another, core components of programmatic party structuration are more likely to subsist.

7 ✦ Positional Issue Voting in Latin America

ANDY BAKER AND KENNETH F. GREENE

Many accounts of voting behavior, party competition, democratic representation, and the political accountability of elected officials in the new democracies of the developing world are downright depressing. These countries are often said to be mired in clientelist or populist political arrangements, their voters bought off—often quite cheaply—or beholden to quasi-charismatic political figures, and their democracies of such low quality that some question whether they would be better classified as something else (Ames 2001; Mainwaring, Bejarano, and Leongómez 2006; Zakaria 2003).

A key element of these devastating portraits is the notion that citizens cannot (or choose not to) act like those in the ideal democracy by voting for the candidate whose publicly announced platform most closely matches their own policy preferences. Many analysts of new democracies assume that this practice of "positional issue voting" does not exist and focus their work on other influences on vote choice. But if voters are in fact exercising roles as issue voters, then there may be more political representation and more accountability than indicated by many existing accounts.

We argue that positional issue voting is much more prevalent in Latin America's new democracies than previous research suggests. After all, unless the rise of the left across Latin America between 1998 and 2008 was well-timed luck—a series of simultaneous idiosyncratic outcomes—then it seems plausible that voters are voting their policy preferences (see Baker and Greene 2011). In this essay, we show that positional issue voting has occurred over the past fifteen years in at least fourteen of the eighteen major countries in Latin America, save Guatemala, Honduras, Panama, and Paraguay.

In the first section of this chapter, we define positional issue voting and discuss the stringent requirements among voters and candidates for it to obtain. In the second section, we show why existing studies, including some of our own previous work, have generally not used adequate methods to detect positional issue voting. The third and fourth sections present our empirical analyses using cross-sectional survey data from eighteen countries and panel data from Brazil in 2010 and Mexico in 2006. Though it is not the main goal of our chapter, we also offer an explanation for variation in the degree of positional issue voting across countries. We conclude by discussing the implications of our findings for the study of voting behavior and democratic quality in new democracies.

Positional Issue Voting in New Democracies

Positional issue voting occurs when a voter chooses the candidate whose publicly announced platform best approximates the voter's own policy preferences. The policy issues at play must be meaningful to voters and politicians. Typically, salient policies will motivate political contestation among the candidates and broad debate among major sociopolitical actors. In many democracies, the government's approach to economic development, the degree to which it redistributes material wealth, the means by which the state combats criminality, and the extent to which it regulates certain moral issues are often salient enough to be the focus of positional issue voting. The public nature of the issues that underlie positional issue voting separates the practice from clientelistic voting, which occurs when citizens exchange their vote for access to an individually excludable private benefit (Brusco, Nazareno, and Stokes 2004; Kitschelt and Wilkinson 2007a). The policy basis of positional issue voting also differentiates it from personalist voting that occurs when voters choose candidates due to personal traits that are not associated with their stances on public policies (Bartels 2002; Conover 1981). We also consider positional issue voting to be distinct from valence issue voting (Stokes 1963), in which voters choose the candidate whom they perceive to be the most likely to achieve goals on which there is a societal consensus, such as job creation, national security, or lowering crime rates.

Positional issue voting encompasses two major models of how voters rationally relate their personal policy preferences to those of the competing candidates. One model is the "directional voting rule" (Rabinowitz and MacDonald 1989), in which voters choose the candidate on their side of an issue relative to a neutral point (often thought of as "the center"). In directional voting models, voters prefer the candidate most distant from the neutral point yet inside a vaguely defined "region of acceptability." We do not employ this approach because it struggles to explain the existence of multiparty competition that includes centrist parties, a characteristic that describes virtually all Latin American party systems.[1]

We instead conceive of positional issue voting using the "proximity voting rule," where each voter chooses the candidate whose policy stance is minimally distant from the voter's policy preferences on salient packages of issues. Anthony Downs (1957) employed this voting rule as the foundation for his far-reaching spatial theory of party competition. In his model, voters relate their fixed policy preferences to the publicly announced policies that candidates choose in the attempt to maximize their vote share.[2] To Downs and other spatial theorists, the dimension that structures partisan competition is an ideology or a package of issues that politicians yolk together for convenience and advantage (Enelow and Hinich 1984). Politicians have incentives to reduce the number of salient issue dimensions to help voters differentiate among the competing candidates and facilitate homogeneity in the messages espoused by candidates from the same party running in different constituencies (Enelow 1986). Most empirical studies on Latin America find that, at the elite level, one or two issue dimensions structure political contestation in countries where public policy issues are salient enough to organize partisan politics (Kitschelt et al. 2010; Wiesehomeier and Benoit 2009).

Other requirements for positional issue voting to exist give the practice a strong normative appeal (Ames, Baker, and Rennó 2008; Kitschelt et al. 2010; Stokes 2001). Voters must have enough relevant political information to possess preferences over the public policy matters that feature in campaigns and know where at least two candidates stand on these matters. Voters must also downplay candidates' traits that are not correlated with their issue positions, such as attractiveness, fund-raising ability, personal wealth, place of origin, race, ethnicity, and gender. Voters must also eschew attempts by politicians to buy their support with short-term clientelist payoffs. Positional issue voting also carries requirements for politicians' behavior. For starters, they must engage in public policy debates rather than obfuscate their positions on major issues. If politicians successfully hide their stances on the issues, then voters cannot differentiate among them and must instead vote on valence or some other criterion with little policy relevance. In most instances, politicians must also follow through, to a reasonable extent, on their stated policy preferences once in office. If they do not, then voters may heavily discount the policy stances of future candidates and positional issue voting would crumble. Finally, a positional issue voting model also implies responsive elites. If voters have fixed preferences on the issues that inform their vote choices, then election-minded elites will be induced to adopt platforms that mirror those of the large mass of voters, conditional on the number of competitors (Downs 1957; Sartori 1976). Where it exists, positional issue voting thus provides a key means by which elites remain accountable to the preferences of the electorate.[3]

The substantial requirements among voters and politicians to make positional issue voting viable have created skepticism that political systems of all sorts could support the practice. More than fifty years ago, Campbell and his colleagues argued that just 12% of the American electorate held a coherent ideology and correctly identified the ideologies of the Democratic and Republican Parties (Campbell et al. 1960, ch. 10). The authors concluded that positional issues cannot drive vote choices except among highly educated and politically knowledgeable citizens.

Whereas this skepticism has abated somewhat for the U.S. case (Ansolabehere, Rodden, and Snyder 2008), it has become well rooted in scholarship on democracies in the developing world. Latin American party systems are often characterized as "inchoate," "volatile," or "clientelistic," but rarely as "programmatic" (Mainwaring and Scully 1995b). For example, Kitschelt and his collaborators (2010) classify virtually all Latin American party systems as less programmatically structured than those of the new democracies of Eastern Europe (320). None of the twelve Latin American systems they examine qualify as high or even moderately high on their scale of programmatic party structuration, and just two (Chile and Uruguay) rise to the intermediate level.

Research on voting behavior in Latin America is similarly skeptical that positional issue voting can exist, in part because the raw ingredients necessary to support it would seem to be absent. Voters are alleged to have lower levels of relevant political knowledge (Gronlund and Milner 2006), material deprivation may inhibit voters' willingness to gamble on asynchronous and uncertain payoffs from policy (Kitschelt and Wilkinson 2007b), and policy switches by politicians encourage voters to discount their campaign promises (Stokes 2001). Arnold and Samuels (2011, 33) sum up the sentiment echoed by many analysts when they argue that Latin American "citizens' voting behavior is, at the aggregate level at least, largely devoid of policy or ideological content." Analysts instead focus on other elements in voters' decisions, including the influence of candidate traits, partisanship, demographics, clientelist payoffs, retrospective evaluations of economic performance, and (oft-tendentious information channeled through) the mass media.[4]

Challenges in Testing for Positional Issue Voting in Latin America

Providing a cross-national test of positional issue voting is fraught with methodological challenges. It is no surprise then that research shows contradictory findings. As we discuss in this section, some studies on Latin America show null results using time-series data at the aggregate or individual level. But poor instrumentation in these studies enhances the probability of finding no effect of positional issues on vote choices even when such effects exist (i.e., type II error). Other studies use cross-sectional individual-level data that can bias findings in support of positional issue voting due to endogeneity (i.e., type I error). Obtaining contradictory results about the validity of positional voting using alternative research strategies is by no means limited to Latin America. Tomz and Van Howeling (2008) reference some fifty studies on the subject—many on voting in the United States—that together yield no firm conclusion. We review existing findings in more detail below and then suggest an approach to diminish the various sources of measurement error and bias.

Research on Latin America that examines elections and voting over time has concluded that positional issue voting does not occur. In one approach, Stokes (2001) points out that many presidential candidates who campaigned as economic statists in the 1980s and 1990s and then implemented market-friendly policies after inauguration (e.g., Alberto Fujimori in Peru and Carlos Menem in Argentina) won reelection anyway. This implies that voters may not hold economic policy preferences in the first place or, at a minimum, that such preferences did not inform their vote choices. Either way, Stokes concludes that the spatial model has limited relevance for Latin America (2001, ch. 1). Presidents' policy switches themselves also imply that, even if voters had clear preferences over economic policy at the outset, they might discount candidates' promises so much in the future that positional issue voting would fade. We find Stokes's argument compelling, but without a direct test of positional issue voting, we do not know whether shifts in voting behavior over time in the countries she studies simply reflect shifts in voters' issue preferences.

Another approach uses individual-level panel survey data that permit a time-series test of the relationship between voters' issue preferences and their vote choices. Using data from the Mexico 2000 Panel Study, McCann and Lawson (2003) argued that voters' beliefs about the main economic issues fluctuated wildly over just a six-month campaign period. From this evidence, they conclude that "the notion that citizens might base their voting decisions on candidates' issue positions seems implausible at best" (75).

Using data from the Mexico 2006 Panel Study, Greene (2009) also argued that vote choice revolved more around candidate images than positional issues.

The Mexico case is particularly instructive because the panel survey findings would seem to reinforce the earlier conclusions reached by Domínguez and McCann (1996) in *Democratizing Mexico*, a book that helped initiate a wave of research on voting behavior in Mexico. Using public opinion data from the 1988 presidential and 1991 legislative elections, the authors found that "these Mexican elections were not about the issues" (41). Instead, voters were more concerned with how the Institutional Revolutionary Party (PRI) handled the economy and whether the party would be a good manager going forward, not with the content of economic policy. The conclusion is especially surprising because the incumbent PRI had recently presided over a dramatic market-oriented economic reform program, a significant recession, and massive cuts in spending on social programs (Lustig 1998).

With data spanning nearly twenty years and elections under both dominant-party authoritarian and democratic rule, the conclusion that Mexico's voters do not choose based on the issues would seem to be easy to sustain. Yet each of the studies cited relies on "noisy" indicators of voters' issue preferences that enhance the probability of finding no effect of positional issues on vote choices even when such effects exist (i.e., type II error). For example, McCann and Lawson (2003) looked at the stability of voters' preferences on just two items, electricity privatization and how to combat crime. We recognize that researchers are often hamstrung by a lack of more appropriate data for a variety of reasons, including cost, access, and continuity over time, yet it is not entirely surprising that these scholars found a high degree of attitudinal instability. Null results are just as likely caused by poor or limited instrumentation as they are by the respondents' attitudinal instability or failure to match policy preferences with candidate choice.

Another group of studies has found evidence of positional issue voting in Latin America and elsewhere using cross-sectional survey data, but this approach also suffers from methodological problems. In their region-wide study, Luna and Zechmeister (2005) (parts of which appear in Kitschelt et al. 2010, ch. 4) show "elite-mass congruence," meaning a strong correlation between the average policy opinions of mass partisans and those of partisan elites in Argentina, Chile, and Uruguay.[5] Baker and Greene (2011) use a positional issue voting model to explain the rise of the left in Latin America, and a few other studies show respondents' issue positions to be significant predictors of vote choice (Greene 2007; Moreno 1999; Zech-meister 2008). In the U.S. context, Lewis-Beck and Nadeau (2011) show that positional issue voting on economic issues impacted voters' decisions in the 2008 presidential election even more than retrospective evaluations of economic performance. By measuring respondents' vote choices and issue preferences at the same point in time, all of these studies may suffer from problems of endogeneity and omitted variable bias.

One common version of endogeneity in vote choice models occurs when voters first decide on their preferred candidate and then, out of affinity that has nothing to do with shared policy views, adopt the candidate's policy stance. Voters may develop a sympathy or even an identity with a particular political party in early adulthood because nearby agents of socialization, such as political discussants, localized media, and community opinion leaders, endear them to it for non-policy reasons (Campbell et al. 1960; Green, Palmquist, and Schickler 2002). Subsequently, such socialized voters "learn" their issue stances from their preferred party's elites and candidates, adopting them largely without criticism or reflection. A substantial body of evidence from the United States supports the idea that elites can cue or lead voters' preferences on public policy (Zaller 1992). In these situations, cross-sectional correlations between issue beliefs and candidate choice make it appear as if voters choose candidates because of shared policy preferences, but in fact the causal ordering is the reverse. If elites do lead voters in this way, and evidence from some work on Latin America suggests that they do (Baker 2009; Kaufman and Zuckerman 1998), then cross-sectional analyses can bias findings in favor of finding support for positional issue voting (i.e., type I error).

Cross-sectional analyses can also artificially bias results in favor of positional issue voting because they suffer from omitted variable bias. Imagine citizens who prefer to consume left-leaning media and also hold anti-market policy preferences. Both tendencies incline these voters to choose a leftist party, but if their media consumption habits are not measured or are measured with error, the researcher may attribute causality to issue positions instead of media influence. The standard strategy of controlling for as many variables as possible is inadequate since it is virtually impossible to control for every variable that influences issue preferences and vote choice, even when survey questionnaires are well designed.

The accumulated methodological challenges seem to suggest that analysts simply cannot determine whether Latin Americans use positional issues when making their vote choices. As is well known, we cannot avoid all sources of type I and type II error using observational data, and we do not currently have access to data from experiments designed to test for positional issue voting (Tomz and Van Houweling 2008). Thus, we cannot offer a definitive solution, but we hope to advance the empirical foundations of the debate over positional economic voting in Latin America by addressing some of the key methodological shortcomings discussed above and by using a variety of data.

We begin with a cross-sectional, region-wide analysis (similar to Luna and Zechmeister 2005) using surveys with questions asked across eighteen countries in the same year. This approach is especially useful for detecting underlying issue dimensions that are common to all Latin American countries. To avoid some of the instrumentation problems discussed above, we construct indices of issue preferences rather than using one or two variables (Achen 1975; Ansolabehere, Rodden, and Snyder 2008). Indices are composites created from the shared variation among multiple items, variation that captures a latent dimension of attitudes toward a particular policy debate. In any single survey item, measurement error can be enormous: respondents may have misunderstood the question, struggled to fit their nuanced or ambivalent beliefs onto the researcher's contrived and oversimplified scale, been distracted, or misrepresented their views for any number of other reasons. Compiling an index of policy attitudes from the covariance across multiple such items helps to represent respondents' true policy preferences since the shared variance is likely to be a meaningful "signal" amidst the measurement error "noise." We think that this simple measurement fix may help resuscitate positional issue voting in Latin America. Indices of voters' policy preferences are also theoretically closer to what Downs had in mind when he argued that voters choose the candidate most proximate to their personal policy preferences (Enelow and Hinich 1984).

By itself, the use of cross-sectional surveys is insufficient. Not only do they suffer from the endogeneity and omitted variables bias discussed above, but when used cross-nationally, they are typically constrained to using the same issue questions, regardless of context. In one sense, standardization is useful for enhancing comparability. At the same time, it raises the possibility of either not measuring the specific issues that arose in each election or measuring these issues with substantial error, thus making it more difficult to detect positional issue voting.

As a partial remedy, we follow our cross-national analysis using cross-sectional data with an analysis of panel survey data from Brazil and Mexico collected before and after single election cycles. By repeating interviews with the same panel of respondents and using election-specific survey questions, we can diminish the problem of using inappropriate indicators of voters' issue preferences. We can also ameliorate the bulk of the endogeneity problem because interviewing the same respondents just weeks apart naturally holds constant many of the confounding variables that are omitted in cross-sectional surveys. We focus on Brazil and Mexico because these are the only two countries in the region where researchers have so far collected panel data on voters during election cycles.

For our analysis, we look only at economic issues as potential sources of positional issue voting. By economic issues we mean policies around material redistribution (such as the size and shape of the welfare state) and economic development (such as the proper role of the state in the market as well as the scope of international trade and investment.) Other issues do structure political contestation in Latin America, including authoritarian versus democratic values (Moreno 1999), socio-religious cleavages (Luna and Zechmeister 2005), and preferences over anticrime policy (Pérez this volume); however, research shows that these "second" dimensions typically appear in addition to a more fundamental economic policy dimension that accounts for the lion's share of party position-taking in Latin American countries (Kitschelt et al. 2010; Wiesehomeier and Benoit 2009). Because we focus only on economic policy issues in this chapter, excluding other issues that could inform vote choices, our results can be viewed as lower-bound estimates on the prevalence of positional issue voting.

Cross-Sectional Results from Eighteen Latin American Countries

We begin with a cross-national analysis that demonstrates the strong potential for positional voting on economic issues in at least fourteen of eighteen countries in Latin America. Our data come from the Latinobarometer project and the AmericasBarometer project, both of which contain (different) questions about the desirability of welfare programs and/or the recent shift to a more market-friendly development model. None of the surveys were designed specifically to measure economic policy preferences, so we use the survey waves that contain the most relevant questions. The 1998–99 and 2007 Latinobarometer survey waves include a sufficient number of questions about privatization, free trade, foreign investment, and core capitalist values. The 2008, 2010, and 2012 waves of the AmericasBarometer survey asked questions about the role of the state in the economy, specifically regarding public ownership and redistribution.[6]

Because the methods used to detect positional issue voting are so important in informing analysts' final conclusions about its existence, we present our approach in detail. Our test relates respondents' self-placement on economic policy issues to the ideology of the party they report that they would vote for in elections. To generate the respondents' preferences over economic policy, we ran a separate factor analysis[7] for each country on the full battery of available economic policy items (eight for Latinobarometer 1998–99, five for Latinobarometer 2007, and four for AmericasBarometer).[8] With minor exceptions, all items were loaded in the expected direction on a latent statist↔liberal economic policy dimension. We then generated each respondent's self-placement on the economic issue dimension from the factor scores, with higher values equating to more liberal sentiments.[9]

Our dependent variable is the ideological location of each respondent's preferred party in a hypothetical presidential election (see also part II introduction, this volume). These scores were generated by a panel of experts where a score of 1 represents the farthest left position and 20 represents the farthest right position (Wiesehomeier and Benoit 2009).[10] Wiesehomeier and Benoit (2009) show that economic policy issues are the main contributor to experts' scores.[11] Yet to use these scores, we must still identify each respondent's preferred party. Here it should be stressed that the Latinobarometer and AmericasBarometer projects are not election surveys and thus most were fielded outside the confines of presidential or legislative election seasons. For Latinobarometer, we use a question that asks respondents which partisan option they would choose if the election were held the day after the interviews were conducted. For AmericasBarometer, we use a question that asked citizens to recall their presidential vote choice in the previous election. Employing the survey wave closest to the most recent presidential election in each country.[12]

Our regression-based approach reveals the correspondence between elites and masses for multiparty systems by testing for a statistically significant individual-level partial correlation between respondents' self-placement on the statist↔liberal economic policy dimension and the expert placement of their preferred party on the left-right scale. We ran fifty-one separate OLS regressions, one for each country-year (within the confines of the timing discussed above) for which data were available. Our models also include the standard demographic control variables of wealth, gender, age, and educational attainment.

Figure 7.1 graphically summarizes the most important finding from each regression. It shows the standardized coefficient and 90% confidence interval for respondents' economic policy preferences aggregated by country. Countries are arrayed from left to right in descending order of the average size of this coefficient in their set of regression models.

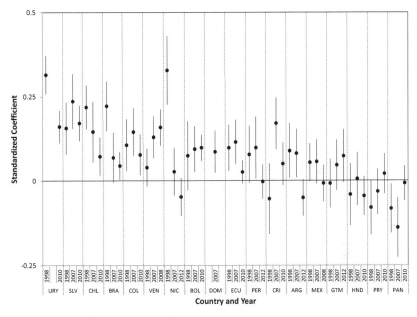

Figure 7.1   Positional Economic Issue Voting by Country and Year.
Sources: Latinobarometer (1998 and 2007) and AmericasBarometer (2008, 2010, and 2012). *Note:* Dots represent standardized regression coefficients on measures of self-placement on the statist↔liberal economic issue dimension. A separate OLS regression was run for each country year (and thus for each entry in the figure). Dependent variables were the ideological location of respondents' preferred party in a hypothetical presidential election (for 1998 and 2007) or who the respondent voted for in the most recent presidential election (for 2008, 2010, and 2012). Vertical bars are 90% confidence intervals on the standardized regression coefficients.

We find evidence of positional issue voting in fourteen of the eighteen countries. Our findings are quite strong for Uruguay, El Salvador, Chile, Brazil, Colombia, Venezuela, Bolivia, Ecuador, and Argentina, where at least two of the three public opinion datasets spanning fourteen years show that voters had party preferences that corresponded to their economic policy views. We have access to just one public opinion poll for the Dominican Republic, and our models using these data also show positional issue voting. In Nicaragua, Peru, Costa Rica, and Mexico, at least one of the polls returns evidence of positional issue voting and in all but Nicaragua, models using a second poll fall just short of reaching statistical significance at the 90% level. Given the persistent characterizations of Latin American voters as pawns of clientelist machines, swayed by charismatic or telegenic individuals, or overly influenced by their demographic profiles, we find it fascinating that the great majority of countries feature some level of positional voting on economic issues.

Only four countries in the region (Guatemala, Honduras, Paraguay, and Panama) do not show any evidence of positional voting on economic issues. It is still possible that *some* positional issues other than economic ones structure vote choices in these countries or that more tailored questions administered during an election campaign would have revealed positional issue voting. But lack of appropriate public opinion data means that we are unable to fashion a useful test, so we treat our fourteen of eighteen mark as a lower-bound estimate for the region.

It is also possible that positional issue voting is activated by contextual variables that are beyond the voters' control. For instance, where party platforms converge and offer voters few meaningful policy differences, we would expect less issue voting. In addition, where politicians can generate clientelist resources and buy many votes, citizens are less likely to vote based on policy. Such contextual influences may shed light on variation in the degree of positional issue voting across all countries in the dataset and account for the four outlier countries.

To test these contextual influences, we constructed a multilevel model (table 7.1). At the individual level (level 1), the model is similar to those constructed above. The dependent variable is the ideological location of each respondent's preferred party in a hypothetical presidential election. The independent variables are self-placement on the statist↔liberal economic policy dimension, wealth, gender, age, and education. We estimate policy preference as a random coefficient that can vary by country (level 2). We also specify three cross-level interactions: we test whether the size of the policy preference coefficient varies with a country's level of polarization in the party system, the degree of clientelist effort exerted by politicians, and the effective number of parties.[13] We expect that party systems that are highly polarized, low on clientelist effort, and minimally fragmented will have a greater degree of issue voting. These conditions make it easier for voters to align their policy preferences with parties that represent distinct ideological options.

As expected, more polarized party systems enable issue voting ($p < 0.01$) whereas more clientelist effort mutes it ($p < 0.05$).[14] These effects are so strong that a highly polarized party system with very low levels of clientelist voting is predicted to generate more than a 3 standard deviation increase in positional issue voting over a system where parties converge on the issues and buy votes routinely. (The coefficient on the effective number of parties variable was not statistically significant.) Overall, this simple

TABLE 7.1   Multilevel Model of Vote Choice in a Hypothetical Presidential Election

Level-1 × Level-2 Interactions	
Self-placement on economic issue dimension × party polarization	−0.108* (0.054)
Self-placement on economic issue dimension × clientelist effort	0.879* (0.174)
Self-placement on economic issue dimension × effective no. of parties	0.033 (0.063)

Level-1 Variables	
Self-placement on statist ↔ liberal economic issue dimension	1.224 (0.883)
Wealth	0.022 (0.065)
Gender	0.236* (0.092)
Age	0.008* (0.003)
Education	−0.034* (0.013)
Constant	12.415* (0.528)

Random Coefficients	
Standard deviation of self-placement on economic issue dimension	0.292* (0.094)
Standard deviation of random intercept	1.951* (0.338)

Source: Latinobarometer 1998.

Note: Entries are multilevel model coefficients with standard errors in parentheses. N = 8,602 clustered in 17 countries. *p < .05, one-tailed test.

contextual model does a remarkably good job at predicting the degree of positional issue voting across countries.

The contextual model also helps explain why Guatemala, Honduras, Paraguay, and Panama do not feature positional issue voting. These countries have less polarizing disagreements over economic policy and relatively high levels of clientelist politics. As a result, more voters are drawn into material exchanges for political support rather than voting their policy preferences.

Panel Data Results from Brazil and Mexico

The shortcomings of cross-sectional surveys imply that the strong support for positional issue voting demonstrated in the prior section could be an artifact of endogeneity or omitted variable bias. To ameliorate these problems, we use purpose-designed panel surveys of voters conducted in single countries and during single election cycles to provide excellent data for detecting positional issue voting. When such surveys begin well before Election Day and include a post-election wave, analysts can assess whether short-term changes between panel waves in issue attitudes are correlated with short-term change in vote choice. Panel waves are often spaced just weeks apart and, as a result, charting change in the same respondents automatically controls for all confounds except those that also change quickly in the short intervals between waves. For our purposes, the great virtue of panel data is that we can control for individuals' past issue preferences and past vote intentions, making confounds that are stable or change only slowly irrelevant to our models because we will have controlled for both of their consequences. Panel data that are collected over reasonably short periods of time thus eliminate a substantial amount of omitted variable bias.[15]

Panel surveys are also well suited to detect positional issue voting because, unlike cross-national surveys that achieve comparability by using the same questions in different political contexts, panel surveys typically use questionnaires designed to tap public opinion during specific election cycles. Such sensitivity to context is important because the issues that matter to voters can differ across countries or even from election to election, even if they tend to belong to the same categories. For instance, the adoption of market-oriented economic reforms may be a hot-button issue in two countries, but in one context the debate may revolve around a proposed free trade pact whereas in another the argument is about privatization of a particular utility. Asking voters questions about the desirability of international trade and privatization broadly defined may measure opinions well in both contexts, but context-specific questions are more likely to elicit valid responses.

Yet panel models also contain a drawback (aside from their limited availability due to high cost) that encourages us to pair analyses of these data with the cross-sectional analysis presented above. Panel models detect positional issue voting only to the extent that changes in voters' issue preferences across panel waves correlate with changes in their vote choices.[16] For this reason, we would not advocate the exclusive use of panel data even if they were available for all countries in the region.

For our panel data analyses, we turn to the Mexico 2006 Panel Study[17] and the Brazil 2010 Panel Study.[18] (The scarcity of panel data in the region does not allow us to include other countries.) Both panels included three waves, with respondents interviewed twice before the election and once immediately after. Unlike statistical models that use cross-sectional data and are thus constrained to examining the static relationship between issue preferences and vote choices at one point in time, panel models are dynamic in that they allow us to examine the impact of prior changes in issue preferences on subsequent changes in vote choices (De Boef and Keele 2008). This structure is particularly appealing for two reasons. First, examining the partial effect of prior issue preferences on subsequent vote choices ameliorates the endogeneity problem. (Our multinomial logit panel models estimate vote choice in waves 2 and 3, using waves 1 and 2, respectively, to measure lagged values.) Second, the structure allows us to control for a series of potential confounds we are able to measure, including past vote intentions and past and present partisan identification, *and* for the potential effects of unmodeled confounds that are unlikely to vary between panel waves. The short intervals between panel waves mean that each respondent's civic activism, union membership, religiosity, social class, education, and a host of other demographic variables are unlikely to have changed. As a result, the structure greatly diminishes concerns over omitted variable bias.

For Mexico, the national sample includes interviews of 2,250 voters in October 2005, May 2006, and just after the July 2, 2006, elections. The May wave occurred during the hard-fought campaigns that pitted the eventual winner, pro-market Felipe Calderón of the incumbent National Action Party (PAN), against Andrés Manuel López Obrador of the Party of the Democratic Revolution (PRD), who criticized free trade, privatization, and the market system more generally. Roberto Madrazo of the centrist and formerly dominant Institutional Revolutionary Party (PRI) finished a distant third. Interestingly, economic issues became more central to the campaigns over time (Hart 2013). After months of campaigning on transparency and conservative values, Calderón abruptly shifted his focus to jobs just three months before the election. A candidate debate on economic issues soon followed. The increasing emphasis on economic issues might have shifted voters' economic policy views and given them enough new information to change their view of the candidates (Greene 2011). Our panel model is well designed to capture such shifts.

The Mexico panel data contain repeated questions on economic policy issues related to privatization, trade, redistribution, and the social safety net.[19] These variables scaled onto a single *Economic Liberalism* dimension in a principal components factor analysis. We then used this variable in panel regression models with the leftist candidate, López Obrador, as the base category. If positional issue voting occurs, the coefficient on the economic issue dimension will be positive and statistically significant.

Table 7.2 shows that voters' shifting preferences on economic policy issues had a notable impact on vote choices.[20] As one would expect, increasing economic liberalism benefited Calderón's market-friendly candidacy and, to a lesser extent, Madrazo's relatively centrist stance, relative to leftist López Obrador. A 1 standard deviation increase in liberal economic sentiment made a voter about 4 to 8 percentage points more likely to support

TABLE 7.2   Panel Model of Vote Choice in Mexico's 2006 Presidential Election

	Calderón	Madrazo
Variable	López Obrador	López Obrador
Economic liberalism^t	0.276*	0.186*
	(0.094)	(0.102)
Economic liberalism^{t-1}	0.104	−0.078
	(0.094)	(0.099)
Party ID		
PAN partisan^t	1.889*	0.743*
	(0.216)	(0.258)
PAN partisan^{t-1}	0.184	0.181
	(0.181)	(0.227)
PRD partisan^t	−2.307*	−1.875*
	(0.269)	(0.326)
PRD partisan^{t-1}	0.026	−0.039
	(0.200)	(0.247)
PRI partisan^t	0.177	1.738*
	(0.233)	(0.208)
PRI partisan^{t-1}	0.204	0.326*
	(0.189)	(0.174)
Independent or DK^t	0	0
	(0)	(0)
Independent or DK^{t-1}	0	0
	(0)	(0)
Lagged DVs		
Calderon vote intention^{t-1}	0.984*	−0.403
	(0.236)	(0.325)
López Obrador vote intention^{t-1}	−1.980*	−1.549*
	(0.218)	(0.265)
Madrazo vote intention^{t-1}	−0.353	1.324*
	(0.283)	(0.283)
Others, abstain, or DK^{t-1}	0	0
	(0)	(0)
Constant	0.388	−0.670
	(0.179)	(0.209)

Source: Mexico 2006 Panel Study.

Note: Entries are multinomial logit coefficients with robust standard errors in parentheses. Standard errors are corrected for clustering by respondent. * $p < .05$, one-tailed test. $N = 2,824$ (1,721 different respondents). T = 3. Coefficients for *Others/López Obrador* and *Abstain or DK/López Obrador* were estimated but are not shown.

Calderón over López Obrador. We should stress that these effects are quite large in the context of a political campaign, especially one that ended with a 0.5% margin of victory. In other words, there is a tight and important relationship between a voter reconsidering her or his view of the overarching economic model during the rhetorical melee of the campaigns and a subsequent change in her or his choice to support the presidential candidate more proximate to her or his newly acquired policy preferences.

For Brazil, the national sample had 2,482 respondents in wave 1 (March and April 2010), 908 re-interviews in wave 2 (August 2010), and 1,221 re-interviews in wave 3 (November 2010 after the October 31 second-round election). Nine candidates competed for the presidency, but as in Mexico, only three rose to prominence: Dilma Rousseff of the incumbent center-left Workers' Party (PT) that held the presidency under incumbent Luiz Inácio Lula da Silva; José Serra of the centrist Brazilian Social Democracy Party (PSDB) that was associated with the pro-market policies of the Fernando Henrique Cardoso administration (1995–2002); and Marina Silva, a former PT member who ran under the Green Party (PV) label. Rousseff won a plurality of the votes in the first round, missing an outright victory by just over 3 percentage points. In the second round, she bested Serra 56% to 44%.

The Brazil panel study contains questions about the desirability of the conditional cash transfer program (Bolsa Família) and government spending on pensions for the poor as well as a preference for government or private ownership.[21] All three variables loaded onto a single *Economic Liberalism* dimension in a principal components factor analysis. We again put the major leftist candidate (Rousseff) as the base category, so that coefficients on the economic liberalism variable should be positive when comparing Serra's supporters to Rousseff's supporters. Silva's campaign focused primarily on environmental sustainability and may have drawn supporters from across the economic policy dimension. We thus do not have strong expectations about the differences between her voters' preferences on economic policy and those of the other candidates.

Table 7.3 shows that voters' shifting economic policy preferences during the campaigns affected which of the major candidates they decided to support. A rightward shift toward more liberal preferences increased the probability of voting for Serra whereas a leftward shift made voters more likely to support Rousseff. As in Mexico, the magnitude of the effect is noteworthy in the context of a closely fought campaign: a 1 standard deviation shift toward liberal sentiments increased the likelihood of supporting Serra over Rousseff by about 4 to 8 percentage points. Our finding that increased liberalism also helped Marina Silva is perhaps mildly puzzling, but the fact that she staked her candidacy on noneconomic issues makes her supporters

TABLE 7.3   Panel Model of Vote Choice in Brazil's 2010 Presidential Election

Variable	Serra Rousseff	Silva Rousseff
Economic liberalism^t	0.715*	0.978
	(0.270)	(0.291)
Economic liberalism^{t-1}	0.217	0.571
	(0.235)	(0.264)
Party ID		
PT partisan^t	−1.267*	−0.896*
	(0.228)	(0.235)
PT partisan^{t-1}	−0.259	0.188
	(0.244)	(0.242)
PSDB partisan^t	2.287*	0.823
	(0.481)	(0.683)
PSDB partisan^{t-1}	0.765*	0.675
	(0.444)	(0.532)
Other party partisan^t	0.328	1.046*
	(0.269)	(0.268)
Other party partisan^{t-1}	0.074	−0.154
	(0.255)	(0.297)
Independent or DK^t	0	0
	(0)	(0)
Independent or DK^{t-1}	0	0
	(0)	(0)
Lagged DVs		
Rousseff vote intention^{t-1}	−0.913*	−0.944*
	(0.200)	(0.217)
Serra vote intention^{t-1}	1.424*	−0.163
	(0.193)	(0.250)
Silva vote intention^{t-1}	0.477	0.845*
	(0.280)	(0.270)
Others, abstain, or DK^{t-1}	0	0
	(0)	(0)
Constant	−0.518	−0.892
	(0.138)	(0.154)

Source: Brazilian Election Panel Study 2010.
Note: Entries are multinomial logit coefficients with robust standard errors in parentheses. Standard errors are corrected for clustering by respondent. * $p < .05$, one-tailed test. $N = 1,621$ (905 different respondents). T = 3. Coefficients for *Others/Rousseff* and *Abstain or DK/Rousseff* were estimated but are not shown.

tougher to pin down on the economic policy dimension. Although it is certainly possible that environmental politics could become a second primary dimension of competition in Brazil's party system, economic issues remain dominant at present. As our findings show, these positional issues clearly informed vote decisions made between the top two candidates.

Panel data on single election cycles offer an excellent opportunity to test for positional issue voting. When they are well designed, panel studies yield context-specific questions that tap salient economic issues better than multi-country cross-sectional surveys that are, by necessity, blunter instruments. Coupled with the ability to construct panel models that control for a host of measured and unmeasured influences on vote choices, panel data provide even more convincing evidence of positional issue voting.

Conclusion

Positional issue voting in new democracies sounds unlikely, on the face of it. Circumstantial evidence such as mandate violations and the common observation that elections turn on clientelist payoffs, demographics, or short-term macroeconomic trends rather than campaign promises make many observers skeptical at the outset. Add to that the very narrow requirements among both voters and candidates for engaging in positional issue voting, and the conclusion seems obvious: Latin America's new democracies involve elite-mass linkages that are either populist, clientelist, or charismatic, but not programmatic.

Yet despite the circumstantial evidence against positional issue voting, when we construct proper measures of voters' economic policy preferences and create models that help minimize biases against positive findings on issue voting, we find compelling evidence that voters really do choose from among competing parties and candidates to a substantial extent based on their personal economic policy preferences. Among the eighteen countries for which we have appropriate data over a fourteen-year period, positional voting on economic policy issues occurs in at least fourteen of them. We would be more convinced by the apparent absence of issue voting in Guatemala, Honduras, Paraguay, and Panama if we had access to well-constructed panel survey data with context-specific questions and the ability to minimize potential problems due to endogeneity and omitted variables bias; however, our best evidence for the moment suggests that voters make their choices based on other criteria in these countries. Our contextual analysis suggests that structural features of the party systems in these countries—features that are less prevalent in the other fourteen countries in the region—may diminish positional issue voting for reasons that are beyond the voters' control.

Our findings suggest that analysts of voting behavior in Latin America have more work to do. There is no doubt that clientelism, candidate traits, media influence, and retrospective economic evaluations all influence vote choices to varying degrees; however, these dominant approaches struggle to explain the causes of partisan waves that have swept across the region, such as the rise of the left from the mid-1990s to the late 2000s and the subsequent resurgence of the right (see Baker and Greene 2011). Constructing better explanations of voting behavior will require scholars to collect more high-quality survey data that replicate issue position questions across countries and over time through large-scale cross-sectional surveys but also through (admittedly expensive) panel surveys on single elections. Analysts will also need to construct better theoretical explanations that go far beyond what we have done here and integrate the multiple influences on voting behavior rather than treating them as separate and conflicting causes. For the time being, our findings that voters do choose in part according to candidates' and parties' issue stances means that Latin American countries may be developing the type of programmatic party systems that most analysts agree enhances democratic representation and accountability, but that were once thought to be out of reach for the average citizen in most countries in the Western Hemisphere.

NOTES

We thank Raymond Duch and Carole Wilson as well as the editors and other contributors to this volume for their comments on earlier drafts.

1. Directional theorists argue that seemingly centrist parties win votes by appealing to voters on issues on which they are non-centrist (Macdonald, Listhaug, and Rabinowitz 1991), an analytical move that is tantamount to dismissing the presence of centrist parties. Moreover, Tomz and Van Houweling (2008) show that few voters employ the directional rule in the United States, where the two-party system should be most propitious for directional theory.

2. We focus on sincere positional issue voting. We do not consider the impact of moderators that can lead to "sophisticated" issue voting, such as strategic defection from preferred losers to less preferred winners (Duverger 1954) or "discounting" whereby voters consider the impact that supporting a particular candidate will have on eventual government policy (Kedar 2009).

3. There are important theoretical exceptions to this melodious result that links voters' choices to politicians' actions in a symphony of democratic harmony (McKelvey 1976, 1986; Shepsle and Cohen 1990).

4. On media and campaign effects, see Baker, Ames, and Rennó (2006); Boas and Hidalgo (2011); Greene (2011); and Lawson (2002). On candidate traits, see Ames, Baker, and Rennó (2008); Lawson et al. (2010); and Merolla and Zechmeister (2011). On clientelism, see Brusco, Nazareno, and Stokes (2004); Greene (2007); Stokes (2005); and Von Mettenheim (1995). On partisanship, see Samuels (2006). On ethno-racial identity, see Madrid (2012). On retrospective economic voting, see the many works cited by Gelineau and Singer (this volume).

5. Elite and mass opinions diverge significantly in the other six countries in their analysis. Similarly, Bruhn and Greene (2009) show that congressional candidates for major parties in Mexico are significantly less centrist than their constituents.

6. The fact that the surveys are not timed with elections could mean that public opinion is captured in some cases at a time when issues are less salient; if this results in a downward bias to the connection individuals make between issues and voter choice, our estimates of issue voting with these data can be considered conservative.

7. This approach allows item loadings to vary across countries, thus taking country-specific context into account. The output of these factors analyses is available in the online appendix.

8. Latinobarometer 1998–99 items are: (1) "The market economy is the most suitable system for the country. Do you strongly agree, agree, disagree, or strongly disagree with this statement?" (2) "The privatization of state-owned enterprises has been beneficial to the country. Do you strongly agree, agree, disagree, or strongly disagree with this statement?" (3) "From the following list of activities, which do you think should be majority-owned by the state and which do you think should be majority-owned by private hands? Petroleum, electricity, telephones, drinking water." (4) "The state should leave productive activity to the private sector. Do you strongly agree, agree, disagree, or strongly disagree with this statement?" (5) "Would you say that your country benefits a lot, quite a bit, a little or not at all for being part of your regional trade agreement?" (6) "Thinking about trade between your country and the United States, how important do you think it is for the economic development of your country? Very important, somewhat important, not very important, not important at all." (7) "Foreign investment should be encouraged. Do you strongly agree, agree, disagree, or strongly disagree with this statement?" (8) "In general, do you consider foreign investment to be beneficial or harmful for the development of the country?"

Latinobarometer 2007 items are 1–3 above plus (4) "Imagine the following situation: two people, of the same age, work as computer programmers doing the same work. One earns 20,000 pesos (equivalent to US $50) more than the other one, but he does his work more quickly, efficiently, and is more trustworthy than the other. In your opinion, do you consider it fair that, in this situation, one programmer is paid more than the other or do you consider it unfair?" (5) "Do you strongly agree, agree, disagree, or strongly disagree with each of the following phrases that I am going to read? Only with a market economy can (country) become a developed country." AmericasBarometer items are the four "role of the state" items described in this volume's conclusion (appendix note 7).

9. Respondents who answered "don't know" to one or more of the items in the batteries were not dropped. Instead, they were scored on the dimension using the questions they did answer. Only respondents who answered "don't know" to *all* of the items (less than 0.5% in Latinobarometer, less than 3% in AmericasBarometer) were casewise deleted and considered not to hold positions on the economic policy dimension.

10. See Baker and Greene (2011) for details.

11. We do not construct the candidate-to-voter issue distances that typically inform empirical models of proximity voting because none of the surveys we employ asked respondents to place the competing candidates on the same economic policy

issues where they placed themselves. Even if they had included such questions, voters often project their own personal preferences onto those of the candidates, thus confounding tests of proximity voting (Conover and Feldman 1982).

12. For both AmericasBarometer and Latinobarometer, responses to the vote choice question of "don't know" or "did not vote" or "would not vote" were dropped from the analysis.

13. See the introduction to this volume for information on the operationalization of these latter three variables.

14. Party polarization data for Panama in 1998 were not available. We used data from 2000 as a substitute. The Dominican Republic was not polled in the 1998–99 Latinobarometer.

15. They do not, however, resolve endogeneity and omitted variable bias problems entirely: only a well-executed experiment can do so.

16. Of course, if voters' issue preferences are highly changeable, then researchers should focus on the variables that cause such instability, even if vote intentions continue to shift with changes in issue preferences.

17. Mexico 2006 Panel Study participants were Andy Baker, Kathleen Bruhn, Roderic Camp, Wayne Cornelius, Jorge Domínguez, Kenneth Greene, Joseph Klesner, Chappell Lawson (principal investigator), David Leal, Beatriz Magaloni, James McCann, Alejandro Moreno (pollster), and Alejandro Poiré. Data available at http://web.mit.edu/polisci/research/mexico06/.

18. Barry Ames, Fabiana Machado, Lucio Renno, David Samuels, Amy Erica Smith, and Cesar Zucco, The Brazilian Electoral Panel Studies (BEPS): Brazilian Public Opinion in the 2010 Presidential Elections, IDB Technical Note No. 508, 2013, http://www.iadb.org/en/research-and-data/publication-details,3169. html?pub_id=IDB-DB-105.

19. Questions are: (1) "Do you believe that more private investment should be allowed in the electricity sector or that the electricity sector should remain almost completely in the hands of the government?" (2) "What would you prefer: that commercial relations between Mexico and the United States increase, decrease, or remain the same?" (3) "In general, what would you prefer? That the government be responsible for the economic wellbeing of individuals or that individuals be responsible for their own economic wellbeing?" (4) "In your opinion, what should the government do to reduce poverty? Give money to the poor and raise taxes on the rich or promote private investment and leave taxes as they are?"

20. It may appear as though the changing economic policy preferences of some voters violate the assumption of fixed preferences in the spatial model, but see Kollman, Miller, and Page (1992).

21. The wordings of the three questions are as follows: (1) "To what extent do you agree with the statement that the Brazilian government, more than the private sector should own the most important firms and industries in the country?" (2) "What should the government do about the Bolsa Família program? Extend it, keep it as is, reduce it, or end it?" (3) "How much should the government spend on non-contributory pension benefits? It should increase taxes and spend more, maintain current expenditure levels, reduce taxes and spend less, or reduce taxes and end the service provision."

8 ✦ Left-Right Identifications and the Latin American Voter

ELIZABETH J. ZECHMEISTER

Navigating complex landscapes is difficult without signposts. In politics, the terms "left" and "right" frequently function as markers that guide individuals through political and ideological terrain. Rather than communicate a profuse number of policy stances to the partially tuned in average citizen, a politician can efficiently convey her or his stance in the political space by claiming to be "on the left" or "to the right" and the citizen can in turn select the candidate closest to his or her own left-right stance. Thus, in their ideal form ideological labels facilitate issue-based vote choice. Yet, they can only do so to the extent that they denote policy content. In practice, the terms often act simply as rough proxies for party labels or, worse, are conceptually nebulous symbols that may or may not be connected to voter choice.[1]

In this chapter I document that on average Latin Americans' left-right identifications correspond to their vote choices. However, this blanket statement masks important variation across countries: first, in the tendency for individuals to use left-right self-placements; second, in the extent to which the left-right semantics link to policy stances; and, third, in the strength of the connection between left-right placements and the vote. In fact, this chapter will demonstrate that, despite their value *in theory*, the terms "left" and "right" are eschewed by many members of the Latin American public, such that nonresponse to left-right placement questions is comparatively high in several countries. Moreover, there is scant evidence of robust ideological significance to left-right labels in Latin America. For example, when considering the classic economic dimension, economic policy stances significantly predict left-right identifications among the mass public in little more than half of the eighteen Latin American countries. Finally, in many countries in the region, self-placements on the left-right scale are not very meaningful predictors of voter choice.

Generally speaking, none of these characteristics makes Latin America exceptional in type (see, e.g., Campbell et al. 1960; Jost, Federico, and Napier 2009). And yet the political significance of the left-right semantics in Latin America is comparatively quite low. There are, of course, a few exceptions. For example, in the contemporary era in Uruguay and Venezuela, the mass public is able and willing to use the left-right semantics for self-placement, left-right identifications reflect key policy divides, and individuals connect their left-right stance to their vote choice. Left-right placements structure vote decisions and policy divides in Chile as well, though Chileans are among the least willing in the region to report a left-right position. In other cases, such as Brazil and Ecuador, there is no evidence of policy significance or vote relevance to left-right identifications.

The core of this chapter evaluates and seeks to explain cross-national variation in Latin America in the extent to which the mass public expresses left-right identifications, connects these to policy stances, and selects elected officials in a manner that corresponds to their left-right position. The first two of these considerations—rates of placement on the left-right scale and policy significance—have received comparatively more attention in previous research (see Zechmeister and Corral 2013). Thus, while addressing all three aspects of left-right identifications, this chapter places more emphasis on examining the connection between left-right identifications and the vote, and the contextual factors that shape this relationship. In so doing, I present and apply a theoretical framework that emphasizes the importance of features of the party system and the substance of party competition to the vote relevance of left-right identifications.

In summary, the main findings in this chapter are as follows. First, placement (versus no placement) on the left-right scale is conditioned by the extent to which individuals are motivated to engage in their political system; in particular, greater levels of left-right identification are found among those with more political interest and those who perceive the party system to be responsive. Second, it is frequently the case in Latin America that the left-right semantics do not reference a classic economic dimension among the mass public. Third, the association between left-right placements and the vote is stronger in systems that are more polarized and that have higher levels of programmatic party structuration; conversely, this relationship is undermined by high levels of fragmentation and clientelism.

The conclusions presented here connect to and are relevant to extant research on the importance of context to left-right identifications (e.g.,

Dalton 2011), and yet the chapter also considers selected factors that are particular to the Latin American context. One of these is the ascendance to power of the political left at the turn of the twenty-first century. Scholars have debated the extent to which this "pink tide" reflected an ideological conversion among the mass public or merely a simple retrospective calculus (under which poorly performing incumbent right parties were voted out). In pooled cross-sectional and case-specific temporal analyses, I find little to no evidence that the pink tide left an imprint on the political significance of the terms "left" and "right" in the region.

On the whole, the results in this chapter affirm that left-right identities in Latin America are often quite anemic and, yet, some substantive content and vote relevance can be infused into the terms conditional on the nature of party competition. The tendency for that to happen does not hinge on the incumbent's ideological stripes. Rather, through their general behaviors and rhetoric in the process of competing for office, political elites can foster information environments that facilitate citizens' roles as voters. The extent to which features of party competition increase the political significance of the left-right semantics varies significantly across countries in Latin America, and thus, while this chapter provides mostly a snapshot of the current period, the patterns detected should lead us to expect change over time. The nature of that change will hinge significantly on how party competition evolves in Latin America and, specifically, whether party systems continue to fragment and prioritize vote-buying and other non-programmatic means of attracting votes or, conversely, stabilize and increase in the extent to which parties distinguish themselves on the basis of relevant policy stances.

Theoretical Perspectives on the Left-Right Semantics and Politics

Left-right labels are highly valued by scholars of democratic politics because, in theory, they create "economies" and "efficiencies" (Converse 1964) for political communication and competition (Fuchs and Klingemann 1990; Thomassen and Schmitt 1997; Hinich and Munger 1996). This is important, because most citizens have little interest in absorbing and understanding the complexities of modern politics (e.g., Campbell et al. 1960; Delli Carpini and Keeter 1996; Kinder and Sears 1985). Left-right identifications carve out easy-to-discern political divisions, and thus can provide an effective tool for decision-making. Yet though such terms are ubiquitous in politics, few political concepts are more deceptively complex.

Left-right labels and identifications are frequently taken as markers of an underlying ideological structure. Ideology, in this sense, refers to a hierarchical and interrelated structuring of beliefs about what is best that is "capped by concepts of a high order of abstraction" (Campbell et al. 1960, 193). In other words, left-right labels can be "symbolic" endpoints of an underlying "operational" ideology composed of bundles of attitudes (Jost, Federico, and Napier 2009). From this perspective, the ideal standard is met when individuals make use of left-right markers by placing themselves on the left-right scale, when those left-right placements correspond to an underlying set of issue positions, and when they connect these identifications to their vote choice.

However, it is well accepted that the mass public typically falls short of this ideal standard. Conventional wisdom offered by scholars of U.S. politics states that levels of ideological rhetoric and structuration within the mass public are quite low (Kinder and Sears 1985; see also Campbell et al. 1960; Converse 1964). Campbell et al. (1960) and Converse (1964) note that there could be individual logics that account for some of the disconnect they find between stances that the sophisticated observer would expect to be correlated (see also Ellis and Stimson 2011). Nonetheless, most individuals' beliefs are "jumbled," many individuals simply do not use ideological markers when discussing politics, and, when they do, there is often a disconnect between their left-right (or liberal-conservative) placement and the specific issue positions that they hold (Converse 1964, 66; Jost, Federico, and Napier 2009).

Given that most individuals have limited time and interest to invest in politics, it makes sense that use of ideological markers can be lower than ideal, with respect to both placement and vote decisions, and that the markers lack robust substantive (policy) significance among the mass public.[2] In fact, an uncomfortable fact for those who would like to assume that "left" and "right" anchor issue divides is that ideological labels tend to be relatively weak in policy content and are often more meaningful as alternatives to party names (Butler and Stokes 1969; Inglehart and Klingemann 1976; see also, among others, Dalton, Farrell, and McAllister 2011; Evans, Heath, and Lalljee 1996; Fleury and Lewis-Beck 1993; Knutsen 1997; Jacoby 2002; Zechmeister 2006b).

Yet, the existence of some degree of substantively meaningful left-right semantics in the political system indicates that effective ideological markers are available for citizens who require assistance in finding elites whose policy stances roughly approximate their own. And, so, rather than lament the generally low levels of ideological structuration in the mass public, we can gain more from applying a comparative lens though which to assess the varying levels of political significance of left-right terms across mass publics.

It is indeed a fact that the political significance of the left-right semantics varies across countries, across time, and even across subgroups of a population (among many, see, e.g., Aspelund, Lindeman, and Verkasalo 2013; Campbell et al. 1960; Dalton, Farrell, and McAllister 2011; de Vries, Hakhverdian, and Lancee 2013; Inglehart and Klingemann 1976; Kitschelt and Hellemans 1990; Nathan and Shi 1996; Evans and Whitefield 1998; Dalton 2008; Weber and Federico 2013). But according to what factors? Classic research has focused most attention on three factors: consistency over time, polarization, and fragmentation.

In the first place, because consistency over time is critical to the establishment of a well-developed ideological structure (Hinich and Munger 1996), scholars have proposed that the comparative youth of democracies in Asia and Latin America makes for less robust ideological semantics (e.g., Jou 2011; see also González and Queirolo 2009). Compared to Western Europe, for example, modern Latin American politics have been characterized by much less stability (Roberts and Wibbels 1999), which should work against the development of high levels of ideological structuration (Zechmeister and Corral 2013). Thus, in general, we should expect comparatively low levels of left-right use and policy significance in Latin America.

In addition, basic features of the party system matter to the degree that they clarify political alternatives. Polarization can make the end points of the political spectrum easier to discern, and may increase the use of ideological labels by elites, leading to more effective use of left-right identifications by the mass public (Ames and Smith 2010; Dalton 2008, 2011; Inglehart and Klingemann 1976; Huber 1989; Singer forthcoming; Zechmeister and Corral 2013). In fact, the relevance of polarization to the political significance of left-right identifications is one of the most well-established findings in research on this topic.

Fragmentation, or the number of parties in the system, may also affect ideological structuration, though this effect differs across cases. A positive relationship between the effective number of parties and substantively meaningful left-right ideological labels is found in research on Europe, where a greater number of parties is thought to increase the utility of left-right semantics (Inglehart and Klingemann 1976; Huber 1989; Knutsen 1997). However, multi-country analyses by Dalton (2008, 2011) find no relationship between fragmentation and the extent to which left-right stances are correlated with vote choice. In Latin America, Zechmeister and Corral (2013) find that the effective number of parties (and, as well, electoral volatility) is *negatively* correlated with individuals' ability or willingness to place on the left-right scale. The authors argue that this relationship makes sense, given that party system fragmentation is highly related to party system flux in the Latin American region. Singer (forthcoming) applies this logic to the question of the connection between left-right identifications and voter choice in Latin America and finds a similar negative relationship.

Other factors can also influence the nature and significance of left-right identifications. At the country level, for example, Dalton (2006, 2011) highlights the relevance of economic and political development (see also Geser 2008, and Freire and Kivistik 2013). Building and expanding on previous research, I draw attention to two additional factors. The first extends directly out of the micro-logic undergirding studies of the relationship between features of the party system and left-right identifications. This logic is that how elites bundle political ideas and package them with distinctive labels influences the degree of ideological structuration in the mass public (Downs 1957; Hinich and Munger 1996). If this is the case, then the substance of party competition should matter for ideological structuration and the significance of the left-right semantics. In a study of ideological labels among citizens in Mexico and Argentina, Zechmeister (2006b) attributes the more robust and politically relevant significance of the left-right semantics in Mexico at the time to Mexican elites' comparatively greater tendency to use the terms in political manifestos and speeches.[3] In a three-country study of left-right attitudes, Harbers, de Vries, and Steenbergen (2013) find evidence that the level of programmatic party structuration (see Kitschelt et al. 2010) in Latin America matters, such that more variation in responses is found in the least structured system, Ecuador, and less variation is found in the most structured system, Chile, with Mexico falling in between.

The second relates to tendencies to place oneself on the left-right scale. Whether an individual self-identifies on the left-right scale can be due to non-rival factors that are cognitive (recognition of the terms) or motivational (willingness to engage). A focus on the former is more frequently found in scholarship on the left-right, and thus scholars have tended to look to individual predictors such as education and/or political sophistication (see Dalton 2011; Zechmeister and Corral 2013). Motivational factors have received comparatively less attention (but see Scholz and Zuell 2012). In the Latin American region, where dissatisfaction with the political status quo has manifested itself in low levels of expressed partisanship as well as more active demonstrations of discontent, we should expect motivation, or *willingness*, to report a left-right identification, to be particularly important. Therefore, this chapter includes an assessment of the relevance of political interest and perceived system efficacy in predicting response to the left-right question in Latin America.

Varying Levels of Left-Right Identification

Figure 8.1 shows the distribution of left-right placements for eighteen Latin American countries in response to the 2012 AmericasBarometer survey by the Latin American Public Opinion Project (LAPOP). The categories are created by taking responses to the left-right self-placement question, asked on a 1–10 scale, and coding "left" those who respond 1, 2, or 3; "center" those who respond 4, 5, 6, or 7; and, "right" those who respond as 8, 9, or 10.[4] Those who indicate they do not know or otherwise do not answer the question are noted as "NR" (this nonresponse option was accepted but not read aloud). The countries are arrayed in order by the percentage of nonresponses.

In seven countries—Nicaragua, Uruguay, the Dominican Republic, Venezuela, Guatemala, Panama, and Brazil—more than one out of every five individuals self-identifies on the left.[5] In nine countries—the Dominican Republic, El Salvador, Panama, Colombia, Paraguay, Mexico, Nicaragua, Venezuela, and Brazil—more than one out of every five people identifies on the right. As others have noted, the public in Latin America leans toward the right (Arnold and Samuels 2011; Došek 2011; Seligson 2007). The AmericasBarometer 2012 reflects this tendency, but only to a very slight degree.[6]

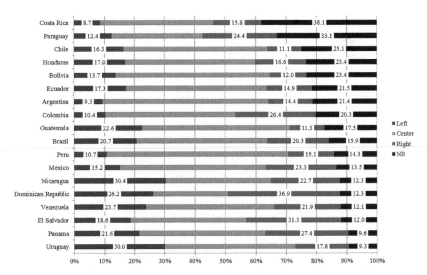

Figure 8.1   Distribution of Left-Right Placements. *Source:* Americas-Barometer 2012 by LAPOP (v49/v50).

Also noteworthy in figure 8.1 are the varying levels of nonresponse to the left-right identification question. Taking the region as a whole, the average nonresponse is 18.6%.[7] As a point of contrast, Mair (2007, 2010) finds mean nonresponse rates between 12.1 and 12.4% in Western Europe and between 16.5 and 22.8% in Eastern Europe. Nonresponse rates are considerably lower for selected Western European countries, such as France, where they range from 2 to 10% (Dalton, Farrell, and McAllister 2011; Lewis-Beck, Nadeau, and Bélanger 2012). In sum, average rates of response to the left-right question in the Latin American region mirror those found in Eastern Europe.[8]

Regional nonresponse rates mask the tremendous variation across countries and, in some cases, over time (see Došek 2011). As per figure 8.1, seven countries have levels of response to the left-right scale that approximate, or are even lower in some cases than, the average nonresponse rate in Western Europe: Uruguay (9.3%), Panama (9.6%), El Salvador (12%), Venezuela (12.1%), the Dominican Republic (12.3%), Nicaragua (12.3%), and Mexico (13.5%). In a number of countries, however, nonresponse rates far exceed the average even in Eastern Europe: specifically, Costa Rica and Paraguay (38.1% and 33.1%, respectively).[9]

Previous research on Latin America has found party system polarization to be positively related to placement on the left-right scale, and the reverse for fragmentation and electoral volatility (Zechmeister and Corral 2013). Yet, failure to self-place on the ideological scale may be driven by other factors as well. One such set of factors particularly relevant to contemporary Latin American politics contains those related to political dissatisfaction and disengagement. Across Latin America, the modern period has been ripe with signs of political discontent expressed both through actions (e.g., demonstrations) and dissociation (e.g., low levels of partisanship) (for a classic framework on voice and exit responses, see Hirschman 1970). Many have placed the blame on failures to engage, include, and respond to the mass public (see, e.g., Agüero and Stark 1998; Hagopian and Mainwaring 2006; Mainwaring, Bejarano, and Leongómez 2006). These perceived system failures might be registered by individuals directly, or simply turn some citizens off from politics. As such, I consider the influence of perceptions of system responsiveness and political interest on willingness to place oneself on the left-right scale.

Figure 8.2 presents results from a logistic regression model based on a pooled dataset for the region. The data are from the 2012 AmericasBarometer. The dichotomous dependent variable, left-right nonresponse, is modeled as a function of basic controls (education, gender, age cohort,

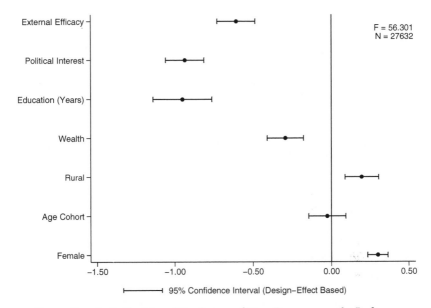

Figure 8.2   Individual Level Predictors of Non-Response to the Left-Right Question. *Source:* AmericasBarometer 2012 by LAPOP (v50).
Note: Analysis based on logistic regression with all independent variables rescaled from 0 to 1. See text for discussion of substantive significance of these results. Country fixed effects included but not shown.

rural residence, wealth,[10] and country fixed effects) and two measures related to motivation: external efficacy and political interest. The external efficacy measure is based on a statement asking respondents the extent to which they agree or disagree that "Those who govern this country are interested in what people like you think." Political interest is measured with a question asking "How much interest do you have in politics?" Responses are coded so that higher values indicate greater efficacy and interest on these 7-point and 4-point scales, respectively.[11] The analysis reveals that, with the exception of the age variable, the independent variables are significant at $p < 0.05$, two-tailed.[12] Women and those in rural areas are less likely to respond to the left-right question; those who are wealthier and more educated are more likely to respond.

As hypothesized, perceptions of system responsiveness and political interest predict left-right response. Individuals who report higher levels of external efficacy and higher political interest are more likely to place themselves on the left-right scale. The three variables with the largest substantive effects are education, political interest, and external efficacy. Logistic regression results are not directly interpretable. Therefore, I use the results of the analysis to calculate a set of predicted probabilities of left-right nonresponse based on moving from the maximum to the minimum value on each of the independent variables in turn, while holding all other variables constant at their means. I find that moving from the lowest to the highest value on education, political interest, and external efficacy increases the likelihood of placing oneself on the left-right scale by 13, 11, and 7 percentage points, respectively.[13]

This result is important because it affirms that high nonresponse rates to the left-right ideological question do not merely signal lack of recognition. Rather, for many Latin Americans, failure to provide a response to the left-right scale is an act of political disassociation. While this point is of general relevance to scholarship on left-right identifications, it also aids in explaining the very high levels of nonresponse to the left-right question in countries such as Costa Rica and Chile (see figure 8.1), both of which have comparatively extensive democratic histories. Levels of confidence in and satisfaction with Costa Rican institutions and democracy have declined in recent years (Alfaro-Redondo and Seligson 2012), and discontent and democratic ambivalence have also been brewing in Chile (Siavelis 2009; Carlin 2011). In the 2012 AmericasBarometer dataset mean levels of external efficacy in Costa Rica are lower than in any other country in the region. Chile ranks in the bottom four on political interest (along with Costa Rica) and in the lower half of countries on external efficacy. In summary, for many in Costa Rica and Chile and for others across the region, *lack of response to the left-right scale is fueled by a motivation to disengage from the political system.*

Weak Correspondence between Issues and Left-Right Identifications

Many members of the public *do* reference left-right semantics as they navigate political space. It therefore is important to consider the extent to which left-right semantics reflect policy divides. That is, in which countries is there substantively rich policy-relevant content to the left-right semantics and where instead are these terms ideologically anemic?

To the extent that ideological labels reflect programmatic orientations, we should be able to detect greater correspondence between policy and left-right stances within the mass public. This correspondence will be low, as the public will tend to only weakly echo back ideological packages conveyed by elites. This is as it should be: possession of a highly detailed conception of the left-right semantics would undermine their utility as short-cuts that create "economies" for political communication and decision-making.

I examine the strength of the connection between policy stances and the left-right semantics, with a focus on five different types of predictors. The first of these, the economic dimension, captures the classic meaning of the left-right terms (Downs 1957; Bobbio 1996) and the principal dimension of party competition in Latin America (Kitschelt et al. 2010; see also Moreno 1999; Wiesehomeier and Doyle 2012; Baker and Greene this volume). The second, the democracy (versus authoritarianism) dimension, has varied in significance in Latin American politics over time and across countries (Moreno 1999) and is kept relevant by debates and incidents in some countries related to the centralization of power in the executive branch at the expense of checks and balances, restrictions on the media, and so on. A third predictor asks about support for tough stances against criminals, in order to tap into the increasing relevance of issues of crime and violence in the region. Fourth, moral issues have been historically important in Latin America, given the history of church-state relations, and specific issues related to gay marriage and abortion rights recently have been debated by politicians, in the media, and by the public (Boidi and Corral 2013; Lodola and Corral 2010). Finally, a fifth dimension—attitudes toward the United States—is included because of its theorized relevance to defining the new left in Latin America (Arnold and Samuels 2011; Remmer 2012).[14]

Table 8.1 is based on a series of regression analyses, one per country, in which left-right self-placement (1–10, with higher values indicating right-leaning tendencies) is predicted by individuals' stances on seven policy measures: *Government Ownership of Key Industries; Welfare Factor; Belief Democracy is the Best; Belief Democracy is Preferred; Tough on Crime; Religion is Important;* and *Trust in the U.S.* The full table of results, with question wordings for these variables, is available in chapter appendix table A8.1. Table 8.1 reports the r-squared statistic, which indicates how much variation in the dependent variable (left-right placement) the issue measures explain in that country, and lists which independent variables (issues) are significant predictors, if any. As the table shows, there is substantial variation across countries in the policy significance of the left-right semantics, a finding consistent with prior work by Zechmeister (2006b) and Zechmeister and Corral (2011, 2013).

Economic attitudes predict left-right placement in only ten of the eighteen cases, and the signs on those measures are negative as expected (such that preferences for a greater role of the state are associated with left-leaning identifications), except in the case of Honduras. Interestingly,

TABLE 8.1 Summary of Multivariate Analyses Predicting Left-Right Placement with Issues

Country	R^2	Significant Variables (with direction of coefficient in parentheses)
Honduras	0.16	Gov't Ownership (+), Welfare (+), Democracy is Best (+), Democracy is Preferred (+)
Uruguay	0.15	Gov't Ownership (-), Tough on Crime (+), Religion is Important (+), Trust in the U.S. (+)
Venezuela	0.14	Gov't Ownership (-), Religion is Important (+), Trust in the U.S. (+)
Chile	0.14	Gov't Ownership (-) , Trust in the U.S. (+)
Argentina	0.12	Welfare (-), Tough on Crime (+), Religion is Important (+), Trust in the U.S. (+)
Panama	0.12	Welfare (-), Democracy is Best (+), Trust in the U.S. (+)
Bolivia	0.06	Trust in the U.S. (+)
Mexico	0.06	Welfare (-), Democracy is Best (+), Democracy is Preferred (+)
Costa Rica	0.06	Gov't Ownership (-), Democracy is Best (+), Religion is Important (+), Trust in the U.S. (+)
Dominican Republic	0.05	Democracy is Best (+), Tough on Crime (+)
Nicaragua	0.05	Trust in the U.S. (+)
Paraguay	0.04	Welfare (-), Trust in the U.S. (+)
Colombia	0.03	Religion is Important (+)
Guatemala	0.03	Religion is Important (+)
Peru	0.03	Welfare (-), Democracy is Best (+), Religion is Important (-)
Brazil	0.02	None
El Salvador	0.02	None
Ecuador	0.02	None

Source: AmericasBarometer 2012 by LAPOP (v49/50).

Note: Table summarizes OLS analyses (adjusted for complex sample design). *R*-squared statistics are from models that predict left-right placement (original linear "l1" measure) with seven independent variables: *Gov't Ownership of Key Industries; Welfare Factor; Belief Democracy is the Best; Belief Democracy is Preferred; Tough on Crime; Religion is Important;* and *Trust in the U.S.* Statistical significance is assessed using a generous $p \leq 0.10$, two-tailed, cut-off. Full regression analysis results and question wording are available in the chapter appendix table A8.1.

in Honduras, those with a greater belief that the government should own key industries and those who prefer a stronger welfare state tend toward the *right*.[15] Attitudes toward the United States are significant predictors in nine cases and in each case the coefficient is positively signed, indicating that greater trust in the United States is associated with placement on the right of the left-right scale. Democratic attitudes are significant, positive predictors in six of the cases. The belief that religion is important shows up as a significant predictor in seven cases and, with the exception of Peru, the coefficients' signs are positive (greater importance to religion is associated with right-leaning identifications). Finally, the tough on crime measure is significant in just three cases and positive in those cases (tougher stances are associated with right-leaning identifications).

In sum, as expected, *the issue-based content of the left-right semantics varies significantly across countries.* We can infer from the analysis that scholars of the region who give in to the temptation to use left-right identifications as proxies for economic divides would only be correct roughly half the time. Further, based on the models assessed here, in a few cases (Brazil, El Salvador, and Ecuador) there is no discernible issue basis to the left-right semantics at all.[16]

Contextual Factors and the Relevance of Left-Right Identities to Vote Choice

Though some individuals select not to place themselves on the left-right dimension and though left-right semantics may be only weakly associated with policy divides, there is nonetheless a general tendency for left-right identifications to predict voter choice in Latin America. But to what extent is this relationship present in all countries and what predicts cross-national variation in the connection between left-right placements and voter choice? This is a worthwhile exercise, given doubts regarding the extent to which the Latin American public conceives of most parties as sitting clearly on either the left or the right of the ideological scale and whether, in fact, members of the mass public actually connect left-right placements to their vote choice (see discussion in González and Queirolo 2009). The extent to which left-right identifications predict the vote gives us one measure of the political relevance of these terms in the Latin American region.

As a first turn at assessing the strength of a connection between left-right placements and individuals' vote decisions across countries in the Latin American region, I ran a series of basic OLS regression analyses. The dependent variable, vote choice, is a measure that arrays the principal candidates in the last presidential election from left to right along a 20-point scale; the measure is described in detail in the part II introduction. The key independent variable is a measure of left-right placement on a 10-point scale (linearly transformed to a 0 to 1 variable). The models also incorporate the individual-level variables included in earlier analysis (see figure 8.2).[17] The core results are presented in table 8.2, with the countries presented in alphabetical order.

In thirteen countries—Bolivia, Chile, Colombia, the Dominican Republic, Guatemala, Honduras, Mexico, Nicaragua, Paraguay, Peru, El Salvador, Uruguay, and Venezuela—left-right self-placement is a significant, positive predictor of the left-right vote. In five countries—Argentina, Brazil, Costa Rica, Ecuador, and Panama—the left-right self-placement

TABLE 8.2   Left-Right Placement as a Predictor of Vote Choice

	N	R^2	Coefficient (std. err.)
Argentina	879	0.07	−0.006
			(0.120)
Bolivia	1,155	0.16	3.288*
			(0.604)
Brazil	1,116	0.01	0.095
			(0.094)
Chile	612	0.32	10.345*
			(0.651)
Colombia	630	0.06	1.388*
			(0.699)
Costa Rica	806	0.02	0.757
			(0.483)
Dominican Republic	927	0.06	0.641*
			(0.180)
El Salvador	644	0.27	11.429*
			(0.661)
Guatemala	431	0.06	0.203*
			(0.060)
Ecuador	966	0.03	0.914
			(0.594)
Honduras	698	0.03	0.794*
			(0.229)
Mexico	781	0.14	4.778*
			(0.716)
Nicaragua	863	0.03	0.722*
			(0.215)
Panama	778	0.05	0.500
			(0.492)
Paraguay	692	0.04	12.823*
			(0.274)
Peru	973	0.07	1.222*
			(0.677)
Uruguay	1,034	0.41	8.362*
			(0.419)
Venezuela	768	0.36	3.430*
			(0.353)
Latin America	14,753	0.08	4.268*
			(0.173)

Source: AmericasBarometer 2012 by LAPOP (v49/v50).

Note: $p \leq$ 0.10, two-tailed. Output is coefficients and standard errors for left-right placement, based on OLS regression analyses for each country (and, in the final row, for the pooled region). Models also include controls for age, gender, education, wealth, rural (versus urban) residence, political interest, and external efficacy; results for those and constants are not presented here for the sake of parsimony. Replication code available in the online appendix and/or from author. Dependent variable is left-right voter choice. Independent variables are scaled 0 to 1.

measure is not a significant predictor of the vote.[18] Not only is there variation in the statistical significance of left-right self-placement as a predictor of the vote, but there is also variation in the substantive relationship between left-right identifications and voter choice across countries. For example, in Chile, moving across the range of the ideological self-identification measure (from far left to far right) results in a shift of 10.4 units on the vote choice dependent variable, which ranges from 1.85 to 17.5 in that country. Conversely, in Peru this same maximum effect is only 1.2 units on the dependent variable, which ranges from 5.36 to 15.72 (for more details, see chapter appendix table A8.2). On average, left-right placement is related to voter choice in Latin America (see the last row of data). Yet, *left-right self-placements are minimally or not at all connected to voter choice in many Latin American countries.*

What predicts cross-national variation in the connection between left-right placements and voter choice? Based on earlier discussion and extending out of extant scholarship, I focus here on four core factors. *Polarization* captures the extent to which parties take distinct stances and should clarify and thus increase the political significance of left-right terms. The *Effective Number of Parties*, in the Latin American case, provides a proxy for system flux (Zechmeister and Corral 2013); greater fragmentation should be associated with less clarity and less political relevance to the left-right semantics. *Programmaticness* should increase the political significance of left-right identifications, while higher levels of *Clientelism* (by diminishing the substantive nature of party competition) should do the reverse.[19]

To assess the relevance of these contextual factors for voters in Latin America, I ran a series of multilevel regression analyses with cross-level interactions. In each case, I predict left-right vote choice with the same individual-level variables reported in figure 8.2. The contextual variables are entered as second-level variables; given degrees of freedom issues associated with a dataset containing only eighteen countries, I assess the second-level variables separately, in a series of four analyses.[20] The results reveal that *Polarization* and *Programmaticness* are associated with a stronger connection between left-right and the vote, while *Fragmentation* and *Clientelism* are associated with a weaker connection. In short, the nature of both the party system and elite competition matters.

Based on the regression analyses, figure 8.3 depicts the significant moderating effect of each of the contextual variables on the extent to which left-right identifications predict the vote choice.[21] In figure 8.3A, we see that there is no significant effect of left-right identities on voter choice at very low levels of polarization; as countries become more polarized, the

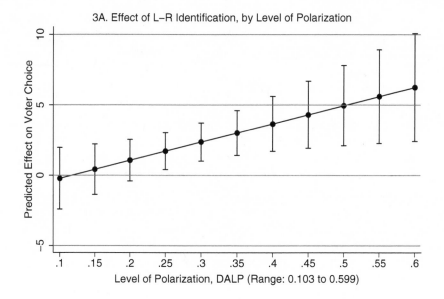

3A. Effect of L–R Identification, by Level of Polarization

Predicted Effect on Voter Choice

Level of Polarization, DALP (Range: 0.103 to 0.599)

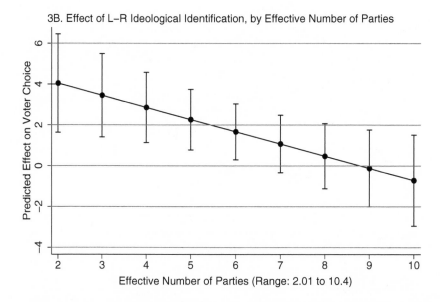

3B. Effect of L–R Ideological Identification, by Effective Number of Parties

Predicted Effect on Voter Choice

Effective Number of Parties (Range: 2.01 to 10.4)

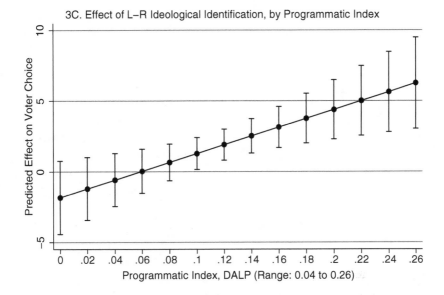

3C. Effect of L–R Ideological Identification, by Programmatic Index

Programmatic Index, DALP (Range: 0.04 to 0.26)

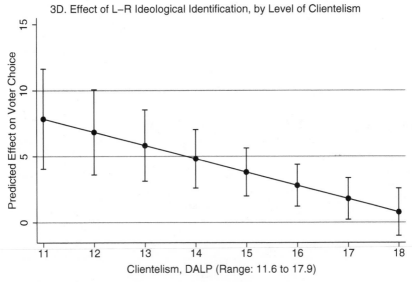

3D. Effect of L–R Ideological Identification, by Level of Clientelism

Clientelism, DALP (Range: 11.6 to 17.9)

Figure 8.3A–D   Predicted Associations between Left-right Identification and Voter Choice. *Source:* AmericasBarometer 2012 by LAPOP (v50)
and DALP. *Note:* Figures based on four separate hierarchical regression
analyses using individual level data from the 2012 AmericasBarometer
and contextual party system data; graphs show predicted average marginal
effects for left-right identifications on voter choice at varying levels on the
contextual (second-level) variables. See chapter appendix Table A8.2 for
regression output.

effect of left-right placement on the vote increases. This result comports with previous research on this contextual variable (e.g., Ames and Smith 2010; Dalton 2008, 2011; Inglehart and Klingemann 1976; Huber 1989; Singer forthcoming). The effect of polarization is estimated to become significant just past the value of 0.20 on the polarization measure. In Latin America, five countries score at or below 0.21: Argentina, the Dominican Republic, Honduras, Panama, and Venezuela. Venezuela is an exception here, as it registers low polarization but a high connection between left-right placements on the vote; it could be that the contentious system is polarized in other ways that generate left-right relevance, or that other factors are shaping that connection.

In figure 8.3B, we see that left-right identifications are significant predictors of voter choice in systems that have low to moderate levels of fragmentation, but not in systems that are highly fragmented. This finding is consistent with previous work on fragmentation and left-right identifications in Latin America (Zechmeister and Corral 2013; Singer forthcoming). The evidence is thus quite strong that the relevance of a high number of parties for voter choice varies across regions. The specific estimates in the figure are driven by an outlier, Brazil, which has an effective number of parties at the high range of the scale, 10.4. Yet, if this case is removed, the interaction remains significant and negative, and in this case the prediction is that a significant relationship exists between left-right placements and the vote for those systems with approximately four or fewer parties. In Latin America, five systems have scores greater than 4.0 on this measure: Costa Rica, Guatemala, Colombia, Argentina, and, of course, Brazil.

In figure 8.3C, we see that left-right identifications have no relationship to voter choice in systems with very low levels of programmatic party structuration, but they do have a positive relationship in more structured systems. The graph estimates that the effect of left-right placements becomes significant at or above the 0.10 level of programmaticness. The same five countries that score in the lowest ranks on polarization also score low (in this case, below 0.10) on programmaticness: Argentina, the Dominican Republic, Honduras, Panama, and Venezuela. Figure 8.3D shows the inverse relationship for clientelism: systems characterized by very high levels of clientelistic effort are predicted to have no significant relationship between left-right identifications and the vote choice, and the association between these variables increases as clientelistic effort decreases. The graph predicts that the effect of left-right placements becomes significant around and below a score of 17. Venezuela and Argentina have scores that round to 17 on this measure, while Panama and the Dominican Republic have slightly higher scores.

Across a number of these analyses, Venezuela stands out as an exception: its low polarization, low programmaticness, and high clientelistic effort scores would predict a lower connection between left-right placements and the vote than we find in practice. One possible explanation for this is Venezuela's comparatively long history of democratic party politics, while another is that Hugo Chávez's Bolivarian revolution (and related politics and rhetoric) infused left-right significance into the system. While identifying which of these explanations is more apt is outside the scope of this chapter, we can assess the general question of whether leftist populist leaders who came into power at the turn of the twenty-first century triggered and/or reflect a left-right ideological shift. The following section turns to that question.

Assessing the Potential Influence of Latin America's Pink Tide

The above section focused on a set of factors found across party systems around the globe. In this last empirical section, I assess the potential relevance of Latin America's pink tide to the political significance of left-right identities in contemporary Latin America. Latin America's "left turn" began in the late 1990s with the election of Hugo Chávez in Venezuela and continued with the subsequent election of left-leaning politicians across many Latin American countries. Given that the nature of party competition matters (as identified in the previous section), then the pink tide may have influenced the political significance of the terms "left" and "right" in the region. Yet, extant scholarship offers two contrasting views of the pink tide and, thus, two different expectations regarding whether it would have influenced left-right identifications.

On the one hand, some scholars have attributed the left's electoral success to standard retrospective accountability voting, suggesting voters tossed out right-leaning incumbents due to performance dissatisfaction rather than ideological conversion (Arnold and Samuels 2011; Levitsky and Roberts 2011a; Queirolo 2013; but see Baker and Greene 2011), and have found little evidence of ideological coherence among this new left (Harbers, de Vries, and Steenbergen 2013; Wiesehomeier and Doyle 2012). On the other hand, the pink tide brought legitimacy to economic programs defined for the mass public as belonging to the "left." Take, for example, a speech by Ecuadoran President Rafael Correa in the fall of 2011 in which he distinguished between the previous economic regime that he stated revolved around capitalism and neoliberalism to the detriment of workers and his new "gobierno de *izquierda* del socialismo" (my emphasis), which he argued has improved the quality of life for the working class.[22] Thus, while many of these victories might *initially* have been due to performance voting, it is conceivable that the consolidation of the left, its programs, and the rhetorical links offered by politicians have pushed the public toward the left and strengthened ideological structuration in at least some countries.

To assess the potential impact of the pink tide on the political relevance of left-right identifications across the Latin American region, I begin by returning to the question of the relationship between left-right identifications and the vote. I develop a new moderating variable, which distinguishes between countries with presidents located on the left and all others.[23] Replicating the models discussed in the previous section, but now with this second-level variable, I find no significant effect for its interaction with left-right identifications ($p = 0.610$). This suggests that the pink tide did not leave an imprint on Latin America with respect to the connection between left-right identifications and voter choice.

But is there any other evidence of an impact of the pink tide on left-right identities in these countries? One way to answer this is to assess left-right identifications across time within a subset of the pink tide countries. To do so, I narrow the focus to the cases of Bolivia and Ecuador. These countries are selected because the AmericasBarometer/LAPOP offers a comparatively long time series, in the middle of which the two current leftist executives were elected.

In Bolivia, President Evo Morales's victory in 2005 came on the shoulders of a broad social movement, the Movimiento al Socialismo (MAS), and a rhetorically charged campaign that emphasized economic equality and opposition to free-market policies (Levitsky and Roberts 2011a; Madrid 2011a). The election was preceded by years of increasingly visible and sometimes volatile expressions of disenchantment with the neoliberal model and traditional political parties and platforms in the country (Madrid 2011). In practice, the economic policies pursued by Morales's administration have been fairly moderate, but nonetheless left-leaning in nature especially with respect to increased state control over resources and increased spending (Madrid 2011).

In Ecuador, President Correa's election in 2006 was fueled by a deteriorated party system and his charismatic appeal. He has pursued a populist leadership style, working around and removing barriers presented by traditional institutions, including some elements of the traditional Ecuadoran left (Conaghan 2011). While not built on the basis of a traditional and deeply rooted left social movement, Correa's campaign and administration have emphasized increasing state spending and programs and often fiery confrontations with big business (Conaghan 2011).

LAPOP surveyed Bolivia every two years from 1998 to 2012, and Ecuador in 2001 and then every two years from 2004 to 2012. To examine whether mean placements on the left-right scale shifted either before or after the elections of Morales and Correa, I first calculated mean left-right placements over time in the two countries. Interestingly, there is very little change in the mean left-right placement among the mass public prior to or after the elections of Morales and Correa.[24] I then examined the percentage of individuals who place on the left in each country across time.[25] In this case, there does appear to be a slight upward trend in the percentage of individuals who place on the left in Ecuador following the election of Correa, but this increase appears starker than it might otherwise appear due to a slight drop in percentage of left identifiers in the year of his election. Conversely, there is no similar trend in Bolivia and, if anything, the percentage of Bolivians placing on the left has decreased in recent years. These results may reflect the nature of the two different left administrations and their paths to power: in Bolivia, the percentage of individuals placing themselves on the left was comparatively greater prior to the election of Morales, perhaps reflecting the presence of the broad left-leaning coalition that supported his victory; in Ecuador, Correa's election was not preceded by, but may have elicited, a small increase in identification with the left among the mass public. Generally speaking, the lack of a strong left surge prior to or after the inauguration of these leaders brings to mind Došek's (2011, 13) statement that "leftist elites are more radicalized than citizens" in these countries.

There are, of course, other ways that one might search for an impact of the pink tide on ideological structuration in Latin America.[26] Yet, the evidence here comports with the perspective that concludes that the pink tide swept across Latin America not because of a wholesale conversion to leftist programs among the mass public but more out of a willingness by the public to support populist leaders who ran counter to poorly performing right-leaning incumbents. In both cross-national and cross-temporal analyses presented here, there is *no evidence that the pink tide significantly altered the nature and political relevance of left-right leanings in Latin America.*[27]

Conclusion

While in theory left-right identifications are effective tools for citizens, a healthy dose of skepticism with respect to the heuristic value of the left-right semantics is warranted when considering the Latin American voter. That said, and in keeping with a core theme in this volume, the portrait offered within this chapter is one of significant variation across countries. High levels of left-right political significance are found in some countries, while in many other cases there is scant to no evidence of substantively meaningful and politically relevant left-right ideological identifications among the mass public.

In conclusion, I emphasize three points. First, in considering placement on the left-right scale in Latin America, it is important to note that while most are willing to express a left-right identification, many do not. Among other factors, nonresponse to the left-right scale is associated with measures of disassociation and dissatisfaction: political disinterest and perceived lack of system responsiveness. This finding is particularly relevant to the Latin American context, where it helps to explain some cases in which we find comparatively long histories of democratic party competition combined with low levels of response to the left-right question (e.g., Chile and Costa Rica). Looking forward, this discussion and finding suggests that others should pay more attention to factors that might motivate individuals to selectively withdraw from identifying on the left-right dimension.

Second, while on average there is some connection between policy stances and left-right identifications in Latin America, this connection is weak in a number of cases and not even discernable in others. For many citizens in Latin America, this suggests that the heuristic value of the left-right semantics for providing policy-rich cues is limited. For scholars, it means that much caution needs to be applied when interpreting the meaning of left-right identities in Latin America.

Third, on average there is a connection between left-right identifications and the vote in Latin America but, once again, this connection is quite weak in a number of countries. When taken together with the evidence of low core issue content to the left-right semantics in a number of countries, we can identify two Latin American countries in which left-right identifications have exceptionally little political significance: Brazil and Ecuador. Likewise, there are a number of countries in which the public makes some connection between policy and left-right stances but does not relate their left-right identifications to their vote choice: Costa Rica, Panama, and Argentina. Conversely, at the other extreme is a case in which the analyses here yielded no evidence of robust left-right policy content, and yet a very high connection to the vote: El Salvador.

There also are a handful of Latin American systems in which left-right identifications are rich in policy content and very relevant to voter choice: Chile, Uruguay, and Venezuela. In these cases, citizens have the ability to use left-right markers as guides to candidates' and parties' policy stances and they make use of these in determining their vote choice. This makes Chile a particularly interesting case, as it is a system in which left-right semantics are robust heuristics for voter choice and, yet, many individuals select not to place themselves on the left-right scale. As I have argued here, high levels of nonresponse to the left-right question in this country likely reflect a deliberative decision to withdraw from engaging in the formal political system, which is a tendency that has also been manifest in recent years in public unrest and, as well, declining levels of partisanship.[28]

Another important conclusion from this chapter is that the vote relevance of the left-right semantics varies in systematic ways according to the nature of Latin American party systems. Those that provide more clearly distinct options, those that are less fragmented, and those in which party competition is characterized by greater levels of programmatic structuration and lower levels of clientelism are those in which left-right identifications take on greater significance with respect to voter choice. It is both interesting and important to note that a number of these findings mirror those found by Baker and Greene (this volume) with respect to the contextual conditions that influence issue-based voting in Latin America.

Collectively, these findings affirm that countries in which parties and political elites give significant emphasis to issues within party competition dynamics and those systems that are more clearly structured are those with higher levels of ideological structuration. In those countries, the mass public is more likely to understand ideological semantics as referencing issues and more likely to connect left-right self-placements to their vote choice. While most of the analyses in this chapter focused on a single point of time, a fair inference from the analyses presented here is one that forecasts continued shifting over time in the political significance of left-right identifications. This shifting will continue as long as Latin American party systems continue to evolve and shift over time, though it is worth noting that the pace at which programmatic structuration is infused into political systems can be slower than ideal (Kitschelt et al. 2010; Singer forthcoming). Ultimately, only when political elites are ideologically driven in their strategies and, by extension, their lexicons, does the public have the potential to reflect and apply a robust and politically relevant left-right structuration.

Chapter 8 Appendix

TABLE A8.1   Individual Country Analyses of Policy Significance to the Left-Right Identifications (see Chapter Table 8.1)

	Mexico	Guatemala	El Salvador	Honduras	Nicaragua	Costa Rica
	Coefficient (std. err.)	Coefficient (std. err.)	Coefficient (std. err.)	Coefficient (std. err.)	Coefficient (std. err.)	Coefficient (std. err.)
Gov't Ownership	−0.042 (0.343)	−0.573 (0.571)	−0.548 (0.379)	1.120 (0.410)	−0.144 (0.330)	−0.745 (0.304)
Welfare	−1.302 (0.637)	0.796 (0.723)	−0.947 (0.791)	1.041 (0.566)	−1.224 (0.923)	0.668 (0.541)
Democracy is Best	1.897 (0.428)	0.755 (0.716)	−0.736 (0.547)	1.576 (0.523)	−0.371 (0.530)	0.663 (0.385)
Dem. is Preferred	0.616 (0.340)	−0.158 (0.477)	−0.312 (0.353)	1.403 (0.452)	−0.439 (0.548)	−0.641 (0.483)
Tough on Crime	0.406 (0.425)	−0.527 (0.524)	0.333 (0.504)	0.290 (0.408)	0.130 (0.514)	0.210 (0.418)
Religion is Imp.	0.532 (0.406)	1.119 (0.630)	0.867 (0.659)	−0.293 (0.487)	0.167 (0.674)	0.826 (0.319)
Trust U.S.	0.344 (0.356)	−0.435 (0.485)	0.352 (0.489)	−0.587 (0.478)	2.047 (0.542)	1.085 (0.422)
Constant	4.133 (0.699)	3.810 (0.855)	6.363 (0.789)	2.516 (0.650)	5.736 (1.216)	4.341 (0.749)
N	557	337	478	423	534	368
R^2	0.06	0.03	0.02	0.16	0.05	0.06

	Panama	Colombia	Ecuador	Bolivia	Peru	Paraguay
	Coefficient (std. err.)	Coefficient (std. err.)	Coefficient (std. err.)	Coefficient (std. err.)	Coefficient (std. err.)	Coefficient (std. err.)
Gov't Ownership	0.486 (0.364)	−0.328 (0.354)	−0.464 (0.302)	−0.419 (0.313)	−0.278 (0.267)	−0.284 (0.482)
Welfare	−0.881 (0.533)	1.020 (0.729)	−0.434 (0.613)	−0.104 (0.481)	−0.792 (0.421)	−1.253 (0.716)
Democracy is Best	2.806 (0.489)	0.677 (0.466)	−0.383 (0.451)	0.629 (0.428)	0.626 (0.362)	0.733 (0.511)
Dem. is Preferred	0.391 (0.352)	−0.188 (0.371)	0.116 (0.352)	−0.423 (0.286)	0.173 (0.269)	−0.048 (0.388)
Tough on Crime	−0.134 (0.389)	0.525 (0.440)	0.046 (0.538)	0.332 (0.358)	0.372 (0.420)	0.759 (0.659)
Religion is Imp.	0.229 (0.468)	0.950 (0.397)	0.611 (0.441)	0.311 (0.339)	−0.661 (0.318)	0.395 (0.602)
Trust U.S.	0.666 (0.397)	0.382 (0.457)	0.458 (0.407)	1.409 (0.346)	0.245 (0.302)	1.345 (0.519)

	Panama	Colombia	Ecuador	Bolivia	Peru	Paraguay
	Coefficient (std. err.)	Coefficient (std. err.)	Coefficient (std. err.)	Coefficient (std. err.)	Coefficient (std. err.)	Coefficient (std. err.)
N	517	442	434	791	505	365
R^2	0.12	0.03	0.02	0.06	0.03	0.04
	Chile	Uruguay	Brazil	Venezuela	Argentina	Dominican Republic
	Coefficient (std. err.)	Coefficient (std. err.)	Coefficient (std. err.)	Coefficient (std. err.)	Coefficient (std. err.)	Coefficient (std. err.)
Gov't Ownership	**−1.245** (0.482)	**−1.044** (0.325)	0.170 (0.433)	**−2.364** (0.386)	−0.009 (0.239)	0.140 (0.428)
Welfare	−1.265 (0.832)	−0.567 (0.604)	0.029 (0.709)	−0.256 (0.698)	**−1.559** (0.657)	1.305 (0.977)
Democracy is Best	0.569 (0.536)	−0.306 (0.502)	0.832 (0.516)	−0.066 (0.583)	0.394 (0.340)	**1.621** (0.531)
Dem. is Preferred	−0.406 (0.459)	−0.617 (0.449)	0.479 (0.349)	−0.974 (0.732)	−0.028 (0.321)	0.377 (0.346)
Tough on Crime	0.135 (0.528)	**1.075** (0.333)	0.642 (0.636)	0.032 (0.470)	**1.281** (0.270)	**1.380** (0.463)
Religion is Imp.	0.163 (0.422)	**0.896** (0.325)	0.396 (0.402)	**0.717** (0.433)	**1.033** (0.253)	0.589 (0.620)
Trust U.S.	**2.253** (0.423)	**1.070** (0.441)	0.275 (0.448)	**1.476** (0.423)	**0.713** (0.324)	0.221 (0.651)
Constant	**5.593** (0.773)	**4.924** (0.699)	**3.457** (0.897)	**6.295** (1.035)	**4.676** (0.589)	**1.473** (1.176)
N	433	408	440	453	434	514
R^2	0.14	0.15	0.02	0.14	0.12	0.05

Note: Output is based on OLS regression analyses for each country. See supplemental file for replication code. Dependent variable is placement on the left-right scale (0–10). Independent variables are scaled 0 to 1. Coefficients in **bold** are significant at $p \leq 0.10$, two-tailed.

Question wordings for above issue variables (from the AmericasBarometer 2012):

Gov't Ownership

Now I am going to read some items about the role of the national government. Please tell me to what extent you agree or disagree with the following statements. We will continue using the same ladder from 1 to 7.

ROS1. The (Country) government, instead of the private sector, should own the most important enterprises and industries of the country. How much do you agree or disagree with this statement?

Welfare (factor)

ROS2. The (Country) government, more than individuals, should be primarily responsible for ensuring the well-being of the people. To what extent do you agree or disagree with this statement?
ROS3. The (Country) government, more than the private sector, should be primarily responsible for creating jobs. To what extent to do you agree or disagree with this statement?
ROS4. The (Country) government should implement strong policies to reduce income inequality between the rich and the poor. To what extent do you agree or disagree with this statement?
ROS6. The (Country) government, more than the private sector, should be primarily responsible for providing health care services. How much do you agree or disagree with this statement?

Democracy is Best

ING4. Changing the subject again, democracy may have problems, but it is better than any other form of government. To what extent do you agree or disagree with this statement? 7-point agree/disagree scale

Democracy is Preferred

DEM2. Now changing the subject, which of the following statements do you agree with the most:

(1) For people like me it doesn't matter whether a government is democratic or non-democratic, or
(2) Democracy is preferable to any other form of government, or
(3) Under some circumstances an authoritarian government may be preferable to a democratic one.

Tough on Crime

I am going to read you some things you hear on the street or in the media when people talk about ways to combat crime. Please tell me if you strongly agree, agree somewhat, somewhat disagree, or strongly disagree with each one of them. The best way to fight crime ... VIC102. The best way to fight crime is to be tougher on criminals

Religion is Important

Q5B. Please, could you tell me how important is religion in your life? [Read options]

(1) Very important (2) Rather important (3) Not very important (4) Not at all important

Trust U.S.

MIL10E. United States. In your opinion, is it very trustworthy, somewhat trustworthy, not very trustworthy, or not at all trustworthy, or do you not have an opinion?

TABLE A8.2   Hierarchical Analyses Predicting Voter Choice (Chapter Figure 8.3A–D)

Contextual Variable	Polarization		Effective Number of Parties		Programmatic Index		Clientelism	
	Coefficient	Standard Error	Coefficient	Standard Error	Coefficient	Standard Error	Coefficient	Standard Error
Constant	13.015*	(2.423)	8.824*	(1.825)	13.488*	(2.089)	-0.941	(5.217)
Female	0.263	(0.168)	0.270	(0.172)	0.257	(0.167)	0.266	(0.173)
Age	0.030	(0.261)	0.028	(0.263)	0.016	(0.251)	-0.032	(0.235)
Rural	-0.097	(0.121)	-0.122	(0.122)	-0.090	(0.122)	-0.114	(0.122)
Wealth	0.423*	(0.178)	0.443*	(0.185)	0.429*	(0.178)	0.440*	(0.182)
Education	0.077	(0.250)	0.008	(0.237)	0.067	(0.249)	0.029	(0.250)
Political Interest	-0.695*	(0.161)	-0.716*	(0.170)	-0.647*	(0.164)	-0.632*	(0.151)
Efficacy	-0.375	(0.358)	-0.299	(0.326)	-0.317	(0.348)	-0.270	(0.337)
LR Non-response	0.024	(0.110)	0.012	(0.103)	0.023	(0.113)	0.021	(0.113)
Left-Right (LR)	-1.509	(1.594)	5.239*	(1.649)	-1.833	(1.325)	18.941*	(5.351)
Contextual Variable	-9.550	(6.423)	0.213	(0.338)	-24.309*	(12.899)	0.671*	(0.338)
LR*Contextual Var.	12.922*	(5.483)	-0.595*	(0.239)	31.123*	(10.581)	-1.009*	(0.320)
Number of Obs.	14,553		14,753		14,753		14,753	
Prob>chi2	0.000		0.000		0.000		0.000	
Random Effects: Country (sd_cons)	3.39*	(0.339)	3.43*	(0.378)	3.371*	(0.356)	3.426*	(0.363)
sd(Residual)	3.517*	(0.383)	3.541*	(0.400)	3.501*	(0.386)	3.521*	(0.407)

Note: $*p < 0.05$, two-tailed. Hierarchical linear regression. Dependent variable is left-right voter choice. Sampling weights were specified at the first level in the multilevel model. Standard errors adjusted for 18 clusters in country (2nd level).

NOTES

1. Another possibility, outside the scope of this chapter, is that the terms are affectively charged political symbols, whether connected or not to particular political groups (see Jacoby 2002).

2. Paradoxically, while low levels of interest make left-right markers and other heuristic aids theoretically even more valuable, it is those who are more interested in and more knowledgeable about politics who are more likely to make use of such shortcuts (Sniderman, Brody, and Tetlock 1991; Lau and Redlawsk 2001).

3. There is pervasive variation in use of and affect toward the terms "left" and "right" across the Latin American region. For instance, referencing Brazil, Power (2000, 94) writes that "left and right tend to be shunned by politicians, though left is still far more desirable than anything right of center." In contrast to that last point, among the Mexican public, there has been greater affect for the term "right" than the term "left" (Zechmeister 2006a).

4. The question was worded as follows: "Now, to change the subject . . . On this card there is a 1–10 scale that goes from left to right. The number one means left and 10 means right. Nowadays, when we speak of political leanings, we talk of those on the left and those on the right. In other words, some people sympathize more with the left and others with the right. According to the meaning that the terms 'left' and 'right' have for you, and thinking of your own political leanings, where would you place yourself on this scale?"

5. Analyses are adjusted for the complex sample designs employed in the AmericasBarometer studies. Replication code for analyses in this chapter is available in the online appendix.

6. The mean left-right response for the region as a whole (among those who answered the question) is 5.5, with 18.1% identifying on the left (placements of 1, 2, or 3) and 20.2% identifying on the right (placements of 8, 9, or 10).

7. Countries are considered units of analysis and therefore weighted equally in the calculation of regional nonresponse levels.

8. The nonresponse rates in some Latin American countries are similar to those found in the United States via the American National Election Study (ANES), which has asked about liberal-conservative self-placements since 1972, *but* which allows an explicit "haven't thought much about it" option. Nonresponse averaged 28.1% between the years 1972 and 2004, per the ANES 1948–2004 cumulative file and the online data analysis portal available at http://www.electionstudies.org /studypages/download/online_analysis.htm.

9. In addition to significant variation across countries, there is some important change across time in nonresponse rates. Three countries experienced changes of more than 10 percentage points between 2010 and 2012. Honduras displays a significantly higher rate of nonresponse in 2012 (23.4%, as shown in figure 8.1) compared to 2010 (when it was 10.9%). Panama and Nicaragua show far less nonresponse in 2012 (9.4% and 12.3%, respectively) than they did in 2010 (21.5% and 22.7%, respectively).

10. Wealth is a measure based on factor-analyzing responses to a battery of household item ownership questions; for more information on its construction, see Córdova (2009). Education is years of education; age cohort is a linear measure in

which voting-age respondents are grouped as follows: 25 or under; 26–35; 36–45; 56–65; 66 or older.

11. The complete table of results, with country fixed effects, is available from the author and in the online appendix as table OA8.1.

12. Upon closer examination, some evidence of a curvilinear relationship can be found between age cohorts and left-right nonresponse, such that those who are in the youngest cohort (25 and under) and those in the older cohorts (56 and above) are marginally more likely to decline to answer the question compared to those in the middle cohorts. This is interesting in part because it parallels findings for age reported by Carlin and Love (this volume).

13. Analysis accounts for the complex sample design and weights each country to an equal number of respondents. Predicted probabilities calculated using *Clarify* (http://gking.harvard.edu/clarify). In separate analyses, I ran the basic regression model for each country separately. For every country, the signs on the coefficients for political interest and external efficacy are negative; however, at $p < 0.10$, two-tailed, the coefficients for political interest are not significant in the case of Panama and Costa Rica and the coefficients for external efficacy are not significant in the Dominican Republic, Uruguay, and Peru.

14. These models should be taken as conservative. By not including issues that are idiosyncratic to particular country contexts, for example, the civil conflict and peace process in Colombia, I may underestimate the substantive significance of left-right semantics. I thank Sandra Botero, Rodrigo Castro, and the rest of the Public Opinion and Elections Working Group Workshop at Notre Dame University for their suggestion that I clarify this point.

15. The positive coefficients on the economic measures for Honduras hold even in a reduced model in which the *Gov't Ownership* measure and the *Welfare* measure, respectively, predict left-right identification, and are similar to a finding reported in Zechmeister and Corral (2011).

16. The result for El Salvador is intriguing given that it may represent a substantial decrease in the policy content of left-right semantics in that country (see Zechmeister and Corral 2011).

17. The results are consistent across models without controls, with the exception that the left-right variable becomes significant in the case of Panama. To avoid list-wise deletion of those who do not respond to the left-right question, I place these individuals at the mid-point of the left-right scale, and then include a dummy variable (dichotomous measure coded 1 if the response was missing and zero otherwise) to account for their presence in the model.

18. Assessment of significance using a generous cut-off level of $p \leq 0.10$, two-tailed. Among those identified for statistical significance, Peru falls closest to this threshold at $p = 0.074$.

19. Each of these measures is described in the introduction of this volume. *Polarization, Programmaticness,* and *Clientelism* are based on data from the Democratic Accountability and Linkages Project (DALP) survey (see introduction, this volume). The result presented here for *Polarization* is consistent if an alternative measure, based on party polarization in Congress, is used (see Singer forthcoming and the introduction of this volume). Likewise, the results for *Clientelism* are consistent with those based on a measure based on the 2010 AmericasBarometer

(percentage of respondents indicating they were offered a material incentive in a recent election; see Kitschelt and Altamirano this volume).

20. As with prior analyses, countries are weighted to an equal number of observations. To capture the hierarchical nature of the data, I use the xtmixed command in Stata. Replication code is available from the author and book editors. If the contextual variables are all included in the same model, the signs on the coefficient stay the same, but the standard errors increase; the effect for programmaticness becomes null because it is so highly correlated with polarization measure (which is a subcomponent of the programmaticness index).

21. Figure 8.3A–D presents the average predicted marginal effects of left-right self-identification at varying levels on the contextual factors; the output is based on margins analysis conducted in Stata 12.0.

22. www.diarioopinion.com/nacional/verArticulo.php?id=812772. Last accessed July 16, 2013.

23. Coded as "left" governments (pink tide countries) are Argentina, Bolivia, Brazil, Costa Rica, Ecuador, El Salvador, Nicaragua, Paraguay, Peru, Uruguay, and Venezuela.

24. Mean values for Bolivia across the years are as follows: 1998: 5.34; 2000: 5.36; 2002: 5.43; 2004: 5.07; 2006: 5.23; 2008: 5.17; 2010: 5.23; 2012: 5.17. Thus, we do see a very slight shift toward the left prior to the election of Correa, but that value inches back toward the center in the subsequent years. In Ecuador mean values are as follows: 2001: 5.46; 2004: 5.35; 2006: 5.78; 2008: 5.37; 2010: 5.43; 2012: 5.33. Thus, in the case of Ecuador, there is a slight tick toward the right in the year that Correa was elected.

25. Bolivia (year: percent placing on the "left," meaning 1, 2, or 3 on the 1–10 scale): 1998: 14.2; 2000: 14.8; 2002: 17.5; 2004: 15.8; 2006: 15.8; 2008: 16.2; 2010: 13.4; 2012: 13.7. Ecuador: 2001: 12.5; 2004: 13.0; 2006: 9.8; 2008: 14.9; 2010: 13.3; 2012: 17.3. There is no clear pattern to nonresponse rates across time in either case except that, if anything, nonresponse has increased over time in Bolivia.

26. Considering the policy significance of left-right identifications, I find no evidence of a cross-temporal increase in the policy significance of left-right identifications in these two countries (see replication code, available from author, for more on these analyses). When looked at for the region as a whole, I also see no clear influence of the pink tide on the policy significance of the left-right semantics (consider the lack of any pattern to the r-squared values reported in table 8.1 and left-incumbency).

27. Many of these left leaders are part of a modern wave of populism. Kitschelt and Altamirano (this volume) find that left-populism is a strong predictor of clientelistic ineffectiveness; it is possible to conclude, then, that Latin America's left-populist victories and administrations have done little to advance elite-mass linkages: on average they fail to inject left-right ideological structuration and, as well, they unsettle clientelistic relations.

28. For more on party-voter links in Chile, see Luna (2014).

9 ✦ Partisanship in Latin America

NOAM LUPU

In advanced democracies, citizens' attachments to a party strongly influence their political behavior. Party attachments often determine not only how people vote, but also how they evaluate their government (Bartels 2000; Campbell et al. 1960; Green, Palmquist, and Schickler 2005). These attachments develop over time, passed down from parents to children and adapted or reinforced over the course of an individual's voting life (Achen 1992; Converse 1969; Jennings, Stoker, and Bowers 2009). Although scholars debate their exact nature and origins, party attachments clearly play an important political role in advanced democracies.

We know far less about mass partisanship in developing democracies. That is partly because many developing democracies only began (or returned to) holding competitive elections in the 1980s and 1990s.[1] For decades, the developing world had been governed by autocrats, obviating scholarly questions about electoral politics and mass political behavior. Even if scholars had wanted to study individual citizens, reliable survey data were rarely available for these contexts.

Once democracies (re-)emerged in these settings, some dismissed the possibility that citizens would develop party attachments (Kinzo 2005; Mainwaring 1999; Widner 1997). They argued that newly available mass media would allow politicians to appeal directly to citizens instead of investing in party-building (Levitsky and Cameron 2003; Hale 2006; Mainwaring and Zoco 2007; Mainwaring and Torcal 2006). Others considered party attachments irrelevant in settings characterized by rampant electoral fraud, ephemeral party organizations, and clientelism (Hagopian 1998; Roberts and Wibbels 1999). As Mainwaring and Torcal (2006, 204) argue, "outside the advanced democracies, more voters choose candidates on the basis of their personal characteristics without regard to party, ideology, or programmatic issues."

Yet there are reasons to expect that mass partisanship in the developing world functions much like it does in advanced democracies. When voters in developing democracies decide which party to vote for, they do so in ways that closely resemble how voters in advanced democracies choose a party (van der Brug, Franklin, and Tóka 2008). There is no clear reason to assume that other behavioral processes operate differently in developing democracies. Moreover, free and fair elections have now been held in many developing democracies for nearly three decades. In many Latin American democracies, political parties that had contested elections during prior periods of democracy returned to political prominence. It seems unlikely that deeply held party attachments from previous democratic periods would simply disappear when electoral competition is interrupted (Lupu and Stokes 2010). In some cases, new political parties have emerged and established themselves over time. But even they often built upon existing political identities that were already politically salient (e.g., Shabad and Slomczynski 1999; Valenzuela and Scully 1997; Wittenberg 2006).

Electoral competition in many developing democracies is imperfect; patronage and clientelism characterize some political linkages in these settings (see Kitschelt and Altamirano this volume). But, in considering the nature of partisan attachments, clientelism alone is unlikely the sole influence. Clientelism and partisanship often complement each other in the portfolio of party strategies; they need not serve as substitutes (Kitschelt and Wilkinson 2007b; Stokes et al. 2013). And if new political parties in advanced democracies can foster partisanship in the era of mass media (Ignazi 1996), why would new political parties in developing democracies be unable to do the same?

This is not merely a question of comparability. Mass partisanship institutionalizes party systems, stabilizes elections, and consolidates new democracies (Converse 1969; Mainwaring and Torcal 2006; Mainwaring and Scully 1995a; Rose and Mishler 1998). As it expands, the menu of parties stabilizes, ensuring that voters are presented with a recurring set of party options. This makes it easier to hold parties accountable for bad performance and reduces the electoral prospects of unknown outsiders. Stable party competition also makes campaign promises more credible, giving voters greater confidence in predicting what each party would do if elected. These are desirable outcomes for developing democracies;

knowing where mass partisanship comes from will help us understand how to achieve these outcomes.

How do we know whether partisanship in developing democracies resembles partisanship in advanced ones? There are at least three ways to address this question. We could examine whether levels of partisanship are the same across countries, although differences in the institutional and social context mean that we should not expect identical rates of partisanship across countries. An alternative would examine whether partisanship is equally stable across countries. Most comparative studies of partisanship—indeed, much of the debate over the concept—has fixated on this metric. But institutional differences may also account for these differences. Even if partisanship functions identically everywhere, it would be more unstable in unstable party environments (Lupu 2013, 2015). A final approach could examine whether the correlates of partisanship are consistent across countries. If the same kinds of individuals form party attachments in developing and advanced democracies, then the origins of partisanship are likely similar across contexts. And if partisanship predicts the same kinds of political behaviors across contexts, then it would appear to function similarly.

This chapter takes the latter approach and examines patterns of mass partisanship and its relationship with political behavior across Latin America. While scholars are increasingly examining the origins and effects of mass partisanship in some Latin American democracies (Baker et al. 2010; Domínguez and McCann 1995; Echegaray 2006; Lupu 2013; McCann and Lawson 2003; Medina Vidal et al. 2010; Moreno 2003; Morgan 2007; Pérez-Liñán 2002; Samuels 2006), we still know little about how these attachments develop in general across the region, and whether they do so in ways that mirror mass partisanship in advanced democracies. I rely on cross-national surveys to see whether, on average, Latin American mass partisanship correlates with the same individual characteristics that are associated with it in advanced democracies. I also examine whether Latin American partisans are more likely to participate in politics, like their counterparts in advanced democracies. To help determine whether these relationships are causal, I analyze panel survey data from Brazil. I find consistent evidence that patterns of partisanship in Latin America closely resemble those in advanced democracies.

Despite these similarities on average, rates of mass partisanship across Latin America vary tremendously. Studying mass partisanship in the region thus also allows us to test and refine comparative theories about how contextual factors condition individual preferences. Why do parties in some countries elicit more widespread partisan attachments than those in other countries? We still know little about how to explain variation in mass partisanship across countries and over time. By expanding our analysis to developing democracies, we will learn much more about the factors that condition mass partisanship.

Mass Partisanship and Political Behavior

The concept of partisanship has occupied scholars of political behavior for decades. Early theories viewed it as a citizen's enduring psychological attachment to a party, inherited like a religious affiliation and tending to persist for a lifetime (e.g., Campbell et al. 1960). A key insight of this conceptualization was the notion that partisanship is a type of social identity (Green, Palmquist, and Schickler 2005). Later authors offered a more rationalistic conceptualization in which citizens evaluate parties over time to form a "running tally" and choose the party most likely to benefit them (Achen 1992; Fiorina 1981). From this perspective, partisanship is not an identity but rather a rational product of citizens' calculations.

Both sets of theories yield similar general implications about the correlates of partisan attachments. The question for scholars of developing democracies is whether similar patterns of mass partisanship exist in these settings. If partisanship of the kind theorized in the advanced democracies also exists in the developing world, then the empirical relationships we uncover in developing democracies should be similar to those extensively documented in advanced democracies.

Among the first of these relationships to be documented is that between partisanship and democratic experience. Partisan attachments solidify either as citizens repeatedly vote for a particular party, as they gain political experience and exposure, or as they update and strengthen their evaluations of parties (e.g., Achen 1992; Dinas 2014; Fiorina 1981). The general implication is that partisanship increases with age (Brader, Tucker, and Bargsted 2013; Cassel 1993; Converse 1969, 1976; Dalton and Weldon 2007). Yet we might not expect a relationship between age and partisanship during the first years of a new democracy. If parties emerge with no prior history, then citizens have no existing experience with them. In Latin America, though, many political parties existed prior to the most recent transitions to democracy. In fact, many had competed in prior periods of democracy (Lupu and Stokes 2010), so citizens may have preexisting attachments to them. Moreover, after nearly three decades of elections in the region, Latin American citizens have by now certainly had experience with their parties.

Ideological positions also influence party attachments in advanced democracies. Citizens tend to identify with the party most ideologically proximate to them (Richardson 1991). However, those on the extremes of the ideological spectrum tend to feel stronger affinities to their parties (De la Calle and Roussias 2012; Pierce 1970). While ideological proximity matters in general for generating party attachments, extremists seem to feel more strongly about their party than centrists.

Partisans in advanced democracies also tend to be more informed and more engaged than nonpartisans. Although early scholars conceived of partisanship as a shortcut that would only be useful for those with limited information about politics (e.g., Shively 1979), empirical studies have consistently found that it is the most informed who are more likely to identify with a party (e.g., Achen 1992; Albright 2009). At least in advanced democracies, it seems that citizens who know something about politics also form meaningful party attachments.[2]

These attachments are also more likely among citizens already engaged in civic life. Membership in voluntary organizations often develops social capital, promoting citizens' interest in politics (Brady, Verba, and Schlozman 1995), and, thus, encourages the formation of party attachments (Norris 2002).[3]

Scholars of developing democracies are often skeptical that partisan attachments will spread in these settings. They argue that mass media now makes it easy for politicians to appeal directly to citizens (Hale 2006; Mainwaring and Scully 1995b; Mainwaring and Zoco 2007). As a result, politicians have little incentive to invest in party-building and parties become irrelevant to citizens. Scholars of advanced democracies offer similar arguments for the recent erosion of mass partisanship there (e.g., Ward 1993). Still others argue that reporting in mass media often denigrates parties and contributes to antiparty sentiment (e.g., Mainwaring 1999; Weyland 1998). Although these arguments are made in terms of aggregate trends, individuals within countries differ in their attention to mass media. If the skeptics are right that mass media weaken aggregate partisanship, we should see that people who pay a lot of attention to media are the least partisan (see also Pérez-Liñán 2002; Seligson 2002).

Partisanship varies not only across individuals; some comparative studies also note variation across countries and over time (e.g., Holmberg 1994; Huber, Kernell, and Leoni 2005; Lupu 2015; Schmitt 2009; Schmitt and Holmberg 1995).[4] These scholars suggest that certain social contexts and party system characteristics may affect a citizen's propensity to form an attachment to a party. Party fragmentation may reduce the likelihood of mass partisanship. Where citizens are asked to keep track of a large number of parties, they may learn little about any one party. Party fragmentation may also mean that governments form via large coalitions, making it difficult for citizens to associate policies or performance outcomes with a particular party.[5] In Latin America, party fragmentation may also be a marker of recent episodes of party instability or collapse (Zechmeister and Corral 2013), episodes often associated with eroding partisanship (Lupu forthcoming).

Other system-level factors may bolster partisanship. Social heterogeneity may push citizens to form stronger attachments to parties, to the extent that membership in ethnic, religious, or linguistic groups is politically salient. Citizens also learn about the parties in their system over time, as the same parties compete for office again and again (Tavits 2007b). As party systems institutionalize, citizens come to know enough about the parties to form more lasting attachments (Dalton and Weldon 2007; Mainwaring and Scully 1995b; Rose and Mishler 1998). Finally, party polarization may clarify the differences between parties. The farther apart the political parties, the easier it is for citizens to distinguish among the options. And if citizens can more clearly distinguish parties, they may find it easier to form a party attachment (Lupu 2015; see also Berglund et al. 2006; Holmberg 1994; Schmitt 2009; Schmitt and Holmberg 1995).[6]

In advanced democracies, these patterns of mass partisanship have important implications for political behavior. Partisans are particularly more likely to participate in politics, whether by voting for their party or by volunteering their time and resources to its campaigns (e.g., Bartels 2000; Campbell et al. 1960; Powell 1986).

Scholars of advanced democracies have documented and explained these patterns of mass partisanship over decades. But their arguments rarely stipulate that they be limited to these contexts. After all, all parties have an interest in cultivating a stable partisan base. If our theories about how citizens in advanced democracies form partisan attachments are right, we should find evidence for them among citizens of developing democracies as well. Still, we should not expect levels of mass partisanship to be the same everywhere. But comparative scholars should seek to explain differences across countries and over time by identifying the institutional and political factors that condition mass partisanship.

Patterns of Mass Partisanship across Latin America

To identify patterns of mass partisanship in Latin America, I employ data from sixty-six AmericasBarometer surveys conducted in 2006, 2008, 2010, and 2012 and covering the eighteen countries that are the focus of this volume. To measure Latin Americans' attachments to political parties I make use of the following question: "Do you currently identify with a political party?" There are well-known debates about the appropriate way to capture party attachment in public opinion surveys, and existing cross-national options are all imperfect (Johnston 2006). This item is one of few defensible options and one that is used widely in the region (e.g., Baker et al. 2010; Pérez-Liñán 2002; Samuels 2006).

I want to know whether partisanship in Latin America correlates with certain individual characteristics, namely, democratic experience, ideological extremism, proximity to a party, political information, and participation in civic associations. In advanced democracies, researchers often measure an individual's democratic experience using her age because most respondents will only have lived under a democratic regime. To see how this might be problematic in the developing world, consider a country that began holding democratic elections thirty years ago and the fact that a respondent who is 30 and another who is 50 will have lived the same amount of time under democracy. Age may still make individuals more partisan because parties may be active even when they cannot compete democratically for public office. But in developing democracies, we can distinguish a person's age from the amount of experience that individual has with democratic competition (see also Brader, Tucker, and Bargsted 2013; Tilley 2003). For each respondent in the AmericasBarometer surveys, I thus calculated the number of years she lived under democracy in addition to her age.[7]

The AmericasBarometer asked respondents to place themselves on a 10-point left-right scale.[8] This allows me to identify three characteristics for each respondent. Most directly, it provides a measure of her ideological leanings (but see Zechmeister this volume). I have no specific expectations about whether left- or right-leaning Latin Americans are more likely to be partisan, but it is possible that ideology could correlate with partisanship. I can also use the respondent's ideological identification to measure her ideological extremism. The farther a respondent places herself from the midpoint of the scale (5.5), the more extreme her ideology, and the more likely she should be to identify with a party. Finally, respondents' left-right self-placements help me determine their ideological proximity to a party. Within each survey, I calculate each party's position based on the average left-right placement of the respondents who said they voted for that party.[9] I then use these party placements to calculate how close each respondent is to a party. In advanced democracies, we expect respondents who are ideologically close to a party to be more likely to form an attachment.

If partisanship in Latin America follows the patterns of advanced democracies, then more informed individuals will be more likely to identify with a party. To measure how informed individuals are, I construct an index using three factual political questions asked in the AmericasBarometer survey.[10] My analysis also includes a measure of education, often a reasonable proxy for political knowledge (e.g., Delli Carpini and Keeter 1996; Highton 2009).[11] We would also expect individuals who are more engaged in civic life to be more likely to identify with a party. To measure participation in civic associations, I construct an index of four questions about the respondent's participation in different kinds of civil society organizations.[12]

Observers of both advanced and developing democracies argue that mass media has made parties less important to politics and eroded citizens' attachments to parties. If this account is right, then individuals who pay more attention to media should be less likely to form party attachments. To capture attention to mass media, I make use of AmericasBarometer questions that ask respondents how frequently they watch television, listen to the radio, or read newspapers.[13] As additional individual-level controls, I include measures of gender, self-identified ethnicity (whites versus nonwhites), urban versus rural residence, and household wealth.[14]

At the contextual level, I want to know whether certain characteristics of the party system and social context correlate with mass partisanship. Therefore, I include measures of party system polarization, institutionalization, and fragmentation, as well as ethnic fragmentation.

Following previous scholars (e.g., Dalton 2008), I measure polarization by summing how far each party is positioned on the left-right scale from the average party position.[15] In systems that are more polarized, parties should be farther away from this mean position, which we might call the system's ideological center of gravity. Where parties are instead clustered together, they will be close to this center. Party polarization thus measures how spread out the parties are in the system. I also account for each party's prominence in the system by weighting its contribution to the system's polarization by its vote share.[16]

Partisanship is likely more widespread when a party system is institutionalized and parties' reputations are widely known. Citizens need to observe party behavior in order to develop party attachments, which may be why older democracies tend to have more partisans (Dalton and Weldon 2007). To account for this possibility, my analysis includes the average age across the major parties for each country, a standard proxy for institutionalization (e.g., Roberts and Wibbels 1999). Because these ages take on very high values for some countries (e.g., Colombia, Uruguay), I use the natural log of this measure. Following Huber, Kernell, and Leoni (2005), I measure how fragmented each party system is electorally by calculating the effective number of parties using electoral vote shares from the presidential election closest to 2007. Finally, I measure social heterogeneity in terms of how fractionalized each society is along ethnic lines. Following Alesina et al. (2003), I measure ethnic fractionalization as the probability that two randomly selected individuals from the survey sample have the same ethnicity, based on their responses to the item on self-identified ethnicity.[17]

Evidence from Cross-National Survey Data

Scholars of Latin American politics have largely ignored mass partisanship, either because they considered it irrelevant to politics or because they did not expect Latin Americans to form strong attachments to their parties. The lack of attention is particularly surprising given how widespread and varied party attachments are in some countries in the region. Figure 9.1 plots the proportion of partisans in each Latin American country at each wave of the AmericasBarometer. As a base of comparison, the figure also includes that proportion for the United States, the case that has motivated decades of scholarship on mass partisanship.

What is striking about figure 9.1 is that three decades after the third wave of democratization began, millions of Latin Americans identify with political parties. In fact, aggregate levels of partisanship in some Latin American democracies rival those of the United States. Citizens in the Dominican Republic and Uruguay seem just as likely to identify with a political party as Americans. Clearly, some form of mass partisanship has emerged in Latin America.

Still, figure 9.1 shows enormous heterogeneity in levels of partisanship across Latin American countries and over time within some of them.[17] At one extreme, only 11% of Chileans identified with a political party in 2010, whereas more than 60% of Uruguayans did that year. This means that even if the underlying behavioral process of partisan identification is the same across developing and developed democracies, other factors seem to condition that process. Social heterogeneity and characteristics of the party system may help to explain these differences.

I turn to cross-national survey data from the AmericasBarometer to simultaneously examine the individual- and country-level correlates of mass partisanship in Latin America. Based on a series of multilevel probit analyses, figure 9.2 plots the estimated changes in the predicted probability of an individual survey respondent identifying with a party when we change the value of each variable from its 25th to its 75th percentile. In other words,

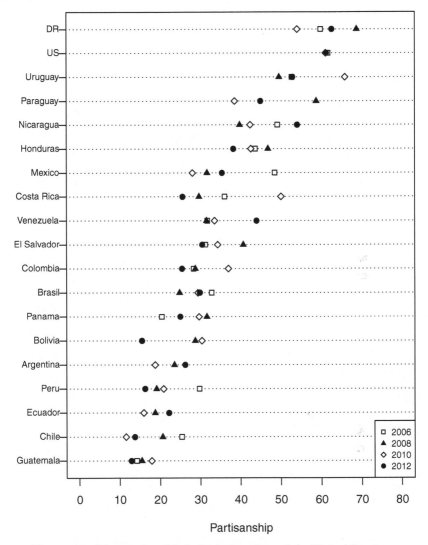

Figure 9.1   Mass partisanship in Latin America and the United States. *Source:* AmericasBarometer 2006–2012. *Note:* Values represent the proportion of respondents who said they identified with a political party in each year.

the figure tells us how much of an effect the inter-quartile range of each variable has on individuals' propensities to form a partisan attachment.[18]

The results in figure 9.2 reveal that patterns of mass partisanship in Latin America resemble those elsewhere in the world. Not only are older individuals more likely to be partisan, but democratic experience

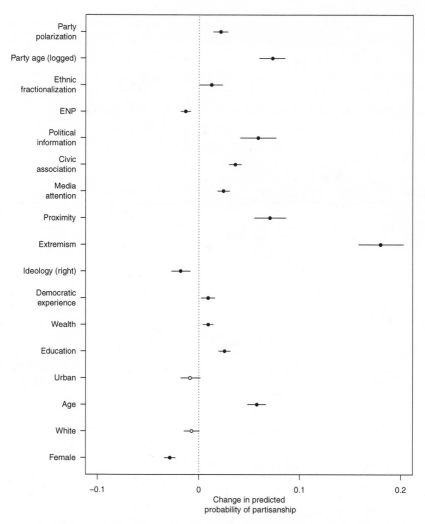

Figure 9.2 Correlates of mass partisanship in Latin America. *Source:*
AmericasBarometer, 2006–2012. *Notes:* Values represent changes in the
predicted probability that a respondent identifies with a party, based
on shifting each variable from its sample 25th to 75th percentile, with
all other continuous variables held at their sample means and ordered
variables held at their sample medians. Solid lines show the simulated
95% confidence interval. Black dots represent values that are significant at
95% confidence, white dots those that fall short of that threshold. These
predicted values are based on the estimates from multilevel probit models
presented in the online appendix to this volume. They represent total
effects, meaning the effects estimated when only causally prior variables
are included.

specifically increases citizens' propensities to form party attachments, as Converse (1969) predicted. As in advanced democracies, Latin American partisans also tend to be more informed and more educated. Those who are ideologically close to a party or hold particularly extreme ideological positions are also more likely to identify with a party. Interestingly, left-leaning Latin Americans are more likely to form party attachments, though this finding may be an artifact of timing: the AmericasBarometer surveys cover the peak of the region's "left turn" (see Levitsky and Roberts 2011b).

Latin American partisans, like their counterparts in advanced democracies, also tend to be more engaged in civic life. And contrary to the suggestion that mass media erodes partisanship or obstructs its development, Latin Americans who pay more attention to media are instead more likely to identify with a party. At the individual level, mass partisanship in Latin America on average follows patterns similar to those found in advanced democracies.[19]

Still, figure 9.1 showed differences in levels of partisanship across countries and over time. Social context and characteristics of the party system contribute to explaining these differences. Where party systems are fragmented, Latin Americans are less likely to form party attachments. On the other hand, ethnic heterogeneity, institutionalized party systems, and party polarization all increase citizens' attachments to parties. These systemic features condition mass partisanship largely in the same ways prior comparative studies of advanced democracies predict.[20]

Does Partisanship Matter?

Latin American partisans on average resemble partisans in advanced democracies. The kinds of systemic factors that condition mass partisanship in advanced democracies also appear to do so across Latin American democracies. But what about the effects of partisanship? Does identifying with a party have the effects on political behavior in Latin America that it has elsewhere?

The chapter on turnout in this volume has already shown the strong correlation between partisanship and reported turnout in the AmericasBarometer surveys (Carlin and Love this volume). I have also examined whether partisanship makes people more likely to work for a political campaign, which is an even more direct way for citizens to engage in the political process.[21] The online appendix for this volume (see figure OA9.1) presents a multilevel probit analysis with the same individual-level predictors as the previous analysis. The results show that Latin American

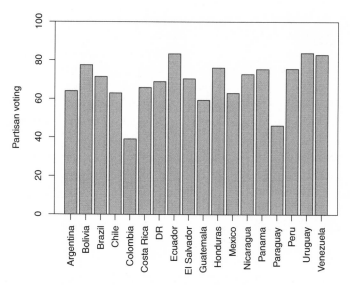

Figure 9.3   Mass partisanship and vote choice in Latin America. *Source:* AmericasBarometer 2006–2012. *Notes:* Bars represent the proportion of respondents who identified with a political party who voted for the candidate of their party in the most recent presidential election. Respondents who identified with a party that did not field a presidential candidate are omitted.

partisans, like their counterparts in advanced democracies, are much more likely to participate in campaigns than nonpartisans. Indeed, an individual's partisanship is among the strongest predictors of participation.

In advanced democracies, which party a citizen identifies with has a substantial effect on her vote choice (e.g., Berglund et al. 2006; Campbell et al. 1960; Richardson 1991). Is the same true in Latin America? For each country in the region, figure 9.3 reports the proportion of respondents identifying with a party who also said they voted for that party's candidate[22] in the AmericasBarometer survey closest to each presidential election.[23] Despite significant variation across the countries, the overall picture is clear: partisans tend to vote for their party. Across the countries and surveys, an average of 69% of partisans voted for their party when it competed. Since these are presidential systems, we would not expect the correspondence between partisanship and vote choice to be as high as in some European parliamentary systems. Even so, rates of partisan voting are remarkably high in Latin America. Like partisans in advanced democracies, Latin American partisans typically vote for their party.

Partisanship and Vote Choice in Brazil

But is this relationship causal? Is it their party attachment that leads partisans to support their party at the polls, or do they bring their party attachment in line with their vote choice? Studies of advanced democracies have found evidence of both effects (e.g., Bartels 2002; Carsey and Layman 2006; Groenendyk 2013). One way to address this problem and identify the causal relationship between partisanship and vote choice is through repeated interviews of the same survey respondents (Bartels 2006). Indeed, part of the definition of a cause is that it occurs prior to an outcome (Finkel 1995). Panel surveys necessarily imply focusing on a specific country and therefore limit generalizability. But we gain confidence in the causal interpretation of correlational analysis if we can better identify that causal relationship with panel survey data.

Fortunately, a team of scholars conducted a four-wave panel survey in two mid-sized Brazilian cities between 2002 and 2006 (see Baker, Ames, and Rennó 2006). The Brazilian party system is considered among the weakest in the region given highly candidate-centered electoral rules (e.g., Mainwaring 1999). Since party attachments are thought to be fairly weak in this context, my analysis presents a hard test of whether partisanship influences how Latin Americans behave.[24]

To analyze the causal effect of mass partisanship on vote intention, I specify a cross-lagged structural equation model frequently used by scholars of U.S. public opinion working with panel survey data (e.g., Highton and Kam 2011; Layman and Carsey 2002; Lupu 2015). This approach uses simultaneous equations to model current partisanship and current vote intention as functions of prior partisanship and prior vote intention. The logic behind cross-lagged causality is that a variable X is said to cause another variable Y if prior observations of X are associated with current observations of Y, holding constant prior observations of Y (Finkel 1995, 25–26). In this context, we want to know whether prior mass partisanship affects current vote intentions while taking account of preexisting vote intentions.[25]

In the Brazilian presidential elections of 2002 and 2006, two main parties—the Workers' Party (PT) and the Brazilian Social Democratic Party (PSDB)—put forward competitive candidates. I therefore analyze two models: one examines intention to vote for the PT and PT partisanship; and a second focuses on intention to vote for the PSDB and PSDB partisanship. The models control for several demographic characteristics: household income, education, ethnicity (whites versus nonwhites), age, and gender.[26] I also include a control variable for residence in cities covered by the survey with a dummy variable for one of the two, Juiz de Fora (by "dummy," we mean the variable is coded 1 if the respondent resides in Juiz de Fora and zero otherwise).[27]

The results reveal a consistent causal effect of partisanship on vote intentions. Figure 9.4 plots the predicted probability of a respondent

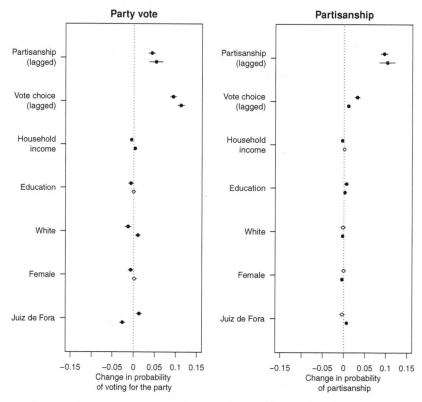

Figure 9.4   Mass partisanship and vote choice in Brazil. *Source:* Brazil Two-City Panel Study, 2002–2006. *Notes:* Values represent changes in the predicted probability that the respondent identifies with the party or intended to vote for a party, based on shifting each variable from its sample 25th to 75th percentile, with all other continuous variables held at their sample means and ordered variables held at their sample medians. Solid lines show the simulated 95% confidence interval. Black dots represent values that are significant at 95% confidence, white dots those that fall short of that threshold. For each variable, the top result refers to the PT and the bottom to the PSDB. These predicted values are based on the estimates from cross-lagged structural equation estimates presented in the online appendix (table OA9.2).

intending to vote for or identifying with the PT or PSDB as we shift each variable over its inter-quartile range.[28] The left panel in figure 9.4 shows that prior partisanship has a substantial causal effect on a respondent's intention to vote for both the PT and PSDB. There is also stability in vote intentions over time.

There is also some evidence of the reverse causation that motivated this analysis. The right panel in figure 9.4 shows that prior vote intentions do affect citizens' party attachments with the PT and PSDB. Prior partisanship, nevertheless, has the strongest effect on current partisanship, suggesting that there is stability in partisan attachments even in this weak party system (cf. Samuels 2006). These results suggest that the relationship between partisanship and vote choice that we observe across Latin America is not entirely endogenous. That is, there is reason to think that partisanship in the region has a causal effect on how citizens vote.

Mass Partisanship in Latin America

In advanced democracies, mass partisanship is both widespread and influential. Yet we know little about whether partisanship in developing democracies functions similarly. In fact, many scholars are skeptical that mass partisanship in the developing world functions like partisanship in advanced democracies. After all, parties come and go regularly in many developing democracies, and clientelism and electoral fraud seem to matter more for individual behavior than partisan identities.

Still, there are good reasons to expect that patterns of mass partisanship in developing democracies generally resemble those in the advanced democracies. The analysis of Latin American partisanship presented in this chapter indeed found much resemblance. Like their counterparts in advanced democracies, Latin American partisans tend to be more experienced, more informed, more attentive, and more engaged. They also tend to participate more in politics, and their partisan attachments significantly influence their vote choices. These findings add to an emerging body of research on mass partisanship in other developing democracies (e.g., Brader and Tucker 2001, 2008; Ishiyama and Fox 2006).

Skeptics suggest that partisanship in developing contexts is merely a product of clientelism. But if clientelism were the main source of partisanship in Latin America, we would see different patterns. There is little reason for clientelistic parties to target citizens who are more informed or those who pay more attention to media. If mass partisanship in Latin America followed the logic of clientelist distribution, we would see very different patterns than those we observe in advanced democracies, where clientelism is rare. The results presented in this chapter do not rule out the possibility that some Latin American partisans are motivated by clientelism, but they do reveal that *most* partisan attachments in the region resemble the ones scholars have studied for decades in the United States and Western Europe.

Still, there are differences across countries that scholars ought to consider. My analysis found that institutional contexts condition citizens' propensities to form partisan attachments. I focused on average effects across the region. But contextual factors may also condition the relationships between individual characteristics and partisanship. An unfortunate consequence of the inattention to mass partisanship in developing democracies is that we have only just begun to understand why levels of partisanship vary dramatically across countries.

Some of these cross-national differences may also reflect differences across parties. In many multiparty countries, partisan attachments are far more widespread for certain parties than for others. Why do some parties foster such attachments more successfully? Are there certain characteristics that make some parties more adept at doing so than others? Or do these differences depend on the competitive environment in which parties operate?

We could ask similar questions about the dynamics of mass partisanship over time. Theories of party identification from advanced democracies offer little guidance for explaining why partisanship might grow or decline. In these contexts, the same parties tend to persist and citizens' attachments to them change slowly (Green, Palmquist, and Schickler 2005). Yet Latin American democracies have seen massive changes in rates of mass partisanship in recent decades, changes that far outpaced the social transformations typically associated with partisan shifts in Western Europe (e.g., Dalton 2000). In Latin America, citizens' attachments to parties declined precipitously in some countries (Lupu forthcoming; Morgan 2007; Sánchez 2002) even as they spread for some parties in others (Samuels 2006). Explaining these trends is vital to understanding the recent development of the region's party systems and the behavior of its citizens. Recognizing that mass partisanship matters in developing democracies poses challenges like these and highlights important avenues for further research.

NOTES

For comments and suggestions, I thank Larry Bartels, Ryan Carlin, Mike Lewis-Beck, Iván Llamazares, Aníbal Pérez-Liñán, Lucio Renno, Lucía Selios, Matt Singer, Liz Zechmeister, the anonymous reviewers, and participants at the Iberoamerica

Institute in Salamanca, the 2012 Workshop on Elections and Democracy at Salamanca, and the 2013 Latin American Voter conference at Vanderbilt. I also thank Arturo Maldonado for assistance with coding the AmericasBarometer data. I gratefully acknowledge the support of the Center for Advanced Study in the Social Sciences at the Juan March Institute. Translations of the Brazil survey are the author's.

1. One exception is India, a democracy since 1947, where mass partisanship received early attention (e.g., Eldersveld 1973).

2. Similar patterns appear in the former Soviet region (e.g., Brader and Tucker 2001, 2008).

3. Note that whether these associations are causal (and in which direction) is not my concern here. I simply want to examine whether the characteristics associated with partisanship in advanced democracies are also associated with partisanship in Latin America.

4. Earlier studies made some cross-national comparisons, but with very limited samples (e.g., Butler and Stokes 1969; Converse and Pierce 1992). All of these comparative studies focus largely on variation within the advanced democracies.

5. Huber, Kernell, and Leoni (2005) test these two effects separately by including the effective numbers of both electoral and legislative parties. I opt against this because the two variables are highly correlated.

6. This is only the case if our analysis controls for an individual's proximity to a party. Parties in more polarized systems may be farther away from a majority of centrist voters. They may readily be able to distinguish the parties, but not find any one party particularly appealing.

7. I identify democratic years as those with a Polity score greater than 5.

8. The item was worded as follows: "On this card there is a 1–10 scale that goes from left to right. One means left and 10 means right. Nowadays, when we speak of political leanings, we talk of those on the left and those on the right. In other words, some people sympathize more with the left and others with the right. According to the meaning that the terms 'left' and 'right' have for you, and thinking of your own political leanings, where would you place yourself on this scale?"

9. Kitschelt (1996) uses a similar approach.

10. The three questions were (1) "What is the name of the current president of the United States?"; (2) "How many [provinces/departments/states] does [country] have?"; and (3) "How long is the presidential term of office in [country]?" Like in Highton (2009), the index is a count of the number of correct responses.

11. Education is based on responses to the question, "How many years of schooling have you completed?" Responses are coded as (1) No schooling; (2) Primary only (6 years or less); (3) Secondary only (12 years or less); (4) Post-secondary, not university (17 years or less); (5) University (18 years).

12. The set began "I am going to read a list of groups and organizations. Please tell me if you attend their meetings at least once a week, once or twice a month, once or twice a year, or never." Respondents were asked about frequency of participation in meetings of (1) "any religious organization," (2) "a parents' association at school," (3) "a community improvement committee or association," and (4) "an association of professionals, merchants, manufacturers or farmers." I construct the index using principal-components factor analysis with orthogonal varimax rotation (eigenvalue = 1.56). The factor loadings are religious organization = 0.48, parents'

association = 0.64, community improvement association = 0.73, professional association = 0.62. Higher values indicate more frequent participation.

13. Beginning in 2010, the surveys asked one item: "About how often do you pay attention to the news, whether on TV, the radio, newspapers, or the Internet?" Prior to that, the surveys asked four separate items: (1) "How frequently do you listen to the news on the radio?"; (2) "How frequently do you watch the news on TV?"; (3) "How frequently do you read the news in newspapers?"; and (4) "How frequently do you read the news on the Internet?" The response options were "every day," "once or twice a week," "rarely," and "never." For the surveys prior to 2010, I generate a combined variable that identifies whether a respondent said she uses any media with each level of frequency.

14. Gender is coded by the interviewer: (0) male; (1) female. Ethnicity is based on responses to the question, "Do you consider yourself white, mestizo, indigenous, black, mulatto, or of another race?" The variable codes responses as (1) white; (0) all other responses. Rural/Urban is from interview/sample-defined codings based on the country's definition: (0) rural; (1) urban. Wealth is measured according to respondents' place in quintile groupings based on an index of household goods constructed following Córdova (2009).

15. Recall that I calculate a party's ideological position using the average self-placement of the respondents who said they voted for it. My measure of polarization thus differs from that used in other chapters in this volume. My measure offers more variation over time, though it focuses on polarization in presidential politics. I opt for this measure for the sake of consistency with my individual-level measure of proximity.

16. Vote shares may not fully reflect the prominence of each party, but they serve as a useful proxy. Moreover, an unweighted measure of polarization risks generating high values as an artifact of small, fringe parties.

17. Note, however, that the rank ordering of countries is quite consistent over time.

18. These predicted probabilities are based on multilevel probit estimates, which are reported in the online appendix (table OA9.1). These are two-level models that nest respondents within surveys. Note that the figure includes only the estimates considered to represent the total effect of each variable. That is, I assume the standard "funnel of causality" of public opinion research in which variables are added sequentially based on their expected stability. The figure, therefore, reports the predicted probability from the model in which each variable is first introduced.

19. In Latin America, rural voters are somewhat more likely to identify with a party, perhaps because rural citizens in the region often participate more in politics (cf. Seligson 1980).

20. The one exception is that Huber, Kernell, and Leoni (2005) predict (and find, in advanced democracies) that electoral fragmentation increases, rather than diminishes, partisanship. Their logic is that more parties provide voters with more nuanced choices. It seems equally plausible to think that more choices mean voters know little about the parties, particularly when those choices are new or change frequently. This may be one instance in which a system-level factor has different implications in developing democracies than it does in advanced ones.

21. The item asked, "There are people who work for parties or candidates during electoral campaigns. Did you work for any candidate or party in the last presidential elections of [year of last presidential elections]?"

22. Vote choice is based on responses to the question, "Who did you vote for in the last presidential elections of [year]?"

23. These proportions omit respondents who identified with a party when that party did not field a presidential candidate. Where the surveys covered more than one election, I calculated the proportion for each election using the closest survey and averaged across elections.

24. I have conducted similar analyses with shorter panel studies from Mexico—a more stable party system—with similar results.

25. This means simultaneously estimating the equations:

$$Vote_{i,t} = \alpha_1 + \beta_1 Vote_{i,t-1} + \gamma_1 PID_{i,t-1} + \varepsilon_1$$
$$PID_{i,t} = \alpha_2 + \beta_2 Vote_{i,t-1} + \gamma_s PID_{i,t-1} + \varepsilon_2$$

26. The dependent variable, vote choice, is based on responses to the question, "If the presidential election were held today, for which of the following candidates would you vote? Ciro Gomes, Lula, Roseana Sarney, José Serra, Anthony Garotinho, Itamar Franco, or some other candidate?" PT vote is coded as (1) Lula (0) all other choices. PSDB vote is coded as (1) Serra; (0) all other candidates. Partisanship is based on responses to the question, "Do you identify with a political party? Yes or no?" and the open-ended follow-up question, "With which one?" PT partisanship is coded as (1) PT; (0) all other party identities or no party identity. PSDB partisanship is coded as (1) PSDB; (0) all other party identities or no party identity. Household income is based on responses to the question, "More or less, what is the total monthly income of your family, including the incomes of everyone who works or has some source of income?" Total income is divided by the square root of the size of the household. The size of the household is based on responses to two follow-up questions: "How many people over 18 live on that income?" and "And how many under 18?" Education is based on responses to the question, "How many years of schooling have you completed?" Coded 0 to 15. Ethnicity is a coding based on interviewer coding as white, brown, black, yellow, or Indian; the variable codes responses as (1) white; (0) all other responses. Gender (female 1, male 0) is also coded by the interviewer.

27. I pool observations of respondents in each two-wave dyad and cluster standard errors by respondent. Controlling for a survey wave dummy variable (dichotomous measure coded 1 for that survey year and zero otherwise) does not substantively change my results.

28. These predicted probabilities are based on the cross-lagged structural equation estimates reported in the online appendix (table OA9.2).

10 ✦ Clientelism in Latin America
Effort and Effectiveness

HERBERT KITSCHELT AND MELINA ALTAMIRANO

In many Latin American democracies clientelism has been one technique for politicians to attract voters and for citizens to secure a modicum of benefits from their governments. For various reasons, in these countries administrative and judicial state capacities are weak and therefore undermine the credibility of politicians' promises to produce "policies" rather than clientelism. Policies involve regulations of citizens' conduct, the extraction of resources from society, and the public production of goods and services—such as local infrastructure, educational opportunities, and social protection—covering codified categories of citizens through legislation and consistently implemented by competent public officials, regardless of whether individuals and groups belonging to such categories voted for the winning coalition of politicians. But when politicians offer voters the lure of immediate, tangible targeted benefits, in exchange for their loyalty to a party, should not common sense dictate acceptance of such offers, particularly when the prospects of effective policy benefits look vague, uncertain, and speculative?

This chapter describes the distribution of clientelistic practices in Latin America. We use an expert survey, the Democratic Accountability and Linkage Project (DALP), in which more than 1,400 respondents—mostly scholars, but also a few journalists—in 88 countries characterized democratic linkages pursued by parties in their home countries.[1] While the variance among political parties within each country is intriguing, this essay focuses on cross-national differences of clientelistic practices among Latin American polities and nested within a global comparison. Generalizations that the subcontinent's electoral partisan politics are mired in clientelism are imprecise, if not misleading, just as the propensity for parties to engage in programmatic competition starkly diverges within the region (cf. Kitschelt et al. 2010). There is no uniformity of democratic linkage mechanisms in the region that would justify invoking a "Latin American" stereotype.

Maybe more surprisingly, the evidence also suggests that the electoral effectiveness of clientelistic efforts to attract voters in the region is not directly proportional to the effort politicians make in their clientelistic outreach. While Latin American countries do not stand out from the rest of the globe in terms of the mechanisms that contribute to politicians' clientelistic efforts, some—but not all—Latin American countries exhibit a striking "effectiveness gap" in that politicians make great efforts to target voters with clientelistic goods, but fail to generate a commensurate number of votes with these practices. This, at least, is the judgment of political science expert juries in a number of Latin American countries.

The first section of the chapter conceptualizes clientelism and describes the data. The second section provides a descriptive overview of clientelism, effort, and effectiveness. The third section gives a summary account of why clientelism is more common in some polities and political parties operating in electoral democracies around the world and what kinds of people are targeted in clientelistic linkage efforts, exemplified by the results of the AmericasBarometer survey. Because intra-Latin American variance can be explained with arguments that apply globally as well, we only render a summary explanation here without detailed analysis. The fourth section then tackles the intriguing problem of why politicians in some Latin American countries, but not elsewhere, make ineffective clientelistic efforts. Here the challenge is to explain variance within the region, but also across regions of the world.

The Logic and Measurement of Clientelistic Linkages

Clientelistic exchange—a targeted, contingent exchange of votes for benefits—is one among many ways voters can link up to politicians and hold them "accountable." Others are universalistic programmatic policies, the attractiveness of a leader's personality (sometimes "charisma"), competence in governance, descriptive representativeness or voters' ascriptive traits (gender, region, ethnicity, etc.), or habit and emotional attachment to parties ("party identification"). We endorse a narrow definition of clientelism that involves both targeting of benefits to individuals and small groups as well as contingency of the exchange (cf. Hicken 2011; Kitschelt 2000,

2011a; Kitschelt and Wilkinson 2007b; Stokes 2005, 2007). We focus on electoral clientelism, but even this comes in many guises and we would like to advance five specifications:

- Clientelism is not necessarily a spot-market, one-time transaction, but more often a temporally extended, durable, iterative relationship that facilitates mutual compliance of principal (citizen) and agent (politician) without the need for continuous monitoring and sanctioning.
- "Vote-buying" is only one specific realization of spot-market clientelism.
- Clientelism is not identical with corruption, understood as the abuse of public office for private purposes, in ways explicitly ruled out by the law. Clientelism may be an open, publically accepted, sometimes even legally enshrined, and from the vantage point of voters an expected form of service performed by politicians. Nevertheless, clientelism often gives rise to corrupt practices to procure the funds deployed in clientelistic exchange (Singer 2009a).
- Unlike economic and bureaucratic clientelism in the past, electoral clientelism is not inimical to political competition or wedded to voters' entrapment in asymmetrical dependency relations. Indeed, recent decades have witnessed a great deal of competition among alternative providers of clientelistic services among which individual voters, or local neighborhoods, may choose (Kitschelt 2012a).
- In many countries for the broad mass of citizens clientelism may be the one expedient way to extract benefits from a weak government apparatus incapable of devising or implementing public policies. This does not make it a form of linkage that lives up to high normative criteria of democratic theory and the sense of justice expressed by intellectuals and educated voters. But it is a reality of democratic accountability where agents deliver a service in exchange for a vote.

The systematic study of clientelism has been hampered by the absence of valid and reliable measures of the phenomenon, if not by the very absence of agreement about conceptual choices. The Latin American Public Opinion Project's (LAPOP) AmericasBarometer survey takes a step toward correcting this deficiency. It offers a question that measures something akin to spot-market vote-buying.[2] The question is not ideal for our purposes, as it misses the long-term, relational, and often collective, group- rather than individual-based character of clientelistic linkages. Moreover, as framed, it may suffer an acceptability bias, with some respondents not confirming the empirical presence of such practices because vote-buying is illegal in many countries. Nevertheless the question may help identify the tip of an iceberg of clientelistic accountability practices.

We therefore supplement these data with responses to a recent global expert survey on Democratic Accountability and Linkage Politics (DALP) that covers all of Latin America. The DALP survey, completed by ten to forty respondents in each country, has four modules concerning (1) party organization, (2) clientelistic effort, effectiveness and channels through which it operates, (3) efforts to monitor voters and enforce exchange relations, and (4) scores of parties' policy positions and left-right placements, if any. The construction and basic measures of the survey to tap clientelism and programmatic partisan appeals, as well as the methodological pitfalls of this research strategy, are covered elsewhere (Kitschelt 2011a, 2011b; Kitschelt and Freeze 2010; see also note 1).[3]

The survey asked experts to assess the effort politicians in each party are making to "promise or provide" targeted benefits as "inducements to gain their vote." With a small anchoring vignette referring to weak and strong efforts in the area of public-sector employment, experts scored parties on five objects: (1) gifts to voters, (2) social policy benefits (access to healthcare, disability insurance, public rental flats, student scholarships), (3) public-sector employment, (4) favorable regulatory decisions, and (5) procurement contracts.[4] For the sake of simplicity, and because scores across the various dimensions are highly correlated, we created an additive index of clientelistic effort for each party over all five modes of clientelistic targeting. At the party level, this yields a measure averaging the jury members' scores for each party (b15). At the national level, it yields a mean effort over all individual party averages, where the contribution of each party to that measure is weighted by the electoral support that party received in the two national legislative elections preceding the point of observation (b15.nwe = b15, national, weighted). The standard deviation of the national average signals the diversification of parties' linkage strategies.

For our concerns a particularly interesting question is whether DALP jury members find that clientelistic effort on the part of the politicians in fact boosts their parties' electoral share. So the question here is one of outcomes: do the juries believe that clientelistic expenses are worth the effort? Again, we work with a party-level average expert score (and standard deviation) of jury responses (b11) and a national-level mean (and standard deviation) of party means weighted by electoral results (b11.nwe).

Expert surveys are fraught with measurement error, random or systematic. Let us report here briefly on two aspects of concern. First, experts may be biased by their own partisan predilections. Even though the survey instrument does not ask them to evaluate "clientelism" (a highly politically charged and contentious notion that might trigger affective responses) but instead leads them to assess operational targeting practices, experts who sympathize with a party may want to claim that (1) their preferred party makes less clientelistic effort than parties less favored and, even if the former does, (2) that effort is less effective so that clientelism is not really a big deal for it. Yet, the expert survey includes a question on the respondents' party sympathies that allows us to establish that sympathies have only a tiny effect on clientelistic effort scores. Whether the correlation is measured at the level of individual experts evaluating each party ($N > 5,700$), or the party averages of experts in all countries ($N = 505$), or the national averages of experts' responses ($N = 88$), there is only a minute negative correlation between experts' party sympathies and their assessment of parties' clientelistic effectiveness (0.5–1.0% explained variance) or parties' clientelistic effort (2.0–5.0% explained variance). So bias is not a major concern here.

Because the survey asks respondents to assess their subjective level of knowledge about the parties, we can also test whether respondents who feel more ignorant about a party give it systematically lower clientelistic effort and/or effectiveness scores. Here, indeed, we find moderate statistical relationships. The explained variance is 4 to 10% of the scores, across the three units of analysis noted in the above paragraph. Yet, in an analysis not detailed here, our conclusions prove robust to controls for expert bias and expert knowledge levels.

Clientelism in Latin America and Around the World

Figure 10.1 reports the national mean values for Latin American parties' clientelistic effort, as measured by the DALP dataset (b15.nwe), as well as the percentage of LAPOP respondents in each country who declare that they have been exposed to vote-buying attempts. Given that what is being measured in the two surveys is quite different—narrow spot-market vote buying in LAPOP versus a broad relational conception of clientelism in DALP—and given that the measurement methods and specific observations are so different—producers of clientelistic efforts in DALP, potential recipients in LAPOP—there is a strikingly high agreement between the

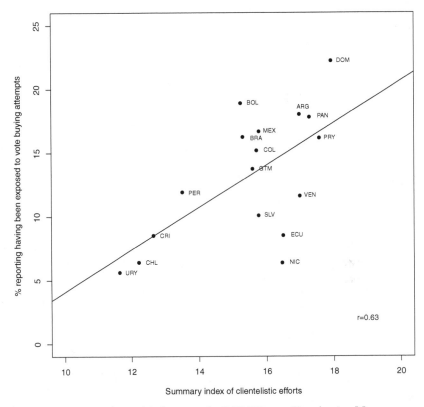

Figure 10.1   Relationship between the LAPOP 2010 Vote-buying Measure and the DALP Index of Clientelistic Effort. *Sources:* LAPOP Americas-Barometer 2010 and DALP.

country scores. Thus, low in both counts are Chile, Costa Rica, and Uruguay, which are the three countries with the strongest programmatic partisan efforts (Kitschelt et al. 2010). Countries high on both counts include the Dominican Republic, Argentina, Panama, Paraguay, and to a lesser, but still substantial, extent the heavyweights of Brazil, Colombia, and Mexico.

Inconsistencies between LAPOP and DALP scores arise for the cases of Nicaragua, Ecuador, and Bolivia, as well as to a lesser extent for El Salvador and Venezuela. Without these five cases, the slope of the regression line would be a bit steeper and almost all the variance would be explained.

Let us turn next to the relationship between clientelistic effort and effectiveness. Figure 10.2 shows a scattergram of national weighted b11.nwe (effectiveness) and b15.nwe (effort) scores. While the figure does not

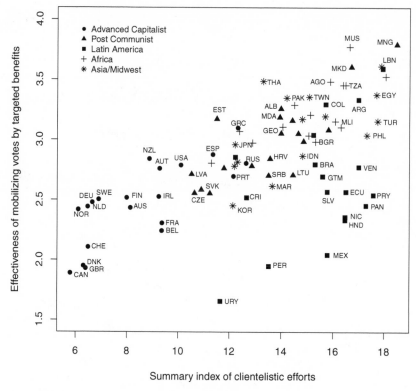

Figure 10.2   Clientelistic Effort and Its Electoral Effectiveness.
Source: DALP.

pick up the variance among parties, a considerable share of the variance is national. In global comparison, Western advanced industrial countries stand out, generally showing low to intermediate clientelistic effort and effectiveness, as do sub-Saharan African countries, demonstrating generally high clientelistic effort and effectiveness. What is more interesting, the other three geographical regions we distinguish have (almost) no clear pattern of concentration: parties in post-communist, Asian and Middle Eastern, and Latin American countries vary almost across the entire spectrum of clientelistic effort.

For the most part, the effectiveness of clientelism is highly correlated with the average clientelistic effort undertaken by parties in a given country. There is just one subgroup of countries concentrated in a single region that sticks out: in some, but far from all, Latin American countries according to experts there is a whole lot less clientelistic effectiveness than effort, regardless of whether levels of effort are intermediate or (very) high. If we standardize the scales for both effort and effectiveness on a 0–1 metric, the difference value indicates the size of the "gap" between these two performance attributes. A large positive gap (effort minus effectiveness) indicates troubling ineffectiveness of clientelistic effort. Where do we find different magnitudes of the effectiveness gap? It turns out that all of the eleven countries with the greatest clientelistic effectiveness gaps in the global set of eighty-eight countries are Latin American, a highly improbable outcome if by pure chance:

- The greatest effectiveness gaps occur in some Latin American countries with strong clientelistic partisan efforts. In an ordinal ranking of gap size, Mexico (1) displays the most yawning gap, followed by Panama (2), Honduras (3), Paraguay (4), Nicaragua (5), and Ecuador (8).
- The gaps are large but against a backdrop of only intermediate clientelistic efforts in Peru (6) and Uruguay (7).
- The gaps are moderately large, paired with strong clientelistic efforts, in Venezuela (9), El Salvador (10), Guatemala (11), and Brazil (12).
- In all other Latin American countries, the gaps are moderately sized or nonexistent, regardless of whether parties' clientelistic effort in these countries is great (Argentina, Bolivia, Colombia, the Dominican Republic) or only moderate to weak (Costa Rica, Chile).
- Elsewhere around the globe, experts judge parties' clientelistic electoral effectiveness to be largely proportional to their clientelistic effort.
- In a few advanced industrial democracies, where clientelistic efforts are judged feeble, experts deem the effectiveness of such tactics to be a bit less weak (negative gap). This may be merely an issue of measurement error and scaling imbalance, as before standardization the effort scale b15.nwe is much more fine-grained (with scores running from 5 to 20) than the effectiveness scale b11.nwe (scores 1 through 4).

Before we turn to the puzzle of clientelistic effectiveness gaps in some Latin American countries, however, let us place the Latin American clientelistic experience in a comparative context. We will summarize arguments that help us understand why clientelistic efforts vary so much across parties and countries and what kinds of voters parties target with their clientelistic efforts.

Why and How Does Clientelistic Effort Vary among Countries and Parties?

Why does clientelistic effort vary among countries and parties and how does it play out in Latin America? This is a broad subject with a large, but idiosyncratic literature, as systematic and globally comprehensive comparative data of even moderate quality have been missing so far. The DALP dataset and its subsequent papers and reports are a first effort to fill this gap.[5]

The dominant argument about the incidence of clientelism in partisan politics has to do with economic development (Kitschelt 2000). Poor people laboring at the bare subsistence threshold are expected to discount the future and prefer an immediate, tangible personal direct gain of clientelistic inducement compared to a distant, less tangible collective indirect policy gain. Conversely, as a citizen's income rises, the material inducements of clientelism become of questionable value, particularly in the case of high-skill professionals for whom patronage appointments and other non-skill-based rewards debase and undermine the return on their educational investment. Moreover, more affluent and educated citizens may realize that clientelistic efforts may drain resources from the provision of public policies that may increase the returns on skill and capital investments. Or compensating them with clientelistic advantages becomes simply too expensive for politicians, even as the corrupt acquisition of party resources and the deployment of public resources for clientelistic targeting escalate.

In an analysis not reported here, we find a negative relationship between economic development (the log of 2008 per capita GDP) and clientelistic effort (b15.nwe). The linear correlation between the two is $r = -0.69$. Higher per capita GDP comes with less clientelistic effort. Upon closer inspection, however, this is not the whole story. An additional quadratic term in the equation, modeling the functional fit in a curvilinear fashion, substantially increases the explained variance. Clientelistic effort initially becomes more intensive at higher income levels. Only above certain intermediate income regions (around $10,000 per capita GDP in 2008), clientelistic partisan efforts begin to drop off decisively and fall to much more modest levels above $20,000 per capita GDP, though even a few outliers remain at that level. What applies on a global scale applies also on the regional scale to Latin America. The income levels of Costa Rica, Chile, and Uruguay, for example, are not that different from those of Argentina, Brazil, Mexico, or Venezuela. But these sets of countries exhibit substantially different levels of clientelistic effort, both when measured with DALP as well as with LAPOP variables (see again figure 10.1).

This result is robust to a wide range of multivariate specifications. Because empirical operationalizations of rival theories of clientelistic linkage formation involve substantial measurement error, even theoretically convincing arguments tend to weaken, but not entirely wipe out, GDP coefficients. Let us specify here relevant complementary theoretical arguments to account for clientelistic effort and either found statistically confirmed in our own or others' statistical research:

- *Cumulative democratic experience* plays a role, but it is not as simple as young democracies having clientelistic parties while older democracies enable politicians to woo voters more cheaply with policy proposals (Keefer 2007). Clientelistic targeting demands organizational networks that require time and resources to build. Hence a three-step model appears to capture the logic of democratic experience and linkage mechanisms: in the first stage, neither programmatic nor clientelistic mechanisms work well; then clientelistic mechanisms gain vigor, only to give way to policy linkage efforts in the third stage (Kitschelt and Kselman 2013). Visual inspection of the Latin American cases suggests this curvilinear argument is plausible. Chile, Costa Rica, and Uruguay cumulatively have the greatest democratic experience within Latin America, albeit with vicious interruptions in at least two cases, and politicians exhibit only moderate propensities for clientelistic targeting. Countries with weaker democratic experience show much stronger clientelistic effort, even if they are equally affluent. And the frailest Latin American countries do not have particularly exalted levels of clientelistic effort.
- *The strategies and results of the developmental state in political economy* play a role in shaping politicians' opportunities for electoral clientelism. Middle-income countries often, but not invariably, have gone through a phase of rapid economic growth based on state-led initiatives to catch up with the developed world. Spurts of growth make resources available to politicians that are not precommitted, thus enabling them to compensate even an expensive middle class with clientelistic benefits, at least initially

before wages and standards of living become very high. The developmental state politicizes allocative decisions that are left to market exchange in advanced capitalist democracies, thus further amplifying the scope of clientelistic targeting by elected politicians. When the developmental state slips into crisis, so do clientelistic practices. As Italy, Japan, and South Korea illustrate, this may happen at rather high levels of development. In Latin America, countries with lower clientelistic effort tend either not to have developed a strong developmental state or to have backtracked from that system after a crisis. In some cases, of course, even a crisis of the developmental state has not produced a thorough economic liberalization and thus maintains clientelistic opportunities in electoral politics.

- *The intensity of party competition*, especially where programmatic differences among parties are weak, can reinvigorate clientelistic partisan efforts. Where the combined share of the largest two parties or party blocks is great, and where simultaneously they run neck and neck in electoral support, clientelistic partisan effort is greater than when there are larger disparities among parties and party camps (Kitschelt 2012a). At the individual level, where party competition is particularly intense, DALP experts tend to assert that politicians generally concentrate their efforts on "core" partisan voters and stimulate their ongoing turnout rather than concentrating on "marginal" strategic voters who are not clearly in any party camp.

- *Ethnic divisions with ethnic income disparities* make a difference, at the margin, intensifying clientelistic efforts (cf. Kolev and Wang 2010). Where there are large disadvantaged ethnic groups represented by distinctive parties, politicians will redouble their clientelistic efforts. Ethnic networks reducing the temptations of opportunism in clientelistic exchange are part of that story. Once again, given the paucity of cases with this configuration in Latin America, with the possible exceptions of Bolivia, Ecuador, Mexico, and Peru, only a global multivariate analysis (outside the scope of this chapter) reveals the effect of ethnocultural divisions.

- A further possible mechanism boosting clientelism is *a patronage state and absence of bureaucratic professionalization* (Shefter 1977). Where administrative positions are awarded based on personal connections rather than meritocracy, the rise of electoral politics could enable politicians to use leverage over the appointment of civil servants to bolster their own constituency. Although empirically not generalizeable for a global comparison, weak state professionalization may account for higher levels of clientelism in some of today's affluent advanced industrial countries (cf. Bustikova and Corduneanu-Huci 2009), but this effect is rather fragile.

One common cause and mechanism often invoked as a definitive boost of clientelistic accountability relations, however, is clearly not borne out in a broad comparative analysis, namely, the impact of democratic institutions on clientelism, particularly that of electoral institutions. Brazil has served as a poster-child for the impact of electoral rules on clientelism. The interaction of multimember districts with voting on open lists and the absence of vote-pooling of candidate preference votes under the auspices of the same list, as well as the *candidato nato* rule that removed parties' control over the nominations process and let an elected legislator decide to run on any party ticket, clearly made Brazil one of the more personalistic systems of democratic governance (Ames 2001; Carey and Shugart 1995; Mainwaring 1999). But when inspecting the full range of Latin American countries, and also that of polities with electoral competition across the globe, the covariance of clientelistic effort with electoral system features disappears (Kitschelt 2011c). It is possible that party organizational structures may compensate for electoral system features deemed inhospitable to targeted contingent and clientelistic accountability relations.

Among democratic institutional features, the only one that appears to influence clientelistic effort is strong presidential legislative and executive powers (cf. Kitschelt 2011c). If presidents wield a wide range of powers, including over office patronage, clientelism tends to thrive, as public resource allocation is under the spell of discretionary political authority. That said, this argument finds little empirical traction, as long as we compare Latin American cases in isolation.

Beyond the aggregate level, what can we say at the micro-level of individual voters about propensities to support clientelism? The Americas-Barometer survey allows us to examine whether poor voters, networked voters, and possibly rural voters who because of their low productivity and sedentary nature have a higher chance to be poor, but networked, are more often the target of clientelistic effort. This, at least, is one insight that can be extracted from previous individual-level survey research on vote-buying in individual Latin American countries such as Mexico and Argentina (cf. Brusco, Nazareno, and Stokes 2004; Calvo and Murillo 2004, 2012; Fox 1994; Stokes 2005).

To explore the determinants of clientelistic targeting at the individual level, we estimated a logit model drawing on the 2010 AmericasBarometer (see also Faughnan and Zechmeister 2011). The dependent variable is the vote-buying item in the survey, asking respondents whether they have been offered material goods in return for their vote. The model includes country fixed effects and incorporates design effects as is available in the online appendix (figure OA10.1). The reported independent variables intend to capture the targeting criteria discussed above. Results are generally consistent with the arguments in the literature and the patterns emerging from the DALP data on party strategies. Household wealth has a negative and significant effect on the likelihood of being targeted with clientelistic offers. Individuals living in rural communities are more likely to be offered material benefits in exchange for their vote. Interestingly, more active participants in partisan organizations are more likely to report experiences related to vote-buying attempts (see also Faughnan and Zechmeister 2011).[6] This finding resonates with arguments emphasizing political networks as mechanisms determining preferential access to certain goods, thus conditioning voters' expectations (Calvo and Murillo 2012). Women and older people tend to report less experience with clientelistic practices, while education does not seem to have a significant effect on targeting, at least net of income. Individuals self-identifying as indigenous are no more likely to report vote-buying attempts than others in our model. But this effect might vary by country depending on the political salience of ethnic cleavages, which tends to be high only in a small number of Latin American countries. LAPOP data indicate that the relatively largest effort parties make to target minorities is in the Dominican Republic, followed by Bolivia, Ecuador, Honduras, and Peru.

Altogether, the LAPOP and DALP data yield a fairly complementary and mutually consistent picture, at least where insights from macro-level and micro-level comparisons can be brought to speak to each other. Poverty and rural isolation, together with partisan networks, promote clientelistic effort, whatever other conditions and strategic opportunities may come into play. While these conditions may also improve the effectiveness of clientelistic efforts in producing votes, it is far from clear, however, whether these are the only conditions that drive clientelistic effectiveness. Let us turn to this topic in the following section.

The Variable Effectiveness of Clientelism across Latin America

The process by which voters cast their votes in exchange for receiving goods or benefits is open to failure. The critical problem of clientelism is the *double contingency of the principal-agent exchange relationship*. With mass enfranchisement and ballot secrecy, it is difficult to enforce clientelistic exchange relations because, in the first place, it has become harder to monitor voter compliance with the implicit contract (Stokes et al. 2013). *Voter opportunism vis-à-vis clientelistic inducements* is thus likely to be rampant, though its frequency and pervasiveness may vary at the margin across parties and countries. Also, the *observability of agent compliance* has changed. On the one hand, politicians can more easily elude their commitments to clients, as the goods and services the latter expect have become more complex and may require protracted efforts to deliver (think public housing of desired quality, public-sector jobs, business procurement contracts, no longer just simple gifts or direct vote-buying). On the other hand, when agents compete for the support of clients it may improve transparency and grant voters leverage that limits politicians' opportunism, particularly in iterative, multiround games of electoral competition.

As the existing country-specific and subnationally comparative investigations of Latin American clientelism show, the presence of networks and the relative stability of partisan relations with poor constituencies, often in rural areas, but sometimes in poor urban neighborhoods, may be constitutive for overcoming the temptations of opportunism felt by both voters and politicians in clientelistic relationships (see especially Auyero 2000; Calvo and Murillo 2012). But iteration of exchange in the face of robust networks, and the resulting trust and reciprocity of voter-patron relations at the party level, may not account for all of the variance in clientelistic effectiveness. As figure 10.2 suggests, there may be central tendencies in national political conditions that render clientelistic efforts more or less effective and that are worth examination. We will focus on these national-level effects in this essay, and note that they are robust even to controls for party-level effects.

How can parties patch, or at least contain, the "leaky bucket" problem to make clientelism a passably effective vote-getting strategy, at least compared to other methods of attracting electoral support that entail their own transaction costs? We see at least four avenues to pursue this question that may then translate into the specification of different operational mechanisms. All four mechanisms we nominate have directly or indirectly to do with "time and learning" in democracies, making it possible to increase the share of those who voluntarily comply with clientelistic inducements, net of associational or coercive efforts. These mechanisms may operate at the systemic level, enabling all parties to improve their constituency linkages, not just individual parties, or setting all parties back, impairing their clientelistic effectiveness.

1. Once democratic party competition gets under way, eventually favorable conditions for deploying clientelistic exchange may weaken, but *politicians may simply need some time to figure out that clientelistic strategies no longer pay off.* We may be observing nonequilibrium results in some Latin American countries, where the decline of clientelistic effectiveness is ahead of the learning curve on which politicians reduce their clientelistic effort. The DALP survey offers one indirect way of getting at this relationship: experts indicated whether clientelistic effort has gone up or down in parties over the ten years preceding the point of observation. A decline in clientelism could predict the presence of a clientelistic effectiveness gap, provided it has not yet been completely wiped out by reductions in effort. Conversely, a judgment that clientelistic effort has increased may follow the experience of particularly strong clientelistic effectiveness.

As a second measure, we rely on Gerring et al.'s (2005) cumulative "political capital" or cumulative democratic experience, where earlier years of democracy are discounted relative to more recent democratic experience. The idea is that during eras of democratic competition politicians can make investments in a democratic associational infrastructure and learn skills of collective political mobilization that pay off later, even if the democratic process is punctuated by spells of authoritarianism. The relationship between democratic experience and clientelistic effectiveness should therefore be linearly positive, or at least curvilinear, with a peak at intermediate experience, before additional experience and iterative interaction between citizens and politicians makes programmatic linkage strategies more attractive and effective relative to clientelism.

2. Ineffective clientelism may also follow from situations of exceptional resource abundance enjoyed by politicians in a new democracy, where a polity is dominated by *the survival of a former ruling party under an authoritarian regime that, now, as an authoritarian legacy party (ALP) exposed to competition* still commands access to scarce resources, for example, through the public administration. These resources may enable it to boost clientelistic political effort, even when such expenditures have only minimal electoral payoffs. ALPs may affect all other parties in the system as well, insofar as the lopsidedness of competition hobbles their efforts to build functionally effective clientelistic networks. ALP presence may therefore boost clientelistic effort, but bust clientelistic effectiveness.

3. *Sudden and profound shocks disorganizing the configuration of entire party systems* may undermine the effectiveness of clientelistic networks in established parties, but also leave new parties scrambling for ways to reduce the volatility or their support base. It is likely that the average effectiveness of

clientelistic vote-getting falls dramatically through the entrance of radically new competitors and the turnover of political parties in the system that may even compel the remaining survivors to reorganize themselves and their constituencies. We will explore this argument by examining the extent to which the *sudden rise of left-wing populist parties in the 1990s and after the crossover to the new millennium* may have affected the effectiveness of clientelistic linkage effort, particularly in a subset of Latin American countries. Such parties may invoke "programmatic" stances on questions of economic and social reform, but often enough they may get bogged down in clientelistic horse-trading to shore up their electoral support and their reputation as future or current rulers. When such new competitors embark on clientelistic exchange, but also when their established competitors threatened by extinction respond in kind, clientelistic efforts may race ahead of clientelistic effectiveness.

As such parties and governments expand their control of economic resources, particularly if they capture the rents of petroleum and gas exports, *the bounty of resource control and their discretionary allocation of benefits may massively expand clientelistic effort, while only moderately contributing to the effectiveness of such effort.* Populist parties may yet have to learn to calibrate their targeted resource expenditures to their electoral objectives and thus initially burn through a great deal of resources without boosting their electoral payoffs. At the same time, their opponents often become so disorganized that they lose whatever clientelistic effectiveness they may have possessed.

Because the phenomenon of left populism reverberates through a polity's entire party system, we conceptualize it not at the party level, but as a systemic phenomenon. We introduce here a dummy variable that codes whether polities experienced such a disruption, signaled by the rise of a left-populist party to prominence, whether it ultimately takes power or not, usually accompanied by the implosion and disappearance of the most electorally successful earlier parties.[7]

4. The *competitiveness of party systems* may also matter for parties' clientelistic effectiveness.[8] High competitiveness forces politicians to deploy their resources in the best possible manner. The prediction, therefore, is that regardless of national affluence, high competitiveness will always make politicians engage in clientelistic targeting if they are fairly certain that it is effective. Competitiveness should drive out irrational, wasteful use of resources on clientelistic effort. *Hence, greater competitiveness should unconditionally reduce the gap between clientelistic effort and clientelistic effectiveness, whether the equilibrium is a high or a low level of clientelistic effort.* We develop an index that shows higher competitiveness, as the margin of

difference between the two largest parties falls and their combined share of the electorate increases, placing two alternatives neck and neck as cores of governments. Taking into account electoral volatility as a tracer of strategically "available" voters, the element of competitiveness makes little empirical difference. Documentation can be requested from one of the authors (see Kitschelt 2012a).

We complement the country-level analysis by including a few micro-level mechanisms as controls in a multilevel model that might more exhaustively explain interparty variance in clientelistic effectiveness. Given that the units of analysis in the DALP survey are political parties, we consider the following variables at the party level (the degree/size of): (1) formal party organization, (2) informal networks of local notables situated at the intersection of community communications networks, (3) contact with civic organizations, (4) client monitoring, and (5) whether parties target loyalist or strategic voters. The key hypothesis here is straightforward: parties' capacity to mobilize and monitor voters (e.g., via social/civic/party networks) will increase clientelistic effectiveness.[9]

We tackle the challenge of accounting for the gap between clientelistic effort and effectiveness in various specifications. Clientelistic effectiveness is the dependent variable (B11) in models displayed. A variety of independent variables are entered, but after controlling for clientelistic effort (B15). Alternatively, we have used the standardized difference between B15 and B11 as the dependent variable, with very similar results, then of course not using B15 as a control. We present estimations with and without regional dummies to explore their resilience, and use the full dataset. Interpreting the B11 and B15-B11 variables as interval scaled, we estimate OLS regressions, with robust standard errors when individual parties are the unit of analysis.[10] Finally, we merge party- and country-level determinants in a hierarchical linear model.[11]

In the online appendix, we test the robustness of these models' results by introducing two additional controls: the level of confidence of experts in their own judgment of the parties and their level of ideological closeness to a given party (see table OA10.1 online). Our main results reported here remain undisturbed by these model modifications and that applies both at the country and at the party level.

Empirical Findings: Country-Level Analysis

Table 10.1 presents a cascade of statistical estimates to account for the clientelistic electoral performance gap with a variety of the national-level

TABLE 10.1 Country-level Models. Dependent Variable: Clientelistic Electoral Effectiveness

	Model 1	Model 2	Model 3	Model 4	Model 5	Model 6	Model 7	Model 8	Model 9
Clientelistic effort (b15nwe)	0.086*** (0.012)	0.071*** (0.015)	0.108*** (0.017)	0.070*** (0.019)	0.070*** (0.019)	0.069*** (0.020)	0.101*** (0.017)	0.098*** (0.017)	0.134*** (0.018)
Programmatic effort (cosalpo_4nwe)		-0.515 (0.342)	-0.418 (0.317)	-0.516 (0.345)	-0.516 (0.351)	-0.546 (0.368)	-0.312 (0.311)	-0.364 (0.305)	-0.365 (0.293)
Democratic tenure (demstock)				-0.000 (0.000)	-0.000 (0.000)	-0.000 (0.000)	-0.000 (0.000)	-0.000 (0.000)	0.000 (0.000)
Change of clientelistic effort (absb7)					-0.001 (0.105)	0.001 (0.106)	-0.114 (0.091)	-0.084 (0.090)	-0.175* (0.081)
Authoritarian legacy party (alpn)						-0.169 (0.254)	-0.337 (0.215)	-0.443* (0.216)	-0.339 (0.191)
Populist partisan rupture (pop1)							-0.772*** (0.130)	-0.748*** (0.128)	-0.392** (0.130)
Competitiveness of the party system (p63)							0.054* (0.025)	0.052* (0.025)	(0.022)
Advanced capitalist			0.643*** (0.146)						0.460** (0.140)
Post-communist			0.550*** (0.101)						0.559*** (0.128)
Sub-Saharan Africa			0.559*** (0.106)						0.530*** (0.108)
Asia and Middle East			0.498*** (0.102)						0.435*** (0.103)
(Intercept)	1.715*** (0.158)	2.059*** (0.277)	1.093*** (0.300)	2.069*** (0.319)	2.069*** (0.321)	2.109*** (0.332)	1.765*** (0.284)	1.648*** (0.283)	0.770* (0.303)
N	88	88	88	88	88	87	87	87	87
R-squared	0.394	0.410	0.621	0.410	0.410	0.412	0.592	0.614	0.726

Note: Standard errors in parentheses. * indicates significance at $p < .05$, ** at $p < .01$, and *** at $p < .001$.

constraints sketched in previous paragraphs. Without doubt, clientelistic effort is the strongest predictor of clientelistic electoral effectiveness (models 1 and 2). Programmatic party appeals[12] are not quite significant by conventional statistical standards, but come close, with t-values approaching but not quite reaching 2.0. The regional dummies substantially boost the explanatory power of the baseline regression with only controls (model 3). Compared to all other regions, Latin American countries have a lower average clientelistic effectiveness of a very substantial 0.5 to 0.65 unit on a scale with a range of 3 units (1.0–4.0), a mean of 2.86, and a standard deviation of 0.46.

Among learning and timing variables, neither democratic experience nor the absolute change of clientelistic effort in the previous ten years account for clientelistic effectiveness in any measurable way (models 4 and 5). The carryover of authoritarian legacy parties (ALPs) generates respectable coefficient sizes in the expected negative direction, but they hover just above or just below conventional levels of significance in the more sophisticated model specifications.

Left-populist partisan mobilization has the strongest (and negative) effect overall on clientelistic effectiveness (models 7–9).[13] The rise of populist parties tremendously disrupts the effectiveness of clientelism. Even though the rupture of party systems may, in fact, contribute to a proliferation of clientelistic effort, it certainly undercuts clientelistic effectiveness. Politicians are compelled to rebuild their entire organizational and associational infrastructure containing opportunism in clientelistic exchange relations. Most likely, several mechanisms are at work that would require detailed case analysis. As the new populist parties are being set up, politicians still have to establish the organizational machinery that makes them effective and efficient vote getters. But in addition, and particularly when left-populists take over the levers of political power and politicize economic decisions, the successful populist politicians lay their hands on valuable economic assets that then can become the disposable mass of discretionary political allocation for clientelistic purposes. When the resource is plentiful, it may not be used very effectively. Natural resource bounties, as in Bolivia, Ecuador, and Venezuela, may be one other channel through which this populist partisan discretion operates.[14]

Finally, a heightened competitiveness in party systems has a positive net effect on the electoral effectiveness of clientelism, presumably because competition provides powerful incentives to use resources in the best possible fashion (models 8–9). Also here the effect is relatively large (the competitiveness index ranges from 1 to 6, going from minimal to maximal value changes clientelistic effectiveness by more than half a standard deviation).

A Hierarchical Analysis of Clientelistic Effectiveness

As a final step, we merged party-level and country-level analysis in a hierarchical linear model using clientelistic effectiveness at the party level or the difference between effectiveness and effort as dependent variables. The hierarchical model in table 10.2 combines the country-level variables included in the models presented in table 10.1 with an array of party-level controls. The results confirm that networks and voter targeting are key elements to making clientelism work well. More important for the present chapter, most of the national-level variables remain robust predictors of clientelistic (in)effectiveness (authoritarian legacy parties, left-populist parties) even when party-specific factors are controlled for. Only the political competitiveness variable is wiped out, but that is because at the party level another competitiveness variable comes into play: clientelistic effectiveness suffers when parties pay off strategic voters who may vacillate between parties rather than focus on their core constituencies or a catch-all of all voters (reference category).

Conclusion

Electoral clientelism in competitive settings is a far cry from what in the past anthropologists and sociologists studied as clientelistic relations between landlords and dependent peasants in primarily monopolistic and highly asymmetric social interactions that afforded neither side the chance to walk away. Much modern electoral clientelism involves competitive situations with exit options and opportunistic strategies available to all actors. This is the case in Latin American countries, where parties in many countries still resort to clientelism as an electoral strategy, but with varying levels of effectiveness. Furthermore, our comparison of party strategies across regions demonstrates the continued relevance of clientelism in Latin America, even though programmatic appeals may be strengthening in some countries. It is all the more important, therefore, to study the conditions that enable politicians and voters to contain opportunism in principal-agent relations. This chapter provides an overview of clientelistic partisan efforts in the region, with a focus both on the individual-level determinants of clientelistic targeting and on the national-level contexts that make clientelistic partisan efforts more or less effective.

TABLE 10.2　HLM Model. Dependent Variable: Clientelistic Electoral Effectiveness

Clientelistic party effort (b15)	0.11*** (0.01)	0.12*** (0.01)	0.12*** (0.01)	0.12*** (0.01)
Electoral support (p11)	0.00*** (0.00)	0.00** (0.00)	0.00** (0.00)	0.00** (0.00)
Executive incumbency (p5_1)	0.02 (0.03)	0.02 (0.03)	0.02 (0.03)	0.02 (0.03)
Local party community (a2)	−0.16* (0.06)	−0.14* (0.06)	−0.14* (0.06)	−0.14* (0.06)
Ties to business groups (a8_2p)	0.06 (0.05)	0.05 (0.05)	0.05 (0.05)	0.05 (0.05)
Ties to religious groups (a8_3p)	0.15** (0.05)	0.15** (0.05)	0.15** (0.05)	0.15** (0.05)
Ties to ethnic groups (a8_4p)	0.23*** (0.06)	0.23*** (0.06)	0.23*** (0.06)	0.22*** (0.06)
Lack of effectiveness of monitoring (c1)	−0.29*** (0.06)	−0.28*** (0.06)	−0.28*** (0.06)	−0.28*** (0.06)
Attracting loyalists only (b12_loy)	−0.02 (0.09)	−0.01 (0.09)	−0.01 (0.09)	−0.01 (0.09)
Attracting strategists only (b12_str)	−0.24^ (0.14)	−0.25^ (0.14)	−0.25^ (0.14)	−0.25^ (0.14)
Programmatic effort (cosalpo_4nwe)	−0.18 (0.24)	−0.43 (0.27)	−0.44 (0.27)	−0.45 (0.28)
Democratic experience (demstock)	0.00 (0.00)	0.00 (0.00)	0.00 (0.00)	0.00 (0.00)
Absolute change in clientelistic effort (absb7)	−0.13^ (0.08)	−0.12^ (0.07)	−0.11 (0.08)	−0.12 (0.08)
Authoritarian legacy parties (alpn)	−0.25 (0.21)	−0.25 (0.20)	−0.26 (0.21)	−0.26 (0.21)
Populist partisan rupture (pop1)	−0.57*** (0.11)	−0.53*** (0.11)	−0.53*** (0.11)	−0.52*** (0.12)
Political competitiveness (p63)	0.01 (0.02)	0.01 (0.02)	0.01 (0.02)	0.01 (0.02)
Average national clientelistic effort (b15nat)		−0.03* (0.02)	−0.03* (0.02)	−0.03 (0.02)
Variance in national clientelistic effort (b15sd)		−0.01 (0.02)	0.03 (0.11)	
b15nat*b15sd				0.00 (0.01)
(Intercept)	2.08*** (0.22)	2.42*** (0.27)	2.43*** (0.28)	2.41*** (0.29)
Log Likelihood	−190.10	−191.17	−193.93	−197.67
N at level 1	488	488	488	488
N at level 2	86	86	86	86

Note: Standard errors in parentheses. ***Significant at .001 **Significant at .01 *Significant at .05 ^Significant at .1

Specific Latin American countries are the showcases in which clientelistic ineffectiveness appears in stark contours. At the national level, conditions facilitating the emergence of durable, stable, iterative relations between patrons and clients boost the effectiveness of clientelism, even without intrusive monitoring or special associational and organizational efforts for which we control in the hierarchical linear model specification of our statistical estimations. The message of our chapter is that the rise of populist left parties is a key disruptive force of clientelistic effectiveness, even though it has more ambivalent effects on clientelistic effort. Of course, a major caveat is that we only have cross-sectional data that can establish correlations, but limit causal inference, and as well we do not sufficiently control for diffusion processes.

Furthermore, our explanation is only moderately successful, as we could not find theoretical mechanisms to account for clientelistic effectiveness gaps that would eliminate the statistical force of the Latin American geographical variable entirely. Thus, there appears to be something about "Latin American" partisan politics that is not entirely captured by analytical variables exposed in this chapter. Further research will have to probe this challenge.

Chapter 10 Appendix

A. QUESTIONS FROM THE DALP EXPERT SURVEY 2008-9

1. **Index of clientelistic effort, individual party score (b15):** Sum of the average scores attributed by all experts i on each of the questions b1 through b5 by all national experts j:

   b1–b5 Question Wording:

   b1: "Consider whether candidates and parties give or promise to give citizens *consumer goods* (e.g., food or liquor, clothes, cookware, appliances, medicines, building materials, etc.) as inducement to obtain their votes. How much effort do candidates and parties expend to attract voters by providing consumer goods?"

   b2: "Consider whether candidates and parties give or promise to give citizens *preferential access to material advantages in public social policy schemes* (e.g., preferential access to subsidized prescription drugs, public scholarships, public housing, better police protection, etc.) as inducement to obtain their votes. How much effort do candidates and parties expend to attract voters by providing preferential public benefits?"

b3: "Consider whether candidates or parties give or promise to give citizens *preferential access to employment in the public sector or in the publicly regulated private sector* (e.g., post office, janitorial services, maintenance work, jobs at various skill levels in state owned enterprises or in large private enterprises with government contracts and subsidies, etc.) as inducement to obtain their vote. How much effort do candidates or parties expend to attract voters by providing preferential access to employment opportunities?"

b4: "Consider whether candidates or parties give or promise to give citizens and businesses *preferential access to government contracts or procurement opportunities* (e.g., public works/ construction projects, military procurement projects without competitive bidding to companies whose employees support the awarding party) as inducement to gain their and their employees' votes. How much effort do candidates or parties expend to attract voters by offering them preferential access to government contracts or procurement opportunities?"

b5: "Consider whether candidates or parties influence or promise to *influence the application of regulatory rules issued by government agencies* (e.g., more lenient tax assessments and audits, more favorable interpretation of import and export regulation, less strict interpretation of fire and escape facilities in buildings, etc.) in order to favor individual citizens or specific businesses as inducement to gain their and their employees' vote. How much effort do candidates or parties expend to attract voters and the businesses for which they work by influencing regulatory proceedings in their favor?"

b1–b5 Value Labels:

[1] A negligible effort or none at all
[2] A minor effort
[3] A moderate effort
[4] A major effort
[99] Don't know

2. **Index of national parties' clientelistic effort (b15.nwe):** national (n) average of the parties' scores of clientelistic effort (b15), weighted (we) by the average of a party's vote shares in the most recent two national legislative elections before the date of the expert survey in 2008-9.

3. **Parties' clientelistic electoral effectiveness (b11):** the average score of all experts *i* given to party *j* on b11:

   b11: "Please assess how effective political parties are in their efforts to mobilize voters by targeted benefits."

   [1] Not at all
   [2] To a small extent
   [3] To a moderate extent
   [4] To a great extent
   [99] Don't know

4. **Experts' assessment of the general change of clientelistic effort for all parties j in country k (b7):** experts' average scores for country k.

   b7: "Do politicians nowadays make the same, greater, or lesser efforts to provide preferential benefits to individuals and small groups of voters than they did about ten (10) years ago?"

   [1] A much lesser effort now
   [2] A somewhat lesser effort now
   [3] About the same effort now
   [4] A somewhat greater effort now
   [5] A much greater effort now
   [99] Don't know

5. **Question wording of items in the DALP expert survey** employed to construct the individual parties' effort to project a programmatic stance. For the index itself (CoSalPo 4 at the party level, CoSalPo_4.nwe at the national level, average programmatic effort of all parties, each weighted by its electoral size in the closest legislative election preceding the expert survey data collection), see Kitschelt and Freeze (2010), downloadable from https://web.duke.edu/democracy/:

   d1: Social spending on the disadvantaged:

   [1] Party advocates extensive social spending redistributing income to benefit the less well-off in society.
   [10] Party opposes extensive social spending redistributing income to benefit the less well-off in society.
   [88] No clear position
   [99] Don't know

   d2: State role in governing the economy:

   [1] Party supports a major role for the state in regulating private economic activity to achieve social goals, in directing development, and/or maintaining control over key services.

[10] Party advocates a minimal role for the state in governing or directing economic activity or development.

[88] No clear position

[99] Don't know

d3: Public spending:

[1] Party supports extensive public provision of benefits such as earnings-related pension benefits, comprehensive national health care, and basic primary and secondary schools for everyone.

[10] Party opposes an extensive state role in providing such benefits and believes that such things as health insurance, pensions, and schooling should be privately provided or that participation in public social insurance programs should be voluntary.

[88] No clear position

[99] Don't know

d4: National identity:

[1] Party advocates toleration and social and political equality for minority ethnic, linguistic, religious, and racial groups and opposes state policies that require the assimilation of such groups to the majority national culture.

[10] Party believes that the defense and promotion of the majority national identity and culture at the expense of minority representation are important goals.

[88] No clear position

[99] Don't know

d5: Traditional authority, institutions, and customs

[1] Party advocates full individual freedom from state inter-ference into any issues related to religion, marriage, sexu-ality, occupation, family life, and social conduct in general.

[10] Party advocates state-enforced compliance of individuals with traditional authorities and values on issues related to religion, marriage, sexuality, occupation, family life and social conduct in general.

[88] No clear position

[99] Don't know

6. **Question wording for individual party level scores (orga-nization, network, party strategy) employed in table 10.2: a2:** "Do the following parties' local organizations maintain a permanent social and community presence by holding social events for local party members or sustaining ancillary social

groups such as party youth movements, party cooperatives, or athletic clubs?"

a8_2: "Do the following parties have strong linkages to *business associations and professional associations?*"

a8_3: "Do the following parties have strong linkages to *religious organizations?*"

a8_4: "Do the following parties have strong linkages to *ethnic/ linguistic organizations?*"

a8_2–a8_4 Question Wording:

[1] Yes

[2] No

[99] Don't Know

c1: "If parties try to check how specific individuals or small groups of citizens voted, how successful are they in getting that information?"

[1] Very Successful

[2] Somewhat Successful

[3] Not at All Successful

[4] Does Not Try to Find Out How Individuals Voted

[99] Don't know

b10: "Considering the special advantages and benefits that accrue to voters of a party, whom do the parties most commonly rely on in their efforts to select the recipients and deliver the benefits to the target constituencies? Please check ALL that apply for each party."

[1] Unions

[2] Business associations and professional associations

[3] Religious Organizations

[4] Ethnic/ linguistic organizations

[5] Urban neighborhood or rural associations/movements

[6] Women's organizations

[99] Don't know

[no response] Not rely on these groups

Clientelistic targeting (b12_loy and b12_str): Recoded from b12: "If parties provide preferential benefits in order to receive votes, which of the following groups of voters do they primarily target?"

a) Partisan loyalists, for whom there is no competition among parties: those who consider voting only for one party and abstain from voting, if that party is not a good prospect.

b) Strategic voters, for whom there is competition among parties: those who consider switching their preferences from one party to another party depending on the past record and the prospective benefits they expect from supporting different competitors.

[1] Primarily to partisan loyalists
[2] Primarily to strategic voters
[3] Both loyal and strategic voters
[99] Don't know

B. DOCUMENTATION OF THE MACRO-LEVEL DATA, SOURCES

1. Electoral support of parties in legislative election closest preceding the DALP expert survey: multiple sources, own coding.

2. Executive incumbency of a party in the legislative term when the DALP expert survey took place: multiple sources, own coding.

3. **Democratic experience (demstock):** Weighted sum of a country's polity scores over the past 100 years, weighting with a discount factor over past Polity scores. Source: Gerring et al. (2005).

4. **Authoritarian legacy party present in country (alpn):** see footnote 214, this paper.

5. **Populist partisan rupture (pop1):** Own coding based on a list of countries with left-populist disruption. In Latin America, we code Bolivia, Ecuador, Mexico, Nicaragua, Paraguay, Peru, and Venezuela as exhibiting a left-populist disruption, but not Argentina, Brazil or Uruguay, to mention only the most likely contentious coding choices.

6. **Political competitiveness (p63):** Own coding, based on the combined vote share of a country's two largest parties in the legislative elections preceding the DALP expert survey, the difference in vote shares received by each of these two largest parties, and the net electoral volatility of all parties' support from the last but one legislative election before the DALP survey took place to the last legislative election preceding the expert survey. For a precise construction of the index, contact Kitschelt to obtain Kitschelt (2012b) and individual country codes.

NOTES

1. Information about the dataset and methodology are available at the project's website at https://web.duke.edu/democracy/, where a wealth of prepublication papers inform about project results.

2. The vote-buying question (clien1) is as follows: In recent years, and thinking about election campaigns, has a candidate or someone from a political party offered you something like a favor, food, or any other benefit in return for your vote? [1] Often [2] Sometimes [3] Never [88] Doesn't Know [98] Doesn't Answer.

3. Question wordings for the relevant DALP questions are provided in the appendix to this chapter.

4. Note that the provision of local club goods that are often not provided in contingent, clientelistic fashion is not included in this list.

5. We are drawing here especially on Kitschelt (2012b) and Kitschelt and Kselman (2013).

6. The exact wording of this question is: I am going to read a list of groups and organizations. Please tell me if you attend their meetings at least once a week, once or twice a month, once or twice a year, or never: Meetings of a political party or political organization? The scale was inverted so that higher values reflect more participation.

7. In Latin America, we code Bolivia, Ecuador, Mexico, Nicaragua, Paraguay, Peru, and Venezuela as exhibiting a left-populist disruption, but not Argentina, Brazil, or Uruguay, to mention only the most likely contentious coding choices. The dummy variable takes on a value of 1 if the polity experienced a disruption and zero if not.

8. Competitiveness is related to the elasticity between marginal changes of parties' electoral support, on one side, and their bargaining power to obtain control over executive government office and authoritative resource allocation on the other. For operationalization, see Kitschelt (2007, 2012a).

9. See the online appendix for a complete description of the hypothesized mechanisms driving the inclusion of this set of party-level variables.

10. When standard errors are computed clustered for countries, the size of standard errors changes somewhat, when compared to the computation of robust standard errors, but without touching the significance level of the variables.

11. The HLM estimations are multilevel models with country-varying intercepts. We explored a few theoretically plausible cross-level interactions, but they yielded nothing interesting. We display the HLM analysis here because it may be the most adequate way to explore the "equilibrium ineffectiveness" argument.

12. The measurement of the variable is explained in Kitschelt and Freeze (2010), available at the DALP project website indicated above.

13. Note that addition of this variable single-handedly drives up the explained variance from 41 to 59%.

14. Since most hydrocarbon-based natural resource extractors and exporters are dictatorships, the number of observations in the set of electoral polities is too small to test whether natural resource abundance, separate from left-populism, also opens up a channel conducive to clientelistic ineffectiveness.

✦ PERFORMANCE AND THE VOTE ✦

Introduction to Part IV:
Performance and the Vote

RYAN E. CARLIN, MATTHEW M. SINGER,
AND ELIZABETH J. ZECHMEISTER

The previous parts of this volume have primarily addressed the vote as a choice wherein voters evaluate the competing candidates based on the demographic characteristics, policies, ideologies, and partisanship that they will represent if elected into office. An alternative perspective is that individuals base their vote on their evaluations of the incumbent government's performance. Indeed, a central tenet in classic theories of voter choice is that if the country's overall situation has improved while the incumbent government has been in power, voters will be inclined to retain his or her party in office. If things have deteriorated, voters are more likely to reject the incumbent party's candidate under the assumption that one of the competing parties will serve as a better steward (Key 1966; Fiorina 1981). These simple decision heuristics do not necessarily supersede considerations of ideological proximity or partisan loyalty because voters view government performance with partisan blinders (e.g., Kramer 1983; Evans and Anderson 2006) and may resist deserting their preferred party regardless of poor performance (Van der Brug, Franklin, and Tóka 2008; Kayser and Wlezien 2011). Performance voting also largely leaves unanswered the question of which alternative to the incumbent voters will select if they decide that change is needed. Nevertheless, the straightforward mechanics of performance voting provide an alternative perspective on how voters decide.

We should not expect voters to behave rashly, punishing the incumbent for anything that goes wrong in their personal lives or in the country or rewarding the ruling party for all good outcomes. In classic accountability theory, voters must decide whether or not the incumbent should be held accountable, which at a minimum entails assessing the degree to which the incumbent is *responsible* for that outcome. While the least sophisticated voters might assume that the government can control everything and that the president controls the government (Gomez and Wilson 2001), accountability theory assumes that most voters are aware of the gap between this stereotype and reality. Many outcomes are beyond the national government's direct control—whether or not the ordinary citizen got a raise or was mugged on the way to work, for example, or whether or not there is a global financial slowdown. Yet voters might judge whether government policies made those personal negative experiences more likely and evaluate how well the national government has responded to international financial swings. Voters also might consider whether the incumbent party was able to implement their preferred policies or had to negotiate with opposition parties in the legislature. If they had to negotiate with other political actors, then those actors will share in the credit for any success that resulted from their collaboration and receive part of the blame for failures (Powell and Whitten 1993).

Voters must also decide which areas of policy performance to *prioritize*. Most of the literature on performance voting focuses on how voters hold politicians accountable for the state of the economy. Yet politicians have the potential to affect a wide variety of policy areas, including crime, corruption, social policy, and foreign policy, and voters may choose to emphasize government performance on noneconomic policy outcomes in their voting decisions (Fiorina 1981; Singer 2011). As voters evaluate politicians who have succeeded in some areas and failed in others, they must decide how to weight these various dimensions of government performance. The electorate's priorities are a partial function of campaign attempts to set the agenda and media coverage of different issues, but they also tend to reflect the pressing issues that have a direct, personal effect on large numbers of voters at election time (see Singer 2011 for a more general review). These differences in priorities mean that incumbent governments in one context might be more likely to be sanctioned for a specific failing than another government in a country where voters prioritize other issues.

The chapters in this part focus on how Latin American voters hold politicians accountable for outcomes under their watch. Doing so requires a different dependent variable from that which formed the basis of many of the analyses in the previous two parts. The nature of this shift in dependent variable reflects both theoretical considerations and questions of data availability. Models of accountability assume that voters look at performance as a way to decide whether or not to retain the incumbent. Voters who feel that the government has performed badly are expected to cast a vote for any alternative, but some might voice their displeasure by abstaining if none of the perceived alternatives is seen as having a credible plan (although in other cases voters frustrated by bad performance may be particularly motivated to participate to demand systemic change). In general, models of performance voting usually focus on the choice to vote for the incumbent or not, a practice that is adopted by each of the three following chapters. Specifically, the dependent variable for this part derives from the following survey question:

"If the next presidential elections were being held this week, what would you do?"

Respondents were given the option of expressing support for the incumbent candidate or party, showing support for a candidate or party different from the current administration, not voting, or casting a blank/null vote. Across the eighteen Latin American countries in the 2012 AmericasBarometer, roughly 36% of respondents said they would vote for the incumbent president, 33% said they would vote for an opposition candidate, 11% would cast a blank/null vote, and the remaining 20% would abstain. Our general expectations for voter choice are straightforward: voters who perceive that outcomes have deteriorated under the incumbent should be less likely to support the ruling party. This question, therefore, allows us to examine *which* outcomes in particular motivate the retrospective vote by comparing the results across this part's chapters, each of which focuses on a different performance topic.

Another reason we focus on this dependent variable is that it asks what respondents would do if the election were held today. In the previous chapters, the authors analyzed voter behavior in the election prior to the survey because the focus was on static or comparatively slow-changing variables like demographics, issue positions, left-right self-identification, and partisanship. Yet policy performance is likely to change more rapidly. Thus, it would be inappropriate to model previous electoral choices as a function of current conditions, especially if the party in power at the time of the survey is different from the one that was in power the last time an election was held. By asking what the voter would do in a snap election, we can gauge how the voter feels about how the incumbent is delivering across a set of different outcome measures.

The chapters in this part focus on three areas of performance: the economy, corruption, and crime. Latin Americans roundly identify these as the most pressing problems facing their countries (see Singer, Carlin, and Love 2012; Singer 2013a; Pérez this volume). All three performance areas tap into key roles of the government: improving citizen wellbeing, governing honestly, and ensuring safety. The evidence in these three chapters finds that government performance plays a strong role in Latin American elections. The chapter by Gélineau and Singer shows that incumbents who preside over a weak economy are generally less likely to be supported than incumbents who have overseen improvements. Manzetti and Rosas also link corruption to reduced support for incumbents. Looking at crime, Pérez finds that voters who feel unsafe are more likely to reject the ruling party. Note that we do not claim that these are the only areas where voters are likely to focus. Politicians who design effective welfare programs, oversee important infrastructure projects, or manage well the nation's relations with other countries, for example, may well reap rewards at the ballot box. Together, these three outcomes establish the important role that electoral accountability plays in Latin America's elections.

Beyond testing the basic performance voting hypothesis, some of the chapters in part IV test a corollary hypothesis as to whether voters emphasize changes in their personal situations or perceived changes in the broader community (for the economy and corruption, the nation; for crime, one's neighborhood). The extant literature on performance voting suggests that voters need not have experienced an economic dislocation personally, been victimized by a crime, or been targeted for a bribe to fear such problems could befall them in the future if policy outcomes have deteriorated under the current administration. Moreover, voters are expected to recognize that national policy outcomes more directly reflect government policies than outcomes in their own lives, which may comport with national trends but also reflect the fruits of the voters' own efforts, talents, and choices (Lau and Sears 1981; Feldman 1982). Since Singer and Carlin (2013) document that perceptions of the national economy play a larger role in Latin American elections than perceptions of changes in voters' personal finances, Gélineau and Singer's chapter does not address that specific topic. Yet the evidence with regards to corruption (in Manzetti and

Rosas's chapter) and crime (in Pérez's chapter) is consistent with this theoretical frame: personal experiences play a less steady electoral role than assessments of the nation's overall trajectory.

A final theme running through the chapters in this part, as with the volume as a whole, is that the electoral impact of policy performance varies across countries and within them over time. Part of this variation reflects differences in the salience of each of these issues to voters and, in turn, which performance domain they prioritize. Both economic performance and corruption receive greater weight from voters when outcomes have been bad. A weak economy also makes voters less forgiving of government corruption. Yet heterogeneity in performance voting not only reflects voters' distinct agendas but also voters' ability to assign responsibility for policy outcomes. Accountability is often muted in fragmented party systems; thus, Gélineau and Singer find that the electoral impact of the economy shrinks as the number of parties in the legislature increases or the president's party's control of the legislature decreases, and Manzetti and Rosas find that voters are also less likely to hold the president accountable for corruption in fragmented party systems, although they find no evidence that voters respond to the number of checks and balances in a system more generally. Voters also take into account how the international financial system may constrain government action. The weight of economic and corruption performance on incumbent support tapers as countries become more heavily integrated into the global financial system. Finally, in the case of the economy, whether the party system provides credible alternatives to the incumbent appears to condition performance voting; that is, as we have seen in previous chapters, a distinct menu of options once again conditions voter choice. In varying ways, the following three chapters thus remind us that the ability of elections to act as mechanisms of accountability is conditional across Latin America. In general, voters' ability to hold politicians accountable is a function of their ability to assign responsibility for policy outcomes and the nature of the choices available on the ballot.

11 ✦ The Economy and Incumbent Support in Latin America

FRANÇOIS GÉLINEAU AND MATTHEW M. SINGER

A central question of the 2006 Mexican presidential election was which party could best manage the economy. Felipe Calderón of the ruling Partido Acción Nacional (PAN) argued that the election offered the choice of "[maintaining] the economic stability we have today and [converting] it into economic growth and jobs through investment, or we can risk losing what we have already achieved."[1] His main rival, Andrés Manuel López Obrador of the Partido de la Revolución Democrática (PRD), declared that the clearest difference between his administration and the previous one would be that under his presidency "[t]here will be economic growth and job growth."[2] The national chamber of commerce also chimed in on the debate, running ads emphasizing the risks of the economic policies offered by the leftist candidate López Obrador and encouraging voters to "defend what we have achieved" instead of risking a return to hyperinflation.[3] While the election was closely contested and voters were divided about the state of the economy, economic improvement in the year before the election was a key factor leading to the incumbent party's narrow victory (Moreno 2009a; Singer 2009b).

The importance of the economy in the 2006 Mexican election is representative of a more general trend in Latin American elections and in elections globally. Challengers often run by promising improvements like "honesty, technology, and work" (Fujimori, Peru 1990) while incumbents try to highlight their record, such as a party telling voters that "because [the president] has done well, we continue with him" (the Dominican Republic, 2008). One former Argentine president seeking to return to office after sitting out a term as required by the Constitution even explicitly reminded voters that "With Menem We Lived Better" (2003 presidential election).

In this chapter, we show that electoral support for presidents' parties in Latin America is strongly conditioned by economic performance.[4] The economy has a large effect because voters consider the economy an important political issue and believe politicians are responsible for economic outcomes. Yet economic voting studies of the United States and Europe suggest that the electoral importance of the economy varies both across countries and within them over time as the conditions that facilitate economic voting shift. In dialogue with these works, we test and find support for the notion that electoral accountability in Latin America is also conditional and is facilitated by incumbents having had clear opportunities to implement their agendas and by elections offering voters alternative visions for how government should be run. When the global economy and party system make it hard to distinguish whether the incumbent is to blame or when elections do not offer meaningful choices, voters have a harder time holding incumbent politicians accountable for the economy or any other policy outcomes.

Under What Conditions Can Voters Hold Politicians Accountable for the Economy?

While the linkage between economic performance and government support is often taken for granted, as illustrated by dictums like "it's the economy, stupid," early studies found no relationship between the two concepts when elections from multiple European and North American countries were pooled (see Anderson 2007 for a review). Why might voters deviate from an economics-based vote? Scholars have identified several rationales, which we briefly review.

First, the economy might not always be *salient* as voters might be focused on issues other than economics. The economy is generally among the most important issues in elections because economic fluctuations affect large numbers of people in a deeply personal way and because information about the economy is easy to obtain. That being said, voters also care about the government's performance in other areas, including crime and corruption (as we will see in the following two chapters), foreign policy and national defense, and education and healthcare (Singer 2011, 2013b). Governments may perform better on some issues than others, forcing voters to decide whether to reward the ruling party's success in one area or to sanction its failures in others. Limitations to cognitive capacity and voter attention also restrict the number of issues voters can learn about. Thus, voters cannot pay attention to everything but instead focus on one or more issues that are personally important to them and these priorities may differ across elections as policy outcomes change. For example, voter and media attention to the economy may increase following a recession as voters clamor for politicians to address the problem (e.g., Bloom and Price 1975; Pacek and Radcliff 1995; Weyland 2000; Echegaray 2005; Singer 2013b; but see Lewis-Beck 1988; Van der Brug et al. 2007). And periods of volatility may generate uncertainty about economic prospects and accentuate the risks associated with weak economic management (Duch and Stevenson 2008; Singer 2011; Singer and Carlin 2013).

A second set of reasons concerns whether the government is held *responsible* for the economy. It makes little sense to hold people accountable for events beyond their control, nor can such outcomes tell the voter anything about the wisdom of the government's economic policies or competence (e.g., Peffley 1984; Gomez and Wilson 2001; Rudolph 2003; Beltrán 2003). But when individuals believe the incumbent is responsible for the state of the economy, they are generally more likely to focus on economic performance when voting. Based on the assumption that presidential responsibility for economic outcomes varies systematically across contexts, two loci of control have received the most emphasis in the extant literature.

One focuses on the degree of *political control* incumbents enjoy. Generally speaking, any factor that concentrates authority in a single party strengthens electoral accountability while any factor that diffuses it makes it harder to evaluate who is to blame (Hellwig 2011). Powell and Whitten (1993), for example, argue that executives forced to negotiate with minority governments or coalition partners are less likely to receive sole credit or blame for the economy. More generally, the economic vote increases inasmuch as the president's party can dominate the legislature (see Anderson 2007 for a review; Duch and Stevenson 2008). A more indirect factor is multiparty competition since it tends to fragment the legislature and, thus, raises the chances of minority control. This, in turn, frustrates voters' attempts to assign responsibility to parties for outputs (Anderson 2000).[5]

More recently, researchers have explored governments' *effective control* over the economy. For example, some voters may blame domestic business actors instead of policymakers for economic swings. Yet domestic economies do not operate independently from global markets, in which case globalization may affect assessments of responsibility. A recession in the United States may spill over into Mexico. A financial panic in Thailand may lead to pressure on the Brazilian currency. Global swings in commodity prices or shifts in export targets may have large effects on the opportunities Latin American firms have to export their wares. In such contexts, the incumbent government has little control over economic outcomes. Thus, voters may ask themselves whether the economic swings they observe solely reflect the incumbent's policy choices. Hellwig (2007), Hellwig and Samuels (2007), and Alcañiz and Hellwig (2011) argue that voters are less likely to sanction governments for economic outcomes in markets highly exposed to trade, the global economy, and international financial institutions.

Finally, the presence of a *credible alternative* (Anderson 2000; Bengtsson 2004) may make voters more likely to sanction the incumbent for past economic performance. Voters can turn to the opposition parties' past records in office to infer whether they might be more competent (Magaloni 1999; Benton 2005). Yet, voters may attribute economic outcomes not to candidate competence but to distinct economic approaches. If voters doubt other parties would (and/or could) make better economic policy choices, then abandoning the incumbent is less viable. But if a challenger advocates a different set of economic policies, he or she may be more attractive to voters when the economy is floundering. In this vein, Hellwig (2010) argues that clear ideological differences between candidates make it easier to frame the challenger as an alternative to the status quo. Thus, a polarized party system makes economic voting more likely because voters can expect changing the ruling party to result in a new economic policy.

In sum, economic voting should be observed when economic issues are salient, when voters hold politicians accountable for economic outcomes under their watch, and when voters have clear and viable alternatives. Whether or not these conditions are met in Latin America should help us understand the extent of economic voting in the region.[6]

Conditions for Economic Voting in Latin America Are Strong on Average

Descriptive evidence suggests that all three conditions necessary for economic voting to occur are regularly observed in Latin America. First, the frequency of economic crises and the high levels of economic vulnerability within the region should serve to focus voter attention on economic performance. Survey data are consistent with that expectation. In every Latinobarometer and AmericasBarometer survey since 1995, a plurality of respondents has consistently identified the economy as the most important problem facing their country (Singer 2013a).[7] Crime and security concerns generally rank as the second most commonly identified problems, followed by social policy, corruption, and governance. A similar pattern emerges from electoral surveys asking voters to identify the most important issue when deciding which candidate to support; in all surveys for which data are available, more respondents favored economic performance over any other issue (Singer 2013a). The economy is sufficiently important to Latin American voters that they even ignore corruption when incumbents generate a strong economy (Manzetti and Wilson 2006; Zechmeister and Zizumbo-Colunga 2013; Manzetti and Rosas this volume).

As for attribution of responsibility, Latin American voters generally hold the government responsible for economic swings. For example, in the 2002 and 2003 waves of Latinobarometer surveys, respondents asked who was responsible for the economic problems of their country were far more likely to blame the government's economic policy than any other organization or group (Alcañiz and Hellwig 2011). This reflects the economic and political reality of Latin America. While external conditionality programs and fears of upsetting credit markets influence policymaking in the region (Kaplan 2013), Latin American economies are less globally exposed than Western Europe's are and thus voters looking to understand the state of the economy may have good reasons to focus on domestic actors.[8] Presidentialism also has a tendency to lead voters to focus their attention on the incumbent because he or she is the face of the government and electoral campaigns focus on leaders and their plans (Samuels 2004). This is particularly true if presidents are largely seen as "proactive" and other political actors as "reactive" (Cox and Morgenstern 2001).

Lastly, while Latin American countries differ in the degree to which elections are structured around programmatic competition (Kitschelt et al. 2010; Kitschelt and Altamirano this volume), economic divisions are the most common issue cleavage in Latin America's legislatures (Kitschelt et al. 2010). Thus, elections are likely to focus on economic policy, which will lead voters to contrast opposition parties with the current government.

Support for the Incumbent Is Strongly Shaped by Economic Performance

The presence of these three conditions raises the likelihood of economic voting in the region. To this day, economic voting is one area of voting behavior that has been widely explored in the Latin American context (there are too many studies to cite, but see Lewis-Beck and Stegmaier 2009 for one review of this extensive literature). All in all, these studies offer evidence that while incumbents in the 1980s and early 1990s were punished for rising inflation, in the past two decades incumbents in the region have been evaluated on their ability to create a growing economy that provides opportunities for its citizens.[9] Government support also seems to fluctuate with individual-level perceptions of economic trends.

We can illustrate the strong relationship between citizens' evaluations of the national economy and their voting intentions in the hemisphere using individual-level data from the 2012 AmericasBarometer. In this survey, respondents were asked if they would vote for the candidate/party of the current president, vote for another candidate, or leave their ballot blank if a national election were held that day.[10] They were also asked about whether the national economy was worse, the same, or better than it was a year before.[11] The basic expectation is that citizens who have positive opinions of the economy should be more likely to support the incumbent than they are to vote for the opposition or cast a blank vote.

As we model the effect of economic perceptions in a multinomial logit model, we control for the respondent's ideological proximity to the incumbent president on a left-right dimension. This allows us to control for the possibility that certain voters will be more optimistic about the economy simply because of the party/ideological position of the president.[12] We also control for perceived government performance in other areas such as respondents' personal experiences with corruption and crime, their evaluations of corruption levels in the government overall, and whether they feel insecure in their neighborhood.[13] Given that incumbents have different demographic types and ideological stripes, our expectations differ from country to country and therefore we do not control for respondents' demographic characteristics. We include fixed country effects to control for differences in incumbents' baseline levels of support.

Complete results of the multinomial logit analysis are available in the appendix (table A11.1) but they suggest that individuals who see the economy as improving are significantly less likely to vote for the opposition or cast a blank vote than those who believe the economy is deteriorating. To illustrate, figure 11.1 estimates the predicted electoral choice for a person who has average values on all the other variables given their evaluations of the national economy. According to these results, a respondent who sees the economy as improving has a probability of voting for the incumbent more than 35 points higher than a respondent who sees the economy as deteriorating. This economic effect is substantially larger than similar

If the Election Were Held Today, Respondent Would:

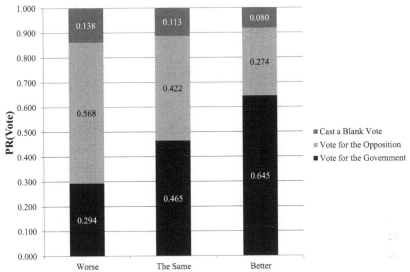

Figure 11.1   Economic Perceptions and Predicted Behavior if an Election Were Held Today. *Source:* AmericasBarometer 2012. *Note:* Predicted probabilities based on a multinomial logit analysis controlling for corruption perceptions, perceived insecurity, crime and corruption victimization, ideological proximity to the incumbent, and country fixed effects, all set at their mean. The model includes 15,549 respondents with responses weighted so that all countries are weighted equally and to control for the survey design. Voters who would abstain are not included. The multinomial logit results are available in the appendix to this chapter as table A11.1.

increases in perceived government corruption or neighborhood insecurity, and is even slightly larger than the predicted impact of ideological proximity.[14]

Citizens who perceive the economy is getting worse are, in contrast, less likely to support the president. The probability that a person votes for the opposition is 29 points higher if she or he thinks the economy is shrinking instead of growing. The probability that an individual casts a blank vote is also slightly higher (6 percentage points) if the respondent thinks the economy is worsening. The choice of the specific opposition party voters supports or, otherwise, their choice to abstain or cast a blank vote is beyond the scope of this analysis but reflects the material, psychological, and programmatic considerations explored in the other chapters in this volume. The primary effect of the economy is on levels of incumbent support while these secondary factors govern voters' choices about which parties they support if they reject the incumbent.

Economic Voting Systematically Differs across and within Latin American Countries

While we observe a strong association between economic assessments and voting behavior on average in Latin America, the conditions that make it possible for voters to hold politicians accountable vary across countries and within them over time. The salience of the economy should vary as conditions change. Presidential control over the policymaking process changes as alignments shift and global exposure also differs across countries. Finally, party systems differ in the range of options they make available to voters. Thus, we expect the strength of the economic effect to vary across the region.

To test for differences in economic voting across countries and over time, we move beyond the 2012 survey used above to maximize the number of contextual settings available for analysis. We pool data from two sources: Latinobarometer surveys conducted annually between 1995 and 2010[15] and AmericasBarometer surveys conducted every other year between 2008 and 2012.[16] We rely on both data sources to obtain the greatest temporal and geographic coverage possible. The resulting sample includes 281 country-years: 230 country-survey-years from the Latinobarometer and 51 from the AmericasBarometer. Both surveys ask respondents whom they would vote for if an election were held shortly and contain comparable economic perception measures that ask about changes in the economy over the past twelve months. There is, however, an important difference in how the vote question is asked. In the Latinobarometer, the vote question is open-ended and the respondent can name any candidate or party. In the AmericasBarometer, it is close-ended and the respondents are asked to say whether they would vote for the candidate/party of the current president, vote for another candidate, or leave their ballot blank.[17] The result of these different frames is a different pattern of voter responses. In the open-ended question, roughly 36% of Latinobarometer respondents with an opinion planned to support the ruling party.[18] In contrast, roughly 46% of AmericasBarometer respondents said they planned to vote for the incumbent. We take these differences into account in the analysis that follows.

To estimate the effect of the economy on incumbent support, we follow the two-stage hierarchical model technique developed by Duch and

Stevenson (2005, 2008) in their work on economic voting in Western Europe and North America and replicated by Gélineau (2013) for a global developing countries sample.[19] We estimate a separate vote choice model for each country-year, with a dichotomous measure of incumbent support modeled as a function of the respondent's economic perceptions, left-right self-identification, and demographic characteristics (namely, age, gender, and education) using binary logistic regression.[20] Responses to the economic perception measure are coded on a 3-point scale such that the current economy is either worse (0), the same (1), or better (2) than it had been previously. The estimated coefficients from the model are used to simulate the predicted change in incumbent support if each respondent were to become 1 point more optimistic on the 3-point economic perception scale; individuals who are already at the top of the scale are left at the highest possible value. This methodology provides a summary measure of the marginal effect of the economy given the distribution of other demographic characteristics within the sample. Estimations of the economy's effect are performed with Monte Carlo simulations using *Clarify* (King, Tomz, and Wittenberg 2000; Tomz, Wittenberg, and King 2001). These estimates of the economic effects can then be modeled (in the second stage) to explore the variation of the strength across contexts (over time and space).[21]

Most (89%) country-years exhibit a positive association between economic perceptions and government support. The consequence of making all voters' economic perceptions 1 point more optimistic on the 3-point scale is to increase the percentage of the vote received by the incumbent by 10.7 percentage points for the closed-list question format and by 5.6 percentage points for the open-list format. Both of these estimates are at least as large as the 5-point effect Duch and Stevenson (2008) find on average in more wealthy democracies and quite comparable to those obtained by Gélineau (2013). The fact that there is a gap depending on whether we are using the open-ended or close-ended vote intention question is not a source of concern. We found that the estimated effects are correlated with each other across data sources in the years for which we have overlapping surveys (2008, 2010) and thus we believe they tap into a common pattern of voting behavior.[22] To develop a single estimate of the size of the economic effect in any given year, we combine them using a strategy developed by Stimson (1991, 55–57) in which the measures are placed on a common scale and then averaged.[23]

Figure 11.2 graphs the estimated economic effects for each Latin American country, sorting them by their median value. These data show that the

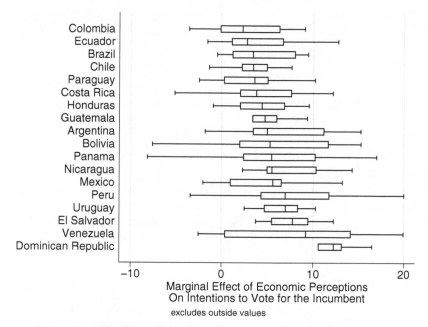

Figure 11.2   The Magnitude of the Economic Vote by Country, 1995–2012. *Source:* AmericasBarometer 2008–2012 and Latinobarometer 1995–2011. The vertical center lines in the box plot represent the country-specific median, the thick rectangles the 25th and 75th percentiles, and the whiskers represent the most extreme values within 1.5 interquartile ranges of the 25th/75th percentiles.

economic effect varies across countries. The economy has a larger electoral effect in the Dominican Republic, for example, than in any other country, and then Venezuela, El Salvador, Uruguay, and Peru also have particularly large economic votes. The smallest economic votes tend to be in Colombia and Ecuador. Yet the large standard deviations within countries remind us that there are significant differences in economic voting over time within countries as well. Particularly in Argentina, Bolivia, Panama, Peru, and Venezuela, for example, the electoral effects of the economy are weak in some periods and strong in others.

These variations in economic voting across Latin America have not gone unnoticed by scholars. Several studies find that Latin American voters adjust their responses to the economy in accordance to the relative level of control the government has over decision-making. Electoral fragmentation, for example, weakens the link between economic outcomes and government support (Echegaray 2005; Johnson and Schwindt-Bayer 2009; Singer and Carlin 2013). Voters also seem to take the broader economic context into account when evaluating incumbent control over the economy. Alcañiz and Hellwig (2011) find that when countries have debt agreements with the International Monetary Fund (IMF), voters are less likely to hold domestic politicians responsible for the economy. Singer and Carlin (2013) show that the link between economic perceptions and government support is weaker in economies with high levels of trade openness. Less attention has been given to factors that explain the economy's salience. Echegaray (2005) argues that economic voting is larger during bad economic times than good ones. The economic agenda may also be affected by longer trends in the economy. Remmer (2003) and Singer (2013a) show that inflation faded as an issue concern with the end of hyperinflation, though periods of economic volatility heighten the economy's effects (Singer and Carlin 2013).

The estimates of economic voting in figure 11.2 allow us to expand on these analyses by illustrating how economic factors, globalization, the concentration of political control, and partisan polarization affect the size of the economy's electoral effect. Specifically, we model the estimated economic vote for each country-year as a function of the context in which respondents were surveyed. To test whether economic voting peaks during an economic downturn, we include a dummy (dichotomous) variable for surveys conducted during a year when the economy is shrinking. To test whether the economy gains salience in countries that have had extended *economic volatility*, we control for the standard deviation of the growth rate in the ten years prior to the survey. We measure the incumbent's *political control* in two ways. In one model specification we use the share of legislative seats held by the president's party. Alternatively, we look at legislative fragmentation more broadly by controlling for the effective number of legislative parties. To measure the incumbent's *economic control*, we include Dreher, Gaston, and Martens' (2008) economic globalization index, which combines trade flows and foreign direct investment levels with policies on tariffs and exports to generate a summary measure of exposure to the world economy.[24] Economic voting should increase with executive control of the legislature and decrease with electoral fragmentation and globalization. Since the breadth of policy differences from which voters can choose differs across contexts, we include a measure of *ideological polarization* within the legislatures developed by Singer (forthcoming) and expect polarization to amplify economic effects.[25]

A preliminary inspection of the data suggests that there is autocorrelation in predicted economic effects within countries.[26] We thus estimate a pooled cross-sectional time series model with a unique autocorrelation coefficient for each country and standard errors adjusted for heteroskedasticity across panels. Missing data on some independent variables reduce the number of observations to 233 country-years.

The results presented in table 11.1 show that voter responses to the economy fluctuate in predictable ways. First, the economic effect increases when the economy is shrinking. Yet, the influence of the economy is not affected by short-term swings in the economy. Indeed, there is no evidence that the marginal effect of economic perceptions is larger when the economy is volatile. In results not reported here, we find no evidence that short downturns in other economic indicators like inflation or unemployment sharpen voters' attention on the economy. Instead, longer-term trends of economic volatility appear to affect the salience of the economy.

By way of illustration, in Peru the average economic effect went from a high of 12.56 percentage points in 1995–2000 to a low of 5.39 points in 2005–12. This decline in economic voting is consistent with the overall long-term economic volatility. The 1995–2000 period followed a decade of high economic instability in Peru. While the economy had somewhat recovered during Fujimori's first term, it continued to suffer episodes of volatility as economic reforms were implemented, and then again in the

TABLE 11.1   Pooled Time Series Model of the Economy's Electoral Effect

	[1]	(SE)	[2]	(SE)
Country in a Recession	0.487	(1.039)	0.165	(1.043)
Economic Volatility	0.525*	(0.214)	0.582**	(0.214)
Share of Seats Held by the President's Party	5.754*	(2.702)		
Effective Number of Parties in the Legislature			−0.687**	(0.223)
Economic Globalization	−0.082*	(0.036)	−0.114**	(0.039)
Partisan Polarization	1.405**	(0.498)	1.418**	(0.492)
Constant	4.696	(2.691)	11.229*	(3.058)
Number of Observations	233		233	
Number of Countries	18		18	
R^2	0.254		0.254	
χ^2	23.40***		25.71***	

Source: AmericasBarometer 2008–2012 and Latinobarometer 1995–2011.

Note: OLS Regression Standard Errors in Parentheses Corrected for Panel Specific Autocorrelation and Heteroskedasticity. * $p < 0.05$, ** $p < 0.01$, *** $p < 0.001$

aftermath of the 1997 Asian financial collapse. In contrast, the 2001–12 period was relatively stable, with steady growth rates during most years. As the economy stabilized, its electoral impact declined.

Second, the clearer the incumbent's political control, the stronger the economic vote. Voters are more likely to hold incumbents accountable as they gain control of the legislature. High levels of incumbent in control of the legislature at least partially explain the high levels of economic voting in the two countries where we observe the greatest average economic effect: the Dominican Republic and Venezuela. In the former, the average incumbent (2004–12) controlled 46% of the legislature and in Venezuela average incumbent support was 53% (1996–2012). Alternatively, the economy's effect falls with electoral fragmentation. The three highest levels of electoral fragmentation in this period are in Colombia, Ecuador, and Brazil—the three countries with the smallest median estimated economic effect in figure 11.2.

In the same vein, globalization also contributes to reducing the economic effect. As Latin American economies become more open to trade and integrated into the global economy, domestic economic actors and policies cease to be the prime drivers of economic trends. Not surprisingly, then, the region's most globalized economy, Chile, also features one of the smallest economic votes. Honduras also illustrates this trend. Its KOF globalization score increased from 55 in 1996 (right around the 28th percentile for the hemisphere) to nearly 70 in 2010 (above the 85th percentile), but the estimated economic voting effect shrunk. Even if we exclude the survey conducted in the aftermath of the 2009 coup, in which economic voting was very small for the new government, the average estimated economic vote in the 1990s was 6.32 compared to 3.1 in the 2005–12 period.

Third, the analysis offers support for the hypothesis that ideological polarization helps voters identify alternatives to the incumbent. For example, the two most polarized countries in Latin America, El Salvador and Nicaragua, also have estimated levels of economic voting that rank among the region's highest. Yet, polarization is not a necessary condition for high levels of economic voting to occur. The Dominican Republic has strong economic voting despite a legislature largely devoid of ideological structure.

In sum, the economy's electoral effect is largest when countries have experienced extended periods of economic volatility, when domestic economies are not closely tied to international markets, when the ruling party has to negotiate with few other parties, and when there are clear governing alternatives.

Conclusion: Holding Latin America's Presidents Accountable

The data in this chapter leave little doubt that voters in Latin America respond to the economy in ways that are quite comparable to those of other regions. Voters are more likely to base their vote decision on the economy when economic performance is a salient issue, but will focus on other issues when they instead dominate the public debate. Voters are less likely to base their vote on the economy when the incumbent lacks control over the policymaking process in the legislature and when the domestic economy is strongly exposed to shocks from the international economic system. Finally, voters less reliably focus their vote on the economy in the absense of ideological alternatives to the incumbent, although the evidence on this question is less consistent than for the other factors. Further empirical work needs to be done to confirm these empirical findings, but the literature on economic voting in Latin America has essentially caught up with the literature on economic voting in Western Europe and the United States.

It is more difficult to say what these findings mean for democracy in the region. It is easy to see the strong empirical association between economic performance and voter behavior and assume that elections are working to hold politicians accountable. However, a strong association between economics and voter choices could also merely reflect the high salience of the economy in a region that has experienced multiple periods of economic uncertainty in its recent history. Yet, the patterns across countries suggest that voters do not reflexively blame the president for economic outcomes, but instead take into account the larger political and economic context. While presidentialism channels voter attention to the incumbent, voters do not seem to be ignorant of the presidents' limits in economic policymaking. Moreover, the data suggest that a party system that offers clear alternatives makes it easier for voters to abandon the incumbent if things go bad. Thus, a strong economic vote often reflects the ability of the party system to frame the choice to keep or replace the incumbent in a substantively meaningful way.

Bolivia provides an extreme example of how a shifting partisan environment can make it easier for voters to hold politicians accountable through elections. At the start of the period under study, Bolivia's party system was best described as "inchoate" (Mainwaring and Scully 1995b). Elections were fragmented but there were few ideological differences between parties, electoral competition focused on leaders' personalities, and presidents had to rely on broad and frequently divided coalitions to get legislation passed. Under these conditions, it should have been difficult to hold the president accountable given the lack of clear responsibility or clear alternatives, and that is what we see in the data. During the 1997–2004 period, the average economic voting effect was only 2.94 percentage points. Yet, the collapse of the traditional parties in the 2002–5 period and the rise of Evo Morales and the Movimiento al Socialismo (MAS) have since resulted in a substantive increase in the president's ability to control the legislative process and higher levels of political polarization. Thus, it is not surprising that our data show that economic voting increased to an average of 10.97 points during the 2005–12 period. As the governing party's control over the legislative process became more consolidated and choices became more meaningful, the conditions for economic accountability to take place were enhanced and voter behavior shifted accordingly.

However, while our data show that incumbent support in the region swings in accordance with economic fluctuations, only two presidents in Latin America seeking immediate reelection have failed to win their electoral contest (Ortega in Nicaragua in 1990 and Mejía in the Dominican Republic in 2004). Incumbent presidents whose performance falls short are likely to lose votes, but manage to stay in office. While we do not know precisely why this incumbency advantage exists, it reminds us of the limits of electoral accountability. Voters also consider the politicians' personalities, their personal characteristics, and their partisanship. The prevalence of clientelism in the region may also work against voters holding politicians accountable for the management of national affairs if they are able to deliver personalized benefits to potential supporters. Finally, in many countries the party system makes it difficult for voters to tell who is responsible for the final outcome that is produced or fails to offer voters a meaningful policy choice. Despite these obstacles, our analysis demonstrates that Latin America's votes are conditionally shaped by the economy in ways that suggest that voters judiciously evaluate the incumbent and carefully weigh their electoral alternatives.

Chapter 11 Appendix

Figure 11.1 graphs predicted voting behaviors among those who think the national economy is getting worse/staying the same/getting better using the 2012 AmericasBarometer. In table A11.1, we present the multinomial logit on which the estimates are based.

TABLE A11.1 Who respondent would vote for if the election were held today

	Vote for Opposition	(SE)	Blank Vote	(SE)
National Economy is Improving	−0.758***	(0.031)	−0.663***	(0.043)
Corruption among Government Officials is Common	0.266***	(0.025)	0.126***	(0.036)
Corruption Victim	0.168**	(0.054)	0.221**	(0.070)
Neighborhood is Insecure	0.086***	(0.025)	0.156***	(0.036)
Crime Victim	0.001	(0.001)	0.001°	(0.001)
Proximity to the President on the Left-Right Scale	−0.181***	(0.012)	−0.107***	(0.015)
Argentina	−0.371*	(0.147)	0.051	(0.244)
Bolivia	0.518***	(0.157)	1.744***	(0.203)
Brazil	−0.949***	(0.147)	0.519*	(0.221)
Chile	0.871***	(0.163)	1.228***	(0.242)
Colombia	−0.379**	(0.144)	1.566***	(0.207)
Costa Rica	0.190	(0.133)	0.405	(0.247)
Dominican Republic	−0.320*	(0.126)	−0.844***	(0.237)
Ecuador	−0.894***	(0.143)	1.033***	(0.192)
El Salvador	−0.461***	(0.128)	0.238	(0.220)
Guatemala	−0.466**	(0.160)	−0.140	(0.234)
Honduras	0.039	(0.139)	0.335	(0.232)
Nicaragua	−1.074***	(0.130)	−0.947***	(0.243)
Panama	0.861***	(0.168)	1.600***	(0.250)
Paraguay	1.067***	(0.141)	1.512***	(0.214)
Peru	0.500***	(0.148)	1.663***	(0.200)
Uruguay	−0.222°	(0.128)	1.339***	(0.186)
Venezuela	−0.834***	(0.139)	−1.961***	(0.380)
Constant	0.344*	(0.135)	−1.867***	(0.214)
Number of Observations	15,549			
F	46.32***			
R^2	0.118			

Source: AmericasBarometer 2012.

Note: Multinomial Logit, Standard Errors Adjusted for Survey Design in Parentheses. Individuals who intend to abstain are excluded, reference category is vote for the incumbent. ° $p < 0.10$, * $p < 0.05$, ** $p < 0.01$, *** $p < 0.001$

NOTES

1. "Mexico's Calderon Names 100 Proposals for Presidency," *Bloomberg*, June 20, 2006.

2. "Conversations with Mexico's Presidential Candidates: A Talk With Andres Manuel Lopez Obrador," *Washington Post*, Sunday, June 18, 2006, B03.

3. See, for example, http://www.youtube.com/watch?v=j7Alu_eehiE.

4. Our analyses focus on presidential voting for both practical and theoretical reasons. On the practical side, current survey data do not allow us to distinguish voting intentions for presidential or legislative elections. On the theoretical side, the literature has clearly established the central role Latin American presidents play in the policymaking process, especially in economic affairs (Mainwaring and Shugart 1997; Crisp 2000; O'Donnell 1994). Thus, the economic vote should be strongest in the context of presidential elections, as documented by Samuels (2004).

5. Electoral fragmentation might also make it more difficult to determine what the plausible alternative governing coalition would be (Bengtsson 2004).

6. Although there is potentially a lot to be said about the individual sources of variation in economic voting across economic groups or between partisans and independents, in this chapter, we restrict the analysis to the aggregate sources of variation in economic voting. We address some of the individual-level sources of heterogeneity in Latin American economic voting in Singer (2011a) and Singer and Gélineau (2012); see also Gomez and Wilson (2006) and Beltrán (2003).

7. This question is not a perfect measure of issue salience (although it is widely used as one) because it asks respondents specifically about *problems* and thus might lead voters to not discuss issue areas where government performance has been good (Wlezien 2005).

8. The average values on the KOF economic globalization measure is 60.6 for the 18 Latin American countries and 77.7 for Western Europe, the United States and Canada, and Australia, New Zealand, and Japan. Latin America has smaller trade/foreign direct investment (FDI) flows and more restrictions on trade and capital flows. The data are available at http://globalization.kof.ethz.ch/.

9. Remmer (1991, 2003); Cuzán and Bundrick (1997); Echegaray (2005); Benton (2005); Gélineau (2007, 2013); Johnson and Schwindt-Bayer (2009); Johnson and Ryu (2010); Alcañiz and Hellwig (2011); Singer (2013a).

10. The survey question also included abstention as an option. Rejection of the incumbent may take the form of abstention, as weak performance leads voters to withdraw from politics more generally (see also Tillman 2008). However, in this chapter we limit the analysis to those individuals who have decided to participate.

11. We use the sociotropic indicator instead of an egotropic one because Singer and Carlin (2013) show that in most Latin American countries sociotropic concerns have a much larger effect than egotropic ones do.

12. We control for the respondent's proximity to the incumbent on the left-right scale, estimating the incumbent's position using the Wiesehomeier and Benoit (2009) expert survey. Wiesehomeier and Benoit code ideology on a 19-point scale (1–20) while the AmericasBarometer survey asked respondents to place themselves on a 1–10 left-right scale. So we first rescaled the Wiesehomeier and Benoit scores for incumbents or their party on the 1–10 scale. We then measure proximity to the incumbent as $|I_R - I_G|^* - 1 + 10$ (where I_G is the ideology of the government and I_R is the left-right identification of the respondent) so that high values represent having a similar left-right score to the incumbent. This specification results in dropping respondents who did not answer the left-right identification question. In an alternative specification we code all respondents who did not answer the proximity question as having the mean proximity score and then included a dummy variable identifying these non-left-right respondents (by coding them as 1 and all others as

zero), and the substantive conclusions regarding government performance do not change.

13. Perceived corruption levels are measured using the question "Taking into account your own experience or what you have heard, corruption among public officials is very common, common, uncommon, or very uncommon?" We include a dummy variable scored 1 if the respondent was targeted for a bribe by a policeman, government employee, court, or local government official, or in the workplace, school, or health system. The crime perception question asks, "Speaking of the neighborhood where you live and thinking of the possibility of being assaulted or robbed, do you feel very safe, somewhat safe, somewhat unsafe, or very unsafe?" Finally we include a dummy variable that takes the value of 1 if a member of the household has been a victim of a crime in the past year.

14. As feelings of insecurity go from their minimum to their maximum, the predicted probability of supporting the incumbent falls by 0.07. A similar change in perceiving the government as corrupt reduces predicted government support by 0.17. Corruption victims are 0.04 less likely to support the incumbent and households while crime victims are 0.03 less likely. Finally, as ideological proximity increases from its minimum to its maximum, the probability of supporting the incumbent increases by 0.32.

15. The Dominican Republic is only included in Latinobarometer surveys after 2004. The 1995 survey was restricted to Argentina, Brazil, Chile, Mexico, Paraguay, Peru, Uruguay, and Venezuela. The 2007 surveys did not ask the full battery of economic perception questions and are thus excluded from the analysis. No survey was conducted in 1999. Surveys conducted in 2011–12 were not available for purchase at the time of writing.

16. The 2008 wave was the first AmericasBarometer survey to ask respondents whom they would vote for if an election were held today; previous waves only asked about whom they had supported in the previous election.

17. In both surveys, voters who abstained are excluded from the analysis. In an alternative analysis we estimated the economic vote when counting abstaining voters as rejecting the incumbent and found that the estimated economic voting effects correlate with those used here at the $r = 0.965$ level.

18. Because the variable is a measure of incumbent support, those who state a firm rejection of all candidates as they plan to vote for "no candidate" are included as non-incumbent supporters.

19. Singer and Carlin (2013) analyze the Latinobarometer surveys to explore how economic voting varies across contexts in Latin America using a one-stage hierarchical model instead of the two-stage approach used here and the results are comparable.

20. Age: in years; Education: Years of education of respondent, ranges from 0–17; Possessions: A count of the following objects owned by the household: Color television, Refrigerator/Icebox/ freezer, Own home, Computer, Washing machine, Telephone, Car, A second home or holiday home, Drinking water, Hot water, Sewage system; Gender: Male (1) or Female (0); Catholic: From the open-ended question "What is your religion?" [1] if Catholic, and [0] otherwise; No Religion: From the open-ended question "What is your religion?" [1] if "None" or "Atheist" or "Agnostic," and [0] otherwise.

21. Two-stage models are particularly appropriate when the goal of the analysis is to appropriately specify the individual-level predictors (as in this case) and if the variables' effects differ within the sample (Franzese 2005). The use of two-stage models also allows us to minimize concerns about pooling data with differences in question wording (e.g., in the control variables) across survey houses because there is no single pooled dataset.

22. The largest difference from the years when we have both surveys is from Venezuela in 2008, which has an estimated economic vote of 19.6% in the 2008 AmericasBarometer survey and 0.92 percent in the 2008 Latinobarometer survey. Yet the bivariate correlation between the two estimates of the economy's effect in 2008–10 is 0.7 if Venezuela 2008 is excluded from the analysis.

23. An inspection of the data suggests that the two series have different means but comparable standard deviations. We re-center the AmericasBarometer data series so that it has the same mean as the Latinobarometer series and then take the arithmetic average for the years that overlap.

24. We use this measure to follow Hellwig (2014) who uses it as his primary measure of global financial exposure. For the 2010 and 2012 survey years we use 2009's estimates of economic globalization as a baseline.

25. While this measure focuses on overall levels of polarization and not specific differences in economic policy, the most consistent dimension underlying elite cleavages in Latin America is economics (Kitschelt et al. 2010) and so these data likely track differences in economic policy preferences.

26. The Wooldridge test for autocorrelation in panel data generates a statistic of 4.423, and rejects the hypothesis of no autocorrelation with $p = 0.051$.

12 · Corruption and the Latin American Voter

LUIGI MANZETTI AND GUILLERMO ROSAS

Why do citizens support corrupt leaders? This phenomenon has significant implications for democratic accountability and good governance, particularly in a region like Latin America that has struggled to establish trustworthy institutions. One of the most common and well-accepted answers to this question is that people are willing to support politicians as long as they deliver on their needs. In the 1950s, followers of São Paulo governor Ademar de Barros proudly said of him, *rouba mas faz* (he steals but he gets things done), and in Mexico during the same decade people made similar comments about President Miguel Alemán (Goertzel 2005).

These unfortunate events have also occurred in recent times. In Argentina, for instance, Carlos Menem (1995) and Cristina Fernández de Kirchner (2011) easily won reelection, earning 50% and 54% of total votes, respectively, in spite of mounting corruption scandals in part because voters credited them for the good economic conditions that the country enjoyed until the previous year. However, there are also cases where good economic conditions have not sufficed to help incumbents. In 2013, Kirchner's party received only 30% in midterm congressional elections, despite her good record in creating employment and economic growth in previous years, as a number of major corruption allegations against her and her entourage broke out that year. We could see these contradictory events as indication that, as in North America and some European countries, Latin American citizens may reason along the lines of the "responsibility hypothesis" (Downs 1957), according to which voters hold elected officials accountable for their behavior at least some of the time.

The academic debate around the responsibility hypothesis is quite extensive, but some of the most essential findings regarding how the responsibility hypothesis relates to corruption can be quickly summarized. One stream of research finds that corruption discourages voters in Mexico (Domínguez and McCann 1998), in Eastern Europe (Kostadinova 2009; Klašnja, Tucker, and Deegan-Krause 2014), as well as in a broad cross-section of less developed countries (Stockemer, LaMontagne, and Scruggs 2013). Another stream contends instead that increased levels of corruption actually galvanize citizens to oust crooked officials through the ballot box in some African countries (Bratton, Mattes, and Gyiman-Boadi 2005; Inman and Andrews 2010). Likewise, Ferraz and Finan (2008) find in Brazil that public disclosure of corruption cases at the municipal level had a significant negative effect on the incumbent mayor's electoral performance. In advanced industrial democracies the evidence is similarly mixed. Several analyses on Japan (Reed 1999), Italy (Chang, Golden, and Hill 2010), Spain (Costas, Solé-Ollé, and Sorribas-Navarro 2010), and the United Kingdom (Eggers and Fisher 2011) point to a mild impact of corruption on reelection rates.

Mindful of these previous findings, we proceed with an analysis of how corruption *perceptions* and *experiences* affect the pro-incumbent vote in Latin America during the period between 2008 and 2012. We employ in the following sections survey data from the AmericasBarometer project. We find evidence of a varying effect of perceptions on vote choice that is driven by contextual variables relating to economic performance and clarity of responsibility. In other words, to the question "Does the Latin American voter behave in accordance with the responsibility hypothesis?" we respond with a conditional statement: voters who perceive corruption do not always vote against the incumbent, but they are very likely to do so in inflationary environments and in settings that facilitate attribution of responsibility for bad policy outcomes to the incumbent government.

We build this argument in four sections. First, we explore the individual-level correlates of corruption perceptions. Second, we consider the types of voters who are more likely to report experiences of corruption victimization, and hence to potentially develop a pocketbook motivation to vote against the incumbent. Third, we look at the power of corruption perceptions and corruption experiences to explain pro-incumbent vote choice. In the fourth section, we show that the correlation between corruption perceptions and vote choice varies dramatically depending on contextual indicators of economic performance and clarity of responsibility.

Correlates of Perceptions of Corruption: Who Sees Evil?

Our focus is on the Latin American voter's support of incumbents at the ballot box based on perceptions of general corruption and corruption victimization. In this section, however, we first consider the determinants of perceptions of corruption. As a starting point, table 12.1 summarizes the average distribution of responses to the question "Is corruption among public officials very common?" in eighty-three AmericasBarometer surveys conducted between 2004 and 2012 broken down by country. Potential answers to this question go from "very uncommon" (1) to "very common" (4). We also include the Transparency International Corruption Perceptions Index scores of each country in our analysis, averaged over the period 2004 to 2012. One obvious conclusion from inspection of these data is that, at the individual level of analysis, Latin American citizens tend to be rather pessimistic. Almost universally, the modal respondent declares corruption to be very common in her or his country. This happens in all countries except Chile, Bolivia, and Uruguay, where the modal response is still a rather gloomy "corruption is common." Interestingly, Chile and Uruguay

TABLE 12.1   Corruption Perceptions and Victimization

Country	AmericasBarometer Corruption Perceptions		Transparency International Corruption Perceptions Index		AmericasBarometer Corruption Victimization	
	Mean	SD	Mean	SD	Mean	SD
Argentina	3.43	0.69	2.98	0.22	6.8	1.3
Bolivia	3.07	0.81	2.85	0.27	18.2	11.9
Brazil	3.05	0.97	3.69	0.29	4.1	1.3
Chile	2.99	0.81	7.10	0.21	1.8	0.4
Colombia	3.25	0.85	3.71	0.20	3.5	0.9
Costa Rica	3.26	0.80	4.90	0.50	4.9	1.1
Dominican Republic	3.35	0.87	2.83	0.38	5.9	1.4
Ecuador	3.33	0.81	2.44	0.39	11.4	3.4
El Salvador	3.02	0.94	3.79	0.29	5.7	0.6
Guatemala	3.26	0.89	2.95	0.34	4.7	1.6
Honduras	3.25	0.83	2.56	0.12	13.6	2.7
Mexico	3.24	0.81	3.34	0.21	3.7	1.5
Nicaragua	3.17	0.93	2.59	0.14	3.7	1.8
Panama	3.24	0.81	3.41	0.22	9.1	1.2
Paraguay	3.30	0.81	2.31	0.19	14.4	9.3
Peru	3.35	0.79	3.54	0.16	2.9	0.9
Uruguay	2.90	0.81	6.71	0.41	2.4	0.3
Venezuela	3.35	0.75	2.03	0.18	7.4	2.8

Source: AmericasBarometer 2004–2012, Transparency International.

Notes: Country means (and standard deviations) of individual-level corruption perceptions in AmericasBarometer surveys (outcomes are 1 (least) to 4 (most corruption)), of Transparency International Corruption Perceptions Index (outcomes are 1 (most) to 10 (least corruption), and of percentages of individuals in AmericasBarometer surveys reporting exposure to bureaucratic corruption.

are two of the countries that Transparency International scores as least corrupt within the region; in fact, these two countries are the only ones in Latin America that consistently score higher than 5 in the Transparency International scale, which goes from 1 to 10. That Latin American citizens would consistently report very high levels of corruption perceptions where Transparency International registers more ample cross-national variation is in line with the notion of Latin Americans as extremely pessimistic.

A second conclusion is that, at least at the aggregate level, respondent views are persistent. However, enough within-country variation exists to make us wonder whether individual-level traits correlate with perceptions of corruption. Some of the theories reviewed in earlier chapters provide guidance about which individual-level traits could matter. First, socioeconomic status indicators are likely to influence a respondent's propensity to perceive generalized corruption, but this effect is likely to change from survey to survey arguably depending on the identity of the incumbent government. For example, where a leftist party governs, we might expect a well-off, older voter to be more likely to express a perception of generalized corruption. Accordingly, we include *age, income, education, gender*, and *urban/rural status* as relevant socioeconomic predictors of perceptions of corruption. The question wording is available in the appendix to this chapter.

Second, we anticipate that the degree of proximity of respondents to the incumbent government would affect their perceptions of corruption. Voters who feel close to the executive are less likely to see corruption everywhere. We get at this proximity effect by including respondents' *vote recall* (i.e., whether they voted for the winning ticket in the most recent presidential election).[1] Third, perceptions of corruption may well be driven by the actual experience of corruption. In particular, voters who have been asked in the past to pay bribes to bureaucrats might be more likely to infer that corruption is generalized. We include a question on payment of bribes to bureaucrats as our indicator of corruption experience.

To get a sense of which citizens perceive corruption, we estimate a series of models where the outcome variable is the ordered categorical indicator coded from 1 ("corruption is very uncommon") to 4 ("corruption is very common") that we summarize in the first column of table 12.1. As predictors on the right-hand side we simultaneously include all of the indicators described above: socioeconomic indicators, indicators of closeness to the incumbent, and indicators of corruption experience. Between 2004 and 2012, there are seventy-six surveys that contain information on all the variables that we require for our analysis.[2] For the sake of space, we show in the left panel of table A12.1 in the appendix an estimate of the "pooled" effect of each indicator (along with its standard error), as well as the standard deviation of the set of survey-level random effects; we relate our main conclusions below based on these statistics. We hasten to add that the table does not show the full panoply of effect estimates of these models; these are included in the online appendix material.

First, we find evidence that victims of bureaucratic corruption are more likely to perceive generalized corruption. The pooled effect of bureaucratic victimization on corruption perceptions is 0.49 (± 0.04), which means that a victim of bureaucratic bribery will on average increase her or his odds of choosing a higher "corruption perception" category by a factor of about 1.6 in comparison with an otherwise identical individual not exposed to bureaucratic corruption.[3] Some survey-specific variation exists around this pooled effect; the standard deviation of survey-specific random effects is 0.36, which suggests that in most country-years the impact of victimization on corruption varies between 0.13 and 0.85 (i.e., 0.49 ± 0.36).[4] Second, a respondent's degree of proximity to the incumbent drives perceptions of corruption downward. Specifically, *pro-incumbent* voters tend to be less likely to report pessimistic perceptions than *abstainers* (the pooled effect is -0.1 ± 0.02); in contrast, *anti-incumbent* voters are more likely to have high corruption perception scores (0.14 ± 0.03).[5]

Third, perceptions of corruption in Latin America are driven by the socioeconomic status of respondents, though, as one would expect, these effects vary more widely across countries, depending perhaps on characteristics of the incumbent government. Even then, a couple of relatively general statements can be supported. Throughout the region, older citizens are more likely to hold more pessimistic views of the extent of corruption.[6] Uruguay is a notable exception in this regard. We remarked before that Uruguayans on average perceive much more generalized corruption than experts and economic elites assign to their country. We find that these pessimistic views are, if anything, more extended among younger citizens. This finding paints a picture of an exceptional Uruguayan electorate, especially because younger citizens are presumably the voters who have formed the backbone of the Broad Front's electoral success in recent national elections.

Fourth, more educated and affluent voters tend to hold more pessimistic views about corruption, though there is in this case wider variation across surveys. For example, though wealthier citizens tend to express higher corruption perceptions in Venezuela, the 2008 round was exceptional in that these same citizens were more likely to express *less* pessimistic views on corruption (see figure OA12.1 in the online appendix). Finally, we do not see any systematic effects of sex or urban status on corruption perceptions: from one survey to the next, these variables could have a small positive effect, a small negative effect, or no effect at all. This fact is reflected in the relatively large size of the standard deviation of random effects compared to the magnitude of the pooled effect.

Correlates of Corruption Victimization: Who Suffers Evil?

One can similarly ask about reported patterns of personal experience of corruption or, as we also call it, corruption victimization. The Americas-Barometer survey includes several items that we could inspect to describe these patterns; on account of data availability we concentrate on respondents' reports of bribe solicitations from bureaucrats. This item speaks to corruption experiences very likely suffered while interacting with national government representatives, which is not true of other items like corruption experienced at the hands of the police.

For the most part, the story of stability we told before describes personal experiences of corruption as well (the average country-level scores for all countries appear in table 12.1). Based on data from four surveys (2006, 2008, 2010, 2012), Chileans report by far the lowest levels of corruption victimization in the region (1.8% of Chilean respondents report being victims of corruption). Uruguayans closely follow them; across surveys, only 2.4% of Uruguayan respondents report being victims of corruption, a datum that contrasts with their relatively pessimistic views about the extent of corruption in the country. On the other end of the spectrum, Peru and Bolivia suffer extremely high rates of corruption victimization, though in both cases the averages are driven upward by what might well be an outlying datum in 2008: in that year, close to one out of every three Peruvians and two out of every five Bolivians reported a corruption experience involving bureaucrats. These two countries, along with Mexico (13.6%), appear to report much higher corruption victimization than we would have expected based on their average Transparency International scores over the period 2004–12.

As we did for the case of corruption perceptions, we try to understand whether there are systematic socioeconomic differences among citizens who report being victims of corruption. As before, we refer the reader to the summary analysis in the appendix to this chapter and to further detailed analyses in the online appendix and, here, summarize our findings about the types of citizens who tend to report experiences with bureaucratic corruption.

Because of a lack of exit options, poorer individuals in Latin America are more likely to request government services and to have to pay bribes to obtain services to which they are in principle entitled (cf. Casey 2014). The pooled effect of income does suggest that across the board wealthier individuals are more likely to report bureaucratic victimization (0.07 ± 0.01), but the standard deviation of random effects is relatively large (0.09) and the standard errors of the individual random effects are themselves broad (online appendix figure OA12.2). Consequently, it is hard to conclude that income correlates highly with reports of bureaucratic bribery. Respondents in urban settings in Bolivia, Ecuador, and Honduras are less likely to experience bureaucratic corruption, but elsewhere the urban/rural status of respondents does not appear to matter (–0.76 ± 0.3, with a large standard deviation of 2.58 for survey-specific random effects). We would not expect "closeness" to the incumbent government to determine corruption victimization, though it may well be that respondents who dislike the incumbent exaggerate the incidence of victimization. In fact, the expectation that pro- or anti-winner voters would not differ from nonvoters in their propensities to suffer bureaucratic corruption is for the most part borne out empirically.[7] The only socioeconomic indicators that appear to systematically predict a respondent's proclivity to denounce bureaucratic bribery are sex and education: men and more educated respondents are more likely to succumb to the scourge of corruption, or at least to recognize it as such and to report it, though here again we see ample variation across countries and years.

In short, we conclude that victimization reports in Latin America are not easy to predict based on individual characteristics. This is not to say that instances of corruption victimization are truly random: men are disproportionately more likely to suffer corruption (or at least to report it) at the hands of bureaucrats. However, we cannot distinguish whether (1) bureaucrats are equal-opportunity bribe-elicitors and women simply happen to access services more often, (2) bureaucrats are equal-opportunity bribe-elicitors and women are disproportionately willing to denounce acts of corruption, or (3) bureaucrats disproportionately target women. More educated voters also tend to report corruption victimization disproportionately. Again, we cannot know the reason that more educated voters are more likely to report corruption, but we venture that this is a result of increased ability to recognize bribe attempts, rather than some ill-guided bureaucratic attempt to target more educated individuals.

Sociotropic Effects on the Pro-Incumbent Vote in Latin America

We have commented on the types of Latin American citizens who are likely to be victims of corruption and to perceive generalized corruption. With this knowledge in hand, we can now seek to understand whether these individuals are in fact less likely to declare support for the incumbent. We offer evidence of the existence of a "sociotropic effect" of corruption perceptions on vote choice, that is, Latin American citizens support or punish incumbent governments based on perceptions of societal corruption even after controlling for personal experiences of corruption they may have suffered.

In the rest of this chapter, we focus on the respondent's decision to support the incumbent. The outcome variable we inspect is a respondent's answer to the question "If elections were held this week, who would you vote for?" The options include "I would vote for the president's party," "I would vote for the opposition," "I would not vote," or "I would deposit a blank ballot." Our focus is on the pro-incumbent vote, which is why we turn this variable into a dichotomous response coded zero when the respondent chooses to vote for the opposition, to abstain, or to turn in a blank ballot. Unfortunately, the prospective vote choice question was not included in early AmericasBarometer rounds, so we work with a reduced set of fifty-three available surveys fielded in or after 2008.

Our view of the precursors of pro-incumbent vote choice appears in figure 12.1. We see corruption experiences as prior to the formation of beliefs about the ubiquity of corruption.[8] Socioeconomic conditions determine how individuals form opinions about corruption—and, in the case of sex and education, also their propensity to report bureaucratic bribery attempts. In our view of citizen behavior in a democracy, the causal link runs from processing information about corruption to acting on these perceptions in the voting booth. However, respondents to public opinion surveys are not always bound to follow this impulse. Instead, it is entirely possible that a respondent who dislikes the incumbent will also tend to report pessimistic corruption perceptions, if only to justify his or her declared vote choice. Alternatively, some other individual trait might drive both the decision to vote against the incumbent and the pessimistic report of corruption. Including the recalled vote choice of respondents, as we do here, may alleviate potential bias induced by the confounding effects of many of these traits—though one also wonders if vote choice recall is itself driven by opinions about the incumbent.[9]

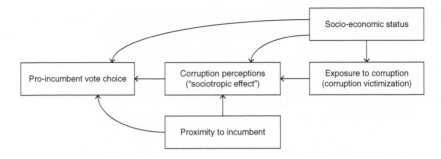

Figure 12.1 Hypothesized relationships among respondents' socio-economic status, prior attitudes toward the incumbent, sociotropic and pocketbook corruption motivations, and vote choice. *Note:* In estimating the "sociotropic effect" on pro-incumbent vote choice, we control for socioeconomic status, prior proximity to the incumbent, and pocketbook experiences.

In the previous sections we reflected on the socioeconomic and po-litical precursors of perceptions of corruption. The patterns of association between perceptions and experiences of corruption, on the one hand, and pro-incumbent vote choice, on the other, are summarized in figure 12.2 and figure 12.3. The coefficients depicted in these figures are from models estimated on fifty-three different datasets where we control for socioeco-nomic variables (age, income, sex, urban status, and education) and for pro- and anti-winner vote recall.[10] We note briefly that the recall variables have coefficients that are signed in predictable directions: those who recall voting pro-(anti-) winner are more likely to support (oppose) the current incumbent than individuals who recall not voting. The coefficients for the socioeconomic variables are not signed consistently, which makes sense given the varied ideological hue of incumbent governments.

We do not expect to find evidence of a strong effect of corruption expe-riences on vote choice once we control for corruption perceptions (see note 8). Figure 12.2 reveals that any direct association between bureaucratic bribery and pro-incumbent vote choice is estimated so imprecisely that we cannot reject a hypothesis of null effect in most surveys. The "pooled" estimate of this coefficient is negative—suggesting that corruption victims are less likely to support the incumbent—but small. In contrast, figure 12.3 illustrates that most of the corruption perception coefficients are negative and clearly bounded away from zero, consistent with the existence of a so-ciotropic effect. The pooled estimate is about the same size as the pooled

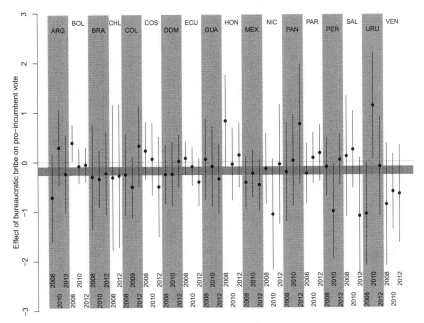

Figure 12.2   Unpooled estimates of the effects of bureaucratic bribe ("pocketbook") on pro-incumbent vote choice. *Source:* AmericasBarometer 2008–2012. *Note:* For each survey, we include point estimate and 95% confidence interval of the coefficient of corruption perception in a logit regression model that includes the following individual-level covariates: age, income, sex, urban status, education, recalled vote choice in previous election (pro-, anti-incumbent, no vote).

bureaucratic bribery estimate, but because the corruption perception scale runs from 1 to 4, the average effect across all surveys is larger. Thus, a respondent who declares that "corruption is very common" lowers her or his odds of voting for the incumbent by more than half (0.58) compared to an otherwise identical voter who declares corruption to be "very uncommon."

There are a number of nuances that warrant elaboration. Some governments in the region were voted into office on broad reformist agendas that prominently included pledges to end generalized corruption. This description fits the experiences of governments in Argentina, Bolivia, Ecuador, and Venezuela, and to a lesser extent the Uribe government in Colombia. What we see in Bolivia could well be described as a loss of patience with the anticorruption pronouncements of the Morales government. In the Bolivia 2008 survey, for example, we cannot statistically distinguish a sociotropic

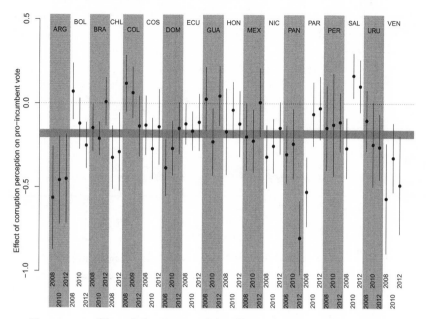

Figure 12.3   Unpooled estimates of the effects of corruption perceptions ("sociotropic") on pro-incumbent vote choice. *Source:* AmericasBarometer 2008–2012. *Note:* For each survey, we include point estimate and 95% confidence interval of the coefficient of corruption perception in a logit regression model that includes the following individual-level covariates: age, income, sex, urban status, education, recalled vote choice in previous election (pro-, anti-incumbent, no vote).

effect on pro-incumbent vote choice. We interpret this as evidence of carte blanche support for Morales's attempts at controlling corruption. But by 2012, Bolivians are no longer willing to give Morales the benefit of the doubt and appear to be more in line with voters in the rest of the region in chastising the incumbent government for perceived corruption. We see a similar loss of patience in the Broad Front governments of Uruguay, as well as in Colombia and Venezuela.

We do see a couple of countries where perceptions of corruption lead to a very clear rejection of the incumbent. These large effects appear in countries undergoing periods of extreme political polarization, as in Argentina or Venezuela, or in Paraguay before the election of President Fernando Lugo (the 2008 survey likely reflects some of the issues that defined the presidential election in April of that year), though it is true that other polarized polities, like Nicaragua, do not show similarly large effects.

Surprisingly, Mexican voters do not translate their perceptions of generalized corruption into extreme punishment for Calderón's presidency in the latter half of the decade. It would seem that Mexicans do not blame the executive for corruption in the country, even though they may blame it for about everything else, especially the increase in violence related to the war on drugs.

Let us now explore systematically the contextual factors that determine the varying effects of corruption perceptions on vote choice. In the following section, we speak to this question by considering economic, ideological, and political factors, measured at the *survey level*, which might exacerbate the sociotropic effects we have detected.[11]

Understanding Variation in the Magnitude of the Sociotropic Effect

As is obvious from figure 12.2 and figure 12.3, estimating a single completely pooled effect of corruption on vote choice ignores the ample cross-survey variability that we have uncovered in the magnitude of the sociotropic effect. In some surveys, the sociotropic effect we detect is minute or nonexistent; in other surveys, this effect is extremely large. We want to know if the sociotropic effect on voting behavior varies predictably based on context. Previous contributions suggest that the electorate's willingness to punish incumbents based on corruption perceptions is mediated by contextual factors. Here, we consider four such factors:

1. *Corruption salience.* The salience of corruption may beget a sociotropic effect. Individuals who perceive generalized corruption are more likely to act on this perception in polities where these perceptions are widely shared than in polities where they are not.
2. *Domestic economic performance.* The sociotropic effect may be activated only where domestic economic performance is dismal. The literature on corruption and political behavior has suggested that those who perceive generalized corruption blame incumbents, but are especially prone to do so when economic conditions are poor (Zechmeister and Zizumbo-Colunga 2013; Klasnja and Tucker 2013; Carlin, Love, and Martínez-Gallardo 2015).
3. *Clarity of responsibility.* The sociotropic effect on vote choice may be large only where voters can clearly attribute responsibility for generalized corruption to the incumbent government (Powell and Whitten 1993; Tavits 2007a). In particular, the sociotropic

effect is more likely to be large under unified than under divided governments.

4. *Economic globalization*. The clarity of responsibility logic can also operate through a country's links with the global economy. Voters with sociotropic concerns may be more forgiving of their governments in countries that are open to trade and integrated into global capital markets. As Hellwig (2001) suggests, these voters might have more trouble assigning blame to governments that are not entirely in control of economic outcomes, which is more likely in contexts of economic openness.

We consider whether any of these factors predict the magnitude of the effect of corruption perceptions. We hasten to note that though the ample number of surveys at our disposal allows more than a single-year snapshot of the attitudes and behaviors of Latin American citizens, the surveys span a very short period (2008–12) characterized by a combination of slow growth or outright recession in the core economies of the world and a leveling-off of the Latin American export-led boom of the first decade of the new century. In other words, our findings—particularly those that relate to the influence of economic factors on the pro-incumbent effect of corruption perceptions—might turn out to be extremely idiosyncratic.

We estimate the varying size of the sociotropic effect within a one-stage multilevel modeling framework. The basic specification is a logit regression model, where the outcome variable, *pro-incumbent vote choice*, is a function of a number of predictors measured at the individual level. On the right-hand side, we include a set of predictors with "fixed effects," that is, variables for which we estimate a single effect pooled across surveys. This set includes *education*, *age*, *sex*, and *urban status*, variables for which we failed to detect drastic variations in the unpooled coefficients estimated in the previous section. We also include on the right-hand side a set of predictors for which we estimate "random effects." These include the *pro-* and *anti-winner* behavior of voters in the previous election, as well as *income* and *bureaucratic bribery*.[12] The most important piece of these models is the inclusion of modeled random intercepts and random coefficients for *corruption perceptions* that allow us to track how its effect varies across surveys. The model for these parameters includes a number of contextual variables observed at the survey level. We include these contextual variables one at a time in alternative specifications.[13]

In the multilevel models, we capture the impact of survey-level covariates on the size of the corruption perception coefficient. Though these models deliver a rich and detailed view of the determinants of the pro-incumbent vote, we comment exclusively on the coefficient estimates of contextual variables since these are the quantities of interest in our analysis.

Table 12.2 displays these relevant coefficients, along with estimated standard errors, providing information about the varying magnitude of the sociotropic effect. For starters, the intercept is an estimate of within-survey effects. Because all indicators at the survey-level are mean-centered, the intercept estimate can be understood as the effect on the log-odds of voting for the incumbent of an individual that increases by 1 point her or his perception of corruption in an average country. As is obvious from inspection of intercept estimates across all models, the within-survey sociotropic effect is always negative and statistically significant.

In contrast, the coefficient of *average corruption perception* captures the between-survey effect of corruption perceptions. Again, this effect is reliably estimated as negative. If we take a country's average corruption perception score as an indicator of how extensive this problem is, we can substantiate the following inference: an individual who perceives high levels of corruption is much more likely to vote against the incumbent in a country where corruption is extensive than in a country with less generalized perceptions of ample corruption. Let us rephrase this latter point in a more recognizable manner: our models confirm that corruption is more salient (i.e., more likely to drive the anti-incumbent vote) where corruption is more extensive. In this particular regard, the Latin American voter behaves in a readily understandable manner: those who perceive high corruption are more likely to vote against the incumbent, especially in countries where corruption is perceived as more extensive.

Turning now to other influences on the size of the sociotropic effect, we inspect first the impact of a country's economic performance. Our expectations are straightforward: we anticipate that citizens will be more likely to let corruption perceptions inform their vote choice during hard economic times characterized by low economic growth, high inflation, or high unemployment.

The first four models in table 12.2 evaluate these expectations. For economic growth and inflation, we consider both contemporaneous values and first lags of economic growth, and contemporaneous values of inflation and unemployment.[14] Unfortunately, the World Development Indicators data have not been updated yet to include 2012 values, which means that for unemployment and economic growth we lose all of the surveys fielded that year. Our data for inflation come from the Inter-American Development Bank, which includes information for 2012.[15] As can be seen in

TABLE 12.2 Contextual Predictors of Sociotropic Incumbent Voting

	Model 1	Model 2	Model 3	Model 4	Model 5	Model 6	Model 7	Model 8
Main predictor is . . .	Growth	Growth (L1)	Inflation	Unemployment	Government Fractional	Checks	Capital Openness	Trade Openness
Coefficient main predictor	-0.004 (0.01)	-0.009 (0.01)	**-1.066** (0.37)	0.013 (0.01)	**0.292** (0.10)	-0.003 (0.02)	0.002 (0.03)	**0.034** (0.02)
Intercept	-0.17 (0.02)	-0.179 (0.02)	-0.177 (0.02)	-0.197 (0.02)	-0.181 (0.02)	-0.172 (0.02)	-0.182 (0.02)	-0.182 (0.02)
Avg corruption perception	-0.596 (0.18)	-0.425 (0.14)	-0.371 (0.14)	-0.916 (0.18)	-0.606 (0.16)	-0.5 (0.18)	-0.547 (0.17)	-0.575 (0.16)
Avg education	-0.016 (0.02)	-0.043 (0.02)	-0.056 (0.02)	0.002 (0.02)	-0.018 (0.02)	-0.018 (0.02)	-0.019 (0.02)	-0.02 (0.02)
Avg age	0.012 (0.01)	-0.003 (0.01)	-0.009 (0.01)	-0.007 (0.01)	0.003 (0.01)	0.012 (0.01)	0.012 (0.01)	0.006 (0.01)
Avg income	0.007 (0.03)	0.011 (0.02)	0 (0.02)	0.032 (0.03)	0.040 (0.03)	0.012 (0.03)	0.015 (0.03)	0.033 (0.03)
Prop female	-4.159 (1.71)	-1.167 (1.11)	-0.978 (1.09)	-4.266 (1.52)	-4.624 (1.67)	-3.8 (1.89)	-3.969 (1.71)	-4.525 (1.70)
Prop urban	0.188 (0.23)	0.089 (0.20)	-0.139 (0.20)	-0.019 (0.25)	0.235 (0.20)	0.188 (0.25)	0.219 (0.25)	0.222 (0.21)
Avg bribe victimization	0.81 (0.77)	1.031 (0.72)	1.392 (0.68)	0.636 (0.77)	-0.037 (0.78)	0.697 (0.78)	0.684 (0.76)	0.329 (0.79)
Avg incumbent support	0.074 (0.25)	0.303 (0.21)	0.26 (0.20)	0.228 (0.23)	0.103 (0.22)	0.128 (0.24)	0.125 (0.24)	0.157 (0.22)
Avg vote against incumbent	-0.936 (0.39)	0.09 (0.29)	-0.034 (0.28)	-0.488 (0.32)	-0.751 (0.35)	-0.876 (0.37)	-0.839 (0.42)	-0.921 (0.35)
N (surveys)	33	53	53	32	35	33	35	35

Source: AmericasBarometer 2008–2012.
Note: Survey-level predictors of individual-level random coefficients (estimate and standard error in parenthesis; significant coefficients in bold, $p < 0.05$).

table 12.2, the only expectation borne out by data concerns inflation. In countries with high contemporaneous inflation, individuals who perceive generalized corruption are much less likely to vote for the incumbent. The top panel of figure 12.4 plots clearly how the size of the sociotropic effect varies across different levels of inflation. The worst inflation outcomes correspond to Venezuela, a country where those who perceive generalized corruption are very happy to declare a disposition to vote against the incumbent. In contrast, economic growth and unemployment do not appear to have a statistically significant impact on the sociotropic effect of corruption perceptions.

Aside from the economic indicators, we include in models 5 through 8 four factors that have been associated with clarity of responsibility conditions in the economic voting literature. The clarity of responsibility hypothesis holds that voters find it easier to blame incumbents for bad outcomes when key decision makers are easy to identify. In Latin American presidential democracies, the identity of the chief executive is obvious, but the president's party may not always be in control of a majority share in Congress. Under such conditions of divided government, responsibility for bad outcomes may be blurred.

To assess whether diffuse responsibility may dampen the sociotropic effect, we consider two different indicators in models 5 and 6, both from the Database of Political Institutions (Inter-American Development Bank 2013). The first indicator, *government fractionalization*, captures the probability that two deputies selected randomly from among the parties in government will in fact belong to different parties. Thus, higher values of this variable correspond to situations of diffuse responsibility in which several parties form the governing congressional coalition. The second indicator, *checks*, purports to measure the number of veto points in a country's political institutions. Since a larger number of veto points would also obfuscate responsibility, we would expect positive coefficient estimates for both of these indicators. A positive coefficient estimate would indicate that the pro-incumbent effect of corruption perceptions is dampened (i.e., is *less* negative) under conditions of diffuse responsibility.

We do not find evidence in model 6 that the number of veto players modulates the effect of corruption perceptions on pro-incumbent vote choice. Model 5, however, tells a story consistent with clarity of responsibility arguments. Though our coefficients at the survey level are based on a smaller set of observations, the middle plot in figure 12.4 makes abundantly clear that outliers do not drive this result. Model 5 confirms that the probability of voting for the incumbent is much larger for an average

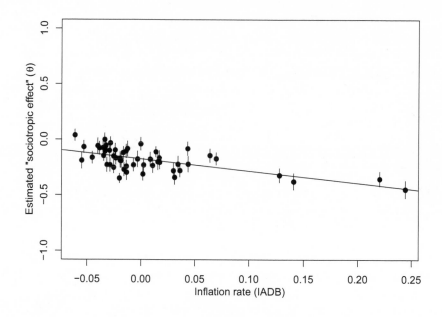

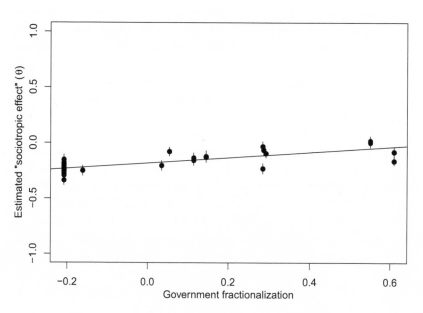

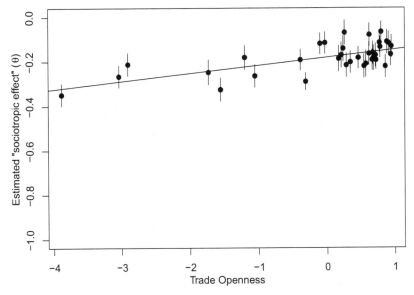

Figure 12.4   The effect of three survey-level contextual variables on the "sociotropic effect." *Source:* AmericasBarometer 2008–2012.

voter in an average country that has a multiparty congressional coalition supporting the president than in an otherwise identical country with a unified government.

Finally, in models 7 and 8 we consider a different angle of the clarity of responsibility hypothesis. Hellwig (2001) has argued that the same psychological mechanism that makes it difficult for voters to blame multiparty governments is at play in contexts of economic openness. In the extreme, bad outcomes in a country with a closed economy cannot be blamed on outside forces. Typically, clarity of responsibility hypotheses concerning openness are tested by considering both *trade openness* (basically, the logarithm of the ratio of exports plus imports over GDP, from the Penn World Tables [Heston, Summers, and Aten 2011]) and *capital openness* (we use the Chinn-Ito index based on the International Monetary Fund [IMF] AREAR indicators of openness of an economy to capital flows). Our results in model 6 are consistent with Hellwig's conjecture, a fact that is easier to verify in the bottom plot of figure 12.4: in countries that are more open to trade, incumbents are not only more likely to be reelected (northwest panel), but the sociotropic effect is also much less severe.[16]

In a nutshell, we can substantiate the following points:

1. Corruption begets punishment. The sociotropic effect is much larger in countries where citizens perceive corruption to be more extensive.
2. Economic performance matters. The period under consideration was not characterized by recession, which may be why we fail to uncover an effect of economic growth or unemployment on the sociotropic effect. However, high inflation increases the size of the sociotropic effect.
3. Clarity of responsibility matters. The size of the sociotropic effect is much reduced where the executive depends on a multiparty governing coalition in Congress.
4. Economic globalization matters. Trade openness mitigates the negative sociotropic effects on incumbents' reelection prospects, a fact that is also consistent with a clarity of responsibility explanation.

Conclusion

Consistent with the theoretical thrust of this book, our goal was to understand how corruption affects the Latin American voter's calculus of support for the incumbent. One message of this chapter is that Latin American voters allow their perceptions of corruption to influence their vote choices. We find that this sociotropic effect of corruption perceptions on the incumbent vote is of varying magnitude, which could be an indication of the validity of the so-called trade-off hypothesis according to which citizens may tolerate corrupt governments that deliver economic growth (*rouba mas faz*). We further analyzed the varying effects of corruption on incumbent support through a multilevel modeling framework to test four hypotheses about the effects of contextual factors commonly found in the voting behavior literature. The first, which follows directly from the trade-off hypothesis, contends that economic conditions have significant effects on how corruption affects vote choice. The second posits that the salience of corruption may increase the sociotropic effect of corruption perceptions. The third argues that the ability to attribute responsibility over policy outcomes to the incumbent government increases the possibility that voters will hold it accountable for bad outcomes. The fourth deals with the degree of a country's insertion in the global economy through international trade. The more globalized an economy is, the lower the chance that the incumbent's electoral support will depend on domestic economic conditions.

Our models support a number of conclusions, which we summarize as follows. First, the examination of the effect of macro-economic indicators shows that, in a context of high inflation, those who perceive a generalized pattern of corruption are much less likely to vote for the incumbent. However, neither economic growth nor unemployment appears to amplify or diminish the sociotropic effect of corruption perceptions. Second, the clarity and accountability factors display a similar outcome. The number of veto players does not seem to be relevant in accounting for the sociotropic effect, but the sociotropic effect tends to be larger in a country run by a unified government than in one run by a multiparty presidential coalition. Third, the impact of trade openness seems quite robust. Indeed, those who perceive corruption are still more likely to vote for the incumbent in an open economy than in a closed one. The most novel contribution of our analysis has been to show the important role of globalization in modulating a sociotropic effect. This is a recent phenomenon, which has been ignored in previous works on corruption, but whose ramifications have puzzling effects and should be further investigated.

Our results show a much-nuanced pattern of how corruption perceptions impact vote choice. To put it differently, the *rouba mas faz* explanation may still apply but up to a point and under certain conditions. You may "deliver," as the old Brazilian slogan said, but whether your deliverables offset your tarnished reputation as a politician who tolerates or fosters corruption depends on how they affect citizens. You may promote growth, but if that growth promotes tangible improvements only for a small segment of society, it remains an elusive concept for most citizens. Similarly, you may increase employment, but if the purchasing power of wages is eroded by inflation, then new jobs alone are not enough. Thus, a corrupt incumbent who prioritizes growth and employment at the expense of inflation control is likely to be held accountable by voters and be penalized. This is an important finding challenging previous studies, which contended that growth and unemployment are closely associated with corruption perceptions in shaping people's support. The 2013 midterm congressional elections in Argentina are a case in point. President Cristina Fernández de Kirchner refused to enact anti-inflationary policies, fearing a significant drop in economic growth and employment, at a time when allegations of corruption involving her, her vice president, and a host of close aides were at an all-time high. Consistent with our findings, her candidates suffered embarrassing defeats, particularly in the most economically developed districts of the country. Much of the same can be said for Venezuela, where the embattled administration of President Nicolás Maduro (plagued by the same problems as Argentina) saw its electoral support in the 2013 local elections being further relegated to rural areas heavily dependent on government subsidies.

Obviously, the combination of globalization's effects, country-specific circumstances, and the limited reliability of employment data (in many cases the impact of the informal economy is vastly underestimated) and of some official statistics (Argentina and Venezuela in recent years have doctored their inflation data) all caution against sweeping generalizations. Nonetheless, what this chapter shows is that in many Latin American countries people are increasingly displaying signs of keeping their rulers accountable and are not as easily swayed as in the past by leaders who assume that their corrupt practices can be forgiven simply by dispensing clientelistic benefits and by pursuing growth policies that concentrate benefits in a small sector of society or that are unsustainable in the long run.

Chapter 12 Appendix

In the text we discuss models of who perceives the government to be corrupt and who was asked to pay a bribe. For each we present an estimate of the "pooled" effect of each indicator (along with its standard error) as well as the standard deviation of the set of survey-level random effects; our summary of the main conclusions in the text is based on these statistics. We hasten to add that table A12.1 does not show the full panoply of effect estimates of these models; see online appendix figure OA12.1.

Table A12.1 Variables, Question Wording, and Codes for Chapter 12

Variable (LAPOP Item)	Question wording	Codes
Corruption perceptions (EXC7)	Is corruption among public officials very common?	1 = very uncommon 4 = very common
Corruption experience (EXC6)	Has any public employee asked you for a bribe during the past year?	0 = No 1 = Yes
Education (ED)	How many years of schooling have you completed?	0 to 20
Age (Q2)	How old are you?	16 through 101

Variable (LAPOP Item)	Question wording	Codes
Income (Q10)*	Into which of the following income ranges does the total monthly income of this household fit, including remittances from abroad and the income of all the working children?	Standard normal distribution of scores within survey
Previous turnout (VB2)	Did you vote in the last presidential elections?	0 = No 1 = Yes
Previous vote (VB3)	For which party did you vote in the last presidential elections?	Country-specific parties
Vote choice (VB20)	If the next presidential elections were being held this week, what would you do?	0 = Vote for opposition, abstain, vote blank 1 = Vote for incumbent party

Note: The AmericasBarometer introduced a new 16-category indicator of income in the 2012 round to substitute the old 10-category indicator. Upon inspection, it was not straightforward to fold some of the new categories into the old ones. We opted to consider all measures as continuous and to standardize them by subtracting the survey-level mean and dividing by the survey-level standard deviation.

Variable	Description	Source
Economic growth	Annual rate of growth of per capita GDP	World Development Indicators
Unemployment	Share of the labor force that is without work but available for and seeking employment	World Development Indicators
Inflation	Consumer Price Index, year-on-year growth, annual average, in percent (expected inflation used for 2012)	Inter-American Development Bank
Government fractionalization	The probability that two deputies picked at random from among the government parties will be of different parties (GOVFRAC)	Database of Political Institutions
Checks	Number of veto points in a political system based on regime characteristics (CHECKS)	Database of Political Institutions
Trade openness	Ratio of exports plus imports over GDP	Penn World Tables
Capital openness	First principal component of restrictions on cross-border financial transactions from the IMF's *Annual Report on Exchange Arrangements and Exchange Restrictions*	Chinn-Ito (2006), 2011 update

NOTES

1. Following Lupu's essay in this volume, we controlled alternatively for whether respondents declared sympathy for the incumbent's party or for a party in the incumbent's coalition ("pro-incumbent sympathy") or for any party in opposition ("anti-incumbent sympathy"). "Pro-incumbent sympathy" and "pro-winner vote in the previous election" are positively correlated in all surveys, though at relatively low levels (around 0.4). Because our basic results are very similar regardless of which indicator of "closeness" we use, we only discuss models that include the pro-winner vote indicator, which allows us to include seventy-six (as opposed to sixty-six) AmericasBarometer surveys.

2. The ordered-logit models we report are based on listwise-deleted datasets, where observations with missing values on any variable are dropped. The online appendix contains details on the number of usable observations per survey. By dropping observations with missing values, we explicitly assume that patterns of missingness are completely random.

3. We take this with a grain of salt, as it is obvious that experiences of bureaucratic corruption are not necessarily assigned randomly to individuals. We have no way of telling whether incumbent supporters may not be underreporting bribery victimization.

4. Only in a few surveys (i.e., Colombia) is bureaucratic corruption not a statistically significant predictor of statements about how common corruption is (see figure OA12.2 in the online appendix).

5. As noted in note 3, we controlled in alternative models for pro-incumbent or anti-incumbent partisanship. We find that pro-(anti-)incumbent partisans are less (more) likely than nonpartisans to report high corruption perception scores on average, though there are many exceptions to this rule across surveys.

6. The estimated coefficient (0.01 ± 0.001) is small, but age is measured in years, so a comparison of an 18-year-old to a 40-year-old, for example, would lead us to expect a relatively large substantive effect on corruption perceptions.

7. The substantive magnitude of this effect is small even where some coefficient estimates are statistically distinguishable from zero (e.g., among pro-winner voters in Bolivia). Variation in the random effects is extremely large (0.56 and 0.41)

8. In our view, corruption perceptions follow in part from corruption experiences. For this reason, if we wanted to estimate the full effect of corruption experiences on vote choice, we would avoid controlling for corruption perceptions, which can be seen as a "post-treatment variable" in our theoretical account. We estimate the full effect of corruption experiences on presidential approval in a larger set of AmericasBarometer surveys in Rosas and Manzetti (2015).

9. One might wonder if respondents may perceive or experience corruption, but find it entirely justifiable. This possibility could be further explored by analyzing an item that asks the respondent's opinion on whether paying a bribe may ever be justifiable. This proportion can be very high, especially in the 1998 Bolivian and Peruvian surveys, where it reached upwards of 40%. We leave open for future research the question of whether respondents who justify bribes may be more lenient with incumbents.

10. *Education*: How many years of schooling have you completed? 0 to 20. *Age*: How old are you? 16 through 101. *Income*: Into which of the following income ranges does the total monthly income of this household fit, including remittances from abroad and the income of all the working children? The AmericasBarometer introduced a new sixteen-category indicator of income in the 2012 round to substitute for the old ten-category indicator. Upon inspection, it was not straightforward to fold some of the new categories into the old ones. We opted to consider all measures as continuous and to standardize them by subtracting the survey-level mean and dividing by the survey-level standard deviation. *Previous turnout*: Did you vote in the last presidential elections? 0 = No, 1 = Yes. *Sex:* 0 = Female, 1 = Male. *Urban-Rural:* 1 = Rural, 0 = Urban. *Previous vote*: For which party did you vote in the last presidential elections? Country-specific parties.

11. It is not worth our while to carry out a similar exploration of the contextual determinants of the pocketbook effect, given that this effect is substantively minuscule even in the handful of surveys where it appears to be statistically significant.

12. The coding for these variables is described in previous notes.

13. A more detailed description of the model appears in the online appendix.

14. *Economic growth:* Annual rate of growth of per capita, GDP World Development Indicators; *Unemployment:* Share of the labor force that is without work but available for and seeking employment, World Development Indicators; *Inflation:* Consumer Price Index, year on year growth, annual average, in percent (expected inflation used for 2012), Inter-American Development Bank (IADB).

15. The IADB information is based on country reports. This is problematic for the Argentina case, where officials doctored inflation data from 2007 to early 2014.

16. The reader may be interested in the "direct" effect of the contextual variables on vote choice. For that purpose, the online appendix includes two additional tables. One includes the modeled random intercepts for models 1 through 8. Lastly, the coefficients for all individual-level variables appear in a second table; this table confirms that self-reported victims of bureaucratic bribery are ineluctably less likely to vote for the incumbent.

13 ✦ The Impact of Crime on Voter Choice in Latin America

ORLANDO J. PÉREZ

Crime and insecurity have emerged as critical issues in Latin America and the rest of the developing world. Studies have shown that citizens view crime as one of the most pressing problems facing their nation (Quann and Hung 2002). Moreover, crime is believed to have important political consequences. Some research links crime with reduced democratic values (Beirne 1997; Newman and Pridemore 2000; Pérez 2003, 2011; Prillaman 2003; Bateson 2012). Moreover, the failure of security and judicial institutions to maintain order and protect citizens' life and property has been connected to decreases in government credibility (Wilkinson 1986) and the crisis of representation in parts of Latin America (Mainwaring et al. 2006). However, despite the importance of the issue, there are only a few studies that examine the link between crime and electoral behavior (Bateson 2012; Trelles and Carreras 2012), and nearly none that examine the link between insecurity and electoral behavior in the region. This chapter examines the effect of crime and insecurity on voters' choice. The specific focus is on the impact of crime and insecurity on the choice to support incumbent versus opposition parties.

While crime and insecurity are issues of great concern for citizens (Pérez 2003), most of the literature on the impact of performance indicators on voter choices has focused on economic factors. Gélineau and Singer (this volume) indicate that voting based on economic performance is nearly ubiquitous in the Latin American region, even if the specific weight given to economic factors varies by context. Manzetti and Rosas (this volume) add to that by showing that corruption affects voter choices. Crime has largely been overlooked in the study of political accountability.

Crime is potentially a key performance indicator for an incumbent government. High levels of crime reflect the state's failure to provide an essential public good and thus we should expect voters to hold incumbents accountable for this failure. Yet only a few studies have analyzed the impact of crime on voters' choices. In the context of the United States, Cummins (2009) found that crime significantly influences gubernatorial races and has a larger impact in states with a more educated population, and that state-level conditions are more salient than national ones. Canes-Wrone, Minozzi, and Reveley (2011) find that crime has a significant impact on holding U.S. congressional candidates accountable but the effect is mediated by issue saliency and candidates' partisan affiliations. Examining cases in Latin America, such as Peru, scholars have found a link between drops in violence and increases in presidential approval (Arce 2003; Holmes and Amin Gutiérrez de Piñeres 2003). In Colombia, Holmes and Amin Gutiérrez de Piñeres (2012a, 2012b) find that persistent political violence causes permanent damage to the party system, and that voters hold incumbent presidents accountable for both economic as well as security performance. Yet we know very little about how systematically voters punish governments for increases in crime nor whether this response is limited to crime victims or reflects a more general societal reaction to an increase in insecurity that puts citizens at risk of becoming victims.

This chapter presents a theoretical framework for understanding how crime might relate to electoral behavior and then tests the individual-level relationships among crime victimization, insecurity, and incumbent support in Latin America. First, personal experiences could seem idiosyncratic and, thus, make it difficult for crime victims to attribute responsibility to the national government (Gomez and Wilson 2001). Second, it is often the case that responsibility for crime prevention falls on local, not national. governments, though the involvement of the national government in police reforms and related venues varies across Latin America. To foreshadow the results, I find support for an effect of perceived insecurity on incumbent support, but not for crime victimization.

Crime and Electoral Behavior

In theory, crime can affect electoral outcomes by influencing the decision to turn out at the polls or by affecting support for the incumbent. With respect to the former, crime victimization can affect both resource-based and attitude-based factors of participation. Crime can pose tangible and intangible costs that reduce an individual's likelihood of participation, but can also provide benefits relating to social solidarity and concrete practices associated with helping to resolve some of the underlying causes of crime. Victims of crime may see active political participation as a way of mitigating the negative effects of victimization. By the same token, while we would expect crime victims to express lower levels of political efficacy, particularly external efficacy since crime represents a failure of the state, we may also see victims express higher levels of efficacy relating to the motivational effects of suffering a personal tragedy. Additionally, in situations where crime is a major national issue individuals touched by this phenomenon might exhibit higher levels of internal efficacy as they feel more "connected" to an important national problem. Logistical regression models assessing data from the AmericasBarometer, not shown here to save space, indicate that crime victimization is indeed associated with higher levels of internal efficacy. However, as would be expected, crime victims exhibit lower levels of external efficacy.

Generally speaking, extant research linking crime and violence to participation point in opposite directions. On the one hand, studies have found that crime victims are more susceptible to depression, anxiety, and post-traumatic stress disorder (Kilpatrick and Acierno 2003; Burris 2006; Macmillan 2001; Norris and Kaniasty 1994). Generally, studies have found that victims of crime exhibit lower levels of interpersonal trust (Brehm and Rahn 1997). Crime victims have been found to be personally alienated (Cárdia 2002; Elias 1986; Marks and Goldsmith 2006; Melossi and Selmini 2000; Skogan 1990) and unhappy (Powdthavee 2005). On the other hand, several studies have shown that crime victims develop attitudes and behavior conducive to greater political engagement. For example, Bellows and Miguel (2009), Blattman (2009), and Voors et al. (2012) found that individuals who personally experienced wartime violence exhibited increased rates of voting, community leadership, and civic engagement. Other studies find that individuals living in war-torn communities have greater levels of social capital, altruism, and political participation (Gilligan, Pasquale, and Samii 2011; Kage 2011).

When considering the influence of crime and violence on candidate choice, a number of studies have examined the extent to which crime can affect voter preferences on the platforms advocated by candidates. The findings tend to support the notion that conservative (right-wing) candidates are more likely to be helped by the crime issue (Estrada 2004; Mayer and Tiberj 2004; Hamai and Ellis 2006). The extant literature shows that crime becomes important to the extent that citizens believe it is a significant problem (Garland 2001; Godoy 2006). In fact, crime seems to be a determining factor on voter preferences even where crime rates are low (Cullen, Clark, and Wozniak 1985; Beckett 1997; Davey 1999). In such circumstances the behavior of the media and the rhetoric of political leaders might heighten the effects of crime (Romer, Jamieson, and Aday 2006). Media coverage can highlight the magnitude of the problem and put pressure on politicians to respond forcefully (Kaniss 1991; Vermeer 2002). As a result, candidates seek to "out do each other" in expressing strength to fight crime and keep law and order. The rhetoric often pits candidates who accuse each other of being weak or "soft" on crime (see Krause 2009; Holland 2013). Early findings indicated that voters tended to favor conservative politicians instead of leftists on the issue of fighting crime (Budge and Farlie 1983; Petrocik 1996). Weyland (2000) found that in Peru Alberto Fujimori's popularity rose significantly in response to the perception of fighting crime. In the context of Central America, the most violent subregion in Latin America, several right-wing candidates such as Alfonso Portillo and Otto Pérez Molina of Guatemala, Ricardo Maduro and Juan Orlando Hernández of Honduras, and Ricardo Martinelli of Panama, used crime and the rhetoric of fighting it with strong measures to win political power.

Crime was the central theme of the campaign in the 2013 elections in Honduras, by many standards the most violent nation in Latin America (see table 13.1). The candidate of the ruling National Party, Juan Orlando Hernández, differentiated himself from his main rival, Xiomara Castro, wife of former president Manuel Zelaya, by emphasizing increasingly tough measures to combat crime. Hernández focused on increasing the collaboration of the military and police by fusing elements of both into a militarized police (*policía militarizada*) that would number about five thousand strong and would take the lead role in combating criminal networks across the country. By contrast, Castro promoted the idea of community policing and criticized human rights abuses by the extant police institution. In the end, Hernández won a narrow victory with 37% of the votes. While it is difficult to discern the exact impact crime played in Hernandez's victory, particularly given that economic conditions were also central in the campaign, the fact remains that Honduras has the highest rate of homicide in the region, that violence is a major concern for citizens in the Central American nation, and that the campaign rhetoric centered on the issue of combating violence.

Another case in which crime played a central role in the campaign was the 2011 presidential elections in Guatemala. Otto Pérez Molina, a retired army general and former head of military intelligence, campaigned on implementing *mano dura* policies to combat the increasing levels of crime. Guatemala's homicide rate is among the highest in the hemisphere (see table 13.1), and the country is increasingly affected by Mexican drug cartels operating in the border regions. Molina's policies included additional deployment of military troops in the streets to assist the police. Molina used his background as a military officer to bolster his credentials as a tough individual with the discipline, knowledge, and training to be an effective leader against gangs and other criminal networks. His opponent, a wealthy hotel owner and former congressman, emphasized populist policies to assist the poor. In the end, Molina won in a second-round run-off election with nearly 54% of the votes. Molina's victory came after narrowly losing the 2007 elections to center-left candidate Álvaro Colom. Colom campaigned on changing the focus of crime policies away from repressive measures toward prevention and economic development. However, increasing violence prompted Colom to rely increasingly on the military to assist the police in combating crime. Molina's emphasis on tough policies to rectify the perceived failures of the Colom administration, plus a general conservative political culture, seemed to have paid off for the former military officer.

Coinciding with the recent wave of crime in Latin America, the past two decades have seen the rise of a new form of repressive policing called *mano dura*, or "strong hand," as well as relative high levels of support for authoritarian measures. As Pérez explains: "Crime undermines support for democratic regimes. As crime rates increase, pressure mounts for 'strong' government action which in many instances results in highly repressive and undemocratic measures" (2003, 638).

At its core, *mano dura* necessitates curtailing individual rights and re-empowering the military and police. These sets of policies normally include deploying the military for internal policing, in addition to lengthening prison sentences, suspending due process guarantees and other protections for alleged criminals, and aggressively arresting youths suspected of gang membership.

Related, some authors suggest that fear of violent crime drives citizens to demand punitive and repressive measures against alleged criminals (Sanjuán 2003), often in the form of *mano dura* policies. Fear can generate demand for strong governance, leading to support for authoritarianism and dictatorship (Corradi, 1992, 267–92). Concern about violent crime in Latin America appears to be so severe that citizens are "willing to sacrifice certain liberties in order to feel more secure" (Tulchin and Ruthenburg 2006, 5). Pérez found that in El Salvador up to 55% of the population would support a military coup if there were high levels of crime (2003). In Africa, for example, fear of crime also has been associated with decreased support for democracy (Kuenzi 2006). Recent studies have found a relationship between trust in institutions and crime victimization in Mexico (Blanco 2013; Malone 2013), and between crime and support for the political system in the Latin American region (Carreras 2013).

Using the 2008 AmericasBarometer, Pérez (2011) found that crime victims were significantly less likely to express confidence in the key institutions of the state. Furthermore, perception of insecurity had an even greater influence than crime victimization. Individuals who felt insecure in their neighborhood were less willing to extend rights to the opposition, had significantly lower interpersonal trust, had lower support for the idea that democracy is the best political system, and exhibited far less confidence in political institutions.

In summary, there are three avenues through which crime might affect electoral outcomes. The first is through its influence on the decision to turn out versus abstain. As the above indicates, the existing theory and evidence is mixed on this question. As the introduction to this part shows, the more insecure Latin American voters feel, the less likely they are to support the incumbent party. The second is that high levels of crime, crime victimization, and insecurity can fuel support for right-leaning platforms that advocate hardline, *mano dura* responses to the problem. The conclusion to this volume presents data showing that this is indeed the case in Latin America in 2012, as respondents who supported hardline tactics to fight crime were more likely to have supported right-leaning parties in the previous election. The third, and comparatively much less studied, is that crime victimization and insecurity can affect incumbent support, to the degree that individuals withdraw their confidence not just from political institutions in general but from the administration that is overseeing these difficult times. This latter link is tested in the analyses below. But, first, I draw a portrait of crime as a pressing issue across most of Latin America.

Context of Crime in Latin America

Data on homicides reveal that Latin America has the dubious distinction of having the highest rates of crime and violence in the world (Geneva Declaration Secretariat 2008). Table 13.1 displays homicide rates for the world, selected sub-regions around the globe, and the individual Latin American countries. Homicide in Latin America is five times higher than in most other places in the world (Fajnzylber, Lederman, and Loayza 1998), and

TABLE 13.1   Intentional Homicide Rate per 100,000 Inhabitants (2009)

Region/Country	Rate
World	7.6
Central America	29.3
South America	25.9
Africa	20
Caribbean	18.1
East Europe	8.1
North America	6.5
West and Central Europe	1.5
Argentina	3.4
Chile	3.7
Uruguay	6.8
Bolivia	6.9
Peru	10.3
Costa Rica	11.4
Paraguay	13.4
Nicaragua	14.0
Mexico	17.7
Ecuador	18.4
Brazil	21.7
Panama	23.6
Dominican Republic	24.2
Colombia	34.6
Guatemala	46.3
Venezuela	49.0
El Salvador	70.6
Honduras	70.7

Source: United Nations Office of Drugs and Crime. 2009 was the last year data was available for all countries.

the differences from the rest of the world are growing larger (Gaviria and Pagés 1999).

There are important sub-regional trends not illustrated in the table that are worth noting. Homicide rates in the Caribbean and Central America have risen since 1995, whereas elsewhere in the region they have decreased or remained stable. Homicide rates have fluctuated in South America but have now returned to levels similar to those observed in 1995. One notable exception to the latter trend is Colombia, which, although it still has one of the world's highest homicide rates, has seen a massive drop from 72 to 33 per 100,000. Central America, however, reflects a troubling pattern of decline between 1995 and 2005, but sharp increases since 2007.

The lower part of table 13.1 shows the homicide rates for eighteen countries in Latin America. The highest rates are found in Honduras and El Salvador, and the lowest in Argentina and Chile. Only Argentina, Chile,

Uruguay, and Bolivia exhibit homicide rates below the world average (7.6). The data illustrate variation on the rate of homicides across time. Between 1990 and 2008, homicides rose sharply in Venezuela, Guatemala, Honduras, the Dominican Republic, and Brazil. Some countries, such as Argentina, Chile, and Colombia, showed positive trends.

Of course, crime victimization goes beyond homicide rates. Crimes such as robbery, burglary, assault, fraud, blackmail, extortion, and violent threats can have a profound effect on people's lives and impact the manner in which they behave politically. Unlike homicide rates, data from the United Nations indicate that rates of assault, robbery, and sexual assault are higher in South America than in Central America or the Caribbean.[1] This variation may reflect differences in socioeconomic development between the sub-regions, with wealthier countries susceptible to higher rates of crime against property.

The AmericasBarometer uses the following question to measure crime victimization:[2] "Now, changing the subject, have you been a victim of any type of crime in the past 12 months? That is, have you been a victim of robbery, burglary, assault, fraud, blackmail, extortion, violent threats or any other type of crime in the past 12 months?" Figure 13.1 illustrates the percentage of respondents who, in response to the 2012 survey, expressed being a victim of a crime in the past twelve months.[3]

The highest levels of victimization are found in Ecuador, Peru, and Bolivia, with 28% of respondents reporting being victims of crime. Mexico, Uruguay, Argentina, and Colombia are the next highest, with 21 to 23% of citizens having been victims of crime in the previous year. The country with the lowest rate of crime victimization is Panama, with only 6.9% of respondents reporting being victims of a crime in the previous twelve months. This rate is significantly lower than that of all the other countries in the study.

Another way in which crime and violence can affect political behavior is through the perception of insecurity. Perception of insecurity is measured using the question from the AmericasBarometer: "Speaking of the neighborhood where you live and thinking of the possibility of being assaulted or robbed, do you feel very safe, somewhat safe, somewhat unsafe or very unsafe?" The original 1–4 scale is recoded here to run from zero to 100, with higher values indicating greater levels of insecurity.

Figure 13.2 demonstrates significant variations in levels of insecurity. Perceptions of insecurity are especially high in the Andes (Peru, Venezuela, Bolivia, and Ecuador) but also in El Salvador, the Dominican Republic, and Mexico. Ironically, perceptions of insecurity are generally higher in South America than in Central America despite the higher rates of homicides

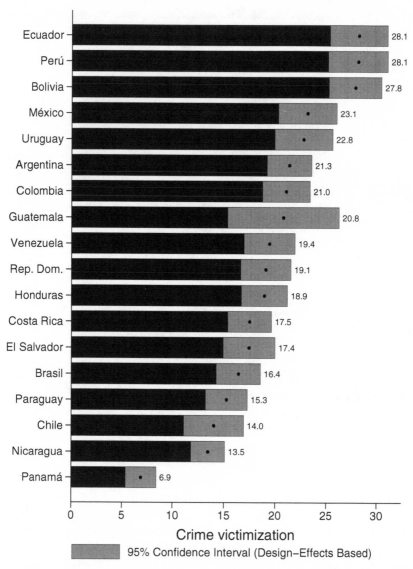

Figure 13.1   Crime Victimization by Country. *Source:* AmericasBarometer 2012.

in the latter. This result may be explained by the fact that, as stated earlier, according to United Nations' data, rates of assault and robbery are higher in South America than in Central America.[4] The data reveal a gap between relatively low levels of insecurity and relatively high levels of victimization in Honduras and Paraguay. Conversely, reported victimization

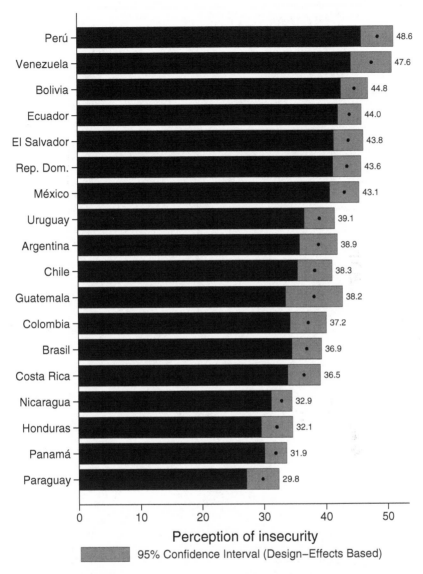

Figure 13.2 Perceptions of Insecurity by Country. *Source:* Americas-Barometer 2012.

rates are lower than one would expect based on the levels of insecurity in Chile, the Dominican Republic, and El Salvador. Just as with perceived insecurity, residents of South America were more likely to report being victims of crime than residents of Central America or Mexico. Further analysis reveals that the correlation between the measures of victimization and insecurity is rather weak, with a Pearson's r of only 0.19 for the pooled sample.[5] Thus, the measures of victimization and insecurity respond to varying factors and, as we will see below, affect voting differently.

Crime and Voter Choices

Crime and violence are key public policy failures for the state. Thus, while these issues might have relevance for turnout and for policy preferences, a classic performance accountability perspective of voting behavior would suggest they should affect incumbent support. That is, if elections provide a mechanism by which citizens can reward or punish incumbent performance, then citizens should hold political leaders accountable for security-related failures.

In exploring the question of how voters respond to crime, one question is whether voters focus on their personal experiences or on broader societal trends. One possibility is that crime victims are the most likely to express disappointment with the incumbent. These individuals suffer both physical losses and emotional turmoil through this negative experience. If they perceive that it was state failure that put them at risk of being victimized, this group may be motivated to hold politicians to account for their failures. Such an expectation draws a conceptual parallel to the egotropic voting hypothesis in the literature on economic voting (see Gélineau and Singer this volume), in which vote choices are based on one's personal economic situation. This chapter tests the following hypotheses:

> H1: Crime victimization will reduce the likelihood of support for incumbent parties or presidents.

Yet the literature on economic voting suggests that voters do not always hold politicians accountable for their personal circumstances (see Gomez and Wilson 2001 for a review of how most voters do not vote egotropically). In the case of crime victims, they might attribute their circumstances to bad luck or focus on the motives of the attacker and holding him or her responsible, not the state. Moreover, individuals who have not been crime victims but who perceive high levels of insecurity might be motivated to hold the government accountable for crime. Higher levels of insecurity may be evidence of a failure of the state to handle effectively the problems of violence and crime. While insecurity levels, as discussed earlier, can be induced by ancillary factors, such as the media, rather than objective crime rates themselves, the psychological effects of insecurity could in fact have a greater impact on political behavior. Perceptions of a problem often create the "reality" of such a phenomenon more readily than actual facts. In this sense, if citizens perceive high levels of insecurity they may view this as a lack of competence on the part of the incumbent. Citizens may also punish the incumbent for perceived insecurity because they assume that, if left unaddressed, it will eventually endanger them. These expectations generally follow the sociotropic thesis of economic voting (Duch and Stevenson 2008; Gélineau and Singer this volume). Therefore, I test the following hypothesis:

H2: Higher levels of insecurity will reduce the likelihood of support for incumbent parties or presidents.

An important element of whether crime and insecurity have an impact on political behavior is the level of issue salience. Salient issues are politically important. People care about these issues and hold opinions about them (Singer 2011; Epstein and Segal 2000; Edwards, Mitchell, and Welch 1995; Weaver 1991). Therefore, these opinions are likely to structure voting behavior. One measure of issue salience is the extent to which crime is considered an important problem facing the country. I would expect crime and insecurity to have greater impact on voter choices to the degree that individuals believe the most important problem facing the country is crime. But, as well, it is possible that individuals' assessment of crime as the most important problem has a direct effect on incumbent support. This expectation can be phrased as follows:

H3: Individuals who indicate the most pressing problem for the country is one related to crime and violence will be less likely to vote for the incumbent.

Table 13.2 presents the distribution of responses on the main problem facing the countries. I have highlighted those in which security is identified as the most important problem. Only in Venezuela and Uruguay do majorities of respondents choose security. Pluralities of respondents chose security as the main problem in Guatemala, El Salvador, Costa Rica, Colombia, Chile, and Argentina.

Assessing the Links among Crime, Insecurity, and Incumbent Support

The data used for the analyses in this chapter are from the 2012 wave of the AmericasBarometer survey, and focus on the eighteen Latin American countries at the core of this volume. The dependent variable is a measure

TABLE 13.2   Main Problem Facing the Country (%)

	Economy	Security	Basic Services	Politics	Other
Mexico	34.19	31.88	5.27	15.94	12.72
Guatemala	32.57	**40.24**	14.54	8.08	4.58
El Salvador	46.22	**48.97**	0.83	3.03	0.96
Honduras	24.45	20.86	9.15	33.37	12.17
Nicaragua	76.75	7.71	5.78	5.42	4.34
Costa Rica	27.06	**41.54**	2.98	16.24	12.18
Panama	34.80	25.60	16.02	16.14	7.44
Colombia	31.65	**39.63**	3.99	16.22	8.51
Ecuador	42.16	29.32	8.24	13.24	7.03
Bolivia	58.12	20.15	5.15	9.31	7.27
Peru	42.74	30.33	5.02	14.38	7.53
Paraguay	53.48	21.28	7.78	11.32	6.14
Chile	19.79	**34.32**	16.84	9.51	19.54
Uruguay	21.10	*51.59*	10.76	3.72	12.83
Brazil	13.70	19.72	33.09	15.37	18.11
Venezuela	17.59	*64.68*	4.06	6.22	7.44
Argentina	35.47	**39.84**	5.32	6.14	13.23
Dominican Republic	46.98	30.07	8.86	7.11	6.98

Source: AmericasBarometer 2012.

Note: Entries are coded responses to an open ended question asking respondents what they consider to be the main problem facing the country.

of support for the incumbent governments that asks: "If the next presidential elections were being held this week, what would you do?" Respondents could indicate that they would support the incumbent candidate or party, would support a candidate or party different from the current administration, would not vote, or would cast a blank vote. In the analyses presented here, the variable is dichotomized by recoding as missing values those respondents who either did not vote or said they voted blank. While an argument could be made that respondents who choose not to vote or vote blank are implicitly rejecting the incumbent leadership, this assumption would require a significant level of speculation and I prefer to restrict our analysis of this variable to the categories in which voter choices are explicit. The data indicate that among the 18 countries under examination, 43.8% would support the incumbent president or party and 56.1% would not.

The main independent variables are the aforementioned crime victimization question and perception of insecurity question. Because of the well-established importance of economic factors for voter choice (see Gélineau and Singer this volume), I include as covariates measures of respondents' evaluations of the national and personal economic situation in the past twelve months.[6] Each model also includes covariates measuring the classic socio-demographic variables of age, color of skin, education, gender, urban/rural, and wealth.[7] Additionally, a covariate is added to measure the impact of issue salience for security problems.[8]

Binary logistic regression models are estimated to examine the relationship between (egotropic) crime victimization and (sociotropic) perception of insecurity measures, on the one hand, and voter choice, on the other. Model 1 shows results with only the socio-demographic covariates. Model 2 adds the economic performance variables, and model 3 includes all the covariates. Though not shown, all models include country fixed effects (table 13.3).

The results of the analysis indicate that perception of insecurity is negatively related to voting for the incumbent; the effect is statistically

TABLE 13.3 Binary Logistic Regression for Support for Incumbent Party or President

	Model 1	Model 2	Model 3
Perception of Insecurity	−0.00488***	−0.00325***	−0.00326***
	(0.000538)	(0.000563)	(0.000751)
Crime Victimization	−0.000595	−4.14e-05	−0.000375
	(0.000393)	(0.000403)	(0.000541)
Perception of National Economic Situation		0.0213***	0.0206***
		(0.000849)	(0.00115)
Perception of Personal Economic Situation		0.00359***	0.00337***
		(0.000950)	(0.00128)
Security Most Important Problem			−0.000317
			(0.000476)
Women	−0.0235	0.0399	0.0140
	(0.0309)	(0.0319)	(0.0437)
Urban	−0.00102***	−0.00135***	−0.00140***
	(0.000374)	(0.000388)	(0.000532)
Age	0.00493***	0.00611***	0.00922***
	(0.00106)	(0.00109)	(0.00150)
Color of Skin	0.0446***	0.0464***	0.0393***
	(0.00991)	(0.0102)	(0.0133)
Education	−0.0217***	−0.0276***	−0.0201***
	(0.00426)	(0.00439)	(0.00603)
Wealth	−0.0499***	−0.0791***	−0.0880***
	(0.0120)	(0.0125)	(0.0170)
Constant	−0.246**	−1.307***	−1.377***
	(0.114)	(0.127)	(0.171)
Number of Countries	18	18	18
Observations	19,177	19,031	10,533
Wald chi^2	1687.62***	2305.42***	1336.65***
Pseudo-R^2	0.0727	0.1080	0.1113

Source: AmericasBarometer 2012.
Note: Robust standard errors in parentheses. Country fixed effects included but not shown. *** $p <$ 0.01, ** $p < 0.05$, * $p < 0.1$

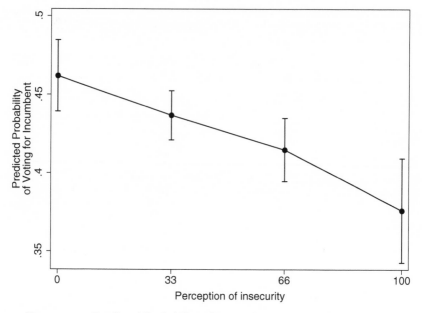

Figure 13.3   Predicted Probability of Voting for the Incumbent by Perception of Insecurity. *Source:* AmericasBarometer 2012.

significant in all three models, even when economic performance variables are included. Crime victimization is not significantly associated with voting for the incumbent, and neither is the extent to which security issues are considered the most important.[9] Thus, the results provide support for hypothesis 2, but not for hypotheses 1 and 3.

Figure 13.3 shows the predicted probabilities of voting for the incumbent party or president by levels of insecurity for the pooled sample holding all covariates constant at their means or modes (see model 3). The probability of voting for the incumbent diminishes by nearly 9 percentage points between respondents who perceive low levels of insecurity and those who perceive very high levels. Respondents who feel very secure in their neighborhood have a 46.2% predicted probability of voting for the incumbent versus 37.6% for those who express high levels of insecurity.

Table 13.4 illustrates the marginal effects of insecurity on voting for the incumbent. Marginal effects show the change in probability when the predictor or independent variable increases by 1 unit. The results indicate that the probability of voting for the incumbent when perception of insecurity goes from "very secure" to "somewhat secure" decreases 10.1% and

TABLE 13.4   Marginal Effects of Voting for the Incumbent by Levels of Insecurity

Perception of Insecurity	(1) Marginal Effects
Somewhat Secure	−0.101*
	(0.0568)
Somewhat Insecure	−0.191***
	(0.0640)
Very Insecure	−0.353***
	(0.0869)
Observations	10,533

Source: AmericasBarometer 2012.
Note: Effects for other variables held at their means. Standard errors in parentheses. Reference category: Very Secure. *** $p < 0.01$, ** $p < 0.05$, * $p < 0.1$

is significant. The probability of support for the incumbent decreases by 19.1% when respondents move from very secure to somewhat insecure, and by 35.3% when citizens perceive very high levels of insecurity. It is worth noting that the marginal effect for crime victims is extremely small and non-significant.

To what extent does the pattern found in the pooled analysis hold for individual countries? As shown earlier, the countries with the highest levels of victimization are Ecuador, Peru, and Bolivia, followed by Mexico, Uruguay, Argentina, and Colombia. Conversely, perceptions of insecurity are highest in Peru and Venezuela. To assess country-level differences, I conducted binary logistic regression models for each country in the study (not shown to save space).[10] Interestingly, I find that crime victimization does not affect support for the incumbent president or party in *any* of the eighteen countries. A null finding for this egotropic measure is interesting because we know from the extant literature that victimization affects other levels of political participation (Bateson 2012), and that it affects trust in institutions and system support (Pérez 2011; Blanco 2013; Malone 2013). Thus, it may be that crime victimization's effect on incumbent support is entirely indirect, traveling through its influence on turnout, conditionally affecting incumbent support under particular circumstances, and/or indirectly affecting incumbent support to the degree it influences insecurity.

To follow up with more detail on the relationship between insecurity and incumbent support at the country level, table 13.5 illustrates the marginal effects of insecurity on voting for the incumbent for each country. In most countries, support for the incumbent decreases as perception of

TABLE 13.5   Marginal Effects of Voting for the Incumbent President or Party by Levels of Insecurity by Country

	Somewhat Secure	Somewhat Insecure	Very Insecure
Mexico	0.0180	−0.153**	−0.405***
	(0.0647)	(0.0685)	(0.0629)
Guatemala	0.0192	−0.00656	−0.114
	(0.0609)	(0.0695)	(0.0980)
El Salvador	−0.0651	0.0219	−0.133*
	(0.0656)	(0.0723)	(0.0806)
Honduras	−0.133**	−0.149**	0.0817
	(0.0606)	(0.0741)	(0.114)
Nicaragua	0.0199	−0.0148	0.0993
	(0.0439)	(0.0523)	(0.0606)
Costa Rica	−0.0436	−0.0726	−0.158
	(0.0639)	(0.0750)	(0.104)
Panama	0.0612	−0.00570	−0.105
	(0.0524)	(0.0758)	(0.0880)
Colombia	−0.0950	−0.0460	−0.149*
	(0.0579)	(0.0659)	(0.0826)
Ecuador	−0.221***	−0.213***	−0.209**
	(0.0568)	(0.0636)	(0.0851)
Bolivia	−0.0770	−0.103**	−0.103
	(0.0480)	(0.0507)	(0.0652)
Peru	−0.00109	−0.0225	−0.0812
	(0.0472)	(0.0470)	(0.0574)
Paraguay	0.0153	0.106*	0.0592
	(0.0483)	(0.0638)	(0.105)
Chile	0.0367	0.00878	0.0160
	(0.0456)	(0.0551)	(0.0810)
Uruguay	−0.132**	−0.0726	−0.293***
	(0.0604)	(0.0674)	(0.0947)
Brazil	0.0418	0.0240	0.0308
	(0.0369)	(0.0458)	(0.0533)
Venezuela	0.0520	−0.136	−0.0756
	(0.0854)	(0.0875)	(0.113)
Argentina	−0.00905	0.00667	−0.0397
	(0.0654)	(0.0733)	(0.118)
Dominican Republic	0.0419	−0.0109	0.0403
	(0.0600)	(0.0675)	(0.0808)

Source: AmericasBarometer 2012.

Note: Effects for other variables held at their means. Standard errors in parentheses. Reference category: Very Secure. Results after logistic regression for each country replicating Model 3 from table 13.3. *** $p < 0.01$, ** $p < 0.05$, * $p < 0.1$

insecurity increases. The effects, however, vary and for most countries are not statistically significant at the $p < 0.05$ level.

The impact is greatest in Mexico, Ecuador, Honduras, and Uruguay. Significant effects are also found in Bolivia and Colombia. In Mexico, crime and violence have been the central issues since the election of Felipe Calderón in 2006, and the 2012 elections were framed by a debate over the success or failure of Calderón's "war on the drug cartels." The results indicate that Mexicans who perceive "some" levels of insecurity are 15.3% less likely to vote for the incumbent party than respondents who are "very" secure, and the difference is statistically significant. Citizens who express the highest levels of insecurity are 40.5% less likely to support the incumbent party than those who perceive themselves to be "very" secure. As discussed earlier, Honduras is among the most violent countries in the world and is the most violent in Latin America; crime has been a central issue in presidential elections since the early 2000s, and particularly salient during the last two elections, 2009 and 2013. The marginal effects indicate that moving from perceptions of "very" to "somewhat" secure reduces the likelihood of voting for the incumbent party by 13.3%. Moving from "very secure" to "somewhat insecure" decreases the probability of voting for the incumbent by 14.9%. Ironically, perceiving the highest levels of insecurity actually increases the likelihood of voting for the incumbent by 8.2% but the effect is not statistically significant. The results for Ecuador indicate that moving from "very secure" reduces the probability of voting for the incumbent by at least 20% for each additional level of insecurity. It is worth noting that according to the AmericasBarometer data, Ecuador is the country with the highest level of crime victimization in Latin America (see figure 13.1) and the fourth highest on insecurity (see figure 13.2). In Uruguay, voting for the incumbent is reduced by 13.2% for those citizens who are "somewhat secure" versus those who are "very secure." Respondents who are "very insecure" are 29.3% less likely to vote for the incumbent than the most secure citizens. While aggregate data suggest that Uruguay's crime levels are relatively low, the AmericasBarometer results indicate the country is in the top ten for victimization and insecurity. Additionally, nearly 52% of Uruguayans chose security issues as the most pressing problems facing the country (see table 13.2). Finally, table 13.5 shows that in Colombia citizens who perceive the highest levels of insecurity are 14.9% less likely to vote for the incumbent than those who are "very secure." In Bolivia, the key difference is experienced by those who express "some" level of insecurity since support for the incumbent president declines by 10.3% for those citizens compared to individuals who are very secure, and the difference is statistically significant. Thus, presidents are particularly likely to be held accountable for crime when it is widespread.

Conclusion

This chapter assessed the link between crime and voters' choice between the incumbent and opposition. As a major problem facing the democracies of Latin America, and an issue that reflects the state's inability to resolve key governance dilemmas, crime violence and perception of insecurity can represent serious debilitating problems for citizen attitudes toward the political system. Crime can alienate citizens from their governments, plus it can exacerbate psychological problems that induce anomie and personal dysfunctions. The extant literature shows that crime victimization lowers trust in institutions and negatively affects support for democratic values.

The results presented in this chapter, however, show that victims of crime are not necessarily more likely to vote for the opposition. Victimization rates vary across the countries of the region, as indicated by the results of the AmericasBarometer; however, even in the most violent countries, victimization does not affect voter choice between the incumbent party or president and the opposition. Using the pooled sample, and accounting for country fixed-effects, the analysis finds that perception of insecurity is a significant predictor of support for the opposition, even when we account for the impact of economic evaluations. So, on average, the public is more likely to hold incumbents to account for crime in a sociotropic, not an egotropic, manner. Closer inspection at the country-level analysis shows that Mexico, Ecuador, Uruguay, and Honduras are the only countries in which perception of insecurity significantly reduces support for the incumbent. The evidence from the AmericasBarometer shows that citizens in the first three countries express relatively high levels of insecurity and victimization. In turn, Honduras is the most violent country in the region.

Finally, the discussion and evidence above indicated that insecurity levels are not necessarily linked to actual victimization levels, and thus the findings here indicate that voter choices are affected more by fear of rather than by personal experience with crime. Insecurity, of course, can be affected by media coverage and by fluctuations in levels of victimization; sudden increases in crime that then engender heightened scrutiny by the media and the state are likely to affect voter calculations as they weigh electoral choices. Protecting citizens from crime and violence is a major area of responsibility for the state. High levels of crime and insecurity are evidence of a failure of the state to provide an important public good. While victimization is not a predictor of voter choices, fear of becoming a victim is, at least in some cases. Therefore in the context of a region that exhibits the highest levels of crime and violence in the world, insecurity plays a comparatively prominent factor in voters' electoral decisions.

Chapter 13 Appendix

The Impact of Crime on Voter Choice in Latin America

Incumbent Vote: Dichotomy measure of intention to vote for the incumbent president or party at the next elections: 0 = No and 100 = Yes. Derived from recoding the following question: If the next presidential elections were being held this week, what would you do? [Read options] (1) Wouldn't vote; (2) Would vote for the incumbent candidate or party; (3) Would vote for a candidate or party different from the current administration; (4) Would go to vote but would leave the ballot blank or would purposely cancel my vote. Response 1 is recoded as missing, and responses 3 & 4 are recoded as 0.

Crime victim: Have you been a victim of any type of crime in the past 12 months? That is, have you been a victim of robbery, burglary, assault, fraud, blackmail, extortion, violent threats or any other type of crime in the past 12 months? 0 = No and 100 = Yes.

Perception of Insecurity: Speaking of the neighborhood where you live and thinking of the possibility of being assaulted or robbed, do you feel very safe, somewhat safe, somewhat unsafe or very unsafe? High values represent feeling unsafe.

Education: Responses to the question: How many years of schooling have you completed?

Gender: 0 = Male and 1 = Female

Age: Responses to question: How old are you?

Wealth: Wealth is measured as a scale of possession of capital goods but based on relative wealth. For more information on this indicator, see: Córdova, Abby B. 2009. "Methodological Note: Measuring Relative Wealth using Household Asset Indicators." In *AmericasBarometer Insights Series.* (http://www.vanderbilt.edu/lapop/insights.php).

Urban: Binary variable category derived from sample stratification for respondents living in urban or rural areas.

Security Most Important Problem: Recoded version of the following question: In your opinion, what is the most serious problem faced by the country? 1 = Security and 0 = all other problems.

Perception of National Economic Situation: How would you describe the country's economic situation? Would you say that it is very good, good, neither good nor bad, bad or very bad? High values represent positive assessments of the economy.

Perception of Personal Economic Situation: How would you describe your overall economic situation? Would you say that it is very good, good, neither good nor bad, bad or very bad? High values represent positive assessments of the economy.

Color of Skin: Measured on a scale of 1 = lightest skin color and 11 = darkest skin color, derived from an interviewer classification using a color palette and the following instructions: [When the interview is complete, WITHOUT asking, please use the color chart and circle the number that most closely corresponds to the color of the face of the respondent].

NOTES

1. http://www.unodc.org/unodc/en/data-and-analysis/statistics/data.html.

2. In 2010, the survey introduced a second question measuring crime victimization in the household; combining the first and second questions results in greater levels of victimization. For purposes of this analysis I am only using the question about personal experience with crime.

3. The gray area represents the confidence interval around the mean. When the areas overlap the differences between bars are not statistically significant. Larger gray areas represent a less reliable mean.

4. http://www.unodc.org/unodc/en/data-and-analysis/statistics/data.html.

5. Correlation analyses for each country reveal a weak relationship between victimization and insecurity in all eighteen countries. The highest Pearson's r, 0.27, is found in Argentina, and the lowest, 0.11, in the Dominican Republic.

6. *Perception of National Economic Situation* is coded from the question "How would you describe the country's economic situation?" while *Perception of Personal Economic Situation* is from the question "How would you describe your overall economic situation?" Responses are very good (100), good (75), neither good nor bad (50), bad (25), or very bad (0).

7. *Education* Responses to the question: How many years of schooling have you completed? 0 = men and 100 = women. *Age* Responses to question: How old are you? *Wealth* measured as a scale of possession of capital goods but based on relative wealth. For more information on this indicator, see Abby B. Córdova, "Methodological Note: Measuring Relative Wealth using Household Asset Indicators," (2009), *AmericasBarometer Insights Series*, http://www.vanderbilt.edu/lapop/insights.php. *Urban* Category derived from sample stratification for respondents living in urban or rural areas. 100 = rural, 0 = urban. *Color of Skin* is measured on

a scale of 1 = lightest skin color and 11 = darkest skin color, derived from an interviewer classification using a color palette and the following instructions: [When the interview is complete, WITHOUT asking, please use the color chart and circle the number that most closely corresponds to the color of the face of the respondent].

8. Recoded version of the following question: In your opinion, what is the most serious problem faced by the country? 1 = security and 0 = all other problems.

9. Interacting crime victimization with security as the most important problem has no measurable effect on the results.

10. In each case the regression analysis mirrors that for model 3 in table 13.3.

14 ✦ Conclusion

RYAN E. CARLIN, MATTHEW M. SINGER,
AND ELIZABETH J. ZECHMEISTER

Elections serve both symbolic and instrumental purposes, uniting individuals under a common set of procedures by which each participant has an opportunity to participate in the process of refining, changing, or continuing the nation's political agenda. Elections generate shared experiences and increase habitual and deliberative commitments to democratic procedures. But elections do more than that in modern democracies: elections provide a mechanism by which voters select and sanction representatives. Nowhere are elections' diverse roles more crucial than in consolidating democracies, where experiences with and commitments to the basic rules of the game are comparatively limited. Latin America is such a region, populated with democratic systems that, by comparison to the long-standing democracies of the West, are young, fluid, and fragile. Given the value of elections to the process of democratic consolidation and functionality, it is important to examine what motivates turnout and voter choice in Latin America to understand the extent to which elections are fulfilling these roles.

The role of the voter is, under the best of circumstances, a challenging one. In well-established democracies citizens are socialized into systems that remain largely stable with respect to general electoral processes, the nature of political discourse, and the menu of political options. And even there the process of turning out and selecting an option on the ballot requires no small amount of individual capability and motivation. Across a number of dimensions, electoral environments in less established democratic systems are more fragmented and volatile, which makes collecting information about the political options even more challenging. For this reason scholars have previously identified party system institutionalization as an important factor in fueling programmatic electoral linkages between citizens and elites (Dalton and Anderson 2011).

As we noted from the outset of this volume, the modern wave of democracy arrived in Latin America more than three decades and more than three hundred national elections ago. And yet "fault lines" continue to appear in democracies across the region, party systems display significant instability, and elites engage in frequent experimentation in platforms and appeals. This raises three important questions. First, to what extent do traditional models of voter choice travel to the less consolidated democracies in the Latin American region? Second, within the region, what factors condition the influence of inputs that are considered staples of voter turnout and choice models? And, third, what will determine the future of democratic voting in Latin America?

In the following sections we will address each of these questions in turn. As we do, we will underscore a central conclusion of this volume: while elections in the region on average reflect group interests, policy concerns, and accountability, the substance (societal divides, candidates, platforms) and the structure (party system features) of political competition significantly shape the behavior of Latin Americans at the polls in ways that move individual voting behavior either toward or away from the ideal of programmatic competition. Modern democracy is a system of rule by which citizens use elections to decide who will represent them and who deserves credit or blame for political outcomes. Participation in elections by the mass public is often taken as an indirect indicator of democratic legitimacy (e.g., Lijphart 1997). Yet, the collective efforts in this volume underscore for us the fact that, when it comes to who turns out and on what basis voters make decisions, factors outside the public's direct control are of immense importance. Briefly put, political institutions and elites play critical roles in creating the conditions that facilitate or impede the public's efforts to secure representation and accountability.

Models of Voter Choice in Latin America

Inspired by classic research on voter behavior and motivated to test its traveling capacity, we structured this volume around a number of standard voting models. Following an assessment of the decision to turn out, we addressed three core models of voter choice. Each emphasizes a different set of considerations in attempting to identify the basis on which individuals select political leaders. What are these considerations?

Individuals can, first, base their vote on their membership in a particular societal subgroup, and thus achieve descriptive or policy representation. In the former case, they are represented to the degree that the winning candidate has personal characteristics that mirror their own, and in the latter case they are represented to the degree that the winning candidate pursues policies that promote the interests of their subgroup; disentangling these two forms of representation can be difficult since in reality the two likely exist in tandem. Classic perspectives on the relevance of group identities to voter choice focused on long-enduring cleavages, which took extensive periods of time and opportune "critical junctures" to develop (Lipset and Rokkan 1967). Yet in most of Latin America politically relevant and enduring societal cleavages are either just beginning to emerge or still developing (Dix 1989; Mainwaring, Bejarano, and Pizarro Leongómez 2006; but see Scully 1992), though the rise of the populist left and indigenous parties may be helping to redefine some of these social cleavages (e.g., Mainwaring et al. this volume).

As a second option, voters can ground their vote choice in issues, left-right identifications, and party affiliations. This requires parties to compete by offering clear and distinct substantive packages to voters, capped with left-right or party labels. While elections in Latin America frequently feature discussion of pertinent issues, the depth and clarity of these discussions as well as the extent to which parties have developed consistent, long-standing reputations on these issues varies, especially as new parties have formed and old parties have collapsed in at least some systems over the past few decades.

Finally, as a third option, voters can consider performance. Government performance with respect to the economy, corruption, and crime prevention has been very salient in modern Latin American politics. Although failings in some of these areas have reached critical levels in recent years in Latin America, the connection between those outcomes and national politics is not always evident to voters. Indeed, conditions such as fragmented legislatures and deep insertion into global markets can complicate voters' attempts to determine how responsible national governments are for policy outcomes.

Given the challenges not only at the individual level but also inherent in the complex political environment of emergent democracies, one overly stylized version of voting behavior in Latin America paints a portrait of individuals captivated by the superficial appeals of charismatic personalities, lured into "catch-all" parties with little regard for programmatic offerings, and/or bribed with short-term material private incentives to refrain from holding incumbents accountable for their broader performance in office (see, among others, Dix 1989; O'Donnell 1994). The Latin American voter, in the most extreme version of this accounting, merely uses elections as a mechanism to delegate power to elected officials, leaving the politician in office free to "govern as he or she sees fit" (O'Donnell 1994, 64), unconstrained by mandate or scrutiny. To a greater or lesser extent, this portrait, fired in the opening salvos of the scholarly debate about the role of elections in Latin America's third wave of democracy, has constituted one type of conventional wisdom ever since. And while students of the region two decades hence may suspect that the picture is more nuanced, this intuition has been backed by strikingly little empirical analysis of individual voting behavior across the entire region. While this dearth of research can be explained in part by the fact that the requisite individual-level data for a region-wide treatment of the topic were not easily and amply available until recently, it is simply the case that there have been few previous attempts to identify the Latin American voter.

Together the chapters in this volume offer a rich and comprehensive account of electoral decision-making in the region. In so doing, we offer compelling evidence that the real Latin American voter defies both caricature and stereotype. In the first place, voters in many Latin American countries do systematically consider group interests, programmatic packages, and government output when making vote decisions. In fact, when tested from the perspective of the region as a whole, the evidence suggests that each of the three models contributes to a description of the average Latin American voter. To enhance our regional perspective, we conducted a series of analyses using a pooled dataset containing responses from individuals surveyed in the eighteen Latin American countries as part of the AmericasBarometer 2012.[1] For the sake of space, we only report our conclusions here. The appendix to this chapter includes more details on the models and a replication file is available with the online appendix materials.

We list below several conclusions we can draw from our pooled analyses about vote decisions in contemporary Latin America "on average." As the chapters in the volume have shown and this list affirms, voters' societal subgroup identities, partisanship, issue stances, and left-right identifications; and performance judgments all have some relevance to choice. First, with respect to socioeconomic, demographic, and other descriptive factors, the *average* Latin American voter is more likely to vote for a left-leaning candidate to the degree that this voter is:

- less wealthy
- someone who attends church infrequently or never

- non-Christian or nonreligious
- male
- indigenous

Second, we find that *on average* across the Latin American region:

- Partisans tend to be more likely to support candidates from their own parties.[2]
- Voters who prefer a small economic role for government, want tougher anticrime policies, disapprove of same-sex marriage, and trust the United States are more likely to support candidates on the right.[3]
- Independent of issue stances, left-right identifications predict voter choices.

Third, with respect to performance issues, we find the following *average* effects for the region:

- Individuals who perceive the national economy has strengthened are more likely to vote for the incumbent.[4]
- Individuals who perceive high levels of corruption in the government are less likely to support the incumbent than are those who believe the government is clean.
- Corruption victims are more likely to reject the incumbent than non-victims.
- Compared to individuals who feel safe in their neighborhood, those who feel insecure are less likely to support the incumbent.
- Crime victimization does not have a significant effect on voter choice or abstention rates in this sample.

In short, these results imply that the average Latin American voter bears a resemblance to the average voter in places such as the United States and Europe. Pioneering scholarship on Western advanced democracies identified group identities, issue stances, ideological orientations, party attachments, and performance evaluations as fundamental to the vote choice. The evidence from the chapters in this volume and the pooled models noted above strongly suggests that these classic models travel fairly well to this very different region. Just as importantly, these patterns remind us that—caricatures and stereotypes notwithstanding—Latin American voters' decision-making calculi generally include more than charisma and clientelism. This is not to say that these factors are insignificant.

To the degree that charismatic appeals can be crafted by leaders, they constitute another aspect of the substance of the election environment that we would ascribe to the efforts of political elites. Yet research on charisma across Latin America is stymied by a lack of relevant survey questions across studies of multiple countries (but see Madsen and Snow 1991; Merolla and Zechmeister 2009b; Merolla and Zechmeister 2011). The influence of charisma on elections thus necessarily lies outside the scope of the comparative research in this volume, in the residual variance our models leave unexplained. Clientelism and related vote-buying efforts likewise also matter to Latin American elections; survey data in the Latin American region confirm the varying presence of such linkage strategies and their relationship to political behavior and attitudes (e.g., Carlin and Moseley 2015; Cohen, Faughnan, and Zechmeister 2012; Gonzalez-Octanos et al. 2012; Nichter 2008; Stokes 2005). Not only do levels of vote-buying vary across the region, but so too does the degree to which vote-buying efforts are effective (see Kitschelt and Altamirano this volume). As a direct influence on individual voter choice, the exchange of material incentives for electoral support, like charisma, candidate personality traits, and other proximate campaign effects, is relegated to the unexplained variance in the models in this volume. While in varying ways we do make connections to these factors, we also hope that future scholarship will address these influences in more detail and in comparative studies. Our core emphasis in this volume has been on the extent to which—and when—more programmatic factors related to the pursuit of representation and accountability influence voter choice. To that end, the findings in this volume allow us to conclude that Latin American voters, *on average*, tend to vote for candidates they believe will best advocate for and represent their social group; vote for candidates with whom they share similar issue positions, party identities, and left-right orientations; and use their votes in an attempt to hold leaders accountable for their actions. Yet, to stop at that point would belie the considerable heterogeneity that exists across the region.

The Significance of Cross-National Variation to the Latin American Voter

Establishing the empirical foundations of the average Latin American voter constitutes a significant contribution in and of itself. Yet we have in this volume pursued an objective that extends the project theoretically and empirically beyond descriptive analyses: locating voters' decision-making calculi within the structure and substance of party competition as constructed by political entrepreneurs, candidates, and parties. The classic canon suggested, and in some cases demonstrated, that the relevance of individual-level factors influencing voting decisions varies across electoral systems and contexts. The chapters in this volume show that this is particularly true for the case of Latin America. While the average regional effects we report here show the possibility for electoral behavior to be structured by the same factors that govern political choices in other contexts, they obfuscate significant intraregional heterogeneity with respect to voter decision-making in Latin America and, by implication, the ability of elections to effectively serve as mechanisms of representation and accountability. To that end, let us first offer additional perspective on cross-national variation in determinants of voter choice in Latin America before marshaling evidence from across the chapters in support of our claim.

One way to gauge intraregional heterogeneity is to compare how much variation in voter choice owes to individual- versus country-level factors. To do so we ran a simple multilevel vote choice model of our left-right voter choice measure (described in detail in the introduction to part II) to determine the variance components for the individual and country levels. We then calculated the proportion of total variance that is attributable to the country level by calculating the intra-class correlation coefficient (ICC). Our estimate of 0.48 for the ICC means that 48% of the variance in the dependent variable comes from differences across countries, while 52% of it comes from differences across individuals. Essentially, then, country and individual factors are nearly of equal importance to understanding voter choice in Latin America.

Such a conclusion resonates with the body of work assembled in this volume, where much of the effort has focused on the role played by country-level factors in conditioning those at the individual level. Each chapter shows how country-level factors influence the effects of tried and true individual-level predictors of voter choice. The theoretical upshot of this empirical evidence is that context—the structure and the substance of electoral politics—plays a vital and, compared to individual factors, an underappreciated role in the vote decision in Latin America, and perhaps more generally. Individuals' vote calculi cannot be understood or predicted without reference to the context in which they operate. Previous comparative research on voting behavior across new and old democracies has, to be sure, acknowledged the role of the stability and clarity of political options in shaping vote choice (Dalton and Anderson 2011). But by harnessing the intraregional variation in Latin America, this volume has affirmed the traveling capacity of that overarching framework (that context matters) to a region composed of less established democracies that vary particularly in their commitment to programmatic politics and, as well, unpacked these mechanisms within the Latin American context. In Latin America there exists tremendous diversity within countries, over time, and across borders along social, economic, and political lines. As we indicated in the volume's introduction, a natural consequence of taking this diversity seriously is that we must conclude there is no one true Latin American voter, but a myriad.

To demonstrate this, we highlight findings from each part of the volume that speak to the importance of particular features of the electoral environment's structure (e.g., institutions and the menu of choices) and substance (e.g., activation of particular identities, issue emphasis). In considering turnout, part I presented evidence that individual-level predictors of turnout commonly identified as relevant in other contexts matter in Latin America as well, especially demographic differences and the degree of psychological engagement. At the same time, compulsory voting and party system polarization spur turnout high enough to blunt the effects of both sets of individual-level variables. Part II's chapters on socioeconomic and demographic cleavages documented that entrepreneurial parties and candidates can activate latent cleavages, thus increasing the relevance of group identities to voter choice in some cases. Programmatic party systems, where parties differentiate from each other on the basis of substantive offerings, can serve to magnify some forms of group-based voting. In part III, the chapters showed that issues, left-right identifications, and party affiliations can matter for vote choice in the region, especially to the extent that party competition is programmatically structured around issues and a limited set of options whose polarization helps voters see parties' differences. The type of party-based linkage frequently juxtaposed with programmatic linkages—clientelism—appears to varying degrees across the region and is often inefficient, but yet can displace voting based on issues and left-right identifications. And, finally, the chapters on performance factors in part IV documented that Latin American voters generally hold politicians accountable for outputs, principally sociotropic evaluations of the economy and perceived levels of corruption and insecurity. At the same time, the analyses of the economy and corruption clearly suggest that the weight of these factors depends on the political and economic environment as these issues change in salience and as policymaking becomes more concentrated in the executive's party.

An important conclusion that emerges from the preceding chapters is that, for as many countries in which identities, issues, and performance matter and despite the importance of these factors on average across the region, there are countries in which at the present time they are of little or no consequence to voter choice. While this is a disappointing conclusion to the extent that it suggests deficiencies in the capacity of the electoral process to deliver on promises of substantive representation and accountability, here the intraregional diversity provides important insights into which conditions are most auspicious for programmatic voting behavior. On the whole, the chapters in this volume point to the important role that political parties and elites in particular can play in shaping the nature of voting across the region and elsewhere. More specifically, the analyses in this volume support a number of inferences about how the electoral environment's *structure* and *substance* influence Latin American voters. In particular, where parties and political entrepreneurs make salient relevant group divisions, societal cleavages can exert important influences on voter choice. And when politicians campaign and differentiate themselves on the basis of policy stances and capabilities without appearing overly fragmented, the region's voters can ground their electoral choices in a wide range of issue preferences, left-right identifications, and performance evaluations.

What Does the Future Hold for the Latin American Voter?

Studying voting behavior in the diverse and shifting region of Latin America is like looking through a kaleidoscope. The portrait that emerges is rich in texture, variegated, and yet coherent under the right conditions. From our study, we conclude that Latin American voters are able to work toward the ideal of representative democracy, but that elites do not always and everywhere meet them halfway by populating the ballot with meaningful choices. Fortunately, the analyses in this volume point to at least five incentives for elites to develop clear, consistent, distinct, and substantively rich menus of choice to voters interested in advancing their group interests, policy preferences, and general welfare. While we discuss these here, we also note our reservations about the likelihood of a rapid and wholesale embrace of the incentives that will profoundly increase Latin American voters' ability to use the ballot to secure programmatic representation and accountability. Building programmatic linkages takes time, and they are more easily destroyed than created (Kitschelt et al. 2010).

In the first place, Carlin and Love's study of turnout in part I tells us that advancing clear, distinct programmatic agendas draws citizens into the process of elections. Increased turnout may not directly benefit every party. But the very fact that voting habituates citizens to work through conflicts at the polls benefits all parties to the extent it increases the durability of the democratic system. Thus, if time horizons are sufficiently long, political elites and parties have some incentive to present themselves to citizens in ways that increase the public's participation in elections.

Second, the evidence presented in part II suggests that the social divisions on which voters form socioeconomic and demographic identities have the potential to be transformed into politically relevant "cleavages" if parties make the effort to mobilize them. The persistent relevance of group identities to broader social and economic issues in Latin America means that class, gender, ethnicity, and religion are resources available to entrepreneurial politicians interested in currying the favor of new groups of voters by activating these dimensions in the political realm. The chapters on class and religion in particular showed how political entrepreneurs have mobilized these cleavages in recent elections. The focus on such factors allows us insight into some of the ways in which candidate images matter to elections in Latin America. But, as Moreno's chapter on ethnic voting reminds us, in some cases the process of politicizing such divisions is not a simple, much less surefire, path to power if the party cannot successfully build the necessary networks to link voters to the party. Regardless, by attempting to convert these social identities into cleavages to garner votes, elites can foster descriptive representation. Of course, achieving descriptive representation may or may not correspond to policy-based or mandate representation. This shortcoming appears to be reflected in the recent rise of the left in Latin America. According to Mainwaring, Torcal, and Somma's chapter, left-populist candidates have engendered class-based voting in many cases in the region. At the same time, the broader imprint of left-populist leaders on Latin American party systems has been disruptive at the worst or of no clear benefit at the best. For example, their presence is associated with a lower efficiency of clientelistic networks, as argued by Kitschelt and Altamirano in their chapter. And, according to Zechmeister's chapter, there is little evidence that left-populist leaders increased the electorates' left-right ideological structuration. Taken together, the chapters in parts II and III suggest that the rise of the left in Latin America may have done more to achieve descriptive representation along class (and, in some cases, ethnic) lines than to enhance ideational or material linkages between voters and politicians.

Yet in a region with deep social inequalities that have served, historically, to marginalize large swaths of the electorate from the formal political arena, it can be of genuine consequence for politicians from traditionally excluded groups to take office. In fact, the positive externalities of such a development have been noted recently even in the U.S. case, where the election of a president with African American roots enhanced political efficacy among African Americans in the electorate (Merolla, Sellers, and Fowler 2012). Moreover, in some cases electing politicians with characteristics that mirror one's own can be a shortcut to programmatic representation. Thus, as Morgan's contribution to this volume suggests, the tendency for women to vote for women in Latin America may derive from an expectation that female politicians will advance issue agendas of particular importance to many women in the region, such as abortion rights or laws protecting against domestic violence. Similarly, Boas and Smith's chapter detects a tendency for the religious to favor the ideological right in Latin America, an orientation consistent with achieving more conservative political programs.

Third, an incentive for parties and elites in Latin America to offer clear, coherent, and distinct options is related to the relatively high costs of an alternative linkage mechanism: clientelism. Kitschelt and Altamirano (this volume) find that clientelism is inefficient, particularly as economic development continues to make vote-buying costly and especially in Latin America where the practice is surprisingly ineffective according to their measures. While they develop a compelling portrait of a "leaky bucket" scenario for clientelism in Latin America, the situation is fueled by elites' persistence in refilling that bucket and voter demands for services that are not being provided through other means. Therefore, we may be observing an out-of-equilibrium situation that will eventually settle into a new equilibrium in which clientelism fades as a preferred linkage mechanism. Should this happen, it would even further raise incentives for politicians to compete for votes on the basis of identities, policy programs, and public goods.

A fourth set of incentives politicians and parties face in developing clear, coherent, and stable programs is voters' sensitivities to them. Rather than merely delegate politics to elites, in this volume chapters by Baker and Greene, Zechmeister, and Lupu document that electorates across Latin America tend to engage in issue voting, relate left-right identifications to politics, and attach to political parties *when given the opportunities*. In fact, these respective contributions explicitly make the point that the way these processes and constructs work in Latin America is often strikingly similar to how they function in advanced industrialized democracies where parties compete programmatically on a more consistent basis. Politicians looking to mobilize support, thus, have an untapped opportunity in parts of Latin America to develop—or redevelop—programmatic linkages more fully in future elections.

The fifth and final incentive for politicians to compete on the basis of substance is that Latin American voters can be good stewards of the political system. Indeed, analyses in part IV render strong evidence that they monitor elected officials' performance and use it to inform their vote choice. Together, chapters by Gélineau and Singer, Pérez, and Manzetti and Rosas demonstrate that Latin American voters are not only (but particularly) sensitive to economic outcomes. They also weigh incumbents' output in the areas of corruption and security (crime). Here the incentives cut two ways. On the one hand, incumbents may benefit to the degree that they can obscure responsibility for poor output for which voters would punish them. But, on the other hand, they will likely face just as many opportunities to benefit from claiming credit for positive shifts. And the same goes for the opposition parties, though in this case, they should be motivated to link incumbents to poor performance while rebuffing incumbents' attempts to claim responsibility for good output. While these varying tactics may challenge voters' ability to "throw bums out" and to reward high performers, they nonetheless function to keep campaigns focused on issues relevant to the public good. As a result, Latin American elections frequently turn on the question of whether or not politicians have delivered and many among Latin America's voters are willing to vote against those politicians who fail to do so.[5]

Conclusion

In our introductory chapter, we motivated our comparative survey of voting behavior in Latin America by asking three questions: (1) Who votes? (2) What attributes and judgments influence voter choice? and (3) What contextual factors distinguish voters in Latin American countries from each other and from voters in other contexts? Our approach to these questions included a study of turnout and subsequent parts that explored how socioeconomic and demographic characteristics, parties' substantive and material offerings, and performance outcomes influence voting behavior in the region. What have we learned about the Latin American voter?

Regarding the first two questions, we can securely conclude that the average Latin American voter bears many similarities to voters in other democratic systems around the world. To varying degrees, the same core elements emphasized in classic scholarship—group identities, party programs, and performance—matter to voter choice in the region. And with some nuances, the factors that influence central components of voter choice, such as the decision to turn out and partisanship, are largely similar to those found in other regions. We trust these conclusions square with the intuitions of many observers of Latin American elections, yet such broad-based empirical evidence is necessary to counter those with more pessimistic intuitions regarding electoral decision-making in the region as well as to demonstrate that classic voting models can travel to a region stocked with comparatively less established democracies.

Yet it is our answer to the third question that grants us the most theoretical purchase and room for empirical nuance, and it leads us ultimately to conclude that, in reality, there is no one Latin American voter who stands as characteristic of the region as a whole. Whereas voters in less established Latin American democracies and in long established democracies outside the region employ the same basic elements in their turnout and vote choice calculi, these elements' weights in the overall decision depend on key features of the electoral environment's substance and structure. Substantive factors include, but are not limited to, social cleavages that foment interests and identities, entrepreneurial parties and politicians who activate latent group-based identities, and candidates who campaign on policy issues and ideologies. When electoral conditions allow voters to ground their choices in substance, the liberal democratic ideal of representation is at least possible in Latin America. Structural factors include party system fragmentation and polarization, which, respectively, obscure or illuminate electoral choices and the shifting salience of the most important problems facing a country. Where electoral competition is structured by a few clearly defined and distinct options, and lines of policy responsibility are easy to establish, the ideal of accountability can become a reality in the region. Nonetheless, we hasten to add that variation in the substance and the structure of electoral competition can only partially explain the divergence from the theoretical predictions of classic voting models that we do witness in Latin America. We leave it for future scholars to identify other variables that deepen our understanding of why in certain instances stock measures from classic voting models roundly fail to predict individuals' preferences at the polls.

The scarcity of more robust models of programmatic voter choice in many countries across the region would leave us remarkably pessimistic if it were not for this last conclusion: parties and political elites have both the capacity and incentives to put effort into developing campaigns, institutions, and reputations that fuel voters' abilities to elect politicians into office who represent their group interests and/or individual interests and to hold those elected accountable for their performance once in office, to at least the same degree that voters in advanced industrialized countries are able to achieve these same objectives. The chapters in this volume and the findings about average patterns across the hemisphere provide evidence that programmatic-based voter behavior occurs in Latin America when conditions favor it. We are aware, of course, that tremendous debate remains over the effectiveness of elections in bringing about economic and political development and the importance of other modes of democratic accountability (see, e.g., Achen and Bartels 2004; Smulovitz and Peruzzotti 2000; Mainwaring and Welna 2003). And yet we believe that voting with the intention to increase representation and accountability reflects and, at least at the margins, can promote democratic functionality and quality. So while we will not conclude with an overly sanguine statement about what future electoral environments hold for the Latin American voter, we can conclude from the work presented in this volume that the capacity for individuals to achieve representation and accountability through voting exists and, under certain conditions, is realized in the Latin American region.

Chapter 14 Appendix

In the first part of the conclusion we present a summary of results from an analysis of pooled models of the left-right vote choice and the pro-incumbent vote across the eighteen countries in our sample, using fixed effects to control for factors that our models may miss. The goal is to look at what structures voter behavior "on average" in Latin America. In this appendix we present the details of these models. As we note in the chapter, we see them as providing strong evidence that the basic voting models travel well to Latin America and of the possibilities for programmatic competition and electoral accountability. Yet we remind the reader that beneath these "on average" findings are significant variations across countries that speak to the importance of contextual factors that structure voter choices. We proceed in three steps that correspond to the three main parts of the book: demographics, substantive offerings, and performance.

Demographics

The dependent variable in this model is the left-right vote measure introduced in part II and used as the dependent variable in most of parts II and III. We model it as a function of the demographic variables that the authors of this volume emphasize: class, religion, gender, and ethnicity. We expect traditionally economically or socially marginalized groups, such as lower classes and indigenous groups, will be more likely to support left-leaning parties. Church attendance, as a proxy for the religious-secular divide, should lead voters to support right-leaning candidates. Our expectations for female voters are less straightforward; per Morgan's chapter in this volume, Latin American women customarily espouse conservative social values and support right-leaning parties, but life circumstances, choices, and societal differences in women's social and economic roles may make them more likely to vote for left-leaning candidates.

We measure the demographic variables in the same way that the authors do in the chapters in the volume. The respondent's *wealth* is based on an index of household access to water and electricity and ownership of television, vehicles, appliances, and other household goods (see Mainwaring, Torcal, and Somma in this volume for a description). *Religiosity* is operationalized with a question about church attendance, with high values representing greater frequency (see Boas and Smith this volume). We also include a series of dummy variables for the respondent's religion, differentiating mainline Protestants, evangelical Protestants, Mormons and Jehovah's Witnesses, non-Christians, and those without any religion from Catholics. *Female* is a dummy variable scored 1 if the respondent is female. Finally, we gauge *ethnicity* with dummy variables for ethnic identity as white, indigenous, black, and mulatto; mestizo is the reference category.[1] Additional controls include the respondents' education,[2] age cohort, and size of the town where they reside.[3] The model includes fixed effects that control for clustering in the standard errors and country differences in average ideologies (either due to differences in how experts interpret the left-right scale across countries, differences in average levels of the explanatory variables across countries, or unmeasured characteristics of the party system). To conserve space, we do not present those country-specific coefficients here but they are available from the authors on request.[4] All variables are rescaled from zero to 1 to facilitate interpretation.

The results are in figure A14.1.[5] As described in the text, wealthy and religious individuals tend to support conservative parties as do women and

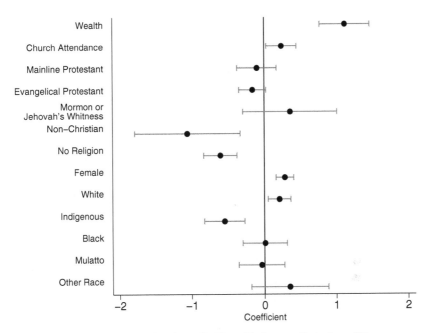

Figure A14.1   Model of Left-Right Vote Choice as a Function of Demographics. *Source:* AmericasBarometer 2012. *Note:* Coefficients are from an OLS Model with additional controls for respondents' education level, age cohort, and the size of the town the respondent lives in as well as country fixed effects. The range plots graph the 95% confidence interval. The baseline category for religion is Catholic and for race is mestizo. N = 15,053, Adjusted R^2 = 0.457, F = 343 (p < 0.001).

whites while indigenous, non-Christians, and non-religious individuals support left-leaning candidates on average.

Left-Right and Issues

We next analyze whether voter preferences in Latin America, on average, reflect policy divisions and general left-right identifications. The dependent variable used here is again left-right vote choice. While the nature of the available survey data requires that we analyze previous electoral behavior as a function of current attitudes, we believe these attitudes are relatively stable and thus the results should reflect the opinions of voters whose preferences are most fully formed. Inasmuch as issue preferences do change over time, it should hurt our chances of observing any consistent patterns in these data.

We focus here on five policy areas that we believe are likely to reflect electoral divisions in Latin America (see Rosas 2005, though note our addition of anti-Americanism). By focusing on five policy areas, we can broaden the perspective beyond the economic issues Baker and Greene study in their chapter, but our analysis will necessarily lack the nuance and richness of multidimensional indicators and country-specific investigations of their analysis.

The first concerns economics, in particular, the role of the state in directly involving itself in the economy to fund industry and create jobs. Traditionally, leftist governments in Latin America have adopted a more hands-on approach to economic management (Murillo 2001, 2009). Baker and Greene (2011) show that while voters have not rejected markets or globalization, the "left turn" in Latin America over the past decade reflects voter desires for governments to take a larger role in managing the economy. There is less evidence in Latin America, however, of ideological differences in how social spending is managed (Huber, Mustillo, and Stephens 2008), and public opinion data reach mixed conclusions as to whether there are ideological disagreements over the government's role in job creation and increasing protections for the poor (Corral 2009a, 2009b).

A second potential set of divisions reflects democratic attitudes. Many rightist parties in Latin America have traditionally been ambivalent to democracy (Middlebrook 2000) and attitudes toward the depth and speed with which democratization should occur frequently emerge as a major cleavage in new democracies (Moreno 1999). Thus, we might expect that skepticism about democracy leads voters toward right-leaning parties. Yet recent analyses disagree about whether there are any ideological differences in democratic attitudes within the general population now that democracy is well established in the region (Arnold and Samuels 2011; Carlin and Singer 2011).

The next two issue areas we examine emphasize the state's social role. As crime continues to be a major problem in many Latin American societies,[6] voters may demand that parties crack down on criminals. This so-called *mano dura* (heavy-handed) approach is generally associated with parties on the right (Holland 2013; Pérez this volume). Support for the right might also correspond to preferences on moral issues such as abortion and gay marriage (Lodola and Corral 2010; Zechmeister and Corral

2013) although the left has varied in its advocacy for the pro-life and pro-LGBT policies (Freidman 2009; Corrales and Pecheny 2010).

The last issue under study refers to international politics. In Latin America, a large ideological divide exists with regards to the role the United States plays in the region (Arnold and Samuels 2011). Remmer (2012) links the use of anti-American rhetoric by many leftist political candidates to their electoral success in the recent decade. Thus, anti-American attitudes might be expected to reflect support for leftist parties.

We begin our analysis by measuring the degree to which respondents support government taking a strong role in the economy, including owning businesses, reducing the gap between rich and poor, taking the lead in promoting citizen wellbeing, and creating jobs.[7] We measure respondents' stated levels of support for democracy as a political system.[8] Attitudes toward crime prevention are measured by asking whether being tougher on criminals is necessary to fight crime.[9] Questions on abortion[10] and same-sex marriage[11] were asked in one half of the sample, while a question on whether the United States is trustworthy[12] was only asked of the other half of the sample. Thus, in the analysis that follows we estimate a version of the model without questions on either of these topics and then estimate models separately, first with questions on the two moral issues and then with the question on the United States. We control for the demographic variables and country dummy variables used in the previous analysis that looked only at demographics.

After looking at these five specific issues and their association with the vote, we re-estimate the models with a variable capturing respondents' left-right self-identifications. In general, we expect voters who place themselves on the "right" to support candidates that experts code on the right, and vice versa. However, an additional question is whether the inclusion of left-right identifications in the models will weaken the relationship between specific policy attitudes and the vote. Yet while left-right identifications in Latin America may indicate distinct policy stances (e.g., Arnold and Samuels 2011; Zechmeister and Corral 2013), in many countries these semantics might primarily reflect partisan or other divides with little to no policy content (Zechmeister 2006a, 2006b; Zechmeister this volume).

In the models below, we do not control for partisanship in the present analysis for one simple reason: as Lupu notes in his chapter, voters in Latin America who self-identify with a party are almost certain to vote for that party. The bivariate correlation between the expert-coded ideology of the party with which a voter self-identifies and the party he or she reported

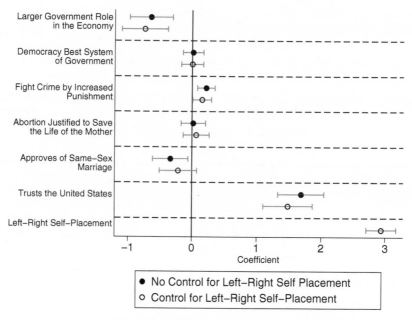

Figure A14.2   Model of Left-Right Vote Choice as a Function of Issue Preferences and Demographics. *Source:* AmericasBarometer 2012. *Note:* Coefficients from OLS regression with controls for demographics and country fixed effects with the 95% Confidence Intervals. Goodness of fit statistics are available in the online appendix Table A14.2 along with the results for the other controls.

voting for in the last election is 0.90. Thus for party identification, it is less a question of how is it related to the vote and more a question of where is it strongest and what factors bolster party attachments.

The main results of these analyses are in figure A14.2. Voters who prefer a small economic role for government, want tougher anticrime policies, disapprove of same-sex marriage, and trust the United States are more likely to support candidates on the right. It is worth noting that even after controlling for left-right identification, these issue variables remain significantly associated with the vote and their estimated coefficients change very little. This suggests that the relationship between Latin Americans' left-right self-placement and their electoral choices does not necessarily reflect a strong association between respondents' issue positions and their self-identification as "left" or "right," a theme found in the chapter by Zechmeister. Thus issue appeals and left-right labels emerge as potential packages that Latin America's parties can use to earn votes.

Performance

To analyze how voters hold politicians accountable for various outcomes, we estimate a multinomial logistic regression of voter intentions to vote for the incumbent party, to vote for an opposition party, to cast a blank/null vote, or to abstain. We analyze the variables emphasized in the chapters by Gélineau and Singer, Manzetti and Rosas, and Pérez. Respondents were asked to evaluate both the national economy and their personal finances with respect to change (or not) over a twelve-month period.[13] Positive evaluations of the economy are expected to correlate with an increased probability of supporting the incumbent. The corruption question asks, "Taking into account your own experience or what you have heard, corruption among public officials is very common, common, uncommon, or very uncommon?"[14] Respondents who perceive corruption is common should be less likely to support the current administration. Since personal experiences with corruption might undermine support for the sitting incumbent, we include a dummy variable scored 1 if the respondent was targeted for a bribe by a policeman, government employee, court, or local government official, or in the workplace, school system, or health system. Our crime perception question asks, "Speaking of the neighborhood where you live and thinking of the possibility of being assaulted or robbed, do you feel very safe, somewhat safe, somewhat unsafe, or very unsafe?"[15] We expect individuals who feel unsafe to be less likely to support the incumbent. To capture personal experiences with crime, we include a dummy variable that takes the value of 1 if a member of the household has been a victim of a crime in the past month and test whether crime victims reject the incumbent.

Individual-level measures of economic and governance outcomes have been criticized as endogenous to attitudes toward the national government; that is, respondents who support the ruling party may wish to describe the current state of the nation less critically than do those who oppose it (e.g., Kramer 1983; Evans and Anderson 2006), a conclusion Manzetti and Rosas (this volume) echo. The ongoing debate over the sources of intra-country variation in performance indicators (Lewis-Beck, Norpoth, Jacoby, and Weisberg 2008; Duch and Stevenson 2008; Stevenson and Duch 2013) emphasizes the importance of controlling for respondents' baseline levels of support for the incumbent to avoid omitted variable bias. We do so in two ways. First, we control for the respondent's proximity to the incumbent on the left-right scale, estimating the incumbent's position using the Wiesehomeier and Benoit (2009) expert survey.[16] Second, we include dummy variables for each respondent's party identification (making non-identifiers the reference category). Chapters by Zechmeister and Lupu in this volume suggest that these variables should be associated with support for the incumbent.

These models control for various demographic and psychological variables that previous chapters have shown affect turnout. However, because the incumbent governments in these countries come from different ideological positions and have ties to different social groups, we are ambivalent as to how these variables will affect incumbent support.[17] We also include country dummy variables to control for differences in baseline levels of incumbent support across party systems.

The main results from the multinomial logit are available in figure A14.3. Individuals who perceive the national economy has strengthened are more likely to vote for the incumbent, with the national economy

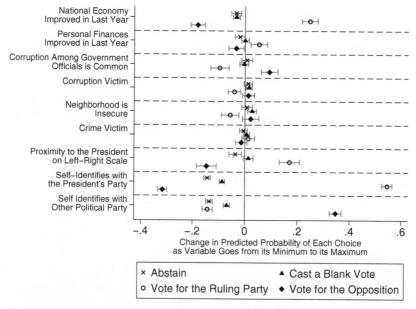

Figure A14.3   Whom Respondent Would Vote for if the Election were Held Today. *Source:* AmericasBarometer 2012. *Note:* Predicted probabilities and their 95% confidence intervals from multinomial logit analysis generated using *Clarify* (King et al. 2000). Model includes controls for demographics and engagement variables as outlined by Carlin and Love Chapter 2 and country fixed effects and are available in online appendix table A14.2. $N = 16,726$, Pseudo-$R^2 = 0.245$, $\chi^2 = 10,490$ ($p < 0.001$).

having a larger effect than personal finances (Singer and Carlin 2013). Individuals who perceive high levels of corruption in the government are less likely to support the incumbent than are those who believe that government is clean. Corruption victims are more likely to reject the incumbent than non-victims. Compared to individuals who feel safe in their neighborhood, those who feel insecure are less likely to support the incumbent. Crime victimization does not have a significant effect on voter choice or abstention rates in this sample, but the individual-level demographic and psychological factors Carlin and Love emphasize in their study of turnout (this volume) do correlate with intentions to abstain.

APPENDIX NOTES

1. In other analyses not presented here, we control for the respondents' skin color and find that darker-skinned individuals are more likely to support leftist parties.

2. Measured as the highest level of school that was completed: none, primary, secondary, or higher.

3. The variable distinguishes whether the respondent lives in a rural area, a small, medium, or large city, or the national capital, with high values representing larger cities.

4. The country dummy variables also explain the model's high R_2 value.

5. See the online appendix for the complete output of the analyses underlying figures A14.1, A14.2, and A14.3.

6. In recent years crime has often tied with economics as the most frequently cited "most important problem facing the country" in Latin America (Singer et al. 2012).

7. We use answers to four questions, originally measured on a 1–7 scale where high values represent strong agreement but we have rescaled them on a 0–6 scale where high values represent a desire for a small state role. The questions are "The (Country) government, instead of the private sector, should own the most important enterprises and industries of the country. How much do you agree or disagree with this statement?" "The (Country) government, more than individuals, should be primarily responsible for ensuring the well-being of the people. To what extent do you agree or disagree with this statement?" "The (Country) government, more than the private sector, should be primarily responsible for creating jobs. To what extent to do you agree or disagree with this statement?" "The (Country) government should implement strong policies to reduce income inequality between the rich and the poor. To what extent do you agree or disagree with this statement?" We then followed Baker and Greene (this volume) and ran a factor analysis of these questions.

8. We measure support for democracy using a dummy variable that takes the value of 1 if the respondent believes that "Democracy is preferable to any other form of government" and zero if the respondent believes either that "For people like me it doesn't matter whether a government is democratic or non-democratic"

or "Under some circumstances an authoritarian government may be preferable to a democratic one." In additional analyses not presented here we have broken apart the two non-democracy answers into separate dummy variables and find no difference across answers. We have also measured support for democracy using agreement with the statement "democracy may have problems, but it is better than any other form of government."

9. Measured from the question "I am going to read you some things you hear on the street or in the media when people talk about ways to combat crime. Please tell me if you strongly agree, agree somewhat, somewhat disagree, or strongly disagree with each one of them. The best way to fight crime is to be tougher on criminals?" Higher values represent agreement with the question.

10. Respondents in the odd-numbered version of the questionnaire were asked "Do you think it's justified to interrupt a pregnancy, that is, to have an abortion, when the mother's health is in danger?" Respondents who answered "yes" are coded as a 1 and those who said "no" are coded as a zero.

11. Respondents in the odd-numbered version of the questionnaire were asked "How strongly do you approve or disapprove of same-sex couples having the right to marry?" High values represent a high level of approval of gay marriage.

12. Respondents in the even-numbered version of the questionnaire were asked "The United States. In your opinion, is it very trustworthy, somewhat trustworthy, not very trustworthy, or not at all trustworthy, or do you not have an opinion?" High values represent considering the United States to be trustworthy.

13. Coded from questions asking "Do you think that the country's current economic situation (your personal finances) is better than, the same as, or worse than it was 12 months ago?" Responses are coded on a 3-point scale, with high values representing positive views of the economy.

14. Responses are coded so that high values represent a high degree of perceived corruption, and the variable is measured on a 4-point scale.

15. This variable is coded on a 4-point scale, with high values representing feeling insecure.

16. The Wiesehomeier and Benoit scale coded ideology on a 19-point scale (1–20) while the AmericasBarometer survey asked respondents to place themselves on a 1–10 left-right scale. So we first rescaled the Wiesehomeier and Benoit scores for incumbents or their party on the 1–10 scale. We then measure proximity to the incumbent as $|IR - IG|*\text{-}1 + 10$ (where IG is the ideology of the government and IR is the left-right identification of the respondent) so that high values represent having a similar left-right score to the incumbent. This specification results in dropping respondents who did not answer the left-right identification question. In an alternative specification we have coded all respondents who did not answer the proximity question as having the mean proximity score and then included a dummy variable identifying these non-left-right respondents, and the substantive conclusions regarding government performance do not change in the larger sample.

17. The performance results change little if we exclude demographic variables.

NOTES

1. Specifically, we modeled left-right vote as a function of demographic predictors and issue concerns and then modeled support for the incumbent as a function of left-right self-placement and the perceived state of the economy, crime, and corruption in the country.

2. The bivariate correlation between the expert-coded ideology of the party with which a voter self-identifies and the ideology of the party he or she reported voting for in the last election is 0.90.

3. We also assessed views on democracy as a political system and belief that abortion is justified to save the life of the mother, and found that neither is a significant predictor of voter choice in the pooled analysis.

4. We also find the impact of personal finances on government support mirrors that of the national economy, but is smaller (cf. Singer and Carlin 2013).

5. Though see the discussion in Gélineau and Singer (this volume) on the strength of incumbency.

References

Aarts, Kees, and Bernhard Wessels. 2005. "Electoral Turnout." In *The European Voter*, edited by Jacques Thomassen, 64–82. New York: Oxford University Press.

Abdelal, Rawi, Yoshiko Herrera, Alastair Iain Johnston, and Rose McDermott. 2006. "Identity as a Variable." *Perspectives on Politics* 4:695–711.

Achen, Christopher H. 1975. "Mass Political Attitudes and the Survey Response." *American Political Science Review* 69:1218–31.

Achen, Christopher H. 1992. "Social Psychology, Demographic Variables, and Linear Regression: Breaking the Iron Triangle in Voting Research." *Political Behavior* 14:195–211.

Achen, Christopher H., and Larry M. Bartels. 2004. "Musical Chairs: Pocketbook Voting and the Limits of Democratic Accountability." Paper prepared for the Annual Meeting of the American Political Science Association, Chicago.

Achen, Christopher H., and Larry M. Bartels. n.d. "Blind Retrospection: Electoral Responses to Drought, Flu, and Shark Attacks." Unpublished paper.

Adcock, Robert, and David Collier. 2001. "Measurement Validity: A Shared Standard for Qualitative and Quantitative Research." *American Political Science Review* 95:529–46.

Agüero, Felipe, and Jeffrey Stark. 1998. *Fault Lines of Democracy in Post-Transition Latin America*. Miami: North-South Center Press/University of Miami.

Aguilar, Edwin Eloy, Jose Miguel Sandoval, Kenneth M. Coleman, and Timothy J. Steigenga. 1993. "Protestantism in El Salvador: Conventional Wisdom versus Survey Evidence." *Latin American Research Review* 28:119–40.

Aguilar, Rosario. 2011. "The Tones of Democratic Challenges: Skin Color and Race in Mexico." *Documentos de Trabajo CIDE* 231.

Albright, Jeremy J. 2009. "Does Political Knowledge Erode Party Attachments? A Review of the Cognitive Mobilization Thesis." *Electoral Studies* 28:248–60.

Alcañiz, Isabella, and Timothy Hellwig. 2011. "Who's to Blame? The Distribution of Responsibility in Developing Democracies." *British Journal of Political Science* 41:389–411.

Alcántara, Manuel. 2012. Proyecto de Elites Parlamentarias Latinoamericanas (PELA). Universidad de Salamanca (1994–2005).

Aldrich, John H. 1993. "Rational Choice and Turnout." *American Journal of Political Science* 37:246–78.

Alesina, Alberto, Arnaud Devleeschauwer, William Easterly, Sergio Kurlat, and Romain Wacziarg. 2003. "Fractionalization." *Journal of Economic Growth* 8:155–94.

Alfaro-Redondo, Ronald, and Mitchell A. Seligson. 2012. *Cultura Política de la Democracia en Costa Rica, 2012: La Erosión de los Pilares de la Estabilidad Política*. Nashville, TN: Latin American Public Opinion Project, Vanderbilt University.

Alford, John, Holly Teeters, Daniel S. Ward, and Rick K. Wilson. 1994. "Overdraft: The Political Cost of Congressional Malfeasance." *Journal of Politics* 56:788–801.

Almond, Gabriel, and Sidney Verba. 1963. *The Civic Culture: Political Attitudes and Democracy in Five Nations*. Boston: Little, Brown & Co.

Altman, David. 2009. "Individual, Economic, and Institutional Causes of Electoral Participation in Latin America." Latin American Public Opinion Project Small Grants Working Paper, http://sitemason.vanderbilt.edu/files/heU6Y0/ALTMAN%20Individual%20Economic%20and%20Institutional%20Causes%20of%20Electoral%20Participation%20in%20Latin%20America.pdf.

AmericasBarometer. Latin American Public Opinion Project (LAPOP), Vanderbilt University. www.LapopSurveys.org.

Ames, Barry. 2001. *The Deadlock of Democracy in Brazil*. Ann Arbor: University of Michigan Press.

Ames, Barry, Andy Baker, and Lucio R. Rennó. 2008. "The Quality of Elections in Brazil: Policy, Performance, Pageantry, or Pork?" In *Democratic Brazil Revisited*, edited by Peter Kingstone and Timothy Power, 107–33. Pittsburgh: University of Pittsburgh Press.

Ames, Barry, and Amy Erica Smith. 2010. "Knowing Left from Right: Ideological Identification in Brazil, 2002–2006." *Journal of Politics in Latin America* 2:3–38.

Amuchastegui, Ana, Guadalupe Cruz, Evelyn Aldaz, and Maria Consuelo Mejia. 2010. "Politics, Religion and Gender Equality in Contemporary Mexico: Women's Sexuality and Reproductive Rights in a Contested Secular State." *Third World Quarterly* 31:989–1005.

Anderson, Benedict. 1983. *Imagined Communities: Reflections on the Origin and Spread of Nationalism*. London: Verso.

Anderson, Christopher J. 2000. "Economic Voting and Political Context: A Comparative Perspective." *Electoral Studies* 19:151–70.

Anderson, Christopher J. 2007. "The End of Economic Voting? Contingency Dilemmas and the Limits of Democratic Accountability." *Annual Review of Political Science* 10:271–96.

Anderson, Christopher J., and Russell J. Dalton. 2011. "Nested Voters: Citizen Choices Embedded in Political Contexts." In *Citizens, Context, and Choice*, edited by Christopher J. Anderson and Russell J. Dalton, 241–96. New York: Oxford University Press.

Anderson, Christopher J., and Matthew M. Singer. 2008. "The Sensitive Left and the Impervious Right: Multilevel Models and the Politics of Inequality, Ideology, and Legitimacy in Europe." *Comparative Political Studies* 41:564–99.

Ansolabehere, Stephen, Jonathan Rodden, and James M. Snyder Jr. 2008. "The Strength of Issues: Using Multiple Measures to Gauge Preference Stability, Ideological Constraint, and Issue Voting." *American Political Science Review* 102:215–32.

Arana, Rubí Esmeralda, and María L. Santacruz Giralt. 2005. *Opinión Pública Sobre el Sistema Político del País y la Participación de la Mujer en la Política.* Colección Género N. 2. San Salvador: FUNDAUNGO.

Arce, Moises. 2003. "Political Violence and Presidential Approval in Peru." *Journal of Politics* 65:572–83.

Arnold, Jason Ross, and David J. Samuels. 2011. "Evidence from Public Opinion." In *The Resurgence of the Latin American Left,* edited by Steven Levitsky and Kenneth M. Roberts, 31–51. Baltimore: Johns Hopkins University Press.

Aspelund, Anna, Marjaana Lindeman, and Markku Verkasalo. 2013. "Political Conservatism and Left-Right Orientation in 28 Eastern and Western European Countries." *Political Psychology* 34:409–17.

Atkeson, Lonna Rae. 2003. "Not All Cues are Created Equal: The Conditional Impact of Female Candidates on Political Engagement." *Journal of Politics* 65:1040–61.

Auyero, Javier. 2000. *Poor People's Politics: Peronist Survival Networks and the Legacy of Evita.* Durham, NC: Duke University Press.

Baker, Andy. 2009. *The Market and the Masses in Latin America: Policy Reform and Consumption in Liberalizing Economies.* New York: Cambridge University Press.

Baker, Andy, Barry Ames, and Lucio R. Rennó. 2006. "Social Context and Campaign Volatility in New Democracies: Networks and Neighborhoods in Brazil's 2002 Elections." *American Journal of Political Science* 50:382–99.

Baker, Andy, and Kenneth F. Greene. 2011. "The Latin American Left's Mandate: Free-Market Policies and Issue Voting in New Democracies." *World Politics* 63:43–77.

Baker, Andy, Anand E. Sokhey, Barry Ames, and Lucio R. Rennó. 2010. "The Sources and Dynamics of Mass Partisanship in a New Democracy." Paper presented at the Annual Meeting of the American Political Science Association, Washington, DC.

Balch, George I. 1974. "Multiple Indicators in Survey Research: The Concept 'Sense of Political Efficacy.'" *Political Methodology* 1:1–43.

Baldez, Lisa. 2002. *Why Women Protest: Women's Movements in Chile.* New York: Cambridge University Press.

Bargsted, Matías A., and Nicolás M. Somma. Forthcoming. "Social Cleavages and Political Dealignment in Contemporary Chile, 1995–2009." *Party Politics.*

Barraca, Steve. 2008. "Why Mexico's Christians Don't Vote Christian Democratic." Paper presented at the Annual Meeting of the Southern Political Science Association, New Orleans.

Barreto, Matt A., and Francisco I. Pedraza. 2009. "The Renewal and Persistence of Group Identification in American Politics." *Electoral Studies* 28:595–605.

Bartels, Larry M. 2000. "Partisanship and Voting Behavior, 1952–1996." *American Journal of Political Science* 44:35–50.

Bartels, Larry M. 2002. "The Impact of Candidate Traits in American Presidential Elections." In *Leaders' Personalities and the Outcomes of Democratic Elections,* edited by Anthony King, 44–69. Oxford: Oxford University Press.

Bartels, Larry M. 2006. "Three Virtues of Panel Data for the Analysis of Campaign Effects." In *Capturing Campaign Effects,* edited by Henry E. Brady and Richard Johnston, 134–63. Ann Arbor: University of Michigan Press.

Bartolini, Stefano. 2000. *The Political Mobilization of the European Left, 1860–1980: The Class Cleavage.* Cambridge: Cambridge University Press.

Bastian, Jean-Pierre. 1999. "Los Nuevos Partidos Políticos Confesionales Evangélicos y su Relación con el Estado en América Latina." *Estudios Sociológicos* 17:153–73.

Bateson, Regina. 2012. "Crime and Political Participation." *American Political Science Review* 106:570–87.

Beaman, Lori, Raghabendra Chattopadhyay, Esther Duflo, Rohini Pande, and Petia Topalova. 2009. "Powerful Women: Does Exposure Reduce Bias?" *Quarterly Journal of Economics* 124:1497–1540.

Beckett, Katherine. 1997. *Making Crime Pay: Law and Order in Contemporary American Politics.* Oxford: Oxford University Press.

Beirne, Piers. 1997. *Issues in Comparative Criminology.* Brookfield, VT: Dartmouth Publishing Company.

Bellows, John, and Edward Miguel. 2009. "War and Local Collective Action in Sierra Leone." *Journal of Public Economics* 93:1144–57.

Beltrán, Ulises. 2003. "Venciendo la Incertidumbre: El Voto Retrospectivo en la Elección Presidencial de Julio de 2000 en México." *Política y Gobierno* 10:325–58.

Bengtsson, Asa. 2004. "Economic Voting: The Effect of Political Context, Volatility and Turnout on Voters' Assignment of Responsibility." *European Journal of Political Research* 43:749–67.

Benton, Allyson. 2005. "Dissatisfied Democrats or Retrospective Voters?" *Comparative Political Studies* 38:417–42.

Berelson, Bernard R., Paul F. Lazarsfeld, and William N. McPhee. 1954. *Voting: A Study of Opinion Formation in a Presidential Election.* Chicago: University of Chicago Press.

Berglund, Frode, Sören Holmberg, Hermann Schmitt, and Jacques Thomassen. 2006. "Party Identification and Party Choice." In *The European Voter*, edited by Jacques Thomassen, 105–23. Oxford: Oxford University Press.

Birnir, Jóhanna Kristín. 2007. *Ethnicity and Electoral Politics.* New York: Cambridge University Press.

Blais, André. 2006. "What Affects Voter Turnout?" *Annual Review of Political Science* 9:111–25.

Blais, André, and Francois Gélineau. 2007. "Winning, Losing and Satisfaction with Democracy." *Political Studies* 55:425–41.

Blais, André, Elisabeth Gidengil, Richard Nadeau, and Neil Nevitte. 2001. "Measuring Party Identification: Britain, Canada, and the United States." *Political Behavior* 23:5–22.

Blais, André, Louis Massicotte, and Agnieszka Dobrzynska. 2003. "Why Is Turnout Higher in Some Countries than in Others?" www.elections.ca.

Blalock, Hubert M., Jr. 1967. *Toward a Theory of Minority-Group Relations.* New York: John Wiley and Sons.

Blancarte, Roberto J. 2009. "The Changing Face of Religion in the Democratization of Mexico." In *Religious Pluralism, Democracy, and the Catholic Church in Latin America*, edited by Frances Hagopian, 225–56. Notre Dame, IN: University of Notre Dame Press.

Blanco, Luisa R. 2013. "The Impact of Crime on Trust in Institutions in Mexico." *European Journal of Political Economy* 32:38–55.

Blattman, Christopher. 2009. "From Violence to Voting: War and Political Participation in Uganda." *American Political Science Review* 103:231–47.

Blofield, Merike. 2012. *Care, Work and Class: Domestic Workers' Struggle for Equal Rights in Latin America*. University Park: Penn State University Press.

Bloom, Howard, and H. Douglas Price. 1975. "Voter Response to Short-Run Economic Conditions: The Asymmetric Effect of Prosperity and Recession." *American Political Science Review* 69:1240–54.

Boas, Taylor C. 2014. "Pastor Paulo vs. Doctor Carlos: Professional Titles as Voting Heuristics in Brazil." *Journal of Politics in Latin America* 6:39–72.

Boas, Taylor C., and F. Daniel Hidalgo. 2011. "Controlling the Airwaves: Incumbency Advantage and Community Radio in Brazil." *American Journal of Political Science* 55:869–85.

Boas, Taylor, and Amy Erica Smith. 2013. "Religion and the Latin American Voter." Paper prepared for the Annual Meeting of the Southern Political Science Association, New Orleans.

Bobbio, Norberto. 1996. *Left and Right: The Significance of a Political Dimension*. Chicago: University of Chicago Press.

Bohn, Simone. 2004. "Evangélicos no Brasil: Perfil Sócio-Econômico, Afinidades Ideológicas e Determinantes do Comportamento Eleitoral." *Opinião Pública* 10:288–338.

Bohn, Simone. 2007. "Contexto Político-Eleitoral, Minorias Religiosas e Voto em Pleitos Presidenciais (2002–2006)." *Opinião Pública* 13:366–87.

Boidi, María Fernanda, and Margarita Corral. 2013. "Public Opinion and Abortion Rights in the Americas." AmericasBarometer Topical Brief, Latin American Public Opinion Project (LAPOP), Vanderbilt University.

Bolzendahl, Catherine I., and Daniel J. Myers. 2004. "Feminist Attitudes and Support for Gender Equality: Opinion Change in Women and Men, 1974–1998." *Social Forces* 83:759–89.

Booth, John A., and Mitchell A. Seligson. 2009. *The Legitimacy Puzzle in Latin America: Political Support and Democracy in Eight Nations*. New York: Cambridge University Press.

Bormann, Nils-Christian, and Matt Golder. 2013. "Democratic Electoral Systems Around the World, 1946–2011." *Electoral Studies* 32:360–69.

Box-Steffensmeier, Janet M., Suzanna De Boef, and Tse-Min Lin. 2004. "The Dynamics of the Partisan Gender Gap." *American Political Science Review* 98(3):515–28.

Brader, Ted, and Joshua A. Tucker. 2001. "The Emergence of Mass Partisanship in Russia, 1993–1996." *American Journal of Political Science* 45:69–83.

Brader, Ted, and Joshua A. Tucker. 2008. "Pathways to Partisanship: Evidence from Russia." *Post-Soviet Affairs* 24:263–300.

Brader, Ted, Joshua A. Tucker, and Matias A. Bargsted. 2013. "Of Time and Partisan Stability Revisited." Unpublished manuscript.

Brady, Henry E., Sidney Verba, and Kay Lehman Schlozman. 1995. "Beyond SES: A Resource Model of Political Participation." *American Journal of Political Science* 89:271–94.

Bratton, Michael, Robert Mattes, and E. Gyiman-Boadi. 2005. *Public Opinion, Democracy, and Market Reform in Africa*. New York: Cambridge University Press.

Bratton, Michael, Yun-Han Chu, and Marta Lagos. 2010. "Who Votes? Implications for New Democracies." *Taiwan Journal of Democracy* 6:107–36.

Brehm, John, and Wendy Rahn. 1997. "Individual-Level Evidence for the Causes and Consequences of Social Capital." *American Journal of Political Science* 41:999–1023.

Brinks, Daniel, and Michael Coppedge. 2006. "Diffusion Is No Illusion: Neighbor Emulation in the Third Wave of Democracy." *Comparative Political Studies* 39:463–89.

Brockington, David. 2009. "It's about the Benefits: Choice Environments, Ideological Proximity and Individual Participation in 28 Democracies." *Party Politics* 4:435–54.

Brody, Richard A., and Benjamin I. Page. 1973. "Indifference, Alienation and Rational Decisions." *Public Choice* 15:1–17.

Brubaker, Rogers. 2004. *Ethnicity without Groups*. Cambridge, MA: Harvard University Press.

Bruhn, Kathleen, and Kenneth F. Greene. 2009. "The Absence of Common Ground between Candidates and Voters." In *Consolidating Mexico's Democracy: The 2006 Presidential Campaign in Comparative Perspective*, edited by Jorge Domínguez, Chappell Lawson, and Alejandro Moreno, 109–28. Baltimore: Johns Hopkins University Press.

Brusco, Valeria, Marcelo Nazareno, and Susan C. Stokes. 2004. "Vote Buying in Argentina." *Latin American Research Review* 39:66–88.

Budge, Ian, and Dennis J. Farlie. 1983. *Explaining and Predicting Elections: Issue Effects and Party Strategies in Twenty-Three Democracies*. London: Allen and Unwin.

Burns, Nancy, Kay Lehman Schlozman, and Sidney Verba. 2001. *The Private Roots of Public Action*. Cambridge, MA: Harvard University Press.

Burris, Scott. 2006. "From Security to Health." In *Democracy, Society, and the Governance of Security*, edited by J. Wood and B. Dupont, 196–216. New York: Cambridge University Press.

Bustikova, Lenka, and Cristina Corduneanu-Huci. 2009. "The Correlates of Clientelism: Economic Development and Historical State Capacity." American Political Science Association Annual Meeting, Toronto.

Butler, David, and Donald E. Stokes. 1969. *Political Change in Britain: Forces Shaping Electoral Choice*. New York: St. Martin's Press.

Buvnic, Mayra, and Vivian Roza. 2004. "Women, Politics and Democratic Prospects in Latin America." *IDB Sustainable Development Department, Technical Paper Series*. Washington, DC: IDB.

Caillier, James. 2010. "Citizens Trust, Political Corruption, and Voting Behavior: Connecting the Dots." *Politics & Policy* 38:1015–35.

Calvo, Ernesto, and Victoria Murillo. 2004. "Who Delivers? Partisan Clients in the Argentine Electoral Market." *American Journal of Political Science* 48:742–57.

Calvo, Ernesto, and Victoria Murillo. 2012. "When Parties Meet Voters: Partisan Networks and Distributive Expectations in Argentina and Chile." *Comparative Political Studies* 46:851–82.

Cameron, Maxwell A., and Eric Hershberg, eds. 2010. *Latin America's Left Turns: Politics, Policies, and Trajectories of Change*. Boulder, CO: Lynne Rienner Publishers.

Camp, Roderic Ai. 2008. "Exercising Political Influence: Religion, Democracy, and the Mexican 2006 Presidential Race." *Journal of Church and State* 50:49–72.

Campbell, Angus, Philip E. Converse, Warren E. Miller, and Donald E. Stokes. 1960. *The American Voter*. New York: John Wiley & Sons.

Campbell, Angus, Gerald Gurin, and Warren Edward Miller. 1954. *The Voter Decides*. Evanston, IL: Row, Peterson and Co.

Campos, Leonildo Silveira. 2005. "De 'Políticos Evangélicos' a 'Políticos De Cristo': La Trayectoria de Las Acciones y Mentalidad Política de los Evangélicos Brasileños en El Paso del Siglo XX al Siglo XXI." *Ciencias Sociales y Religión* 7:157–86.

Campusano, Mauricio. 2005. "Estrategia para Ampliar Votación: Piñera Exhibe Apoyo de Grupo de Falangistas." *El Mercurio*, December 14.

Canes-Wrone, Brandice, William Minozzi, and Jessica Bonney Reveley. 2011. "Issue Accountability and the Mass Public." *Legislative Studies Quarterly* 36:5–35.

Cannon, Barry. 2008. "Class/Race Polarisation in Venezuela and the Electoral Success of Hugo Chávez: A Break with the Past or the Song Remains the Same?" *Third World Quarterly* 29:731–48.

Cárdia, Nancy. 2002. "The Impact of Exposure to Violence in Sao Paulo: Accepting Violence or Continuing Horror?" In *Citizens of Fear: Urban Violence in Latin America*, edited by Susana Rotker and Katherine Goldman, 152–86. New Brunswick, NJ: Rutgers University Press.

Carey, John, and Mathew S. Shugart. 1995. "Incentives to Cultivate a Personal Vote: A Rank Order of Electoral Formulas." *Electoral Studies* 14:414–39.

Carlin, Ryan E. 2006. "The Decline of Citizen Participation in Electoral Politics in Post-Authoritarian Chile." *Democratization* 13:632–51.

Carlin, Ryan E. 2011. "Distrusting Democrats and Political Participation in New Democracies: Lessons from Chile." *Political Research Quarterly* 64:668–87.

Carlin, Ryan E., and Gregory J. Love. 2013. "What's at Stake? A Veto-Player Theory of Voter Turnout." *Electoral Studies* 32:807–18.

Carlin, Ryan E., Gregory J. Love, and Cecilia Martínez-Gallardo. 2015. "Cushioning the Fall: Scandals, Economic Conditions, and Executive Approval." *Political Behavior* 37(1):109–30.

Carlin, Ryan E., and Mason Moseley. 2015. "Good Democrats, Bad Targets: Democratic Values and Clientelistic Vote Buying." *Journal of Politics* 77(1):14–26.

Carlin, Ryan E., and Matthew M. Singer. 2011. "Support for Polyarchy in the Americas." *Comparative Political Studies* 44 (11): 1500–1526.

Carreras, Miguel. 2012. "The Rise of Outsiders in Latin America, 1980–2010: An Institutionalist Perspective." *Comparative Political Studies* 45:1451–82.

Carreras, Miguel. 2013. "The Impact of Criminal Violence on Regime Legitimacy in Latin America." *Latin American Research Review* 48:85–107.

Carreras, Miguel, and Néstor Castañeda-Angarita. 2014. "Who Votes in Latin America? A Test of Three Theoretical Perspectives." *Comparative Political Studies* 47:1079–1104.

Carroll, Susan J. 1988. "Women's Autonomy and the Gender Gap: 1980 and 1982." In *The Politics of the Gender Gap*, edited by Carol Mueller, 236–57. Newbury Park, CA: Sage.

Carsey, Thomas M., and Geoffrey C. Layman. 2006. "Changing Sides or Chang-ing Minds? Party Identification and Policy Preferences in the American Elec-torate." *American Journal of Political Science* 50:464–77.

Casey, Peter. 2014. "Voting for Corruption: How Poverty and Inequality Undermine Democratic Accountability." Ph.D. diss., Washington University, St. Louis.

Cassel, Carol A. 1993. "A Test of Converse's Theory of Party Support." *Journal of Politics* 55:664–81.

Cataife, Guido. 2011. "An Integrated Model of Vote Choice in Argentina, 2009." *Latin American Politics and Society* 53:115–40.

Caul Kittilson, Miki. 2011. "Electoral Supply and Voter Turnout." In *Citizens, Con-text, and Choice: How Context Shapes Citizens' Electoral Choices*, edited by Russell J. Dalton and Christopher J. Anderson. New York: Cambridge University Press.

Chandra, Kanchan. 2001. "Introduction: Cumulative Findings in the Study of Eth-nic Politics." *American Political Science Association* 12:7–11.

Chandra, Kanchan. 2004. *Why Ethnic Parties Succeed*. Cambridge: Cambridge Uni-versity Press.

Chandra, Kanchan. 2006. "What is Ethnic Identity and Does It Matter?" *Annual Review of Political Science* 9:397–424.

Chandra, Kanchan, and David Laitin. 2002. "A Framework for Thinking About Identity Change." Paper presented at the LICEP, Stanford University, Stan-ford, CA.

Chang, Eric, Miriam Golden, and S. J. Hill. 2010. "Legislative Malfeasance and Political Accountability." *World Politics* 62(2):177–220.

Chesnut, R. Andrew. 2003. *Competitive Spirits: Latin America's New Religious Econ-omy*. New York: Oxford University Press.

Chesnut, R. Andrew. 2009. "Charismatic Competitors: Protestant Pentecostals and Catholic Charismatics in Latin America's New Religious Marketplace." In *Reli-gion and Society in Latin America*, edited by Lee M. Penyak and Walter J. Petry, 207–23. Maryknoll, NY: Orbis Books.

Chhibber, Pradeep K., and Mariano Torcal. 1997. "Elite Strategy, Social Cleav-ages, and Party Systems in a New Democracy: Spain." *Comparative Political Studies* 30:27–54.

Ciabattari, Teresa. 2001. "Changes in Men's Conservative Gender Ideologies: Co-hort Change and Period Influences." *Gender and Society* 15(4):574–91.

Clark, Terry N., and Seymour M. Lipset. 1991. "Are Social Classes Dying?" *Inter-national Sociology* 6:397–410.

Clark, Terry N., Seymour Martin Lipset, and Michael Rempel. 2001. "The Declin-ing Political Significance of Social Class." In *The Breakdown of Class Politics: A Debate on Post-Industrial Stratification*, edited by Terry Nichols Clark and Sey-mour Martin Lipset, 77–104. Washington, DC: The Woodrow Wilson Center Press/Johns Hopkins University Press.

Cohen, Mollie, Brian Faughnan, and Elizabeth Zechmeister. 2012. "Reluctant v. Content Clients?: Vote-Buying in the Americas." Paper presented at the An-nual Meeting of the Southern Political Science Association, New Orleans.

Collier, Ruth Berrins, and David Collier. 1991. *Shaping the Political Arena: Critical Junctures, the Labor Movement, and Regime Dynamics in Latin America*. Princeton, NJ: Princeton University Press.

Conaghan, Catherine M. 1995. Politicians Against Parties: Discord and Disconnection in Ecuador's Party System. In *Building Democratic Institutions: Party Systems in Latin America*, edited by Scott Mainwaring and Timothy Scully, 434–58. Palo Alto: Stanford University Press.

Conaghan, Catherine M. 2011. "Ecuador: Rafael Correa and the Citizens' Revolution." In *The Resurgence of the Latin American Left*, edited by Steven Levitsky and Kenneth M. Roberts, 260–82. Baltimore: Johns Hopkins University Press.

Conover, Pamela J. 1981. "Political Cues and the Perception of Candidates." *American Politics Quarterly* 9(4):427–48.

Conover, Pamela Johnston. 1988. "Feminists and the Gender Gap." *Journal of Politics* 50:985–1010.

Conover, Pamela Johnston, and Stanley Feldman. 1982. "Projection and the Perception of Candidates' Issue Positions." *Western Political Quarterly* 35:228–44.

Converse, Philip E. 1964. "The Nature of Belief Systems in Mass Publics." In *Ideology and Discontent*, edited by David E. Apter, 206–61. London: Free Press of Glencoe.

Converse, Philip E. 1969. "Of Time and Partisan Stability." *Comparative Political Studies* 2:139–71.

Converse, Philip E. 1976. *The Dynamics of Party Support: Cohort-Analyzing Party Identification*. Beverly Hills: Sage Publications.

Converse, Philip E., and Georges Dupeux. 1962. "Politicization of the Electorate in France and the United States." *Public Opinion Quarterly* 26:1–23.

Converse, Philip E., and Roy Pierce. 1992. "Partisanship and the Party System." *Political Behavior* 14:239–59.

Coppedge, Michael. 1994. *Strong Parties and Lame Ducks: Presidential Partyarchy and Factionalism in Venezuela*. Stanford, CA: Stanford University Press.

Córdova, Abby. 2009. "Methodological Note: Measuring Relative Wealth Using Household Asset Indicators." AmericasBarometer, *Insights*, I0806, Latin American Public Opinion Project (LAPOP), Vanderbilt University.

Corradi, Juan E. 1992. "Toward Societies without Fear." In *Fear at the Edge: State Terror and Resistance in Latin America*, edited by Juan E. Corradi, Patricia Weiss Fagen, and Manuel Antonio Garretón, 267–92. Berkeley: University of California Press.

Corral, Margarita. 2009a. "Should Government Own Big Businesses and Industries? Views from the Americas." AmericasBarometer, *Insights*, I0808, Latin American Public Opinion Project (LAPOP), Vanderbilt University.

Corral, Margarita. 2009b. "To What Extent Should Government Ensure Citizen Well-Being?" AmericasBarometer, *Insights*, I0816, Latin American Public Opinion Project (LAPOP), Vanderbilt University.

Corrales, Javier, and Mario Pecheny. 2010. *The Politics of Sexuality in Latin America: A Reader on Lesbian, Gay, Bisexual, and Transgender Rights*. Pittsburgh, PA: University of Pittsburgh Press.

Costas, Elena, Albert Solé-Ollé, and Pilar Sorribas-Navarro. 2010. "Do Voters Really Tolerate Corruption? Evidence from Spanish Mayors." Unpublished manuscript.

Cox, Gary, and Scott Morgenstern. 2001. "Latin America's Reactive Assemblies and Proactive Presidents." *Comparative Politics* 33:171–89.

Crisp, Brian. 2000. *Democratic Institutional Design: The Powers and Incentives of Venezuelan Politicians and Interest Groups*. Stanford, CA: Stanford University Press.

Cullen, Francis T., Gregory A. Clark, and John F. Wozniak. 1985. "Explaining the Get Tough Movement: Can the Public be Blamed?" *Federal Probation* 49:16–24.

Cummins, Jeff. 2009. "Issue Voting and Crime in Gubernatorial Elections." *Social Science Quarterly* 90:632–51.

Cuzán, Alfred, and Charles Bundrick. 1997. "Presidential Popularity in Central America: Parallels with the United States." *Political Research Quarterly* 50:833–49.

Dahl, Robert A. 1971. *Polyarchy: Participation and Opposition*. New Haven, CT: Yale University Press.

Dalton, Russell J. 1988. *Citizen Politics in Western Europe: Public Opinion and Political Parties in the United States, Great Britain, West Germany, and France*. Chatham, NJ: Chatham House.

Dalton, Russell J. 1996. *Citizen Politics: Public Opinion and Political Parties in Advanced Industrial Democracies*. Chatham, NJ: Chatham House.

Dalton, Russell J. 2000. "The Decline of Party Identifications." *In Parties without Partisans: Political Change in Advanced Industrial Democracies*, edited by Russell J. Dalton and Martin P. Wattenberg. New York: Oxford University Press. 19–36.

Dalton, Russell J. 2006. "Social Modernization and the End of Ideology Debate: Patterns of Ideological Polarization." *Japanese Journal of Political Science* 7:1–22.

Dalton, Russell J. 2008. "The Quantity and the Quality of Party Systems: Party System Polarization, its Measurement, and its Consequences." *Comparative Political Studies* 41:899–920.

Dalton, Russell J. 2011. "Left-Right Orientations, Context, and Voting Choices." In *Citizens, Context, and Choice: How Context Shapes Citizens' Electoral Choices*, edited by Russell J. Dalton and Christopher Anderson, 103–25. New York: Oxford University Press.

Dalton, Russell J., and Christopher, Anderson, eds. 2011. *Citizens, Context, and Choice: How Context Shapes Citizens' Electoral Choices*. New York: Oxford University Press.

Dalton, Russell J., David M. Farrell, and Ian McAllister. 2011. *Political Parties and Democratic Linkage: How Parties Organize Democracy*. New York: Oxford University Press.

Dalton, Russell J., and Steven A. Weldon. 2007. "Partisanship and Party System Institutionalization." *Party Politics* 13:179–96.

Davey, Joseph. 1999. *The Politics of Prison Expansion*. New York: Praeger.

Davis, Charles L., and Kenneth M. Coleman. 1983. "Who Abstains? The Situational Meaning of Nonvoting." *Social Science Quarterly* 64:764–76.

De Boef, Suzanna, and Luke Keele. 2008. "Taking Time Seriously." *American Journal of Political Science* 52:184–200.

Deegan-Krause, Kevin. 2007. "New Dimensions of Political Cleavage." In *Oxford Handbook of Political Behaviour*, edited by Russell J. Dalton and Hans-Dieter Klingemann, 538–56. Oxford: Oxford University Press.

Degregori, Carlos Ivan. 1998. "Ethnicity and Democratic Governability in Latin America: Reflections from Two Central Andean Countries." In *Fault Lines of*

Democracy in Post Transition Latin America, edited by Felipe Agüero and Jeffrey Stark, 203–34. Miami: North-South Center Press.

De la Calle, Luis, and Nasos Roussias. 2012. "How So Spanish Independents Vote? Ideology vs. Performance." *South European Society and Politics* 17(3): 411–25.

Del Popolo, Fabiana. 2008. *Los Pueblos Indígenas y Afrodescendientes en las Fuentes de Datos: Experiencias en América Latina, Documentos de Proyecto*. Santiago de Chile: CEPAL—CELADE—OPS.

Delli Carpini, Michael X., and Scott Keeter. 1996. *What Americans Know About Politics and Why It Matters*. New Haven, CT: Yale University Press.

Desposato, Scott W. 2006. "Parties for Rent? Ambition, Ideology, and Party Switching in Brazil's Chamber of Deputies." *American Journal of Political Science* 50:62–80.

Desposato, Scott, and Barbara Norrander. 2009. "The Gender Gap in Latin America: Contextual and Individual Influences on Gender and Political Participation." *British Journal of Political Science* 39(1):141–62.

DeVaus, David, and Ian McAllister. 1989. "The Changing Politics of Women: Gender and Political Alignment in 11 Nations." *European Journal of Political Research* 17(3):241–62.

de Vries, Catherine E., Armen Hakhverdian, and Bram Lancee. 2013. "The Dynamics of Voters' Left/Right Identification: The Role of Economic and Cultural Attitudes." *Political Science Research and Methods* 1:223–38.

Diamond, Larry. 2008. "The Democratic Rollback." *Foreign Affairs*. March 2. Accessed June 23, 2014. http://www.foreignaffairs.com/articles/63218/larry-diamond/the-democratic-rollback.

Dinas, Elias. 2014. "Does Choice Bring Loyalty? Electoral Participation and the Development of Party Identification." *American Journal of Political Science* 58:449–65.

Dix, Robert H. 1989. "Cleavage Structures and Party Systems in Latin America." *Comparative Politics* 22:23–37.

Dodson, Michael. 1997. "Pentecostals, Politics, and Public Space in Latin America." In *Power, Politics, and Pentecostals in Latin America*, edited by Hannah W. Stewart-Gambino and Edward L. Cleary, 25–40. Boulder, CO: Westview Press.

Domínguez, Jorge I., and Chappell Lawson, eds. 2003. *Mexico's Pivotal Democratic Election: Candidates, Voters, and the Presidential Campaign of 2000*. Stanford, CA: Stanford University Press and the Center for U.S.-Mexican Studies, University of California, San Diego.

Domínguez, Jorge I., Chappell Lawson, and Alejandro Moreno. 2009. *Consolidating Mexico's Democracy: The 2006 Presidential Campaign in Comparative Perspective*. Baltimore: Johns Hopkins University Press.

Domínguez, Jorge I., and James A. McCann. 1995. "Shaping Mexico's Electoral Arena: The Construction of Partisan Cleavages in the 1988 and 1991 National Elections." *American Political Science Review* 89:34–48.

Domínguez, Jorge I., and James A. McCann. 1996. *Democratizing Mexico: Public Opinion and Electoral Choice*. Baltimore: Johns Hopkins University Press.

Domínguez, Jorge I., and James A. McCann. 1998. "Mexicans React to Electoral Fraud and Political Corruption: An Assessment of Public Opinion and Voting Behavior." *Electoral Studies* 17:483–503.

Domínguez, Jorge I., and Alejandro Poiré. 1999. *Towards Mexico's Democratization: Parties, Campaigns, Elections, and Public Opinion*. New York: Routledge.

Došek, Tomáš. 2011. "Do Left and Right Differentiate Citizens and Politicians in Latin America?" *Boletin PNUD and Instituto de Iberoamérica*, Universidad de Salamanca.

Dow, Jay. 1998. "A Spatial Analysis of the 1989 Chilean Presidential Election." *Electoral Studies* 17:61–76.

Downs, Anthony. 1957. *An Economic Theory of Democracy*. New York: Harper.

Dreher, Axel, Noel Gaston, and Pim Martens. 2008. *Measuring Globalisation—Gauging its Consequences*. New York: Springer.

Duch, Raymond, and Randy Stevenson. 2005. "Context and the Economic Vote: A Multi-Level Analysis." *Political Analysis* 13:387–409.

Duch, Raymond, and Randolph T. Stevenson. 2008. *The Economic Vote: How Political and Economic Institutions Condition Election Results*. New York: Cambridge University Press.

Duryea, Suzanne, Sebastian Galiani, Hugo Ñopo, and Claudia Piras. 2007. "The Educational Gender Gap in Latin America and the Caribbean." *Inter-American Development Bank Working Paper Series*, no. 502. Washington, DC: IDB.

Duverger, Maurice. 1954. *Political Parties: Their Organization and Activity in the Modern State*. New York: Wiley and Sons.

Echegaray, Fabián. 2005. *Economic Crises and Electoral Responses in Latin America*. New York: University Press of America.

Echegaray, Fabián. 2006. "Elecciones en Brasil: Hacia un Sistema Político Moderno y Secularizado." *Nueva Sociedad* 206:27–34.

Edlin, Aaron, Andrew Gelman, and Noah Kaplan. 2007. "Voting as a Rational Choice: Why and How People Vote to Improve the Well-Being of Others." *Rationality and Society* 19:293–314.

Edwards, George C., William Mitchell, and Reed Welch. 1995. "Explaining Presidential Approval: The Significance of Issue Salience." *American Journal of Political Science* 39:108–34.

Eggers, Andrew, and Alexander Fisher. 2011. "Electoral Accountability and the UK Parliamentary Expenses Scandal: Did Voters Punish Corrupt MPs?" Working paper. http://dx.doi.org/10.2139/ssrn.1931868.

Eldersveld, Samuel J. 1973. "Party Identification in India in Comparative Perspective." *Comparative Political Studies* 6:271–95.

Elias, Robert. 1986. *The Politics of Victimization: Victims, Victimology, and Human Rights*. New York: Oxford University Press.

Ellis, Christopher, and James A. Stimson. 2011. "Pathways to Conservative Identification: The Politics of Ideological Contraction in the United States." In *Facing the Challenge of Democracy: Explorations in the Analysis of Public Opinion and Political Participation*, edited by Paul M. Sniderman and Benjamin Highton, 120–50. Princeton, NJ: Princeton University Press.

Enelow, James M. 1986. "The Linkage between Predictive Dimensions and Candidate Issue Positions in American Presidential Campaigns: An Examination of Group Differences." *Political Behavior* 8:245–61.

Enelow, James M., and Melvin J. Hinich. 1984. *The Spatial Theory of Voting: An Introduction*. New York: Cambridge University Press.

Epstein, Lee, and Jeffrey A. Segal. 2000. "Measuring Issue Salience." *American Journal of Political Science* 44:66–83.

Erikson, Robert, and John H. Goldthorpe. 1992. *The Constant Flux: A Study of Class Mobility in Industrial Societies.* Oxford: Clarendon.

Escobar-Lemmon, Maria, and Michelle M. Taylor-Robinson. 2005. "Women Ministers in Latin American Government." *American Journal of Political Science* 49(4):829–44.

Esping-Andersen, Gosta. 1985. *Politics Against Markets. The Social Democratic Road to Power.* Princeton, NJ: Princeton University Press.

Esping-Andersen, Gosta. 1999. *Social Foundations of Postindustrial Economies.* Oxford: Oxford University Press.

Estrada, Felipe. 2004. "The Transformation of the Politics of Crime in High Crime Societies." *European Journal of Criminology* 1:419–43.

Evans, Geoffrey. 1999. *The End of Class Politics?: Class Voting in Comparative Context.* New York: Oxford University Press.

Evans, Geoffrey, and R. Anderson. 2006. "The Political Conditioning of Economic Perceptions." *Journal of Politics* 68:194–207.

Evans, Geoffrey, and Nan Dirk De Graaf, eds. 2013. *Political Choice Matters: Explaining the Strength of Class and Religious Cleavages in Cross-National Perspective.* New York: Oxford University Press.

Evans, Geoffrey, Anthony Heath, and Mansur Lalljee. 1996. "Measuring Left-Right and Libertarian-Authoritarian Values in the British Electorate." *British Journal of Sociology* 47:93–112.

Evans, Geoffrey, and Stephen Whitefield. 1998. "The Evolution of Left and Right in Post-Soviet Russia." *Europe-Asia Studies* 50:1023–42.

Ewig, Christina. 2010. *Second-Wave Neoliberalism: Gender, Race and Health Sector Reform in Peru.* University Park: Penn State University Press.

Fajnzylber, Pablo, Daniel Lederman, and Norman Loayza. 1998. *Determinants of Crime Rates in Latin America and the World: An Empirical Assessment.* World Bank Latin American and Caribbean Studies. Viewpoints. Washington, DC: World Bank.

Faughnan, Brian M., and Elizabeth J. Zechmeister. 2011. "Vote Buying in the Americas." AmericasBarometer, *Insights*, I57, Latin American Public Opinion Project (LAPOP), Vanderbilt University.

Fearon, James. 2003. "Ethnic and Cultural Diversity by Country." *Journal of Economic Growth* 8:195–222.

Feldman, Stanley. 1982. "Economic Self-Interest and Political Behavior." *American Journal of Political Science* 27(3): 446–66.

Ferraz, Claudio, and Frederico Finan. 2008. "Exposing Corrupt Politicians: The Effects of Brazil's Publicly Released Audits on Electoral Outcomes." *Quarterly Journal of Economics* 123(2):703–45.

Finkel, Steven E. 1995. *Causal Analysis with Panel Data.* Thousand Oaks, CA: Sage Publications.

Fiorina, Morris. 1978. "Economic Retrospective Voting in American National Elections: A Micro-Analysis." *American Journal of Political Science* 22:426–43.

Fiorina, Morris P. 1981. *Retrospective Voting in American National Elections.* New Haven, CT: Yale University Press.

Firebaugh, Glenn, and Kevin Chen. 1995. "Voter Turnout of Nineteenth Amendment Women: The Enduring Effect of Disenfranchisement." *American Journal of Sociology* 100:972–96.

Fleet, Michael, and Brian H. Smith. 1997. *The Catholic Church and Democracy in Chile and Peru.* Notre Dame, IN: University of Notre Dame Press.

Fleury, Christopher J., and Michael S. Lewis-Beck. 1993. "Anchoring the French Voter: Ideology versus Party." *Journal of Politics* 55:1100–1109.

Fonseca, Alexandre Brasil. 2008. "Religion and Democracy in Brazil: A Study of the Leading Evangelical Politicians." In *Evangelical Christianity and Democracy in Latin America*, edited by Paul Freston, 163–206. Oxford: Oxford University Press.

Fontaine Talavera, Arturo, and Harald Beyer. 1998. *The Evangelical Movement in Chile: A Sociological Portrait.* Grand Rapids, MI: Acton Institute for the Study of Religion and Liberty.

Fornos, Carolina A., Timothy J. Power, and James C. Garand. 2004. "Explaining Voter Turnout in Latin America, 1980 to 2000." *Comparative Political Studies* 37:909–40.

Fox, Jonathan. 1994. "The Difficult Transition from Clientelism to Citizenship: Lessons from Mexico." *World Politics* 46:151–84.

Franklin, Charles H., and John E. Jackson. 1983. "The Dynamics of Party Identification." *American Political Science Review* 77:957–73.

Franklin, Mark N. 1992. "The Decline of Cleavage Politics." In *Electoral Change: Responses to Evolving Social and Attitudinal Structures in Western Countries*, edited by Mark Franklin, Thomas T. Mackie, Henry Valen, et al., 383–405. Cambridge: Cambridge University Press.

Franklin, Mark N. 2004. *Voter Turnout and the Dynamics of Electoral Competition in Established Democracies since 1945.* New York: Cambridge University Press.

Franzese, Robert. 2005. "Empirical Strategies for Various Manifestations of Multilevel Data." *Political Analysis* 13:430–46.

Freidman, Elisabeth Jay. 2009. "Gender, Sexuality and the Latin American Left: Testing the Transformation." *Third World Quarterly* 30:415–33.

Freire, André, and Kats Kivistik. 2013. "Mapping and Exploring the Use of the Left-Right Divide." *Brazilan Political Science Review* 7(3):61–89.

Freston, Paul. 1993. "Brother Votes for Brother: The New Politics of Protestantism in Brazil." In *Rethinking Protestantism in Latin America*, edited by Virginia Garrard-Burnett and David Stoll, 66–110. Philadelphia: Temple University Press.

Freston, Paul. 2004. *Evangelicals and Politics in Asia, Africa and Latin America.* West Nyack, NY: Cambridge University Press.

Freston, Paul. 2008. *Evangelical Christianity and Democracy in Latin America.* New York: Oxford University Press.

Fuchs, Dieter, and Hans-Dieter Klingemann. 1990. "The Left-Right Schema." In *Continuities in Political Action*, edited by M. K. Jennings, J. W. Van Deth, et al., 203–34. Berlin: Walter de Gruyter.

Gabbert, Wolfgang. 2006. "Concept of Ethnicity." *Latin American and Caribbean Ethnic Studies* 1:85–103.

Gallego, Aina. 2014. *Unequal Political Participation Worldwide.* New York: Cambridge University Press.

Gama, Paulo, and Daniel Roncaglia. 2012. "Russomanno é Alvo da Igreja Católica em Missas Dominicais." *Folha de São Paulo*, September 17.

Garland, David. 2001. *The Culture of Control: Crime and Social Order in Contemporary Society.* Oxford: Oxford University Press.

Garrard-Burnett, Virginia. 2009. "'Like a Mighty Rushing Wind': The Growth of Pentecostalism in Contemporary Latin America." In *Religion and Society in Latin America*. Maryknoll, NY: Orbis Books.

Gaviria, Alejandro, and Carmen Pagés. 1999. "Patterns of Crime Victimization in Latin America." Paper presented at the Inter-American Bank Conference on Economic and Social Progress in Latin America, Washington, DC.

Gélineau, François. 2007. "Presidents, Political Context, and Economic Accountability: Evidence from Latin America." *Political Research Quarterly* 60:415–28.

Gélineau, François. 2013. "Electoral Accountability in the Developing World." *Electoral Studies* 32(3):418–24.

Geneva Declaration Secretariat. 2008. *Global Burden of Armed Violence Report*. Geneva Declaration on Armed Violence and Development, Geneva, Switzerland.

Gerring, John, Philip Bond, William Barndt, and Carola Moreno. 2005. "Democracy and Growth." *World Politics* 57:323–64.

Geser, Hans. 2008. "The Limits of Ideological Globalization." In Prof. Hans Geser: Online Publications. Zürich, September. http://geser.net/internat/t_hgeser5.pdf. Accessed June 20, 2014.

Giger, Nathalie. 2009. "Towards a Modern Gender Gap in Europe? A Comparative Analysis of Voting Behavior in 12 Countries." *Social Science Journal* 46:474–92.

Gil, Federico G., and Charles J. Parrish. 1965. *The Chilean Presidential Election of September 4, 1964*. Washington, DC: Institute for the Comparative Study of Political Systems.

Gill, Anthony. 1994. "Rendering unto Caesar: Religious Competition and Catholic Political Strategy in Latin America, 1962–1979." *American Journal of Political Science* 38:403–25.

Gill, Anthony. 2002. "Religion and Democracy in South America: Challenges and Opportunities." In *Religion and Politics in Comparative Perspective: The One, the Few, and the Many*, edited by Ted G. Jelen and Clyde Wilcox, 195–221. Cambridge: Cambridge University Press.

Gilligan, Carol. 1982. *In a Different Voice: Psychological Theory and Women's Development*. Cambridge, MA: Harvard University Press.

Gilligan, Michael J., Benjamin J. Pasquale, and Cyrus D. Samii. 2011. "Civil War and Social Capital: Behavioral-Game Evidence from Nepal." New York University. Unpublished manuscript. http://papers.ssrn.com/sol3/papers.cfm?abstract_id=1911969. Accessed December 17, 2012.

Glaser, William A. 1959. "The Family and Voting Turnout." *Public Opinion Quarterly* 23:563–70.

Glazer, Amihai. 1990. "The Strategy of Candidate Ambiguity." *American Political Science Review* 84:237–41.

Godoy, Angelina Snodgrass. 2006. *Popular Injustice: Violence, Community, and Law in Latin America*. Stanford, CA: Stanford University Press.

Goertzel, Ted. 2005. "Corruption, Leadership, and Development in Latin America." *Psícologia Política* 31:77–102.

Gomez, Brad T., and J. Matthew Wilson. 2001. "Political Sophistication and Economic Voting in the American Electorate: A Theory of Heterogeneous Attribution." *American Journal of Political Science* 45:899–914.

Gomez, Brad T., and J. Matthew Wilson. 2006. "Cognitive Heterogeneity and Economic Voting: A Comparative Analysis of Four Democratic Electorates." *American Journal of Political Science* 50:127–45.

González, Luis E., and Rosario Queirolo. 2009. "Understanding 'Right' and 'Left' in Latin America." Paper prepared for delivery at the XXVIII Meeting of the Latin American Studies Association, Rio de Janeiro.

Gonzalez-Octanos, Ezequiel, Chad Kiewiet de Jonge, Carlos Melendez, Javier Osorio, and David W. Nickerson. 2012. "Vote Buying and Social Desirability Bias: Experimental Evidence from Nicaragua." *American Journal of Political Science* 56(1):202–17.

Gooren, Henri. 2010. "Ortega for President: The Religious Rebirth of Sandinismo in Nicaragua." *Revista Europea de Estudios Latinoamericanos y del Caribe / European Review of Latin American and Caribbean Studies* 89:47–63.

Green, Donald Philip, Bradley Palmquist, and Eric Schickler. 2004. *Partisan Hearts and Minds: Political Parties and the Social Identities of Voters*. New Haven, CT: Yale University Press.

Greene, Kenneth F. 2007. *Why Dominant Parties Lose: Mexico's Democratization in Comparative Perspective*. New York: Cambridge University Press.

Greene, Kenneth F. 2009. "Images and Issues in Mexico's 2006 Presidential Election." In *Consolidating Mexico's Democracy: The 2006 Presidential Campaign in Comparative Perspective*, edited by Jorge Domínguez, Chappell Lawson, and Alejandro Moreno, 246–67. Baltimore: Johns Hopkins University Press.

Greene, Kenneth F. 2011. "Campaign Persuasion and Nascent Partisanship in Mexico's New Democracy." *American Journal of Political Science* 55(2):398–416.

Greene, Steven. 1999. "Understanding Party Identification: A Social Identity Approach." *Political Psychology* 20:393–403.

Greene, Steven. 2004. "Social Identity Theory and Party Identification." *Social Science Quarterly* 85(1):136–53.

Groenendyk, Eric W. 2013. *Competing Motives in the Partisan Mind: How Loyalty and Responsiveness Shape Party Identification and Democracy*. Oxford: Oxford University Press.

Gronlund, Kimmo, and Henry Milner. 2006. "The Determinants of Political Knowledge in Comparative Perspective." *Scandinavian Political Studies* 29:386–406.

Hagopian, Frances. 1998. "Democracy and Political Representation in Latin America in the 1990s: Pause, Reorganization, or Decline?" In *Fault Lines of Democracy in Posttransition Latin America*, edited by Felipe Agüero and Jeffrey Stark, 99–143. Coral Gables, FL: North-South Center Press/University of Miami.

Hagopian, Frances. 2008. "Latin American Catholicism in an Age of Religious and Political Pluralism: A Framework for Analysis." *Comparative Politics* 40:149–68.

Haggard, Stephan, and Robert R. Kaufman. 2009. *Development, Democracy, and Welfare States: Latin America, East Asia, and Eastern Europe*. Princeton, NJ: Princeton University Press.

Hagopian, Frances, ed. 2009. *Religious Pluralism, Democracy, and the Catholic Church in Latin America*. Notre Dame, IN: University of Notre Dame Press.

Hagopian, Frances, and Scott Mainwaring, eds. 2006. *The Third Wave of Democratization in Latin America: Advances and Setbacks*. New York: Cambridge University Press.

Hale, Henry E. 2006. *Why Not Parties in Russia?* New York: Cambridge University Press.

Hall, Gillette, and Harry Anthony Patrinos, eds. 2006. *Indigenous Peoples, Poverty and Human Development in Latin America*. New York: Palgrave Macmillan.

Hamai, Koichi, and Thomas Ellis. 2006. "Crime and Criminal Justice in Modern Japan." *International Journal of the Sociology of Law* 34:157–78.

Handlin, Samuel. 2013a. "Social Protection and the Politicization of Class Cleavages during Latin America's Left Turn." *Comparative Political Studies* 46(12):1582–1609.

Handlin, Samuel. 2013b. "Survey Research and Social Class in Venezuela: Evaluating Alternative Measures and Their Impact on Assessments of Class Voting." *Latin American Politics and Society* 55(1):141–67.

Hansen, Susan B. 1997. "Talking about Politics: Gender and Contextual Effects on Political Proselytizing." *Journal of Politics* 59(1):73–103.

Harbers, Imke, Catherine E. de Vries, and Marco R. Steenbergen. 2013. "Attitude Variability among Latin American Publics: How Party System Structuration Affects Left/Right Ideology." *Comparative Political Studies* 46(8):947–67.

Hart, Austin. 2013. "Can Candidates Activate or Deactivate the Economic Vote? Evidence from Two Mexican Elections." *Journal of Politics* 75(4):1051–63.

Hartlyn, Jonathan, Jennifer L. McCoy, and Thomas Mustillo. 2008. "Electoral Governance Matters: Explaining the Quality of Elections in Contemporary Latin America." *Comparative Political Studies* 41:73–98.

Hausman, Ricardo, Laura Tyson, and Saadia Zahidi. 2011. *The Global Gender Gap Report*. Geneva: World Economic Forum.

Hawkins, Kirk A. 2010. *Venezuela's Chavismo and Populism in Comparative Perspective*. New York: Cambridge University Press.

Heath, Oliver. 2009a. "Economic Crisis, Party System Change, and the Dynamics of Class Voting in Venezuela, 1973–2003." *Electoral Studies* 28:467–79.

Heath, Oliver. 2009b. "Explaining the Rise of Class Politics in Venezuela." *Bulletin of Latin American Research* 28:185–203.

Hellwig, Timothy. 2001. "Interdependence, Government Constraints, and Economic Voting." *Journal of Politics* 63(4):1141–62.

Hellwig, Timothy. 2007. "Economic Openness, Policy Uncertainty, and the Dynamics of Government Support." *Electoral Studies* 26:772–86.

Hellwig, Timothy. 2010. "Elections and the Economy." In *Comparing Democracies 3: Elections and Voting in Global Perspective*, edited by Lawrence LeDuc, Richard G. Niemi, and Pippa Norris, 184–201. London: Sage.

Hellwig, Timothy. 2011. "Context, Information, and Performance Voting." In *Citizens, Context, and Choice: How Context Shapes Citizens' Electoral Choices*, edited by Russell J. Dalton and Christopher J. Anderson, 149–75. New York: Oxford University Press.

Hellwig, Timothy. 2015. *Globalization and Mass Politics: Retaining the Room to Maneuver*. New York: Cambridge University Press.

Hellwig, Timothy, and David Samuels. 2007. "Voting in Open Economies." *Comparative Political Studies* 40:283–306.

Heston, Alan, Robert Summers, and Bettina Aten. 2011. Penn World Table Version 7.0. Center for International Comparisons of Production, Income and Prices at the University of Pennsylvania.

Hicken, Allen. 2011. "Clientelism." *Annual Review of Political Science* 14:289–310.

Highton, Benjamin. 2009. "Revisiting the Relationship between Educational Attainment and Political Sophistication." *Journal of Politics* 71:1564–76.

Highton, Benjamin, and Cindy D. Kam. 2011. "The Long-Term Dynamics of Partisanship and Issue Orientations." *Journal of Politics* 73:202–15.

Hinich, Melvin. J., and Michael Munger. 1996. *Ideology and the Theory of Political Choice*. Ann Arbor: University of Michigan Press.

Hinich, Melvin J., and Michael C. Munger. 1997. *Analytical Politics*. New York: Cambridge University Press.

Hinton, Nicole, Mason Moseley, and Amy Erica Smith. 2012. "Equality of Participation in the Americas." In *The Political Culture of Democracy in the Americas, 2012: Towards Equality of Opportunity*, edited by Mitchell A. Seligson, Amy Erica Smith, and Elizabeth Zechmeister, 47–86. Nashville, TN: Latin American Public Opinion Project, Vanderbilt University.

Hirschman, Albert O. 1970. *Exit, Voice, and Loyalty*. Cambridge, MA: Harvard University Press.

Hochstetler, Kathryn, and Elisabeth Jay Friedman. 2008. "Can Civil Society Organizations Solve the Crisis of Partisan Representation in Latin America?" *Latin American Politics and Society* 50:1–32.

Hoddie, Matthew. 2006. *Ethnic Realignments: A Comparative Study of Government Influences on Identity*. Lanham, MD: Lexington Books.

Holland, Alisha C. 2013. "Right on Crime? Conservative Party Politics and *Mano Dura* Policies in El Salvador." *Latin American Research Review* 48:44–67.

Holmberg, Sören. 1994. "Party Identification Compared across the Atlantic." In *Elections at Home and Abroad: Essays in Honor of Warren E. Miller*, edited by M. Kent Jennings and Thomas E. Mann, 91–121. Ann Arbor: University of Michigan Press.

Holmes, Jennifer S., and Sheila Amin Gutiérrez de Piñeres. 2003. "Sources of Fujimori's Popularity: Neoliberal Reform or Ending Terrorism?" *Terrorism & Political Violence* 14:93–112.

Holmes, Jennifer S., and Sheila Amin Gutiérrez de Piñeres. 2012a. "Party System Decline in Colombia: A Subnational Examination of Presidential and Senate Elections from 1994 to 2006." *Democracy and Security* 8:175–90.

Holmes, Jennifer S., and Sheila Amin Gutiérrez de Piñeres. 2012b. "Security and Economic Voting: Support for Incumbent Parties in Colombian Presidential Elections." *Democratization* 1:1–27.

Holmes, Jennifer S., and Sheila Amin Gutiérrez de Piñeres. Forthcoming. "Security and Economic Voting: Support for Incumbent Parties in Colombian Presidential Elections." *Democratization*.

Hooker, Juliet. 2005. "Indigenous Inclusion/Black Exclusion: Race, Ethnicity and Multicultural Citizenship in Latin America." *Journal of Latin American Studies* 27:285–310.

Horowitz, Donald. 1985. *Ethnic Groups in Conflict*. Berkeley: University of California Press.

Hout, Mike, Clem Brooks, and Jeff Manza. 2001. "The Persistence of Classes in Post-Industrial Societies." In *The Breakdown of Class Politics: A Debate on Post-Industrial Stratification*, edited by Terry Nichols Clark and Seymour Martin Lipset, 55–76. Washington, DC: The Woodrow Wilson Center Press/Johns Hopkins University Press.

Htun, Mala. 2003. *Sex and the State*. New York: Cambridge University Press.

Huber, Evelyne, Thomas Mustillo, and John D. Stephens. 2008. "Politics and Social Spending in Latin America." *Journal of Politics* 70:420–36.

Huber, John. 1989. "Values and Partisanship in Left-Right Orientations: Measuring Ideology." *European Journal of Political Research* 17:599–621.

Huber, John. 2012. "Measuring Ethnic Voting: Do Proportional Electoral Laws Politicize Ethnicity?" *American Journal of Political Science* 56:986–1001.

Huber, John D., Georgia Kernell, and Eduardo L. Leoni. 2005. "Institutional Context, Cognitive Resources and Party Attachments across Democracies." *Political Analysis* 13:365–86.

Hunter, Wendy. 2010. *The Transformation of the Workers' Party in Brazil, 1989–2009*. New York: Cambridge University Press.

Hunter, Wendy, and Timothy J. Power. 2007. "Rewarding Lula: Executive Power, Social Policy, and the Brazilian Elections of 2006." *Latin American Politics and Society* 49:1–30.

Huntington, Samuel. 1991. *The Third Wave: Democratization in the Late Twentieth Century*. Norman: University of Oklahoma Press.

Ichino, Naomi, and Noah Nathan. 2013. "Crossing the Line: Local Ethnic Geography and Voting in Ghana." *American Political Science Review* 107:1–18.

Ignazi, Piero. 1996. "The Crisis of Parties and the Rise of New Political Parties." *Party Politics* 2:549–66.

Inglehart, Ronald. 1977. *The Silent Revolution: Changing Values and Political Styles among Western Publics*. Princeton, NJ: Princeton University Press.

Inglehart, Ronald. 1984. "The Changing Structure of Political Cleavages in Western Society." In *Electoral Change in Advanced Industrial Democracies: Realignment or Dealignment?* edited by Russell J. Dalton, Scott C. Flanagan, and Paul Allen Beck, 25–69. Princeton, NJ: Princeton University Press.

Inglehart, Ronald. 1990. *Culture Shift in Advanced Industrial Society*. Princeton, NJ: Princeton University Press.

Inglehart, Ronald. 1997. *Modernization and Postmodernization: Cultural, Economic, and Political Change in 43 Societies*. Princeton, NJ: Princeton University Press.

Inglehart, Ronald, and Hans-Dieter Klingemann. 1976. "Party Identification, Ideological Preference and the Left-Right Dimension among Western Mass Publics." In *Party Identification and Beyond*, edited by I. Budge, I. Crewe, and D. Fadie, 243–73. New York: John Wiley.

Inglehart, Ronald, and Pippa Norris. 2003. *Rising Tide: Gender Equality and Cultural Change around the World*. New York: Cambridge University Press.

Inman, Kris, and Josephine Andrews. 2010. "Political Participation in Africa: Evidence from Survey and Experimental Research." Paper presented at the Annual Meeting of the Midwest Political Science Association, Chicago.

Inter-American Development Bank (IADB). 2013. Latin American and Caribbean Macro Watch Database. http://www.iadb.org/Research/LatinMacroWatch /index.cfm. Accessed April 2013.

Ireland, Rowan. 1991. *Kingdoms Come: Religion and Politics in Brazil.* Pittsburgh: University of Pittsburgh Press.

Ireland, Rowan. 1997. "Pentecostalism, Conversions, and Politics in Brazil." In *Power, Politics, and Pentecostals in Latin America,* edited by Edward L. Cleary and Hannah W. Stewart-Gambino, 123–37. Boulder, CO: Westview Press.

Ishiyama, John T., and Krystal Fox. 2006. "What Affects the Strength of Partisan Identity in Sub-Saharan Africa?" *Politics & Policy* 34:748–73.

Iversen, Torben, and Frances Rosenbluth. 2006. "The Political Economy of Gender." *American Journal of Political Science* 50(1):1–19.

Jacoby, William G. 2002. "Liberal-Conservative Thinking in the American Electorate. In *Political Decision-Making, Deliberation and Participation,* edited by Michael X. Delli Carpini, Leonie Huddy, and Robert Y. Shapiro. *Research in Micropolitics,* vol. 6. Oxford: Elsevier.

Jennings, M. Kent, and Gregory B. Markus. 1984. "Partisan Orientations over the Long Haul: Results from the Three-Wave Political Socialization Panel Study." *American Political Science Review* 78:1000–1018.

Jennings, M. Kent, Laura Stoker, and Jake Bowers. 2009. "Politics across Generations: Family Transmission Reexamined." *Journal of Politics* 71:782–99.

Johnson, Gregg, and Leslie Schwindt-Bayer. 2009. "Economic Accountability in Central America." *Journal of Politics in Latin America* 1:33–56.

Johnson, Gregg, and Sooh-Rhee Ryu. 2010. "Repudiating or Rewarding Neoliberalism? How Broken Campaign Promises Condition Economic Voting in Latin America." *Latin American Politics and Society* 52:1–24.

Johnston, Hank, and Jozef Figa. 1988. "The Church and Political Opposition: Comparative Perspectives on Mobilization against Authoritarian Regimes." *Journal for the Scientific Study of Religion* 27:32–47.

Johnston, Richard. 2006. "Party Identification: Unmoved Mover or Sum of Preferences?" *Annual Review of Political Science* 9:329–51.

Jones, Mark P. 1997. "Legislator Gender and Legislative Policy Priorities in the Argentine Chamber of Deputies and the United States House of Representatives." *Policy Studies Journal* 25(4):613–29.

Jost, John T., Christopher M. Federico, and Jaime L. Napier. 2009. "Political Ideology: Its Structure, Functions, and Elective Affinities." *Annual Review of Psychology* 60:307–37.

Jou, Willy. 2011. "How do Citizens in East Asian Democracies Understand Left and Right?" *Japanese Journal of Political Science* 12:33–55.

Jusko, Karen Long, and W. Phillips Shively. 2005. "Applying a Two-Step Strategy to the Analysis of Cross-National Public Opinion Data." *Political Analysis* 13:327–44.

Kage, Rieko. 2011. *Civic Engagement in Postwar Japan: The Revival of a Defeated Society.* New York: Cambridge University Press.

Kaniss, Phyllis. 1991. *Making Local News.* Chicago: University of Chicago Press.

Kaplan, Stephen. 2013. *Globalization and Austerity Politics in Latin America.* New York: Cambridge University Press.

Karp, Jeffrey A., Susan A. Banducci, and Shaun Bowler. 2007. "Getting Out the Vote: Party Mobilization in a Comparative Perspective." *British Journal of Political Science* 38:91–112.

Kaufman, Robert R., and Leo Zuckerman. 1998. "Attitudes toward Economic Reform in Mexico: The Role of Political Orientations." *American Political Science Review* 92:359–75.

Kaufmann, Karen M., and John R. Petrocik. 1999. "The Changing Politics of American Men: Understanding the Sources of the Gender Gap." *American Journal of Political Science* 43(3):864–87.

Kayser, Mark Andreas, and Christopher Wlezien. 2011. "Performance Pressure: Patterns of Partisanship and the Economic Vote." *European Journal of Political Research* 50:365–94.

Kedar, Orit. 2009. *Voting for Policy, Not Parties: How Voters Compensate for Power Sharing.* New York: Cambridge University Press.

Keefer, Philip. 2007. "Clientelism, Credibility and the Policy Choices of Young Democracies." *American Journal of Political Science* 51:804–21.

Key, V. O., Jr. 1949. *Southern Politics.* New York: Alfred A. Knopf.

Key, V. O., Jr. 1955. "A Theory of Critical Elections." *Journal of Politics* 17:3–18.

Key, V. O., Jr. 1966. *The Responsible Electorate.* New York: Vintage Books.

Kiewiet, Roderick. 1981. "Policy-Oriented Voting in Response to Economic Issues." *American Political Science Review* 75:448–59.

Kilpatrick, Dean G., and Ron Acierno. 2003. "Mental Health Needs of Crime Victims: Epidemiology and Outcomes." *Journal of Traumatic Stress* 16:119–32.

Kinder, Donald R. 2006. "Politics and the Life Cycle." *Science* 312:1905–8.

Kinder, D., and D. Sears. 1985. "Public Opinion and Political Action." In *Handbook of Political Psychology*, edited by G. Lindzey and E. Aronson, 659–741. 3rd ed. New York: Free Press.

King, Gary, Michael Tomz, and Jason Wittenberg. 2000. "Making the Most of Statistical Analyses: Improving Interpretation and Presentation." *American Journal of Political Science* 44:347–61.

Kinzo, Maria D'Alva G. 2005. "Os Partidos no Eleitorado: Percepções Públicas e Laços Partidários no Brasil." *Revista Brasileira de Ciências Sociais* 20:65–81.

Kitschelt, Herbert. 1996. *The Radical Right in Western Europe.* Ann Arbor: University of Michigan Press.

Kitschelt, Herbert. 2000. "Linkages between Citizens and Politicians in Democratic Polities." *Comparative Political Studies* 33:845–79.

Kitschelt, Herbert. 2007. "Party Systems." In *Handbook of Comparative Politics*, edited by Carles Boix and Susan Stokes, 522–54. Oxford: Oxford University Press.

Kitschelt, Herbert. 2011a. "Clientelistic Linkage Strategies: A Descriptive Exploration." Paper prepared for the Workshop on Democratic Accountability Strategies, Duke University, Durham, NC.

Kitschelt, Herbert. 2011b. *Democratic Accountability. Situating the Empirical Field of Research and Its Frontiers.* Workshop on Democratic Accountability Strategies. Duke University, Durham, NC. http://www.duke.edu/web/democracy/.

Kitschelt, Herbert. 2011c. "Do Institutions Matter for Parties' Political Linkage Strategies?" Paper prepared for delivery at the Annual Meeting of the American Political Science Association, Seattle.

Kitschelt, Herbert. 2012a. "Clientelism and Party Competition." PowerPoint presentation, Central European University, Duke University, Washington, DC.

Kitschelt, Herbert. 2012b. "Research and Dialogue on Programmatic Parties and Party Systems." Final Report. International IDEA (Institute for Democracy and Electoral Assistance). IDEA Project—PO 134-01/2401.

Kitschelt, Herbert, and Kent Freeze. 2010. "Programmatic Party System Structuration: Developing and Comparing Cross-National and Cross-Party Measures with a New Global Data Set." Paper presented at the American Political Science Association Annual Conference, Durham, NC.

Kitschelt, Herbert, Kirk A. Hawkins, Juan Pablo Luna, Guillermo Rosas, and Elizabeth J. Zechmeister. 2010. *Latin American Party Systems*. New York: Cambridge University Press.

Kitschelt, Herbert, and Staff Hellemans. 1990. "The Left-Right Semantics and the New Politics Cleavage." *Comparative Political Studies* 23:210–38.

Kitschelt, Herbert, and Daniel Kselman. 2013. "Economic Development, Democratic Experience, and Political Parties' Linkage Strategies." *Comparative Political Studies* 46:1339–65.

Kitschelt, Herbert, and Steven Wilkinson. 2007a. "Citizen-Politician Linkages: An Introduction." In *Patrons, Clients, and Policies: Patterns of Democratic Accountability and Political Competition*, edited by Herbert Kitschelt and Steven Wilkinson, 1–52. Cambridge: Cambridge University Press.

Kitschelt, Herbert, and Steven I. Wilkinson, eds. 2007b. *Patrons, Clients and Policies: Patterns of Democratic Accountability and Political Competition*. New York: Cambridge University Press.

Kittilson, Miki Caul, and Christopher J. Anderson. 2011. "Electoral Supply and Voter Turnout." In *Citizens, Context, and Choice: How Context Shapes Citizens' Electoral Choices*, edited by Russell J. Dalton and Christopher J. Anderson, 33–53. Oxford: Oxford University Press.

Klaiber, Jeffrey. 1998. *The Church, Dictatorships, and Democracy in Latin America*. Eugene, OR: Wipf & Stock Publishers.

Klasnja, Marko, and Joshua A. Tucker. 2013. "The Economy, Corruption, and the Vote: Evidence from Experiments in Sweden and Moldova." *Electoral Studies* 32(3):536–43.

Klasnja, Marko, Joshua A. Tucker, and Kevin Deegan-Krause. 2014. "Pocket Book vs. Sociotropic Corruption Voting." *British Journal of Political Science*.

Klein, Ethel. 1984. *Gender Politics: From Consciousness to Mass Politics*. Cambridge, MA: Harvard University Press.

Klingemann, Hans-Dieter, and Bernard Wessels. 2009. "How Voters Cope with the Complexity of Their Competitive Environment: Differentiation of Political Supply, Effectiveness of Electoral Institutions, and the Calculus of Voting." In *The Comparative Study of Electoral Systems*, edited by Hans-Dieter Klingemann, 237–65. New York: Oxford University Press.

Knutsen, Oddbjørn. 1997. "The Partisan and the Value-Based Component of Left-Right Self-Placement: A Comparative Study." *International Political Science Review* 18:191–225.

Knutsen, Oddbjørn. 2004a. "Religious Denomination and Party Choice in Western Europe: A Comparative Longitudinal Study from Eight Countries, 1970–97." *International Political Science Review* 25:97–128.

Knutsen, Oddbjørn. 2004b. *Social Structure and Party Choice in Western Europe: A Comparative Longitudinal Study*. Basingstoke: Palgrave-Macmillan.

Knutsen, Oddbjørn. 2008. *Class Voting in Western Europe: A Comparative Longitudinal Study*. Lanham, MD: Lexington Books.

Kolev, Kiril, and Yi-Ting Wang. 2010. "Ethnic Group Divisions and Clientelism." Paper presented at the Annual Meeting of the American Political Science Association, Washington, DC.

Kollman, Ken, John Miller, and Scott Page. 1992. "Adaptive Parties in Spatial Elections." *American Political Science Review* 86:922–37.

Kostadinova, Tatiana. 2009. "Abstain or Rebel: Corruption Perceptions and Voting in East European Elections." *Politics and Policy* 37(4):691–714.

Kostadinova, Tatiana, and Timothy J. Power. 2007. "Does Democratization Depress Participation? Voter Turnout in the Latin American and Eastern European Transitional Democracies." *Political Research Quarterly* 60:363–77.

Kramer, Gerald H. 1983. "The Ecological Fallacy Revisited: Aggregate- versus Individual-level Findings on Economics and Elections, and Sociotropic Voting." *American Political Science Review* 77:92–111.

Krause, Krystin. 2009. "Iron Fist Politics in Latin America: Politicians, Public Opinion, and Crime Control." Paper presented at the 18th Congress of the Latin American Studies Association, Rio de Janeiro.

Kroh, Martin. 2009. "The Ease of Ideological Voting: Voter Sophistication and Party System Complexity." In *The Comparative Study of Electoral Systems*, edited by Hans-Dieter Klingemann, 220–36. New York: Oxford University Press.

Kuenzi, Michelle T. 2006. "Crime, Security, and Support for Democracy in Africa." Paper presented at the Annual Meeting of the Midwest Political Science Association, Chicago.

Kuenzi, Michelle T., and Gina M. S. Lambright. 2011. "Who Votes in Africa? An Examination of Electoral Participation in 10 African Countries." *Party Politics* 17:767–99.

Laakso, Markku, and Rein Taagepera. 1979. "Effective Number of Parties: A Measure with Application to West Europe." *Comparative Political Studies* 12:3–27.

Laitin, David. 1998. *Identity in Formation*. Ithaca, NY: Cornell University Press.

Lane, Robert E. 1959. *Political Life: Why People Get Involved in Politics*. Glencoe, IL: Free Press.

Lasswell, Harold. 1936. *Politics: Who Gets What, When, How*. New York: Whittlesey House.

Lau, Richard R., and David P. Redlawsk. 2001. "Advantages and Disadvantages of Cognitive Heuristics in Political Decision Making." *American Journal of Political Science* 45:951–71.

Lau, Richard R., and David O. Sears. 1981. "Cognitive Links between Economic Grievances and Political Responses." *Political Behavior* 3:279–302.

Lavezzolo, Sebastián. 2008. "Adversidad Económica y Participación Electoral en América Latina, 1980–2000." *Revista Española de Ciencia Política* 18:67–93.

Lawson, Chappell H. 2002. *Building the Fourth Estate: Democratization and the Rise of a Free Press in Mexico*. Berkeley: University of California Press.

Lawson, Chappell, and Joseph L. Klesner. 2004. "Political Reform, Electoral Participation, and the Campaign of 2000." In *Mexico's Pivotal Democratic Election: Candidates, Voters, and the Presidential Campaign of 2000*, edited by Jorge I.

Domínguez and Chappell Lawson, 67–87. Stanford, CA: Stanford University Press and the Center for U.S.-Mexican Studies, University of California, San Diego.

Lawson, Chappell H., Gabriel S. Lenz, Andy Baker, and Michael Myers. 2010. "Looking Like a Winner: Candidate Appearance and Electoral Success in New Democracies." *World Politics* 62:561–93.

Layman, Geoffrey C., and Thomas M. Carsey. 2002. "Party Polarization and Party Structuring of Policy Attitudes: A Comparison of Three NES Panel Studies." *Political Behavior* 24:199–236.

Lazarsfeld, Paul F., Bernard Berelson, and Hazel Gaudet. 1944. *The People's Choice: How the Voter Makes Up His Mind in a Presidential Election*. New York: Duell, Sloan, and Pearce.

Lehoucq, Fabrice, and David L. Wall. 2004. "Explaining Voter Turnout Rates in New Democracies: Guatemala." *Electoral Studies* 23:485–500.

Leighley, Jan. 2001. *Strength in Numbers? The Political Mobilization of Racial and Ethnic Minorities*. Princeton, NJ: Princeton University Press.

Levendusky, Matthew S. 2010. "Clear Cues, More Consistent Voters: A Benefit of Elite Polarization." *Political Behavior* 32(1):111–31.

Levitsky, Steven. 2003. *Transforming Labor-Based Parties in Latin America: Argentine Peronism in Comparative Perspective*. New York: Cambridge University Press.

Levitsky, Steven, and Maxwell A. Cameron. 2003. "Democracy without Parties? Political Parties and Regime Change in Fujimori's Peru." *Latin American Politics and Society* 45:1–33.

Levitsky, Steven, and Kenneth M. Roberts. 2011a. "Latin America's 'Left Turn': A Framework for Analysis." In *The Resurgence of the Latin American Left*, edited by Steven Levitsky and Kenneth M. Roberts, 1–28. Baltimore: Johns Hopkins University Press.

Levitsky, Steven, and Kenneth M. Roberts, eds. 2011b. *The Resurgence of the Latin American Left*. Baltimore: Johns Hopkins University Press.

Lewis, Jeffery B., and Drew A. Linzer. 2005. "Estimating Regression Models in Which the Dependent Variable Is Based on Estimates." *Political Analysis* 13:345–64.

Lewis, Paul H. 1971. "The Female Vote in Argentina, 1958–1965." *Comparative Political Studies* 3(4):425–41.

Lewis-Beck, Michael. 1988. *Economics and Elections: The Major Western Democracies*. Ann Arbor: University of Michigan Press.

Lewis-Beck, Michael S. 2004. *The French Voter*. New York: Palgrave Macmillan.

Lewis-Beck, Michael S., and Richard Nadeau. 2011. "Economic Voting Theory: Testing New Dimensions." *Electoral Studies* 30(2):288–94.

Lewis-Beck, Michael S., Richard Nadeau, and Éric Bélanger. 2012. *French Presidential Elections*. New York: Palgrave Macmillan.

Lewis-Beck, Michael S., Helmut Norpoth, William G. Jacoby, and Herbert F. Weisberg. 2008. *The American Voter Revisited*. Ann Arbor: University of Michigan Press.

Lewis-Beck, Michael S., and Mary Stegmaier. 2007. "Economic Models of Voting." In *The Oxford Handbook of Political Behavior*, edited by Russell J. Dalton and Hans-Dieter Klingemann, 518–37. Oxford: Oxford University Press.

Lewis-Beck, Michael, and Mary Stegmaier. 2009. "The Economic Vote in Transitional Democracies." *Journal of Elections, Public Opinion and Parties* 18:303–23.

Lijphart, Arend. 1977. *Democracy in Plural Societies*. New Haven, CT: Yale University Press.

Lijphart, Arend. 1997. "Unequal Participation: Democracy's Unresolved Dilemma." *American Political Science Review* 9:1–14.

Lima, Daniela. 2012. "Igreja Católica Ataca Universal e Chefe da Campanha de Russomanno." *Folha de São Paulo*, September 14.

Lindberg, Steffan. 2006. *Democracy and Elections in Africa*. Baltimore: Johns Hopkins University Press.

Linz, Juan J., and Alfred C. Stepan. 1996. "Toward Consolidated Democracies." *Journal of Democracy* 7(2):14–33.

Lipschutz, Alejandro. 1944. *Indoamericanismo y el Problema Racial en las Americas*. Santiago: Editorial Nascimiento.

Lipset, Seymour Martin. 1960. *Political Man: The Social Bases of Politics*. Garden City, NY: Doubleday and Co.

Lipset, Seymour Martin. 1964. "The Changing Class Structure and Contemporary European Politics." In *A New Europe?* edited by Stephen R. Graubard, 337–69. Boston: Houghton Mifflin.

Lipset, Seymour Martin. 2001. "The Decline of Class Ideologies: The End of Political Exceptionalism?" In *The Breakdown of Class Politics: A Debate on Post-Industrial Stratification*, edited by Terry Nichols Clark and Seymour Martin Lipset, 249–72. Washington, DC: The Woodrow Wilson Center Press/Johns Hopkins University Press.

Lipset, Seymour Martin, and Stein Rokkan. 1967. "Cleavage Structures, Party Systems, and Voter Alignments: An Introduction." In *Party Systems and Voter Alignments: Cross-National Perspectives*, edited by Seymour Martin Lipset and Stein Rokkan, 1–64. New York: Free Press.

Lodola, Germán, and Margarita Corral. 2010. "Support for Same-Sex Marriage in Latin America." AmericasBarometer, *Insights*, 144, Latin American Public Opinion Project (LAPOP), Vanderbilt University.

Loewen, Peter John, Henry Milner, and Bruce M. Hicks. 2008. "Does Compulsory Voting Lead to More Informed and Engaged Citizens? An Experimental Test." *Canadian Journal of Political Science* 41:655–72.

Luna, Juan Pablo. 2014. *Segmented Representation: Political Party Strategies in Unequal Democracy*. New York: Oxford University Press.

Luna, Juan P., and Elizabeth J. Zechmeister. 2005. "Political Representation in Latin America: A Study of Elite-Mass Congruence in Nine Countries." *Comparative Political Studies* 38:388–416.

Lupu, Noam. 2011. "Party Brands in Crisis: Partisanship, Brand Dilution, and the Breakdown of Political Parties in Latin America." Ph.D. diss., Princeton University.

Lupu, Noam. 2013. "Party Brands and Partisanship: Theory with Evidence from a Survey Experiment in Argentina." *American Journal of Political Science* 57:49–64.

Lupu, Noam. Forthcoming. *Party Brands in Crisis: Partisanship, Brand Dilution, and the Breakdown of Political Parties in Latin America*. New York: Cambridge University Press.

Lupu, Noam. 2015. "Party Polarization and Mass Partisanship: A Comparative Perspective." *Political Behavior* 37 (2): 331–56.

Lupu, Noam, and Rachel Beatty Riedl. 2013. Political Parties and Uncertainty in Developing Democracies. Special Issue of *Comparative Political Studies* 46(11).

Lupu, Noam, and Susan C. Stokes. 2009. "The Social Bases of Political Parties in Argentina, 1912–2003." *Latin American Research Review* 44:58–87.

Lupu, Noam, and Susan C. Stokes. 2010. "Democracy, Interrupted: Regime Change and Partisanship in Twentieth-Century Argentina." *Electoral Studies* 29:91–104.

Lustig, Nora. 1998. *Mexico: The Remaking of an Economy*. Washington, DC: The Brookings Institution.

Macdonald, Stuart Elaine, Ola Listhaug, and George Rabinowitz. 1991. "Issue and Party Support in Multiparty Systems." *American Political Science Review* 85:1107–31.

Mackerras, Malcolm, and Ian McAllister. 1999. "Compulsory Voting, Party Stability and Electoral Advantage in Australia." *Electoral Studies* 18:217–33.

Macmillan, Ross. 2001. "Violence and the Life Course: The Consequences of Victimization for Personal and Social Development." *Annual Review of Sociology* 27:1–22.

Madrid, Raul. 2005. "Indigenous Parties and Democracy in Latin America." *Latin American Politics and Society* 47:161–79.

Madrid, Raul. 2008. "The Rise of Ethnopopulism in Latin America." *World Politics* 60:475–508.

Madrid, Raul. 2011a. "Bolivia: Origins and Policies of the Movimiento al Socialismo." In *The Resurgence of the Latin American Left*, edited by Steven Levitsky and Kenneth M. Roberts, 239–59. Baltimore: Johns Hopkins University Press.

Madrid, Raul. 2011b. "Ethnic Proximity and Ethnic Voting in Peru." *Journal of Latin American Studies* 43:267–97.

Madrid, Raul. 2012. *The Rise of Ethnic Politics in Latin America*. New York: Cambridge University Press.

Madsen, Douglas, and Peter G. Snow. 1991. *The Charismatic Bond: Political Behavior in Times of Crisis*. Cambridge, MA: Harvard University Press.

Magaloni, Beatriz. 1999. "Is the PRI Fading? Economic Performance, Electoral Accountability and Voting Behavior." In *The New Mexican Party System*, edited by Jorge Domínguez and Alejandro Poiré. New York: Routledge.

Magaloni, Beatriz. 2006. *Voting for Autocracy: Hegemonic Party Survival and Its Demise in Mexico*. New York: Cambridge University Press.

Mainwaring, Scott. 1999. *Rethinking Party Systems in the Third Wave of Democratization: The Case of Brazil*. Stanford, CA: Stanford University Press.

Mainwaring, Scott, Ana María Bejarano, and Eduardo Pizarro Leongómez, eds. 2006. *The Crisis of Democratic Representation in the Andes*. Stanford, CA: Stanford University Press.

Mainwaring, Scott, and Aníbal Perez-Liñán. 2005. "Latin American Democratization since 1978: Democratic Transition, Breakdowns, and Erosions." In *The Third Wave of Democratization in Latin America: Advances and Setbacks*, edited by Frances Hagopian and Scott P. Mainwaring. New York: Cambridge University Press.

Mainwaring, Scott, and Timothy R. Scully, eds. 1995a. *Building Democratic Institutions: Party Systems in Latin America*. Stanford, CA: Stanford University Press.

Mainwaring, Scott, and Timothy R. Scully, eds. 1995b. "Introduction: Party Systems in Latin America." In *Building Democratic Institutions: Party Systems in Latin America*, edited by Scott Mainwaring and Timothy R. Scully. Stanford, CA: Stanford University Press.

Mainwaring, Scott, and Timothy Scully, eds. 2003. *Christian Democracy in Latin America: Electoral Competition and Regime Conflicts*. Stanford, CA: Stanford University Press.

Mainwaring, Scott, and Matthew S. Shugart. 1997. *Presidentialism and Democracy in Latin America*. New York: Cambridge University Press.

Mainwaring, Scott, and Mariano Torcal. 2006. "Party System Institutionalization and Party System Theory after the Third Wave of Democratization." In *Handbook of Party Politics*, edited by Richard S. Katz and William Crotty, 204–26. London: Sage Publications.

Mainwaring, Scott, and Christopher Welna. 2003. *Democratic Accountability in Latin America*. New York: Oxford University Press.

Mainwaring, Scott, and Edurne Zoco. 2007. "Political Sequences and the Stabilization of Interparty Competition: Electoral Volatility in Old and New Democracies." *Party Politics* 13:155–78.

Mair, Peter. 2007. "Left-Right Orientations." In *The Oxford Handbook of Political Behavior*, edited by Russell J. Dalton and Hans-Dieter Klingemann, 206–22. New York: Oxford University Press.

Mair, Peter. 2010. "Left-Right Orientations. In *Oxford Handbooks Online: The Oxford Handbook of Political Behavior*, edited by Russell. J. Dalton and Hans-Dieter Klingemann, 206–22.

Maldonaldo, Arturo. 2011. "Compulsory Voting and the Decision to Vote." *AmericasBarometer Insights* no. 63.

Malone, Mary Fran T. 2013. "Does Crime Undermine Public Support for Democracy? Findings from the Case of Mexico." *The Latin Americanist* 57:17–44.

Manza, Jeff, and Clem Brooks. 1998. "The Gender Gap in U.S. Presidential Elections: When? Why? Implications?" *American Journal of Sociology* 103(5): 1235–66.

Manzetti, Luigi, and Guillermo Rosas. n.d. "Curbing Corruption: Testing the Corruption Performance Trade-off Hypothesis in Latin America." Unpublished manuscript, Southern Methodist University and Washington University.

Manzetti, Luigi, and Carole J. Wilson. 2006. "Corruption, Economic Satisfaction, and Confidence in Government: Evidence from Argentina." *The Latin Americanist* 49:131–39.

Marks, Monique, and Andrew Goldsmith. 2006. "The State, the People, and Democratic Policing: The Case of South Africa." In *Democracy, Society, and the Governance of Security*, edited by J. Wood and B. Dupont, 139–64. New York: Cambridge University Press.

Mayer, Nonna, and Vincent Tiberj. 2004. "Do Issues Matter? Law and Order in the 2002 French Presidential Election." In *The French Voter*, edited by Michael S. Lewis-Beck. Basingstoke: Palgrave Macmillan.

McCann, James A., and Jorge I. Domínguez. 1998. "Mexicans React to Electoral Fraud and Political Corruption: An Assessment of Public Opinion and Voting Behavior." *Electoral Studies* 17:483–503.

McCann, James A., and Chappell H. Lawson. 2003. "An Electorate Adrift: Public Opinion and the Quality of Democracy in Mexico." *Latin American Research Review* 38:60–81.

McKelvey, Richard. 1976. "Intransitivities in Multidimensional Voting Models and Some Implications for Agenda Control." *Journal of Economic Theory* 12:472–82.

McKelvey, Richard. 1986. "Covering, Dominance, and Institution-Free Properties of Social Choice." *American Journal of Political Science* 30:283–314.

Medina Vidal, D. Xavier Jr., Antonio Ugues, Shaun Bowler, and Jonathan Hiskey. 2010. "Partisan Attachment and Democracy in Mexico: Some Cautionary Observations." *Latin American Politics and Society* 52:63–87.

Meixueiro, Gustavo, and Alejandro Moreno. 2014. *El Comportamiento Electoral Mexicano en la Elecciones de 2012*. Mexico City: Centro de Estudios Sociales y de Opinión Pública y ITAM.

Melossi, Dario, and Rossella Selmini. 2000. "Social Conflict and the Microphysics of Crime: The Experience of the Emilia-Romagna Citta Sicure Project." In *Crime, Risk, and Insecurity: Law and Order in Everyday Life and Political Discourse*, edited by T. Hope and R. Sparks, 146–65. London: Routledge.

Merolla, Jennifer L., Abbylin H. Sellers, and Derek J. Fowler. 2012. "Descriptive Representation, Political Efficacy, and African Americans in the 2008 Presidential Election." *Political Psychology* 19(1):169–84.

Merolla, Jennifer L., and Elizabeth J. Zechmeister. 2009a. *Democracy at Risk: How Terrorist Threats Affect the Public*. Chicago: University of Chicago Press.

Merolla, Jennifer L., and Elizabeth J. Zechmeister. 2009b. "Las Percepciones de Liderazgo en el Contexto de las Elecciones Mexicanas de 2006." *Política y Gobierno, special issue*: 41–81.

Merolla, Jennifer L., and Elizabeth J. Zechmeister. 2011. "The Nature, Determinants, and Consequences of Chávez's Charisma: Evidence from a Study of Venezuelan Public Opinion." *Comparative Political Studies* 44:28–54.

Merriam, Charles E., and Harold F. Gosnell. 1924. *Non-voting: Causes and Methods of Control*. Chicago: University of Chicago Press.

Middlebrook, Kevin J., ed. 2000. *Conservative Parties, the Right, and Democracy in Latin America*. New York: Cambridge University Press.

Milbrath, Lester W. 1965. *Political Participation: How and Why Do People Get Involved in Politics?* Chicago: Rand McNally.

Milbrath, Lester W., and Mm. Lal Goel. 1977. *Political Participation*. 2nd ed. Chicago: Rand McNally.

Miller, Warren Edward, and J. Merrill Shanks. 1996. *The New American Voter*. Cambridge, MA: Harvard University Press.

Montero, Maritza. 1975. "Socialización Política en Jóvenes Caraqueños." In *La Psicología Social en Latinoamérica*, edited by G. Marín, 17–25. México: Trillas.

Moore, Laura M., and Reeve Vanneman. 2003. "Context Matters: Effects of the Proportion of Fundamentalists on Gender Attitudes." *Social Forces* 82(1):115–39.

Moreno, Alejandro M. 1999. *Political Cleavage: Issues, Parties, and the Consolidation of Democracy*. Boulder, CO: Westview Press.

Moreno, Alejandro. 2003. *El Votante Mexicano: Democracia, Actitudes Políticas y Conducta Electoral.* Mexico City: Fondo de Cultura Económica.

Moreno, Alejandro. 2009a. "The Activation of Economic Voting in the 2006 Campaign." In *Consolidating Mexico's Democracy: The 2006 Presidential Campaign in Comparative Perspective,* edited by Jorge Dominguez, Alejandro Moreno, and Chappell Lawson, 209–228. Baltimore: Johns Hopkins University Press.

Moreno, Alejandro. 2009b. *La Decisión Electoral: Votantes, Partidos, y Democracia en México.* Mexico City: Miguel Ángel Porrúa.

Moreno Morales, Daniel E. 2008. "Ethnic Identity and National Politics. A Comparative Analysis of Indigenous Identity and Political Participation in Bolivia and Guatemala." Ph.D. diss., Vanderbilt University.

Moreno Morales, Daniel E. 2011. "Percepciones de la Población Indígena Boliviana en Tiempos de Cambio." In *Estado Pluriancional, Institucionalidad y Ciudadanía,* edited by Eduardo Cordova. Cochabamba: CESU–UMSS.

Moreno Morales, Daniel E. 2013. "Ethnicity, Race, and Electoral Preferences in Latin America." Paper prepared for The Latin American Voter Workshop, Vanderbilt University.

Moreno Morales, Daniel E, ed. 2012. *Cultura Política de la Democracia en Bolivia. Hacia la Igualdad de Oportunidades.* Cochabamba: Ciudadania—LAPOP.

Morgan, Jana. 2007. "Partisanship during the Collapse of Venezuela's Party System." *Latin American Research Review* 42:78–98.

Morgan, Jana. 2011. *Bankrupt Representation and Party System Collapse.* University Park: Penn State University Press.

Morgan, Jana, and Melissa Buice. 2013. "Latin American Attitudes toward Women in Politics." *American Political Science Review* 107(4):644–62.

Morgan, Jana, Rosario Espinal, and Jonathan Hartlyn. 2008. "Gender Politics in the Dominican Republic: Advances for Women, Ambivalence from Men." *Politics & Gender* 4(1):35–63.

Murillo, María Victoria. 2001. *Labor Unions, Partisan Coalitions and Market Reforms in Latin America.* New York: Cambridge University Press.

Murillo, María Victoria. 2009. *Political Competition, Partisanship, and Policymaking in Latin America.* New York: Cambridge University Press.

Nathan, Andrew J., and Tianjian Shi. 1996. "Left and Right with Chinese Characteristics: Issues and Alignments in Deng Xiaoping's China." *World Politics* 48:522–50.

Newman, Graeme, and William Alex Pridemore. 2000. "Theory, Method, and Data in Comparative Criminology." In *Criminal Justice 2000,* vol. 4 (July). Washington, DC: U.S. Department of Justice.

Nichter, Simeon. 2008. "Vote Buying or Turnout Buying? Machine Politics and the Secret Ballot." *American Political Science Review* 102:19–31.

Nichter, Simeon. 2012. "Conceptualizing Vote Buying." Manuscript, Department of Political Science, University of California, San Diego.

Nie, Norman H., Sidney Verba, and John R. Petrocik. 1979. *The Changing American Voter.* Cambridge, MA: Harvard University Press.

Niemi, Richard G., Stephen C. Craig, and Franco Mattei. 1991. "Measuring Internal Political Efficacy in the 1988 National Election Study." *American Political Science Review* 85:1407–13.

Nieuwbeerta, Paul, and Wout Ultee. 1999. "Class Voting in Western Industrialized Countries, 1945–1990: Systematizing and Testing Explanations." *European Journal of Political Research* 35:123–60.

Nobles, Melissa. 2000. *Shades of Citizenship: Race and the Census in Modern Politics.* Stanford, CA: Stanford University Press.

Ñopo, Hugo. 2012. *New Centuries, Old Disparities: Gender and Ethnic Earnings Gaps in Latin America and the Caribbean.* New York: IADB and World Bank.

Norris, Fran H., and Krzysztof Kaniasty. 1994. "Psychological Distress Following Criminal Victimization in the General Population: Cross-Sectional, Longitudinal, and Prospective Analyses." *Journal of Consulting and Clinical Psychology* 62:111–23.

Norris, Pippa. 2002. *Democratic Phoenix: Reinventing Political Activism.* Cambridge: Cambridge University Press.

Norris, Pippa. 2004. *Electoral Engineering: Voting Rules and Political Behavior.* New York: Cambridge University Press.

Ochoa, Enrique C. 1987. "The Rapid Expansion of Voter Participation in Latin America: Presidential Elections, 1845–1986." In *Statistical Abstract of Latin America*, vol. 25, edited by James W. Wilkie and David Lorey, 861–910. Los Angeles: UCLA Latin American Center Publications, University of California.

O'Donnell, Guillermo. 1994. "Delegative Democracy." *Journal of Democracy* 5(1):55–69.

O'Donnell, Guillermo A., and Philippe C. Schmitter. 1986. *Transitions from Authoritarian Rule: Tentative Conclusions about Uncertain Democracies.* Baltimore: Johns Hopkins University Press.

O'Donnell, Guillermo, Phillippe Schmitter, and Laurence Whitehead. 1986. *Transitions from Authoritarian Rule: Prospects for Democracy.* Baltimore: Johns Hopkins University Press.

Oro, Ari Pedro. 2003. "A Política da Igreja Universal e seus Reflexos nos Campos Religioso e Político Brasileiros." *Revista Brasileira de Ciências Sociais* 18 (53):53–69.

Oro, Ari Pedro. 2006. "Religião e Política no Brasil." In *Religião e Política no Cone Sul: Argentina, Brasil e Uruguai.* São Paulo: Attar Editorial.

Ortiz, Isabel, and Matthew Cummins. 2011. *Global Inequality: Beyond the Bottom Billion—A Rapid Review of Income Distribution in 141 Countries.* New York: UNICEF.

Oxhorn, Philip. 2011. *Sustaining Civil Society: Economic Change, Democracy, and the Social Construction of Citizenship in Latin America.* University Park: Penn State University Press.

Pacek, Alexander C., and Benjamin Radcliff. 1995. "Economic Voting and the Welfare State: A Cross-National Analysis." *Journal of Politics* 57:44–61.

Page, Benjamin I. 1976. "The Theory of Political Ambiguity." *American Political Science Review* 70:742–52.

Palomares, Alfonso S. 2011. "Los Guatemaltecos se Inclinan por la Mano Dura." *Tiempo*, September 20. http://www.tiempodehoy.com/mundo/los-guatemaltecos-se-inclinan-por-la-mano-dura.

Pascharopoulos, Jorge, and Harry Anthony Patrinos, eds. 1994. *Indigenous People and Poverty in Latin America: An Empirical Analysis.* Washington, DC: World Bank.

Patterson, Eric. 2004a. "Different Religions, Different Politics? Religion and Political Attitudes in Argentina and Chile." *Journal for the Scientific Study of Religion* 43:345–62.

Patterson, Eric. 2004b. "Faith in a Changing Mexico: The Effects of Religion on Political Attitudes, Engagement, and Participation." *Delaware Review of Latin American Studies* 5. http://www.udel.edu/LASP/Vol5-2Patterson.html.

Payne, J. Mark. 2007. "Trends in Electoral Participation." In *Democracies in Development: Politics and Reform in Latin America*, edited by J. Mark Payne, Daniel G. Zovatto, and Mercedes Mateo Díaz, 45–64. Washington, DC: Inter-American Development Bank, International IDEA, and the David Rockefeller for Latin American Studies, Harvard University.

Peffley, Mark. 1984. "The Voter as Juror: Attributing Responsibility for Economic Conditions." *Political Behavior* 6:275–94.

Pérez, Orlando J. 2003. "Democratic Legitimacy and Public Insecurity: Crime and Democracy in El Salvador and Guatemala." *Political Science Quarterly* 118:627–44.

Pérez, Orlando J. 2011. "Crime, Insecurity and Erosion of Democratic Values in Latin America." *Revista Latinoamericana de Opinión Pública (Latin American Journal of Public Opinion)* 1:61–86.

Pérez-Liñán, Aníbal. 2002. "Television News and Political Partisanship in Latin America." *Political Research Quarterly* 55:571–88.

Pérez-Liñán, Aníbal. 2001. "Neoinstitutional Accounts of Voter Turnout: Moving beyond Industrial Democracies." *Electoral Studies* 20:281–97.

Pérez-Liñán, Aníbal. 2007. *Presidential Impeachment and the New Political Instability in Latin America*. New York: Cambridge University Press.

Peters, John G., and Susan Welch. 1980. "The Effects of Charges of Corruption on Voting Behavior in Congressional Elections." *American Political Science Review* 71:697–708.

Petrocik, John R. 1996. "Issue Ownership in Presidential Elections, with a 1980 Case Study." *American Journal of Political Science* 40:825–50.

Pew Research Center. 2006. *Spirit and Power: A 10-Country Survey of Pentecostals*. Washington, DC: Pew Forum on Religion and Public Life.

Pierce, John C. 1970. "Party Identification and the Changing Role of Ideology in American Politics." *Midwest Journal of Political Science* 14:25–42.

Plutzer, Eric. 1988. "Work Life, Family Life, and Women's Support of Feminism." *American Sociological Review* 53(4):640–49.

Plutzer, Eric, and John F. Zipp. 1996. "Gender Identity and Voting for Women Candidates." *Public Opinion Quarterly* 60:30–57.

Popkin, Samuel L. 1994. *The Reasoning Voter: Communication and Persuasion in Presidential Campaigns*. Chicago: University of Chicago Press.

Posner, Daniel. 2004. "The Political Salience of Cultural Difference: Why Chewas and Tumbukas Are Allies in Zambia and Adversaries in Malawi." *American Political Science Review* 98:529–45.

Posner, Daniel. 2005. *Institutions and Ethnic Politics in Africa*. Cambridge: Cambridge University Press.

Posner, Paul W. 1999. "Popular Representation and Political Dissatisfaction in Chile's New Democracy." *Journal of Interamerican Studies and World Affairs* 41:59–85.

Powdthavee, Nattavudh. 2005. "Unhappiness and Crime: Evidence from South Africa." *Economica* 72:531–47.

Powell, G. Bingham, Jr. 1986. "American Voter Turnout in Comparative Perspective." *American Political Science Review* 80:17–43.

Powell, G. Bingham, Jr. 2000. *Elections as Instruments of Democracy: Majoritarian and Proportional Visions*. New Haven, CT: Yale University Press.

Powell, G. Bingham, Jr. 2004. "Political Representation in Comparative Politics." *Annual Review of Political Science* 7:273–96.

Powell, G. Bingham, Jr., and Guy D. Whitten. 1993. "A Cross-National Analysis of Economic Voting: Taking Account of the Political Context." *American Journal of Political Science* 37(4):391–414.

Power, Timothy J. 2000. *The Political Right in Postauthoritarian Brazil: Elites, Institutions, and Democratization*. Philadelphia: Penn State University Press.

Prillaman, William C. 2003. "Crime, Democracy, and Development in Latin America" Policy Papers on the Americas, vol. XIV, Study 6, Center for Strategic and International Studies (CSIS), Washington, DC.

Przeworski, Adam. 1991. *Democracy and the Market: Political and Economic Reforms in Eastern Europe and Latin America*. New York: Cambridge University Press.

Przeworski, Adam, and John Sprague. 1986. *Paper Stones: A History of Electoral Socialism*. Chicago: University of Chicago Press.

Przeworski, Adam, Susan C. Stokes, and Bernard Manin. 1999. *Democracy, Accountability, and Representation*. New York: Cambridge University Press.

Puddington, Arch. 2012. "Latin America's Wavering Democracies." *Freedom House, Freedom at Issue Blog*. Online. Accessed June 23, 2014. http://www.freedom house.org/blog/latin-america%E2%80%99s-wavering-democracies#.U6ho EihwXVw.

Quann, Nathalie, and Kwing Hung. 2002. "Victimization Experience and the Fear of Crime: A Cross-National Study." In *Crime Victimization in Comparative Perspective: Results from the International Crime Victims Survey, 1989–2000*, edited by Paul Nieuwbeerta. The Hague: Boom Juridischeuitgevers.

Queirolo, Rosario. 2013. *The Success of the Left in Latin America*. Notre Dame, IN: Notre Dame University Press.

Rabinowitz, George, and Stuart Elaine Macdonald. 1989. "A Directional Theory of Issue Voting." *American Political Science Review* 83:93–121.

Ranney, Austin. 1954. *The Doctrine of Responsible Party Government*. Champaign: University of Illinois Press.

Reed, Steven. 1999. *Punishing Corruption: The Response of the Japanese Electorate to Scandals. Political Psychology in Japan: Behind the Nails Which Sometimes Stick out (and Get Hammered Down)*. Commack, NY: Nova Science.

Remmer, Karen. 1991. "The Political Impact of Economic Crisis in Latin America in the 1980s." *American Political Science Review* 85:777–800.

Remmer, Karen. 2003. "Post-Stabilization Politics in Latin America." In *Post-Reform Politics in Latin America: Competition, Transition, Collapse*, edited by Carol Wise and Riordan Roett, 31–55. Washington, DC: The Brookings Institution.

Remmer, Karen. 2012. "The Rise of Leftist-Populist Governance in Latin America: The Roots of Electoral Change." *Comparative Political Studies* 45:947–72.

Remmer, Karen, and François Gélineau. 2003. "Subnational Electoral Choice: Economic and Referendum Voting in Argentina, 1983–1999." *Comparative Political Studies* 36:801–21.

Rennwald, Line, and Geoffrey Evans. 2014. "When Supply Creates Demand: Social Democratic Party Strategies and the Evolution of Class Voting." *West European Politics* 37:1108–35.

Rice, Roberta, and Donna Lee Van Cott. 2006. "The Emergence and Performance of Indigenous Peoples' Parties in South America: A Subnational Statistical Analysis." *Comparative Political Studies* 39:709–32.

Richardson, Bradley M. 1991. "European Party Loyalties Revisited." *American Political Science Review* 85:751–75.

Riker, William H. 1988. *Liberalism against Populism: A Confrontation between the Theory of Democracy and the Theory of Social Discourse.* Long Grove, IL: Waveland Press.

Riker, William H., and Peter C. Ordeshook. 1968. "A Theory of the Calculus of Voting." *American Political Science Review* 61:25–42.

Robbins, J. W., and L. Y. Hunter. 2012. "Impact of Electoral Volatility and Party Replacement on Voter Turnout Levels." *Party Politics* 18:919–39.

Roberts, Kenneth M. 1998. *Deepening Democracy? The Modern Left and Social Movements in Chile and Peru.* Stanford, CA: Stanford University Press.

Roberts, Kenneth M. 2002. "Social Inequalities without Class Cleavages in Latin America's Neoliberal Era." *Studies in Comparative International Development* 36:3–33.

Roberts, Kenneth M. Forthcoming. "Market Reform, Programmatic (De) alignment, and Party System Stability in Latin America." *Comparative Political Studies.*

Roberts, Kenneth M., and Erik Wibbels. 1999. "Party Systems and Electoral Volatility in Latin America: A Test of Economic, Institutional, and Structural Explanations." *American Political Science Review* 93:575–90.

Romer, Daniel, Kathleen Hall Jamieson, and Sean Aday. 2006. "Television News and the Cultivation of the Fear of Crime." *Journal of Communication* 53:88–104.

Rosas, Guillermo. 2005. "The Ideological Organization of Latin American Legislative Parties: An Empirical Analysis of Elite Policy Preferences." *Comparative Political Studies* 38:824–49.

Rosas, Guillermo, and Luigi Manzetti. 2015. "Reassessing the Trade-off Hypothesis: How Misery Drives the Corruption Effect on Presidential Approval." *Electoral Studies* 39 (September): 26–38.

Rose, Richard, and William Mishler. 1998. "Negative and Positive Party Identification in Post-Communist Countries." *Electoral Studies* 17:217–34.

Rosema, Martin. 2007. "Low Turnout: Threat to Democracy or Blessing in Disguise? Consequences of Citizens' Varying Tendencies to Vote." *Electoral Studies* 26:612–23.

Rosenstone, Steven J., and John M. Hansen. 1993. *Mobilization, Participation and Democracy in America.* New York: Macmillan.

Rudolph, Thomas. 2003. "Institutional Context and the Assignment of Political Responsibility." *Journal of Politics* 65:190–215.

Sacchet, Teresa. 2009. "Political Parties and Gender in Latin America." In *Governing Women*, edited by Anne Marie Goetz, 148–72. New York: Routledge.

Saiegh, Sebastián. 2009. "Recovering a Basic Space from Elite Surveys: Evidence from Latin America." *Legislative Studies Quarterly* 34:117–45.

Samuels, David J. 2004. "Presidentialism and Accountability for the Economy in Comparative Perspective." *American Political Science Review* 98:425–36.

Samuels, David J. 2006. "Sources of Mass Partisanship in Brazil." *Latin American Politics and Society* 48:1–27.

Samuels, David, and Matthew S. Shugart. 2010. *Presidents, Parties, and Prime Ministers: How the Separation of Powers Affects Party Organization and Behavior.* Cambridge: Cambridge University Press.

Sánchez, Fernando F. 2002. "Desalineamiento Electoral en Costa Rica." *Revista de Ciencias Sociales* 4:29–56.

Sanjuán, Ana María. 2003. "Dinámicas de la Violencia en Venezuela: Tensiones y Desafíos para la Consolidación de la Democracia." In *Entre el Crimen y el Castigo: Seguridad Ciudadana y Control Democrático en América Latina y el Caribe*, edited by Lilian Bobea, 119–26. The Woodrow Wilson International Center.

Sapiro, Virginia. 1983. *The Political Integration of Women.* Urbana: University of Illinois Press.

Sartori, Giovanni. 1969. "From the Sociology of Politics to Political Sociology." In *Politics and the Social Sciences*, edited by Seymour Martin Lipset, 65–95. Oxford: Oxford University Press.

Sartori, Giovanni. 1976. *Parties and Party Systems: A Framework for Analysis.* New York: Cambridge University Press.

Schattschneider, E. E. 1960. *The Semisovereign People.* New York: Holt, Rinehart and Winston.

Schmitt, Hermann. 2009. "Partisanship in Nine Western Democracies: Causes and Consequences." In *Political Parties and Partisanship: Social Identity and Individual Attitudes*, edited by John Bartle and Paolo Bellucci, 75–87. New York: Routledge.

Schmitt, Hermann, and Sören Holmberg. 1995. "Political Parties in Decline?" In *Citizens and the State*, edited by Hans-Dieter Klingemann and Dieter Fuchs, 95–132. Oxford: Oxford University Press.

Schneider, Ben Ross. 2013. *Hierarchical Capitalism in Latin America: Business, Labor, and the Challenges of Equitable Development.* New York: Cambridge University Press.

Scholz, Evi, and Cornelia Zuell. 2012. "Item No-Response in Open-Ended Questions: Who Does Not Answer on the Meaning of Left and Right." *Social Science Research* 41:1415–28.

Schraufnagel, Scot, and Barbara Sgouraki. 2005. "Voter Turnout in Central and South America." *The Latin Americanist* 49:39–69.

Schwindt-Bayer, Leslie. 2006. "Still Super-Madres? Gender and the Policy Priorities of Latin American Legislators." *American Journal of Political Science* 50(3):570–85.

Schwindt-Bayer, Leslie. 2010. *Political Power and Women's Representation in Latin America.* New York: Oxford University Press.

Scully, Timothy R. 1992. *Rethinking the Center: Party Politics in Nineteenth- and Twentieth-Century Chile.* Stanford, CA: Stanford University Press.

Seawright, Jason. 2012. *Party-System Collapse: The Roots of Crisis in Peru and Venezuela.* Stanford, CA: Stanford University Press.

Seligson, Mitchell A. 1980. "Trust, Efficacy and Modes of Political Participation: A Study of Costa Rican Peasants." *British Journal of Political Science* 10:75–98.

Seligson, Mitchell A. 2002. "Trouble in Paradise? The Impact of the Erosion of System Support in Costa Rica, 1978–1999." *Latin American Research Review* 37:160–85.

Seligson, Mitchell A. 2007. "The Rise of Populism and the Left in Latin America." *Journal of Democracy* 18:81–95.

Seligson, Mitchell A., and Daniel E. Moreno Morales. 2010. "Gay in the Americas." *Americas Quarterly*. http://www.americasquarterly.org/node/1316#1301.

Seligson, Mitchell A., Annabelle Conroy, Ricardo Córdova Macías, Orlando J. Pérez, and Andrew J. Stein. 1995. "Who Votes in Central America? A Comparative Analysis." In *Elections and Democracy in Central America, Revisited*, edited by Mitchell A. Seligson and John A. Booth, 151–82. Durham: University of North Carolina Press.

Seligson, Mitchell, Abby B. Córdova, Juan Carlos Donoso, Daniel E. Moreno Morales, Diana Orcés, and Vivian Schwarts Bulm. 2006. *Auditoría de la Democracia: Informe Bolivia 2006*. Cochabamba: USAID—LAPOP—CIUDADANIA.

Seligson, Mitchel A., Amy Erica Smith, and Elizabeth J. Zechmeister, eds. 2012. *The Political Culture of Democracy in the Americas, 2012: Toward Equality of Opportunity*. Latin American Public Opinion Project (LAPOP), Vanderbilt University.

Shabad, Goldie, and Kazimierz M. Slomczynski. 1999. "Political Identities in the Initial Phase of Systemic Transformation in Poland: A Test of the Tabula Rasa Hypothesis." *Comparative Political Studies* 32:690–723.

Shefter, Martin. 1977. "Party and Patronage: Germany, England, and Italy." *Politics and Society* 7:403–51.

Shepsle, Kenneth A. 1972. "The Strategy of Ambiguity: Uncertainty and Electoral Competition." *American Political Science Review* 66:555–68.

Shepsle, Kenneth, and Ronald Cohen. 1990. "Multiparty Competition, Entry, and Entry Deterrence in Spatial Models of Elections." In *Advances in the Spatial Theory of Voting*, edited by James Enelow and Melvin Hinich, 12–45. Cambridge: Cambridge University Press.

Shively, W. Phillips. 1972. "Party Identification, Party Choice, and Voting Stability: The Weimar Case." *American Political Science Review* 66:1203–27.

Shively, W. Phillips. 1979. "The Development of Party Identification among Adults: Exploration of a Functional Model." *American Political Science Review* 73:1039–54.

Siavelis, Peter M. 2009. "Elite-Mass Congruence, Partidocracia and the Quality of Chilean Democracy." *Journal of Politics in Latin America* 1:3–31.

Sieder, Rachel, ed. 2002. *Multiculturalism in Latin America: Indigenous Rights, Diversity and Democracy*. London: ILAS.

Singer, André. 2009. "Raízes Sociais e Ideológicas do Lulismo." *Novos Estudos* 85:83–102.

Singer, Matthew M. 2009a. "Buying Voters with Dirty Money: The Relationship between Clientelism and Corruption." Paper presented at the Annual Meeting of the American Political Science Association, Toronto.

Singer, Matthew M. 2009b. "Defendamos lo que Hemos Logrado: El Voto Económico en México durante la Elección Presidencial del 2006." *Política y Gobierno* 15:199–236.

Singer, Matthew M. 2011. "Who Says 'It's the Economy'? Cross-National and Cross-Individual Variation in the Salience of Economic Performance." *Comparative Political Studies* 44:284–312.

Singer, Matthew M. 2013a. "Economic Voting in an Era of Noncrisis: Economic Voting in Latin America 1982–2010." *Comparative Politics* 45:169–85.

Singer, Matthew M. 2013b. "The Global Economic Crisis and Domestic Political Agendas." *Electoral Studies* 32(3):404–10.

Singer, Matthew M. 2013c. "Should Nervous Workers Make Incumbents Worry about their Own Job Prospects?: Evidence from Developing Countries." *European Journal of Political Research* 52:143–63.

Singer, Matthew M. Forthcoming. "Elite Polarization and the Electoral Impact of Left-Right Placements: Evidence from Latin America, 1995–2009." *Latin American Research Review*.

Singer, Matthew M., and Ryan E. Carlin. 2013. "Context Counts: The Election Cycle, Development, and the Nature of Economic Voting." *Journal of Politics* 75: 730–42.

Singer, Matthew M., Ryan E. Carlin, and Gregory J. Love. 2012. "Questions of Performance: Economics, Corruption, Crime, and Life Satisfaction in the Americas. In *The Political Culture of Democracy in the Americas, 2012: Toward Equality of Opportunity*, edited by Mitchell A. Seligson, Amy Erica Smith, and Elizabeth J. Zechmeister, 125–64. Latin American Public Opinion Project: Vanderbilt University.

Singer, Matthew M., and Francois Gélineau. 2012. "Heterogeneous Economic Voting: Evidence from Latin America 1995–2009." Paper presented at the Annual Meeting of the Midwest Political Science Association, Chicago.

Singer, Matthew M., and Gabriela Tafoya. 2014. "Leaning Left, Right, or Undecided? Voting Patterns in Latin America." Paper presented at the Annual Conference of the Brazilian Political Science Association, Brasilia, Brazil, August 3–8.

Singh, Shane P. 2010. "Contextual Influences on the Decision Calculus: A Cross-National Examination of Proximity Voting." *Electoral Studies* 29:425–34.

Skogan, Wesley G. 1990. *Disorder and Decline: Crime and the Spiral of Decay in American Neighborhoods*. New York: Free Press.

Smets, Kaat, and Carolien van Ham. 2013. "The Embarrassment of Riches? A Meta-Analysis of Individual-Level Research on Voter Turnout." *Electoral Studies* 32:344–59.

Smilde, David. 2004. "Los Evangélicos y la Polarización: La Moralización de la Política y la Politización de la Religión." *Revista Venezolana de Economía y Ciencias Sociales* 10:163–79.

Smith, Amy Erica. 2010. "The Bully Pulpit: Church Influence on Political Socialization in Brazil." Paper presented at the XXIX Conference of the Latin American Studies Association, Toronto.

Smith, Amy Erica. 2013. "Clerical Work: Clergy, Media, and Religious Polarization, Brazil 2008–2012." Paper presented at the Annual Meeting of the Southern Political Science Association, Orlando.

Smith, Brian H. 1998. *Religious Politics in Latin America, Pentecostal vs. Catholic*. Notre Dame, IN: University of Notre Dame Press.

Smith, Christian, and Liesl Ann Haas. 1997. "Revolutionary Evangelicals in Nicaragua: Political Opportunity, Class Interests, and Religious Identity." *Journal for the Scientific Study of Religion* 36:440–54.

Smith, Eric R.A.N. 1989. *The Unchanging American Voter*. Berkeley: University of California Press.

Smulovitz, Catalina, and Enrique Peruzzotti. 2000. "Societal Accountability in Latin America." *Journal of Democracy* 11(4):147–58.

Sniderman, Paul M., Richard A. Brody, and Philip E. Tetlock. 1991. *Reasoning and Choice: Explorations in Political Psychology*. New York: Cambridge University Press.

Steenbergen, Marco R., and Bradford S. Jones. 2002. "Modeling Multilevel Data Structures." *American Journal of Political Science* 46:218–37.

Stegmaier, Mary A., and Michael S. Lewis-Beck. 2013. "Economic Voting." In *Oxford Bibliographies in Political Science*, edited by Rick Valelly. New York: Oxford University Press.

Steigenga, Timothy J. 2003. *The Politics of the Spirit: The Political Implications of Pentecostalized Religion in Costa Rica and Guatemala*. Lanham, MD: Lexington Books.

Stevenson, Randolph T., and Raymond Duch. 2013. "The Meaning and Use of Subjective Perceptions in Studies of Economic Voting." *Electoral Studies* 32:305–20.

Stimson, James. 1991. *Public Opinion in America*. Boulder, CO: Westview Press.

Stockemer, Daniel, Bernadette LaMontagne, and Lyle Scruggs. 2013. "Bribes and Ballots: The Impact of Corruption on Voter Turnout." *International Political Science Review* 34:74–90.

Stoker, Laura, and M. Kent Jennings. 1995. "Life-Cycle Transitions and Political Participation: The Case of Marriage." *American Political Science Review* 89:421–33.

Stokes, Donald E. 1963. "Spatial Models of Party Competition." *American Political Science Review* 57:368–77.

Stokes, Susan C. 2001. *Mandates and Democracy: Neoliberalism by Surprise in Latin America*. New York: Cambridge University Press.

Stokes, Susan C. 2005. "Perverse Accountability: A Formal Model of Machine Politics with Evidence from Argentina." *American Political Science Review* 99:315–25.

Stokes, Susan C. 2007. "Political Clientelism." In *The Oxford Handbook of Comparative Politics*, edited by Carles Boix and Susan C. Stokes, 604–27. New York: Oxford University Press.

Stokes, Susan C., Thad Dunning, Marcelo Nazareno, and Valeria Brusco. 2013. *Brokers, Voters, and Clientelism*. New York: Cambridge University Press.

Stoll, Heather. 2013. *Changing Societies, Changing Party Systems*. New York: Cambridge University Press.

Strate, John M., Charles J. Parrish, Charles D. Elder, and Coit Ford. 1989. "Life Span Civic Development and Voting Participation." *American Political Science Review* 83:443–64.

Studlar, Donley T., Ian McAllister, and Bernadette Hayes. 1998. "Explaining the Gender Gap in Voting: A Cross-National Analysis." *Social Science Quarterly* 79(4):779–98.

Tajfel, Henri, ed. 1978. *Differentiation between Social Groups: Studies in the Social Psychology of Intergroup Relations.* New York: Academic Press.

Tavits, Margit. 2007a. "Clarity of Responsibility and Corruption." *American Journal of Political Science* 51(1):218–29.

Tavits, Margit. 2007b. "Party Systems in the Making: The Emergence and Success of New Parties in New Democracies." *British Journal of Political Science* 38:113–33.

Teixeira, Ruy A. 1987. *Why Americans Don't Vote: Turnout Decline in the United States 1960–1984.* Westport, CT: Greenwood Press.

Telles, Edward. 2004. *Race in Another America. The Significance of Skin Color in Brazil.* Princeton, NJ: Princeton University Press.

Telles, Edward, and Liza Steele. 2012. "Pigmentocracy in the Americas: How is Educational Attainment Related to Skin Color?" AmericasBarometer, *Insights*, I73, Latin American Public Opinion Project (LAPOP), Vanderbilt University.

Telles, Edward, and PERLA. 2014. *Pigmentocracies. Ethnicity, Race, and Color in Latin America.* Chapel Hill: University of North Carolina Press.

Telles, Edward, and Tianna Paschel. 2012. "Beyond Fixed or Fluid: Degrees of Fluidity in Racial Identification in Latin America." Paper presented at the LASA Conference, San Francisco.

Telles, Helcimara, and Alejandro Moreno, eds. 2013. *Comportamento Eleitoral e Comunicação Política na América Latina.* Belo Horizonte: Editora UFMG.

Thomassen, Jacques. 1976. "Party Identification as a Cross-National Concept: Its Meaning in the Netherlands." In *Party Identification and Beyond: Representations of Voting and Party Competition*, edited by Ian Budge, Ivor Crewe, and Dennis Farlie, 63–80. London: John Wiley & Sons.

Thomassen, Jacques, ed. 2005. Introduction. In *The European Voter: A Comparative Study of Modern Democracies*, 1–21. Oxford: Oxford University Press.

Thomassen, Jacques, and Hermann Schmitt. 1997. "Policy Representation." *European Journal of Political Research* 32:165–84.

Tilley, James R. 2003. "Party Identification in Britain: Does Length of Time in the Electorate Affect Strength of Partisanship?" *British Journal of Political Science* 33:332–44.

Tillman, Erik R. 2008. "Economic Judgments, Party Choice, and Voter Abstention in Cross-National Perspective." *Comparative Political Studies* 41:1290–1309.

Tomz, Michael, and Robert Van Houweling. 2008. "Candidate Positioning and Voter Choice." *American Political Science Review* 102:303–18.

Tomz, Michael, Jason Wittenberg, and Gary King. 2001. CLARIFY: Software for Interpreting and Presenting Statistical Results. Version 2.0. Cambridge, MA: Harvard University Press.

Torcal, Mariano, and Scott Mainwaring. 2003a. "Individual Level Anchoring of the Vote and Party System Stability: Latin America and Western Europe." Working Paper 17/2003, Departamento de Ciencia Política y Relaciones Internacionales, Facultad de Derecho, Universidad Autónoma de Madrid.

Torcal, Mariano, and Scott Mainwaring. 2003b. "The Political Recrafting of Social Bases of Party Competition: Chile, 1973–95." *British Journal of Political Science* 33:55–84.

Trelles, Alejandro, and Miguel Carreras. 2012. "Bullets and Votes: Violence and Electoral Participation in Mexico." *Journal of Politics in Latin America* 4:89–123.

Tulchin, Joseph S., and Meg Ruthenburg. 2006. "Toward a Society Under Law." In *Toward a Society Under Law: Citizens and Their Police in Latin America*, edited by Joseph S. Tulchin and Meg Ruthenburg, 1–11. Washington, DC: The Woodrow Wilson International Center.

Tverdova, Yulia. V. 2011. "Follow the Party or Follow the Leader? Candidate Evaluations, Party Evaluations, and Macropolitical Context." In *Citizens, Context, and Choice: How Context Shapes Citizens' Electoral Choices*, edited by Russell J. Dalton and Christopher J. Anderson, 126–48. New York: Oxford University Press.

Uang, Randy Sunwin. 2013. "Campaigning on Public Security in Latin America: Obstacles to Success." *Latin American Politics and Society* 55:26–51.

United Nations Development Programme. 2007a. "Table 29. Gender Empowerment Measure." In *Human Development Indices: A Statistical Update 2008*, 330–33. New York: UNDP. http://hdr.undp.org/en/media/HDR_20072008_EN_Complete.pdf. Accessed 14 August 2009.

United Nations Development Programme. 2011a. "Gross National Income per Capita." http://hdrstats.undp.org/en/indicators/100106.html. Accessed June 16, 2012.

United Nations Development Programme. 2011b. *2011 Human Development Report*. New York: UNDP. http://hdr.undp.org/en/media/HDR_2011_EN_Complete.pdf. Accessed June 17, 2012.

Valenzuela, Arturo. 2004 "Latin American Presidencies Interrupted." *Journal of Democracy* 15:5–19.

Valenzuela, Samuel J., and Timothy R. Scully. 1997. "Electoral Choices and the Party System in Chile: Continuities and Changes at the Recovery of Democracy." *Comparative Politics* 29:511–27.

Valenzuela, Samuel J., Timothy R. Scully, and Nicolás Somma. 2007. "The Enduring Presence of Religion in Chilean Ideological Positionings and Voter Options." *Comparative Politics* 40:1–20.

Van Cott, Donna Lee. 2000a. *The Friendly Liquidation of the Past: The Politics of Diversity in Latin America*. Pittsburgh: University of Pittsburgh Press.

Van Cott, Donna Lee. 2000b. "Party System Development and Indigenous Populations in Latin America: The Bolivian Case." *Party Politics* 6:155–74.

Van Cott, Donna Lee. 2002. "Constitutional Reforms in the Andes: Redefining Indigenous-State Relations." In *Multiculturalism in Latin America*, edited by Rachel Sieder, 45–73. London: Palgrave Macmillan.

Van Cott, Donna Lee. 2005. *From Movements to Parties in Latin America: The Evolution of Ethnic Politics*. New York: Cambridge University Press.

van der Brug, Wouter, Mark Franklin, and Gábor Tóka. 2008. "One Electorate or Many? Differences in Party Preference Formation between New and Established European Democracies." *Electoral Studies* 27:589–600.

van der Brug, Wouter, Cees van der Eijk, and Mark Franklin. 2007. *The Economy and the Vote: Economic Conditions and Elections in Fifteen Countries*. New York: Cambridge University Press.

Verba, Sidney, and Norman H. Nie. 1972. *Participation in America*. New York: Harper & Row.

Verba, Sidney, Norman H. Nie, and Jae-On Kim. 1978. *Participation and Political Equality: A Seven-Nation Study*. New York: Cambridge University Press.

Verba, Sidney, Kay Lehman Schlozman, and Henry E. Brady. 1995. *Voice and Equality: Civic Voluntarism in American Politics*. Cambridge, MA: Harvard University Press.

Vermeer, Jan P. 2002. *The View from the States: National Politics in Local Newspaper Editorials*. Lanham, MD: Rowman & Littlefield.

Von Mettenheim, Kurt. 1995. *The Brazilian Voter: Mass Politics in Democratic Transition, 1974–1986*. Pittsburgh: Pittsburgh University Press.

Voors, Maarten J., Eleonora E. M. Nillesen, Philip Verwimp, Erwin H. Bulte, Robert Lensink, and Daan P. van Soest. 2012. "Violent Conflict and Behavior: A Field Experiment in Burundi." *American Economic Review* 102:941–64.

Wade, Peter. 1994. *Blackness and Race Mixture: The Dynamics of Racial Identity in Colombia*. Baltimore: Johns Hopkins University Press.

Wade, Peter. 1997. *Race and Ethnicity in Latin America*. London: Pluto Press.

Ward, Ian. 1993. "'Media Intrusion' and the Changing Nature of the Established Parties in Australia and Canada." *Canadian Journal of Political Science* 26:477–506.

Weaver, David. 1991. "Issue Salience and Public Opinion: Are There Consequences of Agenda-Setting?" *International Journal of Public Opinion Research* 3:53–68.

Weber, Christopher R., and Christopher M. Federico. 2013. "Moral Foundations and Heterogeneity in Ideological Preferences." *Political Psychology* 34:107–26.

Weitz-Shapiro, Rebecca. 2012. "What Wins Votes: Why Some Politicians Opt Out of Clientelism." *American Journal of Political Science* 56:568–83.

Welch, Susan, and John R. Hibbing. 1997. "The Effects of Charges of Corruption on Voting Behavior in Congressional Elections, 1982–1990." *Journal of Politics* 59:226–39.

Weyland, Kurt. 1998. "The Politics of Corruption in Latin America." *Journal of Democracy* 9:108–21.

Weyland, Kurt. 2000. "A Paradox of Success? Determinants of Political Support for President Fujimori." *International Studies Quarterly* 44:481–502.

Weyland, Kurt. 2002. *The Politics of Market Reform in Fragile Democracies: Argentina, Brazil, Peru, and Venezuela*. Princeton, NJ: Princeton University Press.

Weyland, Kurt G., Raúl L. Madrid, and Wendy Hunter, eds. 2010. *Leftist Governments in Latin America: Successes and Shortcomings*. New York: Cambridge University Press.

Widner, Jennifer. 1997. "Political Parties and Civil Societies in Sub-Saharan Africa." In *Democracy in Africa: The Hard Road Ahead*, edited by Marina Ottoway, 65–82. Boulder, CO: Lynne Rienner Publishers.

Wiesehomeier, Nina, and Kenneth Benoit. 2009. "Presidents, Parties and Policy Competition." *Journal of Politics* 71(4):1435–47.

Wiesehomeier, Nina, and Kenneth Benoit. n.d. "Parties and Presidents in Latin America" dataset. http://ninaw.webfactional.com/ppla.

Wiesehomeier, Nina, and David Doyle. 2012. "Attitudes, Ideological Associations, and the Left-Right Divide in Latin America." *Journal of Politics in Latin America* 4:3–33.

Wilkinson, Paul. 1986. "Maintaining the Democratic Process and Public Support," In *The Future of Political Violence*, edited by Richard Clutterbuck, 177–84. New York: St. Martin's Press.

Wittenberg, Jason. 2006. *Crucibles of Political Loyalty: Church Institutions and Electoral Continuity in Hungary*. Cambridge: Cambridge University Press.

Wlezien, Christopher. 2005. "On the Salience of Political Issues: The Problem with 'Most Important Problem.'" *Electoral Studies* 24:555–79.

Wolfinger, Raymond E., and Steven J. Rosenstone. 1980. *Who Votes?* New Haven, CT: Yale University Press.

World Bank. 2013. World Development Indicators. http://data.worldbank.org/data-catalog/world-development-indicators. Accessed April 2013.

Yanez, Ana Maria. 2001. *Mujeres y Política el Poder Escurridizo: Las Cuotas en los Tres Últimos Procesos Electorales*. Lima: Manuela Ramos.

Yashar, Deborah. 2005. *Contesting Citizenship in Latin America: The Rise of Indigenous Movements and the Postliberal Challenge*. New York: Cambridge University Press.

Yashar, Deborah. 2007. "Resistance and Identity Politics in an Age of Globalization." *Annals of the American Academy of Political and Social Science* 610(1):160–81.

Zakaria, Fareed. 2003. *The Future of Freedom: Illiberal Democracy at Home and Abroad*. New York: W. W. Norton and Company.

Zaller, John R. 1992. *The Nature and Origins of Mass Opinion*. New York: Cambridge University Press.

Zechmeister, Elizabeth J. 2006a. "Qué es la Izquierda y Quién está a la Derecha en la Política Mexicana. Un Enfoque con el Método Q al Estudio de las Etiquetas Ideológicas." *Política y Gobierno* 13(1):51–98.

Zechmeister, Elizabeth J. 2006b. "What's Left and Who's Right? A Q-method Study of Individual and Contextual Influences on the Meaning of Ideological Labels." *Political Behavior* 28:151–73.

Zechmeister, Elizabeth J. 2008. "Policy-Based Voting: Perceptions of Feasible Issue Space, and the 2000 Mexican Elections." *Electoral Studies* 27:649–60.

Zechmeister, Elizabeth J., and Margarita Corral. 2011. "Una Evaluación de la Representación por Mandato en América Latina a través de las Posiciones en la Escala Izquierda-Derecha y de las Preferencias Económicas." In *Algo Más Que Presidentes: El Papel del Poder Legislativo en América Latina*, edited by Manuel Alcántara Sáez and Mercedes García Montero, 132–54. Zaragoza, Spain: Fundación Manuel Giménez Abad de Estudios Parlamentarios y del Estado Autonómico.

Zechmeister, Elizabeth J., and Margarita Corral. 2013. "Individual and Contextual Constraints on Ideological Labels in Latin America." *Comparative Political Studies* 46(6):675–701.

Zechmeister, Elizabeth J., and Mitchell A. Seligson. 2012. "Public Opinion Research in Latin America." In *Handbook on Latin American Politics*, edited by Peter Kingstone and Deborah Yashar, 467–82. New York: Routledge.

Zechmeister, Elizabeth J., and Daniel Zizumbo-Colunga. 2013. "The Varying Political Toll of Corruption in Good versus Bad Economic Times." *Comparative Political Studies* 46(10):1190–1218.

Zuazo, Moira. 2008. *¿Cómo Nació el MAS? La Ruralización de laPpolítica en Bolivia*. La Paz: Friedrich Ebert Stiftung.

Zub, Roberto. 1992. "The Growth of Protestantism: From Religion to Politics?" *Revista Envío* 137:19–30.

Zucco, Cesar. 2008. "The President's 'New' Constituency: Lula and the Pragmatic Vote in Brazil's 2006 Presidential Elections." *Journal of Latin American Studies* 40:29–49.

Contributors

Melina Altamirano is a PhD candidate in the Department of Political Science at Duke University. She is writing a dissertation about social cleavages, informal labor, and political behavior in Latin America.

Andy Baker earned his PhD in political science from the University of Wisconsin–Madison in 2001. Currently, he is Associate Professor of Political Science at the University of Colorado–Boulder, where he teaches courses and conducts research on comparative politics, political economy, global development, and African and Latin American politics. He is the author of *The Market and the Masses in Latin America: Policy Reform and Consumption in Liberalizing Economies* (2009), which examines the nature and causes of citizens' attitudes toward free-market policies in eighteen Latin American nations. He is also the author of *Shaping the Developing World: The West, the South, and the Natural World* (2014), which is a textbook for college courses on global development. His articles have appeared in the *American Journal of Political Science, World Politics, Latin American Research Review*, and *Electoral Studies*.

Taylor Boas is Assistant Professor of Political Science at Boston University. His research examines various aspects of electoral politics in Latin America, including campaigns, voting behavior, religion and politics, and political communication. His publications include articles in the *American Journal of Political Science, World Politics, Studies in Comparative International Development*, the *Journal of Theoretical Politics*, and *Latin American Research Review*. He holds a PhD from the University of California–Berkeley and has been a visiting fellow at the Kellogg Institute for International Studies, University of Notre Dame.

413

Ryan E. Carlin is Associate Professor of Political Science at Georgia State University. His research interests include comparative political behavior, executive approval, the politics of natural disasters, and the rule of law. Recently, his research has appeared in the *Journal of Politics, Comparative Political Studies, Comparative Politics*, the *Political Research Quarterly, Political Behavior*, and *Electoral Studies*.

François Gélineau is Associate Professor and Research Chair of Democracy and Parliamentary Institutions at the Université Laval. His research focuses on voter choice and accountability. His research has appeared in *Electoral Studies*, the *Journal of Elections, Public Opinion and Parties*, the *Political Research Quarterly*, the *British Journal of Political Science*, and *Comparative Political Studies*, among others.

Kenneth F. Greene is Associate Professor of Government at the University of Texas at Austin. He is author of *Why Dominant Parties Lose: Mexico's Democratization in Comparative Perspective*, which won the 2008 Best Book Award from the Comparative Democratization Section of the American Political Science Association. He was Principal Investigator on the Mexico 2012 Panel Study. His current research focuses on voting behavior, democratization, and party systems in new democracies.

Herbert Kitschelt is George V. Allen Professor of International Relations at Duke University. In 2010 Cambridge University Press published his co-authored book *Latin American Party Systems* (together with Kirk A. Hawkins, Juan Pablo Luna, Guillermo Rosas, and Elizabeth J. Zechmeister). He is currently working on a global comparison of clientelistic and programmatic citizen-politician linkages based on an original dataset covering eighty-eight countries and more than five hundred parties.

Gregory J. Love is Associate Professor of Political Science at University of Mississippi. He received his PhD in 2008 from the University of California–Davis. His research focuses on comparative political behavior, democratization, and experimental political science, often examining Latin America. His most recent work has appeared or is forthcoming in *Comparative Politics, Electoral Studies, Public Choice*, and *Political Behavior*.

Noam Lupu is Assistant Professor of Political Science and Trice Faculty Scholar at the University of Wisconsin–Madison. His current book project, Party Brands in Crisis, explores how the dilution of party brands eroded partisan attachments in Latin America and facilitated the collapse of established parties. His research has appeared or is forthcoming in the *American Journal of Political Science*, the *American Political Science Review*, *Comparative Political Studies*, *Electoral Studies*, and *Latin American Research Review*. He received his PhD from Princeton in 2011.

Scott Mainwaring is the Eugene and Helen Conley Professor of Political Science at the University of Notre Dame. His research interests include democratic institutions and democratization; political parties and party systems; and the Catholic Church in Latin America. His latest book, written with Aníbal Pérez-Liñán, is *Democracies and Dictatorships in Latin America: Emergence, Survival, and Fall* (Cambridge University Press, 2013). He was elected to the American Academy of Arts and Sciences in 2010. In 2005 he won the James C. Burns, CSC Graduate School Award, given annually to a Notre Dame faculty member for distinguished teaching of graduate students.

Luigi Manzetti is Associate Professor of Political Science at Southern Methodist University. He specializes in issues that include governance, corruption, and market reforms in Latin America. His latest book, *Accountability and Market Reform Failures: Eastern Europe, Russia, Argentina, and Chile in Comparative Perspective*, was published by Penn State University Press in 2010.

Daniel E. Moreno Morales is Coordinator of Research Activities at Ciudadanía, Comunidad de Estudios Sociales y Acción Pública, a think tank based in Cochabamba, Bolivia. His recent research interests include identities and their relationship with politics, Internet use and citizenship, protests and political mobilization, and survey data collection methods. He coordinates several public opinion studies in Bolivia, including the Latin American Public Opinion Project (LAPOP) surveys.

Jana Morgan is Associate Professor of Political Science and Research Fellow in the Center for the Study of Social Justice at the University of Tennessee. Her research considers issues of inequality, exclusion, and representation in Latin America. She is particularly interested in exploring how gaps in the representation of economically and socially marginalized groups undermine democratic institutions and outcomes. She is the recipient of the Van Cott Outstanding Book award given by the Latin American Studies Association for her book *Bankrupt Representation and Party System Collapse* (Penn State University Press, 2011), which shows how party systems' inability to provide adequate linkages between society and the state precipitate their collapse. Her work has also been published in numerous journals, including the *American Political Science Review*, the *Journal of Politics*, *Politics & Gender*, *Comparative Political Studies*, *Latin American Research Review*, and *Latin American Politics and Society*.

Orlando J. Pérez is Associate Dean of Humanities and Social Sciences of Millersville University of Pennsylvania. He is a member of the Scientific Support Group for the Latin American Public Opinion Project (LAPOP) at Vanderbilt University. He is the author of *Political Culture in Panama: Democracy after Invasion* (Palgrave-Macmillan, 2011) and co-editor (with Richard L. Millett and Jennifer S. Holmes) of *Latin American Democracy: Emerging Reality or Endangered Species* (Routledge, 2009).

Guillermo Rosas is Associate Professor of Political Science at Washington University in St. Louis, where he has taught since 2003. His research focuses on the economic consequences of political regimes and on the effect of political institutions on behavior of political elites in Latin America. He is the author of *Curbing Bailout: Bank Crises and Democratic Accountability in Comparative Perspective* (University of Michigan Press, 2009).

Matthew M. Singer is Associate Professor of Political Science at the University of Connecticut. His research focuses on electoral accountability and the interaction between party systems and political behavior. His work has been published in numerous journals, including the *British Journal of Political Science*, *Comparative Politics*, *Comparative Political Studies*, *Electoral Studies*, the *European Journal of Political Research*, and the *Journal of Politics*.

Amy Erica Smith is Assistant Professor of Political Science at Iowa State University, and she holds a PhD in political science from the University of Pittsburgh. Her research focuses on public opinion, civil society, and democratization cross-nationally, and especially in Latin America and Brazil. She is particularly interested in the roles of religious organizations and informal social ties between elites and ordinary citizens, as well as among citizens. Her work has appeared in a number of peer-reviewed outlets, and she has published a book on civil society and democracy in Brazil.

Nicolás M. Somma is Assistant Professor of Sociology at the Pontificia Universidad Católica de Chile, where he teaches and does research on political sociology, social movements, and comparative sociology. He holds a PhD from the University of Notre Dame. His research has appeared or is forthcoming in *Comparative Politics*, the *Sociological Quarterly*, *Sociological Perspectives*, and the *Journal of Historical Sociology*, as well as several book chapters.

Mariano Torcal received a PhD in Political Science from Ohio State University and a PhD in Political Science from the Universidad Autónoma de Madrid. He is a Full Professor in Political Science at the Department of Political and Social Science at the Pompeu Fabra University in Barcelona and National Coordinator of the European Social Survey in Spain. He is also co-director of the Research and Expertise Centre for Survey Methodology (RECSM) at the Pompeu Fabra University. He has also been a Senior Adjunct Faculty at the Graduate School of International Studies at the University of Denver since 2006.

Elizabeth J. Zechmeister is Professor of Political Science and Director of the Latin American Public Opinion Project (LAPOP) at Vanderbilt University. Her research includes studies of voting, ideology, parties, representation, charisma, and crisis. She is co-author of *Democracy at Risk: How Terrorist Threats Affect the Public* (University of Chicago Press, 2009) and of *Latin American Party Systems* (Cambridge University Press, 2010). In 2012 she was awarded a Jeffrey Nordhaus Award for Excellence in Undergraduate Teaching at Vanderbilt University.

Index

abortion, 145, 153, 161, 205–7, 362–63
accountability voting: corruption, overview
of, 300–301, 318–20; corruption, sociotropic effects of, 307–18; crime, voting
behavior and, 324–29, 334–41; economic
context, overview, 281–84, 294–95;
economic performance of incumbents,
285–88, 335–41; economic voting, cross-
country comparisons, 288–94; electoral
context, overview, 8–11; measurement
methods, 365–67; overview of, 275–79;
voting behavior and, 57, 348, 350, 353,
357; voting behavior models, 4, 5–8,
23–24
African (Afro) descent, people of, 126–27,
131. *See also* ethnicity
age: clientelism and, 258; partisanship and,
229, 236; voter participation and, 33–36,
35, 41, 44–45, 49
Alemán, Miguel, 300
Allende, Salvador, 92
The American Voter (1960), 23
AmericasBarometer survey: clientelism data,
248–49, 257–58; corruption, experience
of, 305–6; corruption, perception of,
301–5; corruption, sociotropic effects
of, 307–18; crime, voting behavior and,
326, 329, 335–41; crime victimization
data, 331–34; data and methods, 19–20;
economic issue data, 284–88; economic
voting, cross-country comparisons,
181–85, 288–94; Erikson-Goldthorpe
class variables and, 80–87; ethnicity
data, 123–25, 129–32; household wealth
measures, 73–74; incumbents, voting
for, 277; left-right identifications data,
201–4; left-right vote choice, 63–64, 65;
main problem facing country data, 336;
partisanship data, 231–37; religion and

vote choice, 105–10; religious affiliations,
voters, 100, 101–3; religious beliefs of
candidates, 110–12
Argentina: class voting, 70, 72, 75, 76, 78,
81, 85–86, 89, 91, 92; clientelism, 251,
253, 255, 257; corruption, 300, 302,
307–10, 319–20; crime, voting behavior
and, 340; crime data, 330, 331–32, 333,
336; economic context, 177; economic
issue voting, 183, 290; employment class
data, 81; ethnicity, self-identification data,
123–25, 130; ethnicity, voting behavior
and, 131; gender-gap, voting behavior,
146, 147; left-right identifications, 200,
201, 206, 207–8, 212, 213; left-right
vote choice, 64; partisanship, 178, 235,
238; political parties, overview of, 15,
16; presidential and legislative elections,
25; religion and voting behavior, 103,
106, 107, 110; religious affiliation data,
101–3; voter turnout data, 32, 52; women,
employment of, 145, 156, 157; women,
voting behavior of, 145
Arrate, Jorge, 110
atheists/agnostics. *See* secularism
authoritarianism *vs.* democracy: clientelism
and, 260, 264; crime, voting behavior
and, 328–29; left-right identifications
and, 205–7, 218–19, 361–64; voting
behavior, overview, 350

Bachelet, Michelle, 78, 89, 110, 111, 158
Baldizón, Manuel, 110, 111
Barros, Aldemar de, 300
Binner, Hermes, 110
blacks, 123–25, 130, 131. *See also* ethnicity
Bolivia: class voting, 70, 75, 76, 78, 79, 81,
85–86, 88, 94; clientelism, 251, 253, 256,
264; corruption, 302, 305, 306,